EVERYDAY POLITICS IN RUSSIA

EVERYDAY POLITICS IN RUSSIA

From Resentment to Resistance

Jeremy Morris

BLOOMSBURY ACADEMIC

LONDON • NEW YORK • OXFORD • NEW DELHI • SYDNEY

BLOOMSBURY ACADEMIC
Bloomsbury Publishing Plc
50 Bedford Square, London, WC1B 3DP, UK
1385 Broadway, New York, NY 10018, USA
29 Earlsfort Terrace, Dublin 2, Ireland

BLOOMSBURY, BLOOMSBURY ACADEMIC and the Diana logo are
trademarks of Bloomsbury Publishing Plc

First published in Great Britain 2025

Copyright © Jeremy Morris, 2025

Jeremy Morris has asserted his right under the Copyright, Designs and Patents Act,
1988, to be identified as Author of this work.

For legal purposes the Acknowledgements on p. xii constitute
an extension of this copyright page.

Cover image © Parshina Olga/Getty Images

All rights reserved. No part of this publication may be reproduced or
transmitted in any form or by any means, electronic or mechanical, including
photocopying, recording, or any information storage or retrieval system,
without prior permission in writing from the publishers.

Bloomsbury Publishing Plc does not have any control over, or responsibility for,
any third-party websites referred to or in this book. All internet addresses given
in this book were correct at the time of going to press. The author and publisher
regret any inconvenience caused if addresses have changed or sites have ceased
to exist, but can accept no responsibility for any such changes.

A catalogue record for this book is available from the British Library.

Library of Congress Cataloging-in-Publication Data

ISBN:	HB:	978-1-3505-0932-0
	PB:	978-1-3505-0931-3
	ePDF:	978-1-3505-0934-4
	eBook:	978-1-3505-0933-7

Typeset by Integra Software Services Pvt. Ltd.
Printed and bound in Great Britain

To find out more about our authors and books visit www.bloomsbury.com
and sign up for our newsletters.

For my mother and father

CONTENTS

List of Figures	ix
Preface	x
Acknowledgements	xii
Note on the Text	xiii

INTRODUCTION: RETHINKING THE MEANING OF
THE POLITICAL IN RUSSIA — 1

Part I
ABSENT PRESENCES

Chapter 1
WAR AND SOCIETY'S RESPONSE: DEFENSIVE CONSOLIDATION — 27

Chapter 2
FEELING FOR AN ABSENT PRESENCE: THE ROOTS OF RUSSIAN
RESSENTIMENT — 45

Chapter 3
ABSURD INHABITATIONS: PORTRAITS OF SUFFERING AND STRIVING — 59

Part II
LINES OF CONTROL

Chapter 4
CAPITALIST REALISM: RUSSIA'S LABORATORIES OF HOPELESSNESS? — 87

Chapter 5
INCOHERENT STATE: ON CO-PRODUCING GOVERNANCE FROM BELOW — 115

Part III
LINES OF FLIGHT

Chapter 6
NOMADS: AN INTERMEZZO ON GARAGES AND OTHER NONPLACES — 149

viii *Contents*

Chapter 7
CRAFT AS POLITICS: FROM SALVAGE ECONOMIES TO MENDING
THE WORLD   167

Chapter 8
'THIS THING WE DO': WARTIME ENTANGLEMENT OF PEOPLE IN
POLITICS   189

Chapter 9
PEOPLING THE EVERYDAY POLITICS OF POSTSOCIALISM   209

References   218
Index   239

FIGURES

1	'The "Z" boys flex their muscles.' Image based on a photograph, used by kind permission of Peter Caffrey	41
2	Uzbek workers in the village	104
3	The Chief and his workers fix a leak	117
4	A garage block in Izluchino	152
5	The folk craft fair in Izluchino	175
6	Collecting signatures opposing a planned rubbish dump in Kaluga region	184
7	Political postering in Izluchino, 2019: 'Leeches on the body of the Town'	187
8	Donbas aid collectors in 2014	191
9	Anti-war sticker saying 'no to military invasion of Ukraine. Peace to the nations, fight the rulers'	198
10	Cakes decorated with 'fuck the war' and an ambiguous Eastertime abbreviation, 2024	215

PREFACE

It might seem strange to begin with what is missing, or what is at least made less visible than it should be in this book. There are many omissions and blank spots over the course of these pages and the main ones are due to the unpredictable consequences of talk in Russia today. In many places in this manuscript, I pull back from the interactions of the field. I obscure people and places to a much greater degree than I have done before. Here, in this 'sequel' to *Everyday Postsocialism*, I am more careful and reticent about 'showing my working'. This is a strange state of affairs for an ethnographer, especially as the majority of my interlocutors continue to talk to me openly and in the full knowledge that a version of our talk and interactions will appear in print someday.

I planned this book in 2018 to explore in greater depth and breadth aspects of the life of the little post-industrial town of Izluchino that I had not been able to cover in my previous work: political subjectivity, the role of the state, the situation of an average wage-earner given the harsh economic situation, the vital and creative life of people despite their 'absurd inhabitation' of a risky and hostile environment. Some of the topics in this book appeared in a sketched-out form in the interim, but none were given full treatment until this book. The scale is kaleidoscopic: I move from national to regional to micro-social and back in the same chapter. The breadth of coverage is also a 'bit too much', as one reader said: I talk, inter alia, about support for the war, socialist values, intergenerational communication, phenomenological theory, libidinal economy, woodwork, anti-war action and patriotic motorbikers. I make no apology for this ambitious and expansive scope. Scholarly readers will dip in and out, but I hope that there is enough connectiveness to sustain the curious educated reader to stick with me. Not least because this kind of book does not tend to get published nowadays given the pressures to sell short and mono-focussed works, piling them higher and deeper.

As a researcher, I am part of the field I study. It's not much remarked upon that many ethnographies still use a post-research 'extraction' model that neatly obviates ongoing ethical dilemmas. Professional ethnographers are supposed to be able to look interlocutors in the face and defend the validity of work written – usually in isolation and much later – about them and their lives. However, for many, the relationship ends with fieldwork, and the reality is that usually the ethical dimension also falls away, especially in 'difficult places' such as conflict zones. My situation – of ongoing 'access' –which just means I continue living in the fieldsite when I can – necessitates my caginess here and elsewhere. Having said that, I intentionally always planned my interactions and relationships so that I have nothing to hide, especially from interlocutors. My bikers commented on the final chapter, as did the anti-war activists. Igor was critical of my initial description of his work in the Far North and demanded more than one re-write until he was satisfied.

Despite the openness of most interlocutors, I have obscured (while retaining actual interview data) the identity of the antiwar activists who would risk many years in prison if the contents of this book could be used as evidence against them. I have also resorted to the use of some 'composite' characters to spread the risk of self-identification and deanonymization. So, for example, while municipal head 'Tamara's' words are all taken from actual interviews and interactions with local politicians, for ethical reasons I combine these multiple interactions with different people into a single ethnographic composite character. I describe how this works in the introduction. Mostly, talk with soldiers, police and security services workers is not deployed in this book, nor are materials from Ukrainians in Russia or elsewhere. This too is for ethical reasons.

ACKNOWLEDGEMENTS

This book began its life as a reflection that while scholars talked a lot about suffering and trauma, in the postsocialist context these remained rather abstracted minus signs – assumed, acknowledged, but hardly thought of as generating any social force. In engaging in many fruitful conversations with colleagues from political science, I was fortunate to encounter critical voices like those of Gulnaz Sharafutdinova, Regina Smyth and Samuel Greene who were engaged in a project to criticize what remain key assumptions: that Russians are atomized, passive, apolitical and largely disconnected. Later I was fortunate to have many challenging talks about Spinoza with Galina Orlova, and monism with Anna Kruglova. Denys Gorbach, Xenia Cherkaev and Alexandrina Vanke also inspired me to continue writing from a left perspective ethnographically. These, along with my many organic intellectual interlocutors, are the real custodians and curators of this book.

No less a debt is due to the many colleagues and friends who were willing to chat and comment on drafts and ideas for the book. They include my colleague at Aarhus, Birgitte Beck Pristed, who was one of the first to both support and critique. Others who sustained me in my writing were Inna Leykin, Hadas Weiss, Alexandra Oberländer, Ivan Maas, Regina Smyth, Lisa Gaufman, Eliot Rothwell, my students in Aarhus, and anonymous reviewers at Slavic Review. I also thank Viktoria, Marina, Andrei, Kolya, Viktor P, Larisa, Olga, Liuda, Alyona, Anton, Sergei Sergeevich but most of all Masha, Zhenya and Ilya. I thank all my colleagues who helped me with pitching such a prickly project, and those who read parts of the manuscript. They include Franck Billé, Nancy Ries, Elizabeth Dunn, Ed Pulford, Choi Chatterjee, Mariëlle Wijermars, Nagihan Haliloğlu, Edward Schatz, Ilya Matveev, Greg Yudin and Natalia Savelyeva. The book was made possible by a Carlsberg Foundation Monograph grant.

There remain numerous supporters in Russia and elsewhere who unfortunately must remain nameless. This book is for them. It represents the ethical necessity of continuing to give voice to currents of experience that are subject to erasure. I hope one day we can write ethnographically about Russia without contributing to invisibility even while trying to overcome it. This also goes for what Karin Knorr Cetina calls 'epistemic cultures' – the way academic disciplinary practices make some objects recede almost to invisibility in the background while others gain prominence.

NOTE ON THE TEXT

For rendering Russian personal names, I have opted for the most reader-friendly transliteration into Latin script. I mainly avoid the many diminutives used to aid readability. Where relevant, in citing interlocutor speech I add transliteration in italics within square brackets. In these cases I use Library of Congress system of transliteration without diacritics, but in the References section I use diacritics.

In 2024, 100 Rubles is around 1 USD, but readers should be aware that the Russian currency devalued over the course of the war. Similarly, rates were quite different ten years ago and where relevant I indicate this in the text.

Attentive readers will note that for more sensitive topics I sometimes do not necessarily fully cite Russian media or Russian public intellectuals and scholars. There are good reasons for not doing this as of 2024.

INTRODUCTION: RETHINKING THE MEANING OF THE POLITICAL IN RUSSIA

It is 2014 and a few months after the annexation of Crimea. I am sitting in the cosy garden gazebo of my neighbour Lyova, the diminutive name for Lev. We are in the village of Kamenka, Kaluga region. Lyova is in his late fifties. He will soon retire from his job as a plumber for the local housing authority. This thought makes him especially gloomy: 'pension means poverty, or rather, even worse poverty', he reminds us.

His eldest son Sasha is also with us. Sasha's wife is cutting up preserved herring and laying it all out neatly on a board. Lena looks up:

> You should be rejoicing about the future. Look at what your grandchildren will have to look forward to. Now they have something they can learn in school and say, 'we are proud to be Russian'.

Lena's husband starts laughing cynically,

> So this Crimea of ours, it will feed and clothe you and the kids? Now we've got to feed a whole bunch of new mouths – you and me. A whole two million of them. And it's not the people on the TV who will feed them. They are singing about how the reunification has made us 'complete human beings'.

Lyova turns to me for support:

> Tell me, you're proud of your country, right? Britain has a great history, like Russia. I don't understand people who don't support their authorities and yet who can go on living there. Youth just seems to complain nowadays. Yet they don't live so badly.

We have some local beer called My Kaluga. Just seeing a bottle of this brew always sets Lyova off on an exposition of how everything local is good and how Moscow hates it and wants to destroy it. Like they did with the best vodka factory in the country, which of course was in Kaluga. He flicks on the TV, but it can only receive the federal Channel One. The president of the country is speaking, but

Everyday Politics in Russia

Lyova talks over him almost as soon as he is 'addressed' by the stern and unsmiling leader. Lyova is careful to turn himself sideways so as not to catch the speaker's eye, though the latter appears to look through the viewer. Finally Lyova says, 'And what have that lot ever done for the likes of me? They look after their friends, for sure.' Lena gives me a look and turns the sound down. Lyova is not particularly inebriated. His son looks up with a boiled potato on a fork, and winks: 'But at least Crimea is ours, eh, dad?'[1]

***

Fast-forward seven years. More than fourteen thousand people have died in the Donbas conflict. It is 2021 and I am washing dishes in the village hotel with the 'chambermaid', Tanya. We have to refer to her using this aristocratic-sounding word in front of the posh Moscow guests. Tanya tells me that she knows there will be a great war soon. Do people in Britain and America know this? I think that for a moment I'm going crazy: what is she talking about? Tanya, however, is one of the calmest and sturdiest people imaginable. She can't survive on a sports teacher's salary, so she comes and works a summer job here. The job is demeaning and her talking to an outsider is a good distraction. To get an extra salary increment, she also runs the extracurricular patriotic education classes at school.

I change the subject to the archaeology of war. They are restoring the German trench network from the Second World War in the next village, I remark. An hour and half later, Tanya has finished telling me in minute detail about the primary research she's been doing as an amateur historian into local sites of battles barely recorded in the literature. The patriotic education classes involve travelling to the sites with school children and reconstructing the past. The sparse Soviet sources are reinvigorated by the children's imaginative retelling based on their feeling of being in this landscape they have known from birth; how they connect each of their own lives to a personal meaning of the past. It is better than the dry intonation of patriotic values handed down from the Ministry of Enlightenment that people tend to purse their lips uncomfortably at. 'We do the parades, and it can be fun for the kids to dress up, sure, but who can afford all the paraphernalia?' Unfortunately, not everyone can afford to be a good patriot.

Her son Dima attends various paramilitary rallies. He likes historical computer games where you can recreate empires or destroy them. He likes World of Tanks too. He goes along with his mother's view that putting on a uniform is the way to get a subsidized university place to study law. After a law degree you might be able to get a position in the Procuracy and that would protect you. From what? 'Well, you'd get a security-services pension early [three times higher than average], you won't be sent to fight. You won't have to worry about money and that kind of

---

1. 'Crimea is ours' is a slogan used ironically, and unironically to reflect on the fundamental changes in Russian foreign policy since 2014 and their domestic effects. We come back to this watershed 'Crimean moment' later.

thing.' Sometimes Dima says it is fun to be the poster child for patriotic education, but most of the time he doesn't really think about it. Like Lyova, he knows that a decent higher education in this country is not for the likes of him. As the war goes on, Dima becomes noticeably withdrawn. He spends more time online reading patriotic social media accounts. A lot of his friends say they don't 'get him' anymore. While a small number of kids are more outwardly patriotic, their peers largely look down on them and even make jokes behind their backs.

***

In late 2022 at the height of the first war mobilization wave, I sit in Alla's spacious central Moscow apartment near the zoo. Alla works for an IT company which makes shopping apps and integrates them with social media accounts. We cook dinner and talk about how to get her 27-year-old son Gosha out of the country and away from military mobilization. He hasn't left the flat during daylight for weeks; everyone is paranoid about kids getting snatched by the recruiters from the street even though it seems the risk in Moscow is negligible. The rumour mill is out of control and few are immune. Gosha likes to walk the dog when it gets dark. 'Mum, just leave me alone, I can look after myself.' Gosha wants to be a music producer in Moscow. He doesn't want to leave because his English is not so good, and it wouldn't work out for him somewhere else. Over the years, he introduces me to many American and Russian bands I have never heard of. His girlfriend drops by and, since it's late evening, persuades him to go to the replacement McDonalds, now called Tasty, Full Stop. While they're out, Gosha's mother takes a call from Kharkiv city in Ukraine where her sister's family live and have recently been under bombardment by the Russian armed forces. Then, Alla's much younger daughter from a second marriage sends a voice message. She's in a Rostov-on-Don café with her friends. She lives with her aunt there. Rostov is a key city serving as a logistics point for the Russian armed forces. Alla plays the conversation on speaker phone:

> Mum, sorry; I spent 104 rubles [around one dollar] more than I should have; I bought sweet waffles. I had to, you see. I've been listening to what is supposedly an adult man for a whole fifty minutes, the teacher of the Life Skills and Personal Safety course at school: he was talking about why the family is the most important thing, why all this LGBT is cringe and why the West is the fucking devil. The guy just stood there and told us why LGBT is a sin, bad and all that. Then he started talking about the West. That, you know, it's full of shit. And then he started talking about that gender order stuff; that women should give birth, and a man should earn. Cringe [*krindzh*].[2]
>
> Then Dasha spoke up and said she wants to be child-free ... She tried to challenge it. And he goes: 'this is what the Lord says, childfree is a sin, LGBT is

---

2. *Krindzh* is a recent borrowing from English 'cringe', and much deployed by young people as of 2022–3.

a sin, fuck all this shit'. In general, he said, 'read the Bible', that kind of shit. Well, of course he said it all without swearing, but you get the general idea, mum. It's all such trash, and the class looks at him like he's insane, but the rest don't say anything – I mean, what's the point?

[…] I just don't understand how can you consider these things from just this one angle? And then Lena says 'child-free is normal', and the instructor pretends to be shocked and says: 'Who told you that? Talk to doctors; they will tell you that it's not normal'. Lena says that she has two parents and both are doctors and her older sister is a doctor. Then the instructor is like, 'Then they must be bad doctors, you know, my girl'. And you know, this fuckwit is from the USSR, I guess, where the bible was banned! Trash! Where do they get these morons who fill kids' ears with shit like this?

The daughter sends another voice message a minute later:

And today we had a geography lesson. And the assignment was to write about how Russia changed since 1700. We had to write about rulers and what they did … So, the first section for Peter's the Great's government. I wrote, 'which opened a window to Europe'. Final section. 'Vladimir Putin. Closed the window to Europe'. And I didn't fill in the middle.

***

The three vignettes give a taste of this book's focus: political subjectivity develops in mundane intersubjective moments. All the vignettes reveal deep political content and reflection – even among the people others might write off as hapless or 'passive' supporters. Is Lyova a 'loyalist'? How does his son feel about his rich neighbour who says Crimean annexation made 'him whole as a person'? The same neighbour got rich thanks to work for a foreign company where he facilitated bribes to a Russian state agency, while plumber Lyova's job was to keep people's homes supplied with hot water. What will happen in the daughter's Rostov school class after a year of such conservative pedagogic 'enlightenment'? Will Dima trace a path from patriotic education to the frontline? What is his mother's true agenda in her history instruction?

Everyday politics is not detached from discourses derived from 'big politics' by any means, but it does take on a life of its own. Similarly, the focus is not just on politics in micro as reflecting the local burning topics of the day. The everyday is about how talking and doing 'the political' makes for a trajectory that has its own productive and tangible power, often 'aside' – as Jacques Rancière calls it – big politics. It doesn't have an 'escape velocity' from 'big power' – what Russians call *vlast*. But it does operate insidiously and insistently (in a demotic way) alongside authoritative power. It moves in what Gilles Deleuze and Félix Guattari call 'lines of flight' stretching away from, but still in contact with power; this is all possible because of the driving mechanism of society – deep tectonic structures of feeling.

The desires for political voice explored in this book are not captured by neat characterizations of 'nostalgia' for great power status, or for Soviet governance more generally. Nor does the political mean articulation of a kind of national authoritarian personality, though it does involve overcoming atomization and apathy, and negotiating the snares of geopolitical resentment.

How do we get at the political in a new way? I closely attend to the words and actions of the people I encounter in a 'triangulation' with big politics. I reverse the usual perspective on politics – that explanation and understanding can only derive from examining 'big and important things' (Hobson and Seabrooke 2009: 290). This simultaneously requires focus on 'the political' content of people's lives rather than just 'politics'. This distinction refers to Chantelle Mouffe's criticism of overly narrow conceptions of political relations (Mouffe 1999: 754). If 'politics' is institutional practices and discourses – realms from which almost all Russians are excluded, 'the political' is a dimension of antagonism inherent in all human society. The war on Ukraine only makes more intense Russians' deliberations about what kind of 'good' society can be imagined. 'Political' discussions about the good are part of everyday experience, even in 'post-democracies', even in militarized dictatorships. Like Pierre Clastres' classic critique of Western notions of politics (Clastres 1977), I insist that contention and negotiation, along with conflicts about the meaning of the 'good', can be grasped beyond the normative frames of formal politics in the public sphere. Politics exist beyond a narrow idea of 'hierarchical subordination' of the individual to power.

Through an anthropological lens, war and authoritarianism take on different meanings. Some support the aims of the regime, come what may, but would be hard pressed to define them. Some look to active or passive resistance. However, such clear definitions are not so helpful unless we move to interpret deep social content of both words and actions. Responses to the war of all types resonate with feelings of social disconnection and voicelessness. These feelings diverge in the everyday lives of people. A silenced majority hope and even strive for social reconstruction, even while a minority stew in resentment and revanchism. This book takes seriously everyday politics as revealing the positive impetus of people's social desires, and the sometimes-invisible content of their struggles. Their readiness to engage with the 'political' can be uncovered if only we stop to listen and watch.

Correspondingly to looking at 'small things' with big resonance, my methodological approach is bottom-up – using people who live in Russia – many of them confronting difficult circumstances, as lay experts. They are treated seriously, as best placed to explain issues often analysed by scholars abstractedly via political speeches, statistics and other secondary sources. The 'experts' in this book are small business owners, pensioners, prison guards, night-watchmen, taxi-drivers, day labourers, 'dropouts', anti-war activists, factory workers, housewives, 'independent' politicians, teenagers seeking gender transitions and many others. No matter how 'lowly' their job or 'narrow' a person's knowledge of the world, such people do the work necessary for society in Russia to function and reproduce itself. Often this knowledge (we could call it their 'lifeworld view') comes to a

Western public so filtered through detached lenses – whether of survey data, journalistic vox pop or 'social media research' – that it becomes distorted, not least by the biases all observers bring.

My interlocutors are treated as co-creators of this book, but while I make their views and values prominent, their knowledge is not taken as the 'final word' because my long-term embedded experience as a researcher is also part of the picture. The purpose of political anthropology is to get inside the subjective experiences that make up the social reality of participants. My method is avowedly immersive based on relationships of trust and mutual intellectual respect with a broad and diverse group of people. In a previous book (Morris 2016), I made ethnographic participant observations with a group of mainly working-class families and young people from Kaluga region in central European Russia. Kaluga is near Moscow – in its strong gravitations pull, so to speak, but can feel to its inhabitants a provincial backwater. Like many parts of Russia, Kaluga's rural population is rapidly shrinking, and the region is dominated by one relatively small city. Nonetheless it remains rural space, about the area of Maryland in the United States, or Normandy in France, but with a tiny fraction of those populations.

Most researchers would be interested in Kaluga because it was the site of experiments in creating Special Economic Zones in the 2000s to encourage high-tech investment by foreign conglomerates. In my previous work, I discussed some of the implications of this experiment – how many younger people looked to build careers in these novel factories set up by Samsung and Volkswagen, among others. This book revisits the two main age cohorts of my previous research participants. These are people now in their thirties and forties, and sixties and seventies. But I also broaden my coverage from those groups to younger people, urbanites from Kaluga city itself, a broader selection of towns and villages in the Kaluga region, as well as Moscow. I also bring into focus conversations and observations with Central Asians in Moscow and Kaluga whom I followed as part of a project on labour activism of food couriers and taxi-drivers after 2018. Furthermore, this book will give space to public political activists as well as underground war-resisters and informal war-supporters. While having to obscure or alter details to protect interlocuters, materials from diverse social groups allow me not only to make observations about society as a whole, but also to reflect on deep currents of continuity and change.

Implicated yet fractured ethnographies

Jan Krause's (2021) solution for scientists conducting risky fieldwork is to choose limited immersion. This is not an option for political anthropologists. I cannot refuse when an anti-war activist desperately wants to talk to someone, anyone, about her graffiti, or when a metalworker calls me, inebriated, just after the invasion of Ukraine and wants to vent about his government. Or, for that matter, should I put down the phone when the relative of a security services worker wants to talk about the terrible conditions and poor pay which result in her husband not really doing his job properly? Furthermore, it's understandable that the limited exposure to the field that Krause (2021: 334) describes allows one to actively choose to avoid 'long immersion' and the 'risk of becoming part of the social, political and economic complexity' of fields in conflict. However, in my case, when I started on this journey (in earnest in 2009)' I could not in my wildest dreams predict the potential risks to me or others. I am implicated in the lifeworlds of my interlocutors whatever their political positioning and can offer only interpretation, not moral judgement.

Ethnographers have long struggled with the ethical dilemma of representing and engaging with the views of others which conflict with their own. Anthropologists, as Hugh Gusterson points out, are 'political citizens' and have to choose between 'objectivist' strategies where they bracket the views of interlocutors against a normative perspective, a 'dialogic' strategy where one's own internal attitude is contrasted to those of interlocutors without trying to privilege it, and a 'polyphonic' strategy where critique comes as much from other characters in the cast of informants as from the author herself (Gusterson 1993: 73–4). The polyphonic effect I present in this book is maximally extensive. I present the diverse views of interlocutors and allow them to come into conflict with each other without overlaying meta-narration or third-person stabilizers. One reader of this book as it was being finalized commented that the result is a frustrated and fractured ethnography and that this was both 'good' and 'bad' from the perspective of the reader. I guess my response is that already dozens of safely 'objectivist' books have been produced about Russia since February 2022. This is not one of those books. Certainly, the war presents a unique challenge to ethnographic approaches. The relationship with some interlocutors changes radically. They may stop answering the phone or messages. Others even go into hiding from all unnecessary social contact. Some, on the contrary, put themselves at risk by breaking anti-war legislation and 'bringing the army into disrepute' in their messages and talk. This prompts me to make difficult editorial decisions of cutting and obscuring. Indeed, many-a-time I have deleted fieldnotes, recordings and other materials because of wartime legislation that could put interlocutors at risk. Then there is the enforced mixing of modes of engagement with the field. As physical access becomes more difficult, I make more extensive use of instant messages and other forms of contact with the people from afar. The result is both a fracturing and patchwork connection in the ethnographic manner described by Günel et al. (2020) and Odierna (2024). Patchwork as a research lens critiques the artificial separation of 'private' and 'professional' lives of ethnographer and her subjects, as well as the often-belated realization of materials' relevance. It aims at a more honest recognition of recombinative work of 'home' and 'field'.

Having given notice of the 'fractured' nature of this ethnography, a further word on the peopling of this book is in order. Evolutionary psychologist Robin Dunbar is now famous for his namesake concept. 'Dunbar's number' describes gradations of intimacy – the number of relationships as 'friends', acquaintances, nodding relationships and ascribes a cognitively comfortable maximum for each. Accordingly, you can sustain reasonably friendly involved relations with 150 people over time, though within this set there is variation. The rest of the people known to you are either more intimate or more distant types of relationship (Mac Carron et al. 2016). As a rule of thumb about a sustainable network, I find this an approximation to the development of my relationships in Izluchino and beyond. While passing acquaintances (beyond a circle of 150) are sometimes useful, the association of a number with the term 'friend' for ethnographers is crucial, because it means one can bother them with some trivial request, usually information, or burden them with one's presence. So, while the number of actual characters in this book is much smaller than 150, it may help the reader to imagine this much larger circle of relations as informing the content. One reason for using composites is to make things manageable for the reader and writer alike.

Composites compress diverse yet sample-saturated materials. I take the words of real people, real situations, but obscure the identity of both by creating a composite person from different sources, and often a composite place as well. Composites present a solution to ethical issues when representing sensitive materials that require the disguising of real identity. While 'representativeness' is a difficult concept to work with in ethnographic research, the material in this book represents a condensed report on the immersion over many years in the field and many thousands of conversations. The main ethnographic persons presented here therefore represent that much wider and larger research community followed by me actively since 2009.

In some respects this book follows the logic of Michael Burawoy's 'extended case method' (ECM).[3] I study conditions in a particular 'case' – the network and web of connections radiating out from the central point of the village and town. These extend to Moscow and even Central Asia, but mainly focus on an axis which replicates the actual movement of most people: Kamenka the village, Izluchino the former Soviet company town of around 20,000 people, the district administrative centre, Kaluga city, Obninsk (a regional city closer to Moscow), and Moscow itself. Physically, the world of my interlocutors represents a skewed line on this axis of 300 kilometres, and 5–9 hours of travel. The line doesn't always draw itself from small-large, or vice-versa. People may bypass Kaluga or avoid Moscow entirely. I understand ECM as allowing research materials to speak to a social shaping process – from external forces to a specific discursive and interpersonal situation to understand it (Burawoy et al. 1991). Rather than generalization and representation, the aim is to show 'societal significance' of the case.

While some of my characters are composites, searching for objectivity via 'real people' is the wrong question. As in my last book, all the dialogue and descriptions of events and interactions stem from personal observations over the last fifteen years, but equally they can only ever be a partial, and highly attenuated glimpse into forms of life. While not anthrofiction, returning to the problem of fragmentation and frustration, I have produced a kind of elliptical and

---

3. I agree with Eliasoph and Lichterman (1999) that ECM may obscure important empirical elements of the field and therefore my own approach is more of a hybrid which adheres to the spirit of 'pragmatic' phenomenological anthropology.

even synecdochic ethnography, combining 'blow ups' of close-focus shots, then zooming out to the level of a wide-shot where faces are hardly discernible even while the actions of groups are obvious. This elliptical ethnography seems to me one solution, neither better nor worse than others, to the problem of fractured representation of conflict.

Despite having had to retreat somewhat from depicting all that I would have liked, elliptical zooming in and out has a rhetorical force of its own. I find people have much more in common, and what drives them is very often the same set of traces of communal potentiality that it overrides what divides them. And we can say the same about the war on Ukraine. 'Resenters' – those readily making use of narratives about betrayal and threat are not really so different from what I call '*ressentiment*' people: those attuned to the social hurt and lost opportunities of the last thirty years. My only two descriptions of Z-patriots (people publicly displaying pro-war propaganda provided by the authorities) are entirely ambiguous scenes: are the kids making selfies about the war being ironic? It seems the answer is 'yes'. Why do so many people react with hostility to those around them putting Z decals on their cars? Because they feel affronted by the deployment of the Second World War memory for an undeserving cause by no-nothing conformists.

***

Having established some bases and angles of this research project, I return to the question: why take a bottom-up approach now? Surely, it is enough to look at the actions of the elite; they made the decision to narrow down the meaning of the political to ritual voting as a mark of loyalty. Political parties and elections are almost meaningless from the perspective of voice and preference. One could also point to the spectacular success in exterminating all traces of independent civil society and media. It was a small, isolated elite that made the decision to invade Ukraine in February 2022, but it seems that society quickly fell in behind the leader. It is often thought that one of the only values that united Russian people was the mantra 'anything but a war' because of the long memory of the Second World War. However, as political scientists like David Lewis (2020) point out, maybe the true success of the regime was in persuading Russians that they live in a time of threats and geopolitical humiliation. In other words, for many it seems that the mobilization of grievance narratives as a central discursive framework was successful in bringing the leader and popular imagination together to express collective resentment (Lewis 2020: 14) and in turn facilitate public alignment with impossibly rash foreign policy 'aims'.

But on what basis do we rush to that conclusion? The main instrument for measuring the political in Russia has been opinion polling. Throughout 2022 and 2023 polling appeared to show broad support for the actions of the Russian armed forces. Similarly, before that, Putin's personal approval rating had rarely fallen even close to 50 per cent. However, there are numerous objections that can be levelled, even at the seemingly independent and scientific polling that is presented as indicating broad support for the decisions of state. I will not rehearse those arguments in full here, but fundamentally they come down to the question of how meaningful a person's expression of 'public opinion' can be in a society that has had the very concept of 'public' and the political stripped down to the minimum. People are much more likely to give the 'expected' answer when talking to pollsters, even in confidence, than express an opinion that goes against the clearly communicated 'correct' narratives blaring at all hours of the day on television. While there is a certain emotional intimacy between people and the familiar faces of propagandists on TV, this book provides an important corrective to the idea that there is strong identification between the regime's favourite media faces (such as Vladimir Soloviev and Olga Skabeeva) and a loyal contingent of propaganda consumers.

My participants provide a much more nuanced view of popular perceptions. They demonstrate that Russians understand they live in a country where elections are not the same as in 'the West'. They also feel the coercive capacity of the state. Most know that the 'preventative' argument for the invasion of Ukraine is tenuous. They know too that the experience of 'authoritarianism', for most of them, is ordinary and more than bearable.[4] They also know that when they talk to a pollster (and here there is also the question of what kind of crazy person would agree to do that), they are not expressing a 'preference'; rather, they are showing themselves to be either a loyalist or a renegade. Criticisms of polling can be philosophical or technical (Yudin 2020, Morris 2023a). I argue that political preferences, values and beliefs are better understood through fieldwork-based examination.

Even in describing a 'high compliance' regime like Hafiz al-Assad's 1990s Syria, researcher Lisa Wedeen (1999: 30) was careful to put 'authoritarian' in inverted commas. This was because even under Baathism, citizens and regime alike knew that performative support was more important than belief or action. In other words, authoritarianism only required symbolic consent, not meaningful confirmation of the authoritative relationship. In the Russian case I agree with Karine Clément (2018) that if anything, people in Russia are more politically critical of their government and state than many in democracies. This is not despite authoritarianism, but because of it – sources of legitimacy are hard to come by. While opinion polling in my view is too problematic to interpret meaningfully, there are plenty of other indicators in what people do, rather than say. Too little has been made of the failure of military mobilization in Russia since 2022 to elicit anything but a negative response. The sources and motivation of 'volunteers' for the war (actually representing various categories) similarly need much closer examination than many are willing to undertake.

Political anthropology has a difficult relationship with its more publicly visible cousin, political science. The latter is characterized by focus on uncovering mechanisms of cause and effect, rationality and generalization between cases. Anthropologists are more likely to reject the idea that political phenomena can be grasped so easily. As an interpretive rather than explanatory philosophy,

---

4. Tom Pepinsky noted that the 'mental image of authoritarian rule in the eyes of Americans is completely unrealistic, and dangerously so'.

anthropology is more likely to see politics as any kind of social practices which reveal the negotiation and interrogation by people of power relations. This is an approach I try to remain faithful to in this book. It is very easy to think about politics in Russia as a thing removed from ordinary life entirely, and many Russians do think about *electoral* politics in that way. In the version for Western consumption, an informalized elite in patron-client relationships and the window dressing of stolen elections and fake institutions are all we need to know. As a result, every single Russian person outside a small circle in the Kremlin is almost irrelevant. There are studies of housing renovation activism and eco protests. There are even some outlandish scholars tracking labour protestors who block roads and stage sit-ins. In the greater scheme of things, however, these are seen as trivial contributions because the 'system', as Alena Ledeneva memorably called it (2013a), supposedly need not consider the voices of such people. Coercion rules supreme and is all-encompassing.

And yet even the most dictatorial society doesn't really work by coercion or bought consent, and 'atomization' or alienation is not really how Russians think of their relationship to politics. We are spellbound by the visually shocking scenes of the paramilitary police dispersing protestors in Moscow, or soldiers in occupied Donbas firing into the air over the heads of Ukrainians defiantly flying their national flag. These are the spectacular exceptions – most political actions whether resistant or compliant lie somewhere beyond coercion and violence. They arise too in contexts where it is hard to truly reduce them to explanations of 'interest', 'loyalty' or even 'ideology'. Since the war, many seem to have forgotten that the visible public sphere – whether rallies or symbols – is carefully curated by the regime, and not a reflection of social reality. Citizens know the boundaries and steer clear of open political opposition, but that seems to be changing and is likely a disruptive force in the making, as witnessed in the actions of soldiers' wives demanding an end to mobilization, and armament factory workers unhappy at low wages and poor conditions. These, rather than the relatively privileged moral protestors against war, are important bellwethers.

In this book I will make the case for the relevance of a frustratingly fuzzy concept. This is a 'structure of feeling': that at different times, different societies make use of a vague sense of the meaning of their era. Raymond Williams coined this phrase in the 1950s. Since then, this idea of a structure has helped problematize strong versions of hegemonic, or dominant thinking. A 'structure of feeling' emerges in a space between official discourses and is sometimes inferred rather than clearly defined.[5] It is 'populist' in the sense that it insists that political meaning-making

---

5. E. P. Thompson's work also strongly suggests that through experience, people actively process antagonisms and conflicts and in doing so 'make themselves' into classes and identifiable groups. Shared experience links individuals and then acts in a dialectical relationship with imposed discourses. Regime propaganda and hegemonic narratives are never just external inputs passively received. Here I am inspired by Ellen Meiksins Wood's (1982) defence of a reading of Thompson which emphasizes the experiential generation of social being.

emerges from below as much as above. It is intimate in that it often escapes words and only emerges fleetingly – like Sasha's ironic wink when he trotted out the patriotic meme: 'At least Crimea is ours'. This feeling about the meaning of the present might be strongly inflected by official discourses and their propagation in the media, but anthropologists are keen to point out that their reflection in reality has a life of its own. Some political anthropologists come close to Williams' intention when they deploy terms like 'vernacular' politics and 'social poetics' (Herzfeld 2016). Whatever concepts scholars use, they are making a claim that the articulation of political ideas and desires need not be dictated solely from above.[6]

The structuring feelings of twenty-first-century Russia are powerful and dangerous. Most observers think these feelings are outward-looking (that Russia's 'greatness' needs to be acknowledged by others), and backward-oriented (that greatness implies recreating a past imperial project). Geopolitical frustration and resentment are not nearly as important as one might think, however. I argue in the next chapters that these political emotions might express themselves through engagement with the geopolitical narratives of elites, but that more powerful forces are at work. These forces emerge from frustrated connectiveness. This is a feeling that derives from decades of denying the value of social needs – whether in hindering people who want to form civic organizations beyond the surveillance of the security state, or in ridiculing political discourses of care and nurture. These stymied imperatives reveal a deep itch of the phantom limb: the absent social 'order' of the socialist-era project. Paradoxically, while the USSR is thought of as an equally 'atomized' society with top-down control over social organization, that is not how Russians 'use' this past. They are much more likely to feel haunted by the possibility of connectiveness, sincerity in personal relations, the overcoming of personal interest, *despite* the acknowledged barriers of communist-era political control.

I argue that we cannot impose clearly defined Western political concepts even to describe the social imaginary of the Soviet era. I propose that the present is haunted by the spirit of *obshchnost* – variously and sometimes inadequately translated as commonality/communality/feeling-in-common (Pesmen 2000).[7] And here we

---

6. Many scholars try to get beyond a view that the public or media sphere represents social reality in Russia and this book will try to engage with most of them. Perhaps the two most formative for me in searching out forms of political autonomy from top-down dictation are Greene (2019) and Clément and Zhelnina (2020). Looking back to earlier periods, Ries (1997) and Pesmen (2000) are scholars who strongly prefigure and influence my own approach: anthropologies by foreigners who were witness to epochal changes in Russian society.

7. The term *obshchnost* is also used explicitly by Russian philosophers to describe putative Eurasian civilizational unity (Bassin 2011) and so may have a political flavouring. For an anthropological treatment of the intersection of community and nationalism in Russia, see Oushakine (2010b). *Obshchnost* can more neutrally refer to a cultural 'commons' (Caffee 2013). Orlova (2021) is close to my use of the term in a more sociological manner when she translates *obshchnost* into a sense of affective 'unity'.

also need a further set of clarifications: the social 'order' of the Soviet Union does not refer to the political and social institutions themselves, but their – often unintentional – effects at the level of the socialized individual. Social order refers to how individuals come to relate to each other and cannot escape confronting these relational categories in everything they do. Secondly, while 'emotions' and 'affect' are symptomatic of such hauntings, the 'structure of feeling' does not refer to an emotional attachment, such as in nostalgia. Instead, 'feeling' is a bit like the relation of a tree to a water source. It is the idea of an inescapable, implicating relationship. The necessity of connection does not require emotional attachment, just innate drives and needs. These drives demand an acknowledgement of the holism of relations. Individuals can be separate, but their identity and meaning as persons are only understood through a relational lens, grounded in place. This is a way of overcoming what is sometimes called 'methodological individualism' in scholarship – that self-centred interests at the level of the person are the ultimate explanatory factor. In the first chapter, I discuss how, regardless of the actual social, political and economic reality, the Soviet period provided a tantalizing taste of the structuring feeling for relations. And a desire for these relations has great resonance today: the need for the individual of social role, mutual acknowledgement as a social person, and a purpose greater than herself.

Peopling political economy

The second aim of this book is to link the situated study of human interactions, meaning-making and social organization with a particular form of 'peopled' political economy. So, instead of thinking narrowly of Russia as another semi-periphery of 'economic statism' (Callinicos 2005), we reverse the analytical lens, not according to traditional political economy, but with a dose of grounded ethnographic knowledge. Where else, if not in Russia, does even a political economist frequently encounter the methodological objection – 'such official statistics are unreliable', or 'do we even have any idea how big the black economy is?' Critical political economy (CPE) has long understood the wider challenge to positivist empiricism – that entire categories and properties of economic behaviour are invisible to a macro approach (Cameron and Palan 2009). While the answer for CPE is more historicism and geographically specific analysis – particularly of states, others go further and call for bringing in 'non-elite actors' to an understanding of how political and economic environments adapt and change (Hobson and Seabrooke 2009). Mine is again an anthropological approach – how the economic is embedded in 'everyday life' choices and practices. Individuals are subordinated to macro processes of 'tight money', or fiscal conservatism (Trickett 2025), or to hire-and-fire firms where they sell labour fearfully against the continual erosion of meaningful labour protections. Nonetheless, meso and micro changes, and even individual economic behaviour (that might not appear explainable according to classical theories of rational interest), can reinforce, subvert or 'retrack' the actions of elites (e.g. Broome 2009, discussed in Hobson and Seabrooke 2009).

My perspective is influenced too by recent feminist scholarship. Juanita Elias and Lena Rethel (2016) emphasize how an 'everyday' lens helps foster an ambitious interdisciplinary conversation. To give an example from the Russian context, nannies' unpaid childcare in 'the provinces' for close or extended family has long facilitated *vakhta* – the large-scale periodic labour mobility from rustbelt towns like Izluchino to Moscow. A typical model is a grandmother caring for a child while the father is away and the mother works full-time (perhaps even on two jobs, sixty hours a week). *Vakhta* is unpleasant: groups of men take a long-distance bus holding plastic bags of provisions and then disappear into the fenced-off construction sites of Moscow. Often, work is entirely without formal contracts, without insurance and without safety or other protections – a situation now more typical of Central Asian migrants (Urinboyev 2021). *Vakhta*'s semi-invisible migration facilitated Moscow's property boom in the early 2000s and its elevation to a global megacity. In turn, Moscow's massive wealth facilitated cutting-edge digital governance and with it, surveillance. Meanwhile perhaps two-thirds of all the petrochemical wealth was offshored and contributed to the consumption economies of places like London, as well as the courtier-like financial services industry there. At home, a form of authoritarian capitalism emerged, underpinned by hard and soft forms of coercion unparalleled outside China (Orlova and Morris 2021), but also with lots of trinkets for the new middle-class.

Nonetheless, *vakhta* migration, while in some ways unique to post-socialist countries, can be applied elsewhere in a comparative analytical sense. Saskia Sassen (2014) tried to draw together different migratory phenomena as 'accumulation by dispossession'. The point is to move beyond the narrow purview of interstate politics and highlight common processes, by virtue of looking at them up close. We then avoid losing sight of the active role played by victims of our time's 'savage sorting' (Sassen's phrase). The Russian displacement and dispossession are ongoing processes since 1991, as Caroline Humphrey pointed out (2002). They are characterized not only by glaring inequality, but also by the role *and* practices of ordinary people themselves in shaping economic outcomes. In the case of *vakhta,* the political powerlessness of older non-metropolitans is exacerbated – marginalizing pensioners in small towns which are emptied of the younger residents. But labour migration also facilitates economic (and political) room to manoeuvre in the rustbelt. People turn hard-won wages from Moscow into a form of defence: building country cottages and turning to forms of self-provisioning. The global scale also interacts: Co-ethnics from Central Asia replace ethnic Russians in various jobs and their relatives back home become dependent on remittances from Moscow.

The everyday lens of critical political economy also helps us unpack desire and agency. In contrast to rust-belt nannies, well-paid metropolitan carers respond to demand from the burgeoning upper-middle-class Muscovites who are also keen to keep the contract informal and exercise control over the arrangement. However, this phenomenon is marked by political and economic desires on the part of older women carers. They wish for a higher standard of living (economic rationality) in a context where pensions only allow subsistence. 'Desire' does not just equate to 'rationality'. They also search for compensation for the loss of status and social role after communism; they reflect on the 1990s as a period of women's declining social mobility. They use nannying to reclaim and restake visibility, worth and their right to both a caring and intellectual contribution (in moulding the upbringing of their wards). To paraphrase Elias and Rethel (2016: 6) – the everyday is essential to grounding global political economic changes, struggles and resistance. More than that though, the lens needs focussing on specific regions to show how ongoing marketization and economic transformation play out in 'variegated ways'. Marketization of labour and the place-specific commodification of roles like nannying that nonetheless remain invisible to the state and taxation do not imply a simplistic two-way relationship between individuals and an amorphous 'market'. The Central Asian migrants, as we will see in Chapter 4, while seemingly subaltern, draw on powerful political networks of co-ethnic solidarity, even at the most mundane level, among Uber-type taxi-drivers. Similarly, the complex relationship between older women and the Russian state, and its (non)roles in the lives of citizens also calls for an everyday approach. There is a continuous interplay between expectations, desires, economic context and changing gender/labour norms. These are 'lines of flight' in the Deleuzian sense – a movement away from control while still in negotiated 'contact'.

Such everyday political economy perspectives have been adopted as part of an attempt to promote an alternative to Western-centric ones. Particularly in postcolonial contexts they presuppose a theorization of social reproduction – the socially necessary work required for generation to produce generation – based on confronting the vectors of spatial and temporal violences in everyday struggles (Elias and Rai 2019). In the Russian and postsocialist cases too, discussions of the particularity of Soviet modernization and the swift shift to marketization tend to separate out elite and 'ordinary' perspectives, unintentionally downplaying such structural violence and its long-term impact. In many accounts, people are presented as victims: reactive, maladaptive or largely bereft of agency. The chapters in this book are organized to bring to the fore the political and economic *vita activa* of the most ordinary people, played out in a landscape dominated by a feeling of experiencing 'slow violence' (Vorbrugg 2022).

Part of the economic perspective in this book aims to drill down to the experience of 'prospectlessness' but refutes the idea that resistance or striving is unthinkable. To help conceptualize this I adapt Mark Fisher's (2009) term 'capitalist realism' to help describe Russian reality. This term is useful in explaining the ground-zero mechanics of Russia's system – where coercion is more about persuading people that 'there is no alternative' to economic submission than in the fear of the police truncheon, or the argument that people need to actively fight a collective West. The war merely accelerates and intensifies the system set up in the 1990s, now with added territories where more open violence can be inflicted and rights further restricted. While some see occupation of Donbas and southeastern Ukraine as neo-colonial forms of extraction, their treatment reiterates the 'compact' of capital-labour in the Russian system as a whole: miser and miserable corporatism where people are the 'new oil' to lubricate the flow of economic rents upwards (Morris 2019a). Indeed, many observers have felt that Russia has always had a 'comprador' internal colonial arrangement. It doesn't matter whether the human resource is in Yakutia in the Far East or the 'new' territories around occupied Mariupol. Russification is about making legible to the state the human material needed for extraction. Plenipotentiaries at all levels mark themselves out as a breed 'above' the rabble they rule, and select the useful or superfluous populations. Any national ideology is skin deep, and certainly most elites are entirely cynical, if not incredulous at pretensions about expanding the 'Russian World'. An economic Darwin is the real figurehead, not that favourite writer of Putin, Ivan Ilyin, or the over-emphasized Eurasianist Aleksandr Dugin.

Rather than thinking of people as subordinate to corrupt state networks or distracting imperialist ideology, the harshest subjectivation is to social Darwinism in the name of market competition. In a notorious public comment that illustrates both the idea of the uncaring state and the indifferent market, a young official in Sverdlovsk Region opined in 2018 during an 'inspirational' speech to assembled youth that 'The state owes you nothing ... the state did not ask your mother to give birth ... it's your life, you must make it yourselves'. Social research on the political in Russia has to deal with material and discursive subordination – the hegemony of the market enforced by a hand holding the whip.

From economic regime to state machine and resistance

One of the founding ideas of political anthropology was that the state is the most important unit of analysis. It is true that political studies have produced ever more sophisticated ways of dealing with this. Neoinstitutionalists acknowledge that political rule-making may be wholly informalized and invisible and yet power is wielded through 'the state'. Douglass North indirectly expresses a core anthropological concern when he defines institutions as 'game rules of a society ... the limitations of human interaction as conceived by people' (1990: 3). In the Russian context the institution of 'clientelism' is one of the most important informal institutions. Clientelist relations of patronage lie like a stifling blanket over all formal organizations. It makes more sense to think of actual institutions in the conventional sense of the word – courts, agencies, political parties – as partly hollowed out by the informal institution of clientelism. Individuals cannot escape this relationship – they 'pay' rents (through collected bribes and non-official services) and more upwards and in return get to keep positions, power, prestige and a livelihood. A few get to enter the sub-elite of judges, rectors, hospital chiefs and make good money on the backs of others they left behind who now have to pay up to them in turn. Certainly, clientelism can go some way to giving an anthropological flavour to how the various Russian state agencies work to their own purpose – enriching various placeholders through corruption. Power struggles are then explained in relation to access to resources. Subsequently, those in a subordinate relationship to regime and state are exploited, coopted, silenced, marginalized: once again, 'internal colonialism' is a useful idea to think with, to a degree. How this occurs has always been a central focus of anthropology. After all, the majority of Russian people are losers in this system. However, clientelism needs to be put into the context of actual contention – there are not only counternarratives but 'insurgent' forms of politics and citizenship that resist. Subordination and domination led to an interest in anthropology in diverse forms of resistance.

James C. Scott made a name for resistance studies in political science and anthropology. This body of work opened a way to conceptualize the 'fugitive political conduct of subordinate groups' and had a smart-sounding name: 'infrapolitics' (1990: xii). I would be the first to argue that Scott's framing, applied to slaves in antebellum United States, and Malaysian peasants in the twentieth century, needs acknowledging in the Russian context. Powerless people are never really so passive or disengaged, and 'weapons of the weak' should be taken seriously. Along with scholars like Christian Fröhlich and Kerstin Jacobsson, one of my aims is to open political studies of Russia to consider 'everyday', or 'micropolitics' as resistant and meaningful too. Even in circumstances of harsh oppression, 'creative and subversive … forms of resistance' mean that claims to active citizenship are possible (Frölich and Jacobsson 2019: 1146). Even now, everyday and microscale anti-war activism remains vibrant, from the mundane to the spectacular: stickering, graffiti, ironic speech in public, underground organized groups promoting escape for soldiers, and even covert sabotage. However, in paying attention to forms of resistance from below, I also heed criticisms of this frame which call for a better contextualization of practices and talk that appears oppositional.

Instead of relying on the elements of social distress in Lyova and his son's talk in the first ethnographic vignette as self-contained examples of political dissent, we should examine them alongside the other political contents of people's lives: how they vote, whether they avoid taxes, the penetration – alongside litanies of the type 'power doesn't speak to or for us' – of narratives that actually perpetuate subordination or deflect blame onto even more marginalized groups. This allows us to understand how this broader definition of the political is linked to perceptions of the war. Did Lyova later come to embrace a view of his 'country, right or wrong' in 2022? Did Lyova nonetheless vote for the ruling party? What were Lyova's views on Central Asian migrants? Did he quickly blame them for economic problems? Where was the emphasis in Sasha's irony about Crimea?[8] In other words, we should always consider and interrogate, and not romanticize what look like infrapolitical

---

8. Most people like Lyova did indeed argue 'my country, right or wrong'; few people willingly voted United Russia by 2018 in my group of working-class families; xenophobia against Central Asians continues to be a significant cause of small-scale social unrest in towns like Izluchino; Sasha, and indeed his father, both quickly came to critique Crimean annexation as the economic costs were perceived as falling on the weakest.

acts of resistance. Do they have substance, and can we move beyond the world of 'talk' to examine micropolitical resistance in sets of practices that may not even be exceptional, but embedded in dispositions and ordinary ways of the lifeworld?

More importantly, the 'resistance' frame cannot be divorced from the interaction of people with state agencies and the world of work in the market economy. Once again, political anthropology tends to emphasize the problem of state reification – that we think too readily of the state as a 'thing' whereas it might be better to attend to its power via effects as a social construct. Specific interactions with bureaucrats and agencies (whether claims-making or resistant) then channel practices and actions. The state is made real in the expectations and lack of expectations people reveal when they talk about it and interact with its representatives. I examine the paradox of people's construction of the Russian state. Powerful ideas about care, paternalism and responsibility abound. They compete with strong counter-currents such as fear of contact with the state and a desire to avoid dependency. Based on experiences where the state has failed to provide basic care or has shown its rapacious capacities, people embrace fundamentalist forms of autonomy from governance and administration. To deal with this paradox, I make a complex two-step move in the second part of the book. A hegemonic idea of social Darwinism is not just internalized and accepted by people. Regardless of the importance of what Michel Foucault called 'governmentality', the internalization of competitive neoliberal values is tempered by subtle moves to reinstate connective values of kinship. Reciprocity, mutual aid and protective responsibility are just as important as the game-like calculation of advantage, interest and debt-credit that the clientelist literature proposes.

People make claims on what they rightly perceive to be an uncaring state. The social imaginary of kinship and care extends even here in powerful yet largely unexamined ways. To get at this we need to take on the challenge of other recent innovations in political anthropology – the decompartmentalization of state institutions. While state organizations and agencies cut across local communities, their actual practices are carried out in specific and very visible local contexts. Observers (and participants, including politicians) make mistakes when they think of the state as 'over' or 'above' the local (Harvey 2005). In some of my recent work I drew attention to the 'incoherence' of Russian state mechanisms. I want to better disaggregate Russia's coercive capacities generalized too readily as 'the strong state'. The legacy of the Soviet state was clear in Russia's capacity to rebuild security architectures. But the service state (the governance and developmental state) was lost with the Party and never rebuilt. Incoherence is the natural outgrowth of this legacy. The ability of clientelist agencies to get basic stuff done, from road building to basic utility infrastructure, continues to be tested. And it shows in the military conduct of war on the home front as much as the warfront.

Grounded anthropological investigation comprehends what 'state capacity' and 'effectiveness' really mean. I argue that incoherence draws ordinary citizens into a highly political relationship with state-making. In dialogue with literature on improvised and devolved state-making, I describe and analyse what happens when regulatory and service providers cannot make the state without ceding ground to the agency of ordinary people and non-state formations such as local businesses. Agency here implies the sociological notion that one can defy social structure to secure change. As a result, metaphors of kinship and care get even more reinvigorated. From the ground up, the overall imaginary of the state is therefore more strongly inflected by ideas of duty, protection and responsibility. Even official ideologies struggle to remain coherent. They are in a rhetorical double bind made even worse by the war on Ukraine. The state offers significant financial incentives to surplus populations to fight in a war, while proposing more social retreat (lower healthcare and education spending). This divergence of 'care' threatens to undermine the foundations of the transactional proposal. In the eyes of many, dangerous criminals, dupes and the feckless are unfairly rewarded by hundreds of thousands of rubles a month at the frontline.[9] This is a structural violence on the rest of society. If you are unwilling to die a senseless death, you are not worthy of care. And yet society is deeply disturbed, and this has real effects. There is good evidence about businesses being unwilling to hire Wagner fighters and others who have been demobilized. The very 'heroes' of Donbas are subject to social sanctions from below even as from above they are incorporated into the social code of reward which the regime wants to impose.

The whole political cosmology of Russia as a 'reality map' was little changed until 2022. 'Keep your head down and shut up; politics is a dirty business, but trust in the boss'. War presents an impossible dilemma. To win, the regime needs both ideological and physical mobilization of the population and yet its *raison d'être* has been to divide, demotivate and silence. The dreamy mantra of 'stability' threatens to collapse under such contorted transactional logics. Tropes taken from the thinking of philosopher Gilles Deleuze such as 'lines of flight' and nomadism nonetheless appear to me highly apt in explaining the active response of people in Russia. In the third part of the book, I descend into the micropolitical realm where the sum of tiny, almost invisible and intimate practices adds up to more than the sum of their modest parts. Much work on political activism is on the spectacular opposition protests of Navalny supporters or the sporadic public outcries at pollution, housing renovation and other specific issues. These are quickly contained by the coercive

9. 100,000rb is about $1000 as of 2024, which in turn is around 30 per cent more than a decent blue-collar salary in a regional town or city. The financial incentive is overplayed in a lot of analysis because it is only really effective in cases of relative poverty, which, admittedly, are plenty. Many returning soldiers report that the state holds out on paying them, especially if they return disabled. There are many other difficulties in accessing war-related benefits which have been widely reported. A common response by the state authorities is that they had not anticipated such high 'demand' for services, for example, the presidentially decreed grant of agricultural land for soldiers. As of June 2024, the 'Mobilization, News, What to Do?' Telegram channel had 130,000 subscribers, and also reported that of funds set aside for the social organization Defender of the Fatherland, 97 per cent were spent on running and staffing expenses.

state. As a result of this and the ill-defined meaning of the political, the 'rest' are seen as disengaged, apathetic, sheep and so on. However, the micropolitical is a way to foreground the content of even the most mundane everyday practices and discourse – their tectonic potential over time.

Not only does village and small-town life pulsate with actual political discussions, people act as agents with their feet, their hands and the resources available to them. Rarely is any of this political intensity visible in public or organized ways, although I devote plenty of space at the end of this book to the limited forms of public activism. Both 'noisy' and 'quiet' or even insidious politics are given equal prominence. Phenomena such as the informal economy of garages and other liminal spaces are underestimated in their political significance. Written off as marginal or compensatory practices of the Russian precariat, in fact they comprise a big part of the real economy. That they stubbornly lie beyond the purview of the fiscal state as well as the administrative (cadastral) state is significant. People's 'flight' into such liminal spaces of production has political meaning as much as economic effects. As Benedict Kerkvliet (2009) has argued, the cumulative effect of 'low profile', and even private behaviour, means 'everyday politics' is worthy of attention. Taking constellations of micropolitical life seriously, we can anticipate changes at the macro level that otherwise defy explanation to those observers satisfied only with the actions of elites. Overall, this book reiterates in the Russian context one of the main insights of political anthropology – that the separation of the political from the social is an ideological construct of Western political science. Just as the autonomy of the 'political' is an illusion in modern democratic societies (Gledhill 2000), this essentially Eurocentric mistake can be critiqued by looking at complex 'authoritarian' societies. At every turn, societies like Russia's serve as an early-warning system for the degradation of the public sphere, the rise of populist and authoritarian politics, the digital control society and many more of the core challenges facing us in the twenty-first century. We ignore these lessons at our peril. Just as we should learn from new forms of resistance and refusal.

Summary of the book

The rest of the book is structured as follows: in Part 1, **Chapter 1**, I address Russia's war on Ukraine directly. Summarizing the immediate impact on ordinary Russians and their responses to it, I propose 'defensive consolidation' of society as a working definition of the majority's response. I also discuss the problems of relying on secondary measurement of public sentiment and the meaning of everyday nationalism. Reactions are defensive because they are characterized by a lack of enthusiasm, fearfulness and practical ways of fending off the effects: material, psychological and moral stemming from the invasion of Ukraine. Consolidation entails cleaving to both national and local forms of authority and identity, but in an unrequited manner. Far from rally round the flag and jingoism, the problem is the absence of meaningful leadership and persuasive ideology to channel consolidation in the way the regime would like.

In **Chapters 2 and 3**, I contextualize *ressentiment* as a sense of hurt about absent social potentiality, and then follow up a theoretical discussion with an ethnographic treatment. My conceptual departure from most political accounts of frustration is partly inspired by Keti Chukhrov's (2020) theorization of Soviet modernity as offering a template of profoundly 'dealienating' political economy. Responses to the war should not be seen as fundamentally different from other forms of disillusionment. They find their roots in broad feelings of *ressentiment* about the last thirty years – feelings that are chiefly not geopolitical in nature but about the dispossessing trajectory in Russia since the transition from the Soviet era. While the actual Soviet project recedes further from view into the past, all people, I argue, remain in some senses 'Sovietized' through contact with family, and through the political institutions and forms of organization which still strongly retain the stamp of paternalistic and 'socializing' identity. Drawing on Didier Fassin's (2013) distinction between anthropological *ressentiment* and geopolitical resentment, I propose an alternative to a narrow geopolitical reading of frustration. In the accompanying ethnographic chapter, I disaggregate reactions among Russians to the war. Here we meet two very different people navigating feelings of hurt. Vanya cannot achieve more than an absurd inhabitation of life – a cruel parody of the striving working-class dignity his Soviet father envisaged for him. Nonetheless, even for him, 'second best' forms of communication and connectiveness present themselves in village and town life. Tamara the striving activist type also shares her historical hurt and suffering. She is spurred on by her sense of loss to pursue social and ecological projects. Both Vanya and Tamara are haunted by potential commonality, or *obshchnost*, rather than geopolitical resentment or nostalgia.

In Part 2, **Chapter 4**, I build a structural explanation for the absurd feelings of hopelessness Vanya experiences. Russia is at the forefront of the production of 'capitalist realism' (Fisher 2009). Capitalist realism cultivates relations which reinforce a feeling of exploitation and despair as inevitable and inescapable. If capitalism is, at the present conjunction, sustained by an increasingly authoritarian neoliberalism underpinned by the state, then we should look to regimes like those in Russia as at the vanguard. I focus on aspects of governance that are less 'disguised' in the authoritarian context. These include the relegation of social welfare, extreme naturalization of market logic and a lock-in of public sector austerity. These are facilitated by the absence of a public sphere or possibilities for open political mobilization, fear of the security state and an exhausted population. I argue that Russia is an example of the success of the rhetorics of capitalism in 'making themselves true' as domesticated forms. I ethnographically explore the domestication of such a dismal ideology and show how ordinary people over the course of thirty years have internalized forms of neoliberalism that are extreme by any standards. However, people also sustain an immanent critique of such relations as well as resisting through hybrid forms of 'bare' and 'unruly' entrepreneurialism, alongside making claims for kinship with corporations.

In **Chapter 5**, I turn to grounded interactions of Russian citizens with bureaucrats and the increasingly militarized techno-policing state. In proposing an 'incoherent state', I draw attention to how different actual experience is from two dominant narratives. The first common-sense narrative is that Russia is strong in terms of coercive capacity. Second, most scholars subscribe to a neo-institutionalist deficiency model of 'state withdrawal' (Thelen 2011). Inspired by Tatjana Thelen, I build my own theory of state incoherence: the experience of encountering over-determining and overlapping jurisdictionally competing bureaucratic rules. After a genuine period of low state capacity in the 1990s, the state returns as a network of competing bodies: entrepreneurial and circulating discourses of regulation, rather than concrete organizations. Regulation seeks citizens to absorb into what Deleuze calls 'antiproduction', where the state operates to constrict and stifle emerging social forms (Robinson 2010). However, the incoherence of the state leads to a return of the genuinely social. Processes emerge of negotiated settlement and deregulation. 'Devolution' of governance is led from below in a dramaturgical encounter of two socially-embedded persons: the supplicant and the clerk. I try to restore a multi-scalar analysis of 'the state'; I see it neither as reified homogenous 'form', nor as merely the sum of competing ideologies of order but as 'built' from below.

Part 3 of this book begins with a theoretical discussion in **Chapter 6** of how to align the many possible approaches to ordinary or mundane resistance with the micropolitical frame inherited and adapted from various post-structuralist interventions on the 'political'. Are 'quiet politics' enough to do justice to a Deleuzian model of resistance stemming from desire? I map the insights from feminist emancipatory perspectives, such as Cindi Katz's 'minor theory' (1996), onto the grounded reality of my research participants. Some of the most vulnerable and dispossessed of people are practical Deleuzians – nomadically resistant in relation to both the Russian state and neoliberal capital. This chapter homes in on the micro-scale and insidious forms of refusal which have cumulative scaling effects: the tens of millions of Russians working informally and only partially visible and legible to the Russian state. I take seriously the networks of mutual aid and reciprocity which undermine efforts to 'modernize' and embed communities into the state-capital matrix. The point here is not just to underline the specificity of the Russian case; the small tricks in the everyday which people actively employ to make their lives fuller and less governed by the logic of capitalist realism are present in all societies.

In **Chapter 7**, I turn to the material processes of households steeped in a gestalt of craft and self-production. Shifting perspective from salvage as provisioning, I take seriously creative making and mending as political categories. Gleaning – the right of the poor to take the harvest remainder – is linked to a prefigurative politics of how to live well despite calamity. The current crisis, even prior to Ukraine, sees the struggle for existence of more and more people resemble a form of gleaning. There are increasing hierarchies of plenty and want, but enclosure and expulsion do not stop the marginalized gaining access to the 'left overs'. Nor does dispossession mean that moral economies of the commons disappear (Palomera and Vetta 2016). The second part of the chapter introduces the provisioner as an emblematic figure. New enclosures contain both meanings and materials, but waste and detritus from

Rethinking the Political in Russia

the destructive effects of change are available as resources. Aware of autonomist cautions against romanticized views of resistance, I nonetheless characterize gleaning as a holistic practice and political in nature. The chapter extends the meaning of provisioning to more diverse socio-economic contexts – we are all, whether we realize it or not, creative provisioners and increasingly so.

Chapter 8 shifts the focus to political subjectivity and the everyday among 'actives' and activists. Building on my previous theorization of activism as entailing 'experiential entanglement' (Morris 2023c), I deploy two case studies drawing on 'expert' testimony and observation to illustrate politicized involvement, networking and activism in the increasingly dangerous domestic Russian environment. While I focus on the intersubjective experiences of activists, these cases bring to light process-tracing, histories of politicization, practical matters of organization, capacity building and migration between sites and causes of contention. I contrast 'pro' and anti-war activism. The latter evolves from environmental protests before the war, pointing to how decentralized activism has the potential to survive the harsh clampdown. This is a story of continually transformative activism; it is hard to define single causes or coherent groups. One week a group works together on flyers highlighting the illegal burial of rubbish in a national park. The next week a single activist 'affiliated' to the environmentalists undertakes covert anti-war vandalism. A month later a smaller core funds legal advice for an elected politician to deny a planning licence to a polluting plant. However, in form and development, anti-war activism differs little from 'pro-war' activism. I devote space to the ambivalent politics of those building organizational capacity to help people in Donbas and Russian soldiers. Nomadic and transverse activism demands a more serious look at the micro-political foundations of contention and commitment.

In a concluding **Chapter 9**, I draw together the materials, people and reflections of the book. Russia is a 'crisis heterotopia' – a disturbing time-space containing what look like the most dysfunctional elements of contemporary neoliberal capitalism and the authoritarian tendencies of the modern state. However, this heterotopia is merely one world within our world where the current crises are played out in greater relative dramaturgical intensity than in our own societies. The situation of ordinary people's subaltern position to the political-economic regime is both banal and taken for granted. But it is also delimited – we can trace its edges. Crisis heterotopias contain dual meanings. They reflect shared challenges but also give glimpses of resolution. They have room for several tendencies and subregions of dwelling that try to escape along lines of flight. Provisioning, informal and delegated governance, everyday politics, activism and solidarity all show us how the small agency and structure of social(ist) feeling link up into the form of 'small lifeboats'.

Part I

ABSENT PRESENCES

Chapter 1

WAR AND SOCIETY'S RESPONSE: DEFENSIVE CONSOLIDATION

The full-scale invasion of Ukraine led to initial shock and then to forms of emotional and cognitive coping for the majority – it was just too painful to acknowledge full-scale war on a neighbour with whom so many millions of Russians had close ties of friendship, family or work. Since summer 2022, the grinding yet mainly distanced violence provoked a specific perception of shrinking prospects: *bezperspektivnost* – a loss of possible futures for some, and *bezyskhodnost* – a frustrated hopelessness, for others. While grief, despair and fear were some reactions early in 2022, they had to be normalized, or emotionally tamed in some way.[1] And the narrowing of future horizons was one consensus that people holding different opinions could agree on.

Little has been written about the palpable fear pervading Russian society before the failed Ukrainian counter-offensive in 2023. There was open talk of the destruction of the Russian state or even 'Russian civilization'. Anxiety and apprehension of sanctions, military mobilization by the authorities and the threat of the war 'coming home' were obvious when speaking to all kinds of people. This was much in contrast to the picture of indifference and cynicism, or even passive support, painted by many at the time.[2] At first, I witnessed a snapshot of reactions,

1. The regular and detailed analytical reports of the research collective the Public Sociology Lab provide a good barometer of changes in public feeling towards the war. It is revealing of the bias towards survey data that the detailed, robust and regular reports based on interviews and ethnography by PSL, including those translated into English, got little coverage in the press or even scholarly engagement so far. For a representative example, see Erpyleva and Kappinen (2023).

2. Not a day went by, when I first drafted this chapter in early 2023, without prominent observers writing that Russians 'don't care' or are indifferent to Ukraine's fate. This seems to me to be a classic misconception based on a lack of sociological and ethnographic imagination. It mistakes silence and reticence for (lack of) feelings. The point of immersive approaches such as mine is to be able to spend time talking to people, which then almost always elicits talk based on deep reflection and feeling about the war. Feelings both 'positive' and 'negative' emerge, but hardly indifference.

first on a minute-by-minute basis as the first rockets fell on Kyiv, and then in even more difficult or defiant exchanges in response to events like the murder of civilians in Bucha, the destruction of the city of Mariupol, and the effect of sanctions and withdrawal of Western companies from Russia.

Many reactions to the war – which those outside Russia interpret as callous or exculpatory – find their origin in the slow eradication of a sense of progress. Future *perspektivy* slipped ever faster away; 'positive prospects' receded beyond the horizon. A majority have sensed the loosening grasp on positive change. It would be hard not to experience in some way a palpable sense of the last dozen or more years as economic stagnation and the increasing turn to culture war. However, few were directly touched by foreign agent laws (stigmatizing and harassing those with any foreign NGO funding or even social media income), anti-LGBT policies or the criminalization of much protest activity. By the same token, the 'feeling' that the regime was itself entrenching itself in an 'us and them' relationship with the West could hardly be ignored by anyone. The war was the final push for more mobile citizens, some of whom experience a sense of relief as much as regret in leaving Russia and cutting ties. My focus is on those with fewer socio-economic resources: those who stay regardless of what their views on the misnamed 'Special Military Operation' in Ukraine might be. We can say that only a small minority experienced real enthusiasm in February 2022 or since. This is in marked contrast to the sense of fulfilment that was documented after the annexation of Crimea and its 'reincorporation', as most saw it, into the Russian 'core lands' (Alexseev and Hale 2016, Lankina 2016, Lipman 2016).

But was Crimea such a watershed moment for public opinion? And what if revisiting the basis for that perception changed our ideas about the current war? Maria Lipman and Tomila Lankina use the word 'euphoria' to describe the public response to Crimea's annexation. However, this characterization emerges only through an interpretation of opinion polling and quickly becomes a 'social fact' without much evidential basis; both authors treat it as self-evident without any need for qualification. Mikhail Alexseev and Henry Hale parse survey data to argue that Crimea saw a measurable shift in the assessment of Putin's leadership in comparison with other Russian politicians. Yet they find only a 34 per cent approval of Putin in terms of his ability to provide a positive basis for building Russian national identity. More critical attempts at discourse analysis reveal how 'euphoric' public sentiment is at least partly a construct of media treatment without robust evidence beyond spectacle – a very unwise barometer of society. Even scholarly responses to the full-scale invasion tend towards the mistaken interpretation of managed public spectacle as evidence for public consolidation.

When Crimea was hurriedly annexed, despite Putin's promise to the contrary a few weeks earlier, widely disseminated positive sentiment (exclusively from social media and not actual sociological research on the ground) was actually matched by ironic, and even reflexively critical responses among the public (Tomášková 2017). Anna Arutunyan (2015) more critically argues for Putin's lack of genuine 'popularity' throughout much of the period of his tenure. Gulnaz Sharafutdinova (2020: 173) also uses the term 'euphoria' about Crimea. But in a comment close

1. Society's Response: Defensive Consolidation 29

to my argument in this chapter, she argues that emotional responses to political events signify 'societal demand for horizontal linkages and collective identities' beyond nationalism. To summarize, it is important to stress how much received opinion about public sentiment is an artefact of polling. Often this lacks what social scientists call 'triangulation' – i.e. checking from multiple perspectives. If we stop to listen ethnographically, we can uncover deeper currents of sentiment, like those Sharafutdinova does: of frustrated social connectiveness.

That feelings of fear and trepidation quickly grew after the annexation because of the war in eastern Ukraine in 2014 shows how ephemeral any positive feedback was to annexation (Sharafutdinova 2020).[3] A quickly waning 'Crimea effect', just like the stifled consolidation after the invasion of 2022, emphasizes the frustrated desire for connectedness and recognition at the root of societal troubles and how the geopolitical 'solution' in no way satisfies this.[4] Like after 2014, the negative economic effects of foreign policy are quickly reflected in public calculus, offsetting or even negating so-called 'patriotic-nationalist' activation (Sherlock 2020). Regarding the 2022 invasion, Ishchenko and Zhuravlev (2022) are close to my position when they argue that aggressive foreign policy took on a 'crystalizing' agency of its own. Even hawkish elites were surprised by their incorporation into a process whereby imperialistic and revanchist narratives were deployed increasingly shrilly. Not only that, but since 2022 it became hard to ignore the waxing and waning of competing and contradictory official narratives – from 'saving the Russians in Donbas', resisting NATO encirclement, defanging fascist Ukrainians, to vague 'civilizational' defence against a degenerate 'collective West'. Social fragmentation and public alienation from formal politics, not to mention confusion from the continuous flip-flop of propagandists, meant that the best adjective to describe Russian public opinion was not 'support', or even 'sympathy' for the foreign policy aims of the state, but a 'startle' reflex (2022: 670).

In this chapter, I connect 'defensive consolidation' – what I see as the chief response among Russians to the war – to a broader arc of postsocialist history. Defensive consolidation is the admixture of frustrated sentiments and narratives, not about a homeland under threat but a society. Consolidation may access 'victim' narratives and link to political propaganda, but a greater part is driven by stronger and deeper currents. Most significant is the imperative – frequently frustrated – to find modes of citizenship and community that would support a society in crisis and lead to its recovery. These are often implicitly or

---

3. For a nuanced view of some counterintuitive effects of the limited scope of positive shifts in patriotic sentiment after Crimea on public opinion which have relevance to the 2022–present context, see Hale (2018).

4. Nadkarni and Shevchenko (2004) use the word 'frustration' to describe responses to the disjunctive post-Soviet event and link it to a general sense of 'hysteresis' or lag. I would go further – frustration is if anything too 'articulate' a feeling. The absurdity of inhabiting this present, when a different pathway was possible, characterizes the meaning of social suffering and is evident in interpretations of reality.

explicitly in conflict with the military mobilization, and of course the war itself. Ironically, the war brings into the open frustrations about society's trajectory over the last thirty-odd years. While the war shuts down criticism of foreign policy, it counter-intuitively seems to open more space for domestic discontent, even while elites talk about the need for harmony and consensus. Consolidation then is a story about dispersed yet visible processes of the reactivation of the social at the base level and is different from 'rally around the flag'.[5]

Take the story about a children's hockey team in Nizhnii Novgorod whose trainer is mobilized and then killed in late 2022. The media reports show pictures of placards held by the children seeing off their beloved sports coach. However, the text of the story reveals that these children are protesting his loss to the community and the risk to their 'well-being'. Interviews with parents support this message. His absence will not only lead to the loss of a teacher and trainer but damage the ethical foundations of the children's lives and personalities, and their future 'realization'. After his death is announced – a few weeks later – the atmosphere is not one of patriotic sacrifice, but of tragedy and woe. Once more, commentators mention his forced mobilization. This drama unfolded on VKontakte – the main social media platform used in Russia and heavily censored and self-censored.[6]

To understand what seems from the outside like muted or passive acceptance of the war, but which is more complex, we have to do two things. First, dig deep into the structure of Russian society – characterized by economic adversity and political disconnection. Second, we need to zoom out – to look at how disappointment and the seemingly fruitless searches for a connective idea to make sense of the new Russia after 1991 find incomplete fulfilment in expressing approval of the decisions of state. In Henry Hale's (2018) parsing of recent survey data, 'approval' of the leader is not so much about effects of patriotic-nationalism or charisma, but the fruitless search for state care, and the lack of a sustainable

---

5. To be against the mobilization does not mean a person does not support the purported aims of the military campaign to 'denazify' Ukraine, or 'save' the Russian-speakers of Donbas from 'genocide'. However, the many ellipses and missing context in coverage of public opinion once more underline the broad lack of enthusiasm and positively articulated support for the war.

6. See https://vk.com/typical_nn (posts from 9 and 19 October 2022, 9 and 11 January 2023). This local news channel for a city of a million people has over 300,000 subscribers. VK (VKontakte translates as 'InContact' and is often thus shortened) is often wrongly thought to be an apolitical space frequented by the passive majority whereas more active citizens are thought to use Facebook. While individuals are less likely to express dissent or socially undesirable and possibly dangerous opinions on VK on their personal pages, this does not apply to the content of, and comments to, community channels where much more diversity is observed. Even after the invasion of Ukraine, VK contains critical postings from channels as well as critical comments from identifiable individuals towards the war. The story of the mobilized sports coach provoked hundreds of comments. Many were critical and many were from Russian citizens using their personal and non-anonymous accounts.

1. Society's Response: Defensive Consolidation

idea of identity.[7] Now is the beginning of the end of Putinism, but it was never a coherent ideology and in many senses is just part of exhausting continuous change that goes back to 1986 and Gorbachev's reforms. The descent of the core elite into militarism, chauvinism and isolationism is a last attempt to offer an answer to the question posed by big politics: 'who are the Russians?'[8] The unexpected risk-taking of political hawks took society by surprise. The fearful and gloomy initial response by most people, apart from a small constituency of ultra-loyalist 'patriots', allows us in retrospect to see what a dead-end the series of political and economic choices represent within the context of a process of change over thirty years in the making. What was initially thought to be a gradualist civil-liberal programme of incorporation of Russia into the global capitalist order (Sharafutdinova 2020: 8) ends in absurdity and an orgy of violence, much of which is now 'coming home' with traumatized veterans, Cargo 200 and with Ukrainian drones.[9]

So much has been written about a rise in nationalism, but perceptive observers, while emphasizing the resonance of imperialistic narratives about the Soviet period (Blackburn 2021: 95–7), question how useful the frame of state-promoted nationalism really is. State patriotic promotion is relatively malleable to entrepreneurial forces from below, and therefore diffuse, while retaining a relative antipathy to ethnicizing or xenophobic nationalism (Goode 2018). While online there are of course many examples to be found of virulent anti-Ukrainian rhetoric, overall there is a marked absence of racialization despite the attempts of regime-linked propagandists to play this card. Instead, the war has progressively seen official propaganda shift towards emphasizing the perfidious role of NATO countries, seemingly because of the difficulty in mobilizing sentiment. As we see below, this is more effective because it links to Soviet-era 'encirclement' narratives. Furthermore, the NATO card is one where 'ordinary' – in the sense of people not

---

7. By state competence I mean the idea that governance serves the common good. Ironically, Putin as decision-maker is not really the focus of 'approval', rather he represents something identifiably familiar and reassuring to the majority who share a Soviet connection, even those who hated the KGB and believe the many anti-corruption reports by people like Alexei Navalny (cf. Gaufman 2023, who argues against the idea of 'cult of Putin'). The president is many things that represent more than the sum of Russian identity even now: social mobility of the Soviet period, co-suffering in war (Second World War blockade parents and sibling), reform-adjacent 'new people' of the late 1980s, battles in the 'unbridled' 1990s, a seemingly reluctant, non-intelligentsia, technocratic, straight-talking type of politics. However cultivated, curated, or downright false these aspects of his image, they resonate. While his personal popularity should not be overestimated, as it frequently is, his socio-historical resonance among people over forty cannot be denied.

8. A more accurate, but cumbersome version of this question would be: 'who are the people who live in the Russian Federation, the former core of a larger state and polity?' This more accurate question would foreground the lack of purchase in ordinary talk of ethnic nationalism.

9. 'Cargo 200' is the well-known code for military transportation home of soldiers' corpses.

following international affairs – political sentiment expresses shared 'common sense'. Resentment against NATO expansion since 1991 is easily linked in a person's mind to what are really disparate processes: such as the unipolar moment of US (over)confidence in foreign policy from 1999 to 2021, EU expansion as a normative legal order, and the decline in Russian hard and soft power. A typical conversation, even with anti-war people, goes along the lines of: 'if the Cold War ended, why did the West push so much for the Baltics and Poland to join NATO? What did they have to fear from us?' Of course, to Balts or many Eastern Europeans, these responses are a sign of a hopeless inability to acknowledge the historical aggression of Russia and the USSR towards them and ample evidence of the way 'imperial-mindedness' actively forgets the past.

Overall, I agree with Marlene Laruelle (2019: 8–9) that for Russian nationalism to have purchase as a broad ideological movement we would have to identify its potential to mobilize beyond its visibility as a state-sponsored discourse or grumbling lay narrative of exclusion. Other approaches stress the relative self-sufficiency of 'everyday nationalism' as it emerges in individual practices as offering 'ontological security' (Goode et al. 2022). The current war would tend to undermine the explanatory power of top-down 'nationalism' not least because of the lack of willing volunteers for a war propagandized as a defence of Russia and Russians. The narrowness of an 'identitarian' frame may mislead us despite the clear resonance of Putin's emotional rhetoric of the post-Soviet period as one of shared 'pain' and 'trauma' (Shirikov 2022).

Many grudgingly express consent by proxy of the decisions of state if cornered in public. But what this means is: 'the elite is distant and has its own agenda – who am I to disagree?' Equally, many harbour deep antipathy to the course taken because they are able to imagine the long-term outcome of further distance from what was just a generation ago called 'our common European home'. In my understanding of 'consolidation', I differ then from observers like Volodymyr Ishchenko and Oleg Zhuravlev (2022) who emphasize ritualistic loyalty as a result of decades-long depoliticization, while I agree with them that a hegemonic crisis in authority accelerates because of the war. Talk for more than a few minutes and difficult topics are acknowledged. There is visible cognitive dissonance about unprovoked aggression towards a neighbour, and autarkic withdrawal from the global economy, and not least, dependence on a mercantile China. Some repeat propaganda tropes but these only lie on the surface of political consciousness. Paradoxically, the war is seen as both inevitable and yet the 'wrong' answer to the question: 'who are we Russians?' Most ordinary people have an entirely different question in mind. This is not really a 'question'; rather, it is a demand for social reparation which the regime does not acknowledge. How to address the loss of a 'feeling', an 'experience' of social coherence and supra-national purpose that the Soviet period – however flawed and coercive in practice – provided? I put those two words about senses of epoch in quotation marks to highlight how my argument is aimed at going beyond a simplistic reading of people's relationship to the USSR as 'nostalgic' based on personal experience or even through intergenerational

1. Society's Response: Defensive Consolidation

communication (Anipkin 2018).[10] While those readings are valid on some level, I take up the critique of the nostalgia-frame in more detail in the following chapter. Before discussing Russia at war further, let us step back and take stock of 'late Putinism' as seen by the average person.

Russia's 'long Covid': Late Putinism in context

The Russian economy had its short boom time in the 2000s with real incomes increasing much faster than inflation. Sometimes overlooked is the bookending of this seven- to eight-year period by over a decade of crisis on either side. The 1990s were effectively a lost decade for most. After the global financial crisis of 2008, Russians saw some of the worst income stagnation in Europe, staggering wealth concentration (far higher than the United States or China), and high levels of extreme poverty.[11] What makes Russia exceptional is that the post-1991 political economy was *designed* with wealth concentration in mind. Large-scale corruption grew, and the wealth of a new breed of the super-rich expanded. After the original oligarchs were politically neutered in the first five years of the twenty-first century, a new network of rich and powerful people emerged among those with political connections via the security services – the so-called *siloviki*.

However, the increasingly online population could no longer claim blissfully ignorance; the tenacious efforts of oppositionist Alexei Navalny to publicize corruption at the highest level meant that no one could ignore the rapacious appetites of the new elite set against deteriorating standards in schooling, health and social infrastructure more generally. While oil and gas revenues continued to make Russia, or rather, Moscow, rich in terms of GDP, average incomes fell behind, and regional inequality remained enormous. Politicians responded with the rhetoric of social Darwinism, my focus in Chapter 4. They lamented the lack of 'entrepreneurialism' or bootstrapping among Russians. More than once a minor scandal ensued after unguarded statements by politicians, such as 'no one asked

---

10. I generally avoid using the term 'nostalgia'. Uses of the past do not so much look back in terms of comparing loss to a superior socialist period (for a discussion of 'restorative' nostalgia versus 'reflective', see Svetlana Boym's (2008) well-known division). Nor is it quite a '"longing for longing" – a reflective nostalgia sensitive to the "past structure of desire"' (Nadkarni and Shevchenko 2004: 503). Reflective nostalgia in places like Russia is said to lament the impossible recovery of a bright and naïve hopefulness that history is not yet ended. Instead, I emphasize a relationship with the past as activating a common groping towards the recovery of social potentiality at a scale mundane, but which extends beyond the individual.

11. By 2018, real incomes had likely declined by 11 per cent since 2014 (Zubarevich and Safronov 2019). The true, and staggering, extent of high poverty and inequality levels in Russia is likely not adequately captured by statistics, but it is reasonable to say that as of 2024 incomes are no higher in real terms than 2013. On inequality, see Remington (2018).

34 *Everyday Politics in Russia*

you to have children', or, 'if you're not already successful then why should I talk to you?' So even before the present crisis, Russia had drifted into a long period of growing social discontent. A weak economy focussed on export of raw materials only benefits a small minority who can extract rents – often via corruption. Furthermore, no one can ignore the largely cynical and distant political class. The main rhetorical strategies of 'political technologists' like Vladislav Surkov revolved around stoking a culture war against symbols of so-called Western permissiveness such as LGBT flags, and proposing backward-looking evocations of imperial greatness, often centred on the 'Russian' victory in the Second World War and on strong-state conservatism. These were omnipresent on TV but mainly consumed passively. In any case they were way down the list of priorities when it came to viewing habits.

The Covid-19 pandemic in 2020–2 hit Russia particularly hard. The federal government cynically delegated responsibility to subnational authorities who medicalized everyday life, riding roughshod over the limited civil rights of Russians (Kuksa 2020). The burden fell on what was already a chronically underfunded health service and ageing, sick population, and by some counts Russia had the highest death rates of any developed country.[12] Moscow and its region, where over 10 per cent of Russians live, instituted relatively harsh lockdowns and used advanced technology to monitor citizens' quarantine. Arbitrary punishment was meted out to thousands of ill people due to the rushed and buggy programming of its self-isolation app.

When vaccination arrived, people didn't trust their authorities and medical personnel. Mass avoidance of the vaccine was not so much about anti-science views but reflected a rational calculus – Russia's state is ineffective at protecting people at the best of times. People's resentment also played a part. 'Why should I risk my health in getting a jab of unknown provenance when the state does nothing for me' was a frequent rejoinder. People refused a call to reciprocal social solidarity, not because they are strongly individualist, but because the experience of poor medical services, corruption and lack of meaningful social protection along with harsh restrictions on civil rights meant they had little confidence or trust in provision (Morris 2021b). The idea that the weakest will have to look after themselves is coded into the callous 'common sense' of Russian politics itself, as later chapters of this book explore.

Two years later, war surprised almost everyone, including even intimates of Putin himself, because Russia was already well past the point where it could follow through effectively on the 2014 military intervention in Donbas. And, one cannot overemphasize, there was no public appetite for foreign policy revanchism. To observers focussed on the rhetorics of chauvinism and 'victim' narratives, it now

---

12. In mid-2021, extrapolating from publicly available mortality statistics, journalists suggested a total of around half a million excess deaths (MKRU 2021). There are plausible estimates that are higher still (leading independent demographer Aleksei Raksha has commented in various interviews that he thinks a million people died).

1. Society's Response: Defensive Consolidation 35

seems reasonable to assume Putin meant what he had been saying since 2007: that international law was a dead letter for so-called Great Powers and that he would take inspiration from the United States to show that might makes right.[13] These narratives relate to complaints about Russia's alleged side-lining in international affairs since 1991, a perception of a lack of genuine incorporation into the global order (such as that afforded to West Germany and Japan after 1945), and the specific charge that 'the West' broke promises by expanding NATO eastwards. It is of course no coincidence that while Putin was exposed to these resenting geopolitical ideas before 2007, it was Russia's economic recovery running out of steam and falls in his popularity that surely focussed his mind on populist calls to 'make Russia great again'.

Commentary on the present Ukraine war for Euro-American public consumption often sees a rehearsal of these points to highlight the effective leveraging of this victim narrative by the Russian regime, coupled with ordinary people's supposed nostalgia for the USSR's Great Power status. The allegation is that Russians have been willing consumers of this Putin-branded Kool-Aid. It is true that some older Russians feel that their country is 'disrespected' and there are even those who think Russia should be feared. Some celebrate Ukraine being 'put in its place'. However, even among my older interlocutors, these are the exception, not the rule. A typical response would be that of bewilderment directly related to a sense of the unfinishedness of the Soviet multi-national project (and certainly, misrecognition about its centre-periphery power relations). More recently (since 2023), there are consolidating feelings of powerlessness which can be misinterpreted as unconditional support for war aims. These feelings certainly wish to accelerate the end to the conflict even at the expense of further suffering by Ukrainians and Russian soldiers like. The jury is out on how much people care whether they 'keep' Donbas or not. Crimea is another matter but not because of its historical (since Catherine the Great) association with Russian imperial power. Much more important is that Crimea represents an aspect of Soviet-Russian emotional wholeness for some, and a feeling of close familialness for others.[14] It became an integral part of the Russo-Soviet 'Riviera' during the twentieth century, and the idea of it being 'a foreign country' goes against lay notions of access to the imaginary of common recreational rights. One does not have to sympathize with Russian complaints that Crimea should not have been administratively attached to Soviet Ukraine to understand the situated rationality behind objections to returning it to a post-bellum Kyiv, Westphalian niceties aside.

Let's take Julia Evgenievna from Moscow whom I've known since 1995. A Russian-Ukrainian with admix of Tatar heritage, Julia was born in Kazakhstan

---

13. On revanchism, see Toal (2017). On chauvinism, see Kuzio (2016). On Russia as 'betrayed' victim of international geopolitics, see Tsygankov (2015).

14. This idea of hurtfulness is a much better explanation of Alexei Navalny's perceptive comment that Crimea wasn't like a 'sandwich' to be given back out of sanguine geopolitical logic.

in the 1940s and after training as an engineer helped construct power plants in Central Asia and then Vietnam. She has a daughter, son-in-law and grandchildren in Zaporozhe City, Ukraine. As the city was shelled and bombed by Russian forces in late 2022, she struggled to align her responses.

> The army will save these people from the bad ones [...] Why are they fighting back and prolonging things? It must be because of the fascists in Kiev.

'But mum', says her other daughter, Katya, who has lived all her adult life in Moscow, 'It's Russians bombing civilians and trying to kill my sister and your grandchildren'. It's no good; on some ultimate level this cannot be rationalized, cannot be assimilated. 'It would be better for them to give up then. To save themselves. Why do they keep fighting then?' responds Julia. Other former Soviet people, and even younger ones, simultaneously acknowledge that Ukraine is a sovereign state, but insist that within the late USSR, Ukraine and Russia were core 'brotherly' constituents.[15] They might well also acknowledge the 1930s Ukrainian famine, or *Holodomor* as part of the political repression of Ukrainian identity. However, they would in the same breath downplay the idea of national targeting, pointing out that the hunger weapon was also used in Russia and Kazakhstan by a multiethnic Soviet leadership. Expropriation was delegated to local communist elites who were often co-ethnics of the people they exterminated or exiled. I do not include this information as historical gloss – these are the rationalizations and exculpations that even people without much education bring up. The problem of the multinational nature of the USSR also returns with a vengeance. People like Julia argue: 'Crimea is Russian [-speaking, and majority ethnically], why do Ukrainians need it? If borders didn't matter before, why do they now?'

While both 'post-colonial' knowledge and guilt exist about the biggest horrors inflicted during the USSR, there is widespread ignorance of other episodes such as the deportation of Crimean Tatars, or the mass murder of tens of thousands of political prisoners in west Ukraine in 1941 by the NKVD. The russification of Ukraine is downplayed in Russian vernacular understandings of history. This is, once again, because of ignorance, but also the knowledge of Russian as lingua franca and as prestige language in Ukrainian cities in the USSR. As a result, lay people and even the educated often still deploy the Soviet official term: 'friendship of peoples' to express their (diverse) feelings about the Russo-Ukrainian war. This term encapsulates the coexistence of a contradictory multinational civic identity alongside an essentialized ethno-nationalist way of thinking. So, in saying 'why can't we have friendship of people's back', or, 'Ukrainians are denying the friendship of peoples between us', Russians sustain the distinctive Soviet-type

---

15. People often make use of the Soviet official term: 'friendship of peoples' to express their (diverse) feelings about the Russo-Ukrainian war. This term encapsulates the coexistence of a contradictory multinational civic identity alongside an essentialized ethno-nationalist way of thinking (Irby forthcoming).

1. Society's Response: Defensive Consolidation

framing of imperial relations where Ukrainians are certainly in a subordinate, and arguably subaltern position. This is an impossible juggling which derives from thinking Soviet in the vernacular: Ukrainians are differentiated but not ethnicized (except for the bad ones resisting) at the same time as their status as supra-national Soviet citizens is preserved or restored (without asking for their consent).[16] This operation is distinct from the Russian state's invention of the ideological category of 'compatriots' used about Ukraine and elsewhere to stake claims on Russian speakers abroad. Nonetheless, both categories – 'brothers' and 'compatriots' – coincide, in that they propose a recuperation of citizenship to a state that no longer exists (but may in the future return).[17]

Looking back to February 2022, I opened my phone messenger with great trepidation on the morning of Russia's invasion. I had been in conversation with many people more frequently in early 2022 as it became clear the situation was getting worse. The initial reaction was disbelief, shock: that roller-coaster vertigo feeling – a giddy anxiety – 'it can't really have happened? How can he [Putin – who is rarely named] have made this decision?', Anton wrote to me from his garage out in the sticks where he takes cash to repair cars. Even in the first twenty-four hours, shock started to morph, and coping mechanisms kicked in. Most people daily consume state-controlled media. People are influenced, sometimes strongly, by the state's messaging, but we should be cautious about propaganda's supposed 'hypodermic needle' effects; a predetermined correct response is never just injected and absorbed into what is misleadingly called 'public opinion'.

The state has shut down most easily accessible sources of trustworthy alternative information. After the war started, a VPN was needed to access many sites such as Facebook and Russian language sites critical of the regime. Many people were rightly afraid to even talk about the war given the immediate move by the government to criminalize the publication of information that 'discredits' the Russian armed forces – a frighteningly wide definition that has been applied to people merely 'liking' a post on social media.

The invasion was officially called a 'special antiterrorist' operation against 'neo-Nazis', but it quickly became clear that things were not going according to plan. By 2023, even the aims of the operation were hard for most people to explain. This fed into coping mechanisms – forms of 'defensive consolidation'. On one level this is a retreat into comforting truths which help individuals deal with cognitive dissonance – so it is a psychological response. Rather than accept that 'our' Russian

---

16. Portraits of virulently anti-Ukrainian nationalist youth, such as those depicted by Ian Garner (2023), are not representative of more than a small minority. Studies such as Garner's show both the value and methodological limitations of social media-based research. One can meet many everyday examples of xenophobia and racism in Russian society; however, we should be sensitive to the stronger alignment between regime propaganda and liberal, middle-class racism, and its historical roots there (Djagalov 2021).

17. On the trope 'druzhba narodov' [friendship of peoples], see Hirsch (2000), cited in a discussion of the legacies of citizenship versus nationality concepts (Irby forthcoming).

troops were indiscriminately using rockets and bombs against targets in Ukraine, people would make similar comments to those of Julia: 'It's better that it's over quickly'; others more callously gravitated to the view that Ukrainians brought this upon themselves: 'it's better that it happens there than here – it was inevitable that the West would provoke a large conflict.'

Reacting to war: From cognitive coping to defensive consolidation

Sociologist Stanley Cohen (2001) wrote a book called *States of Denial* about how people react to unpleasant events, not with critical thinking, but with avoidance. Cohen also problematizes what we mean by 'knowledge'. Most Russian people, even Julia, quite quickly grew to 'know' on some level that her country had invaded Ukraine without genuine provocation, that Russian forces were responsible for the deaths of thousands of Ukrainians including many civilians, and that the massive destruction of eastern Ukraine's urban spaces (where a lot of Russian-speaking people live) was the result. And yet they actively or passively 'did not know'. They on some level continued to make use of narratives about the Ukrainian leadership as guilty, about the West as having provoked the conflict, or propose that Ukrainian resistance only made the conflict worse, or that Ukrainian troops 'chose' to contest or target urban territory, making civilian casualties worse. The popular memory of the defeat of fascism is the most effective 'trump card' manipulated by the regime: 'Russia had to defeat the Nazis almost alone, and now history is repeating itself.' In Julia's case, she would somehow conflate the current conflict with actions in the late USSR, referring to the Russian side as 'the Soviet army' and by implication (unconsciously) demoting Ukrainian sovereignty to an insurgent force.[18] Historians of post-war Germany have long known of this problem: even in defeat, collective punishment did not lead to an enduring or deeply held sense of guilt, only a vague feeling of discomfort. However, once again, I would rather avoid psychologizing and instead focus on social effects. More powerful than guilt or shame are competing claims of victimhood that get re-echoed in social intercourse. Collectively, the war just gets incorporated into already existing feelings of resentment which have a social cause – a structure of feeling.

Even among those with a more instinctive grasp of the coercive capacities of their own state and the injustice of Russia's invasion, the response was chiefly defensive consolidation. I don't use the familiar term 'rally round the flag' because expressions of patriotism, or nationalism, or enthusiasm for the campaign or for the Russian government were few and far between. The Russian government has failed in creating a coherent conservative, or nationalist ideology, or meaningful reasons beyond self-interest and advancement for loyalty to the regime. When talking about the Russian state's opaqueness or incoherence in the eyes of

18. Denys Gorbach (2024) finds similar slips of the tongue which conflate the Ukrainian army as 'Soviet defenders' among his Kryvyi Rih interlocutors.

1. Society's Response: Defensive Consolidation 39

Russians, people often fall back on a variety of instinctive 'lay' narratives – some of which coincide with elite talking points. These narratives also have a life of their own relating to social grievances (Morris and Garibyan 2021). Until the war, what genuinely linked people and the regime was the ever-deferred promise of paternalism – legitimacy was always contingent on projection of an ability to 'sort things out' and return some kind of social justice. By 2018 when the amended constitution allowed de-facto indefinite rule, and the pension age was raised significantly, patience had run out. The government had never been so unpopular, nor did many people have much good to say about the elite's ability to balance their own rapacious appetites with broader social needs. People began to openly balk at the barely concealed coercive enthusiasm of the security state and the now obvious decline in living standards and economic prospects for the majority whose livelihoods did not benefit from hydrocarbon revenues.[19]

Against the impossible-to-acknowledge realities of war, the phrase 'truth [*pravda*] is on our side' is used by some in a kind of magical defensive incantation.[20] It is not said with any sense that the speaker celebrates this 'truth'. An alternative translation of this evocative phrase could be 'our cause is just'. Viktor is a retired provincial engineer in his late sixties whom I've known since 2009:

> There's disinformation on both sides, but we have the greater truth. Yes, it's war: we'll find out later who burned whom; there'll be losses, probably big losses for us, and for you [in the West], but one cannot stop inevitable historical processes. This is not about fascism, I will admit. It's about overcoming a greater injustice – the division of fraternal peoples.

19. In late 2021, Levada Center polled Russians on their chief 'fears'. Beyond personal misfortunes, the top-rated ones were fear of regime 'lawlessness', 'a return to political repression' and 'poverty and destitution'. In 2023, the Russian Academy of Sciences' sociological centre published the results of yearly surveys on the 'social political' situation (Levashov et al. 2023). Despite the war appearing to 'consolidate' society, a significant majority still cite 'inequality', 'class stratification', 'the people versus the authorities' as the three main sources of enmity in Russia. When asked what kind of concepts they thought should underpin Russian 'revival', the top were 'fairness' (32 per cent), 'peace' (29 per cent) and 'order' (21 per cent). Some of the smallest measures were for 'autocracy', 'orthodoxy', 'Russian empire', 'Great Power status', though there were also small measures for 'USSR' and 'socialism'. At the beginning of the war, there was a huge spike in the number of respondents citing 'brotherhood'.

20. Ushakin, in a key essay on trauma (2009: 27–8), focusses on the use of the phrase 'the truth is with us' in tragic/traumatic circumstances where the speaker performs rhetorical victimhood. The focus on 'greater' truth for Ushakin links post-Soviet sociality with an articulation of the experience of loss – whether imagined or real: a fixation with negative experience.

40   *Everyday Politics in Russia*

By contrast, his neighbour Boris says to me:

> This is a war of aggression and conquest and a crime against both Ukrainians and Russians. One person took the decision, but as a society we are all responsible, I suppose. I find it hard to look some of my fellow countrymen in the eye these days.

Boris is a former factory workshop foreman, illustrating that social class is not clearly correlated with war support. Viktor uses the term 'injustice' in relative terms, promoting revanchist meanings, while acknowledging more immediate socio-political issues. At the same time, Viktor's teenage grandson posts a photo of himself and his friends (see Figure 1) to Instagram (blocked in Russia – he must be using a VPN). They are shirtless, flexing their muscles against the backdrop of a tall city building, probably in Kaluga. The lights in the building have been switched on to illuminate the night city with the pro-invasion symbol 'Z'. Viktor's wife is embarrassed and says it is a 'joke'. Viktor, in turn, thinks it highly inappropriate for his grandson to 'ironize' about something so serious. Later, when we talk again about his acknowledgement of disinformation 'on both sides', Viktor expands on this, talking about genuine distrust of Russian TV channels coverage. Dmitrii Zhikharevich and Daria Savchenko (2023: 4) conducted similar conversations with Russians who reflect on knowledge of the war. In their view respondents subscribed to what they call 'a dysfunctional epistemology of *individual* empiricism' as a way of maintaining a depoliticized position and avoiding moral complicity. Viktor, however, denies his is a 'post-truth' position. Like some other 'pro-war' people, he embraces the moral consequences, but justifies them with a kind of utilitarian, or even universalizing argument – that the ends of a renewed supranational state justify the means.[21] We come back to the idea of 'monist', or encompassing values, in the next chapter.

Another young person I know tries to volunteer for the front in the early days of March 2022, but his medical papers are not in order. His social media is full of images glamourizing the Wehrmacht and SS, and yet in conversation he talks of pride in his Soviet great-grandparents (born in Ukraine) for defeating fascism. In contrast, Dima, an unemployed provincial 25-year-old who is training to become a police officer, talks in October 2022 of the 'idiocy' of those in his age group who are considering signing up.

> Is this patriotism? Hmmm, it's a kind of badge of stupidity and greed. They promise to pay so much because there are no other arguments for fighting. But who would believe you'd even see the money? And for what? Fighting

---

21. Personally, I prefer the conceptual vocabulary of 'monism' to explain ends-means reasoning like that of Viktor. I cover this in the next chapter. However, here I use the term 'universalizing' because this term has been used informally by Grigorii Golosov (in social media posts) to explain what he sees as a civilizational trait in Russian history.

1. Society's Response: Defensive Consolidation

Figure 1 'The "Z" boys flex their muscles.' Image based on a photograph, used by kind permission of Peter Caffrey.

our relatives, the Ukrainians? It's like coming home and punching your sister; kicking in your refrigerator because your senile granddad told you it's made in Germany. It's the elders who are the really culpable ones – sending their sons and husbands off in the hope they get killed and then they can buy a car with the pay-out.

He adds that the number of his peers in this group of volunteers is very small, which is why they tend to be ostracized.

Let's return to the 'defensive consolidators', like Viktor the retired engineer. Two of his words stand out – 'injustice' and 'fraternity'. Zooming out to look at the period since 1991, it is easy to see why these are still Soviet-style keywords that have purchase on the thinking, even of younger people. The incomplete recovery of living standards from 2000 to 2009, which could have been Putin's legacy, only papers over the cracks in the bigger picture. By many measures of human flourishing, subjective well-being and social mobility, Russia has barely progressed since the Soviet period. For the majority, despite the shiny façade of a roaring consumer sector – the trappings of a 'market economy' – life is more of a financial and future-fearful struggle than the so-called Soviet 'era of stagnation'

42   *Everyday Politics in Russia*

in the 1970s and early 1980s.[22] Statistics show that Russia is a struggling middle-income country with a GDP per capita comparable to that of Argentina, Malaysia or Bulgaria. Its oil and gas money flatters this statistic; incomes are so skewed towards the rich that the average wealth of a Russian family (beyond ownership of a concrete panel-built apartment from the 1970s) is negligible. The poor are reliant on micro-credit to get by, and many people struggle to pay utilities – even smartphone data packages. Average incomes in Russia were recently surpassed by China for the first time – a remarkably bad milestone for Russia, given its fifty-year headstart on industrialization, its mineral wealth, highly educated and urban population, and China's still-rural millions. Once again, oil-boosted GDP figures hide the fact that real incomes are similar to those in Mexico, Thailand, Turkey and Brazil. In 2023, even the mainstream Russian press was forced to admit that the average family spends more of its income on basic staples than counterparts in Columbia, Costa Rica or Mexico. It is not hard to see why even official surveys show a significant majority of people over the age of forty express 'nostalgia for the USSR', including nearly half of younger people. Typically, this is dismissed as more evidence of chauvinism (a post-Empire people harking back to a period of greatness), or an expression of the inability of some to adapt to change and a stubborn attachment to the state's management of individual risk – i.e. people expect 'paternalism'.

But we should reject this negative assessment of 'Soviet nostalgia', for the term lacks analytic value. 'Nostalgia' laments 'non-repeatable' time and is often deployed as an accusation that the subject is retrograde or anachronistic in their views. Nonetheless, a sense of lost potential – of something worthwhile, whether a political project of relative equality, a vast federal state of some modernizing power, or a coherent sense of social purpose – can act as a glue that binds all kinds of people to an idea, even an elite. Defensive consolidation is an ambiguous and contingent set of responses related to this absence – it includes finding excuses to justify to oneself what's happening which are logically very tenuous and even self-contradictory. What is noticeable even among those who never voted for Putin is a kind of sunk cost fallacy – 'Putin was wrong, mad even, but now it's started we see the world is against us, but because of that we must go on regardless to the bitter end, for to lose will mean a broader disaster'. Here, the ostensibly 'positive' associations of defensive consolidation – the need for social renewal – bleed into victim politics. These politics propose national exceptionalism and encirclement by enemies – highlighted by Sharafutdinova (2020: 22) – as also

---

22. The now-defunct social justice thinktank Centre for Economic and Political Reform reported in 2016 that 70–80 per cent of poor families' income is spent on essentials only, leaving little left over even for basic items like children's clothing. CEPR's archive and website have been inaccessible since 2022. Overall, poverty in Russia should not be compared to that in Western countries; it really means absolute levels of subsistence and bare survival. A summary of poverty issues can be found in Morris (2017).

1. Society's Response: Defensive Consolidation 43

generated by traumatic impacts post 1991. Nonetheless, such thinking is also tied to longstanding feelings of being a periphery and 'other' to the West – what Viatcheslav Morozov (2015) called the 'normative dependency' of Russia on the West as a 'subaltern Empire'. Furthermore, Morozov argues that the 'negative exercise' underpinning Putin's conservative turn and anti-West rhetoric cannot compete as a consolidating ideology with the 'affirmative' achievements, real and imagined, of the Soviet period.[23] Defensive consolidation may also include critique from ordinary people of the political system based on 'common sense'. As Karine Clément has argued in her book on 'patriotism from below' (Kleman 2021), such feelings may arise thanks to the perceived shortcomings of the social compact – and these are the 'fault' of both elites and 'the collective West' in the popular imagination.

Why do I call such a response 'consolidating' if it echoes back emptily? It involves a cleaving to forms of immediate authority when the higher response is inadequate. So, people ask their village 'elder' what to do and he answers – collect diapers to send to IDPs or to mobilized soldiers to use as bandages. While some remain disorientated, one question does emerge – 'what can I do?' People not stunned into disbelief and stasis genuinely have a desire to do something 'as a part of society'. This comes up against the logic of Russia as politically demobilizing due to elites' fear of any independent action and civicness.[24] And in fact, when people 'cleave' they often find an absence of leadership and no answers – authority is so very brittle and hollow. Defensive consolidation would therefore *not* mean a relative closing of the gap between an elite that has lost its way and a tired and disorientated people. Instead, the inevitable attempt to rechannel frustrated desires for social action echoes emptily. What makes this different from the usual way of looking at reactions to war such as 'rally round the flag' is that consolidation is based on desiderata that are quite dislocated in time and space (the 'good' USSR project, reaction against social dispossession, and loss of normative aims for society in general). It is striking that the majority have not responded with overt nationalistic or even patriotic fervour or enthusiasm. Even pro-war demonstrations must be carefully curated (and people bribed to attend) so afraid is the regime of independent mobilizations. Nonetheless, most people are 'patriots' and seek ways

23. See Morozov (2015: 121) for a discussion of how Russia's counter-hegemonic ideology lacks any positive agenda.

24. Regina Smyth (2021) argues that regime stability in Russia rested on a 'cascade' of demobilization of citizens through two related factors: repression resulting in feelings of protest futility, and persuasion about the inevitability of Putin's continuation as leader. Graeme Robertson (2010) puts demobilization as an active political strategy of authoritarian regimes in a long-term perspective, where repression is coupled with co-optation of potential opponents and competitors. However, demobilization can have a broader meaning: a general disbelief in the ability of people to influence government and therefore focus exclusively on aspects of their life they think they can control and change.

of expressing their belief in their country. For those who are unable to see any frame of social action in the local or community level, the only way of doing this is to defensively consolidate behind the 'idea' of the political struggle for nation (which is hardly even a sense of 'Russianness') against the hegemonic part of the world. In the next chapter, we delve deeper into the question of where an enduring sense of hurt comes from how hauntings of the past produce *ressentiment*.

Chapter 2

FEELING FOR AN ABSENT PRESENCE: THE ROOTS OF RUSSIAN *RESSENTIMENT*

The previous chapter argued the war in Ukraine activates frustrated feelings for social recovery but mainly results in defensive consolidation. If consolidation both provokes and responds to a need for a search for social reparation, then the main available model is that of the past: the Soviet project. Here, I take up the shared and experienced-based approach to politics and history by emphasizing the importance of 'feeling' for both social coherence and supra-national purpose that relate to the Soviet period. At the outset I should say that 'feeling' as I use it relates to 'sense for', rather than 'sentiment/emotions for'. Many scholars have traced the sentimental emotions of older people towards both the cultural products and political order of the USSR. Just like with any post-imperial polity, some feel pride in former greatness and regret its loss. My purpose is different. Based on a fusing of scholarly approaches to social suffering and desire, I argue that what haunts the lives of many is a *feeling for an absent presence:* of connection and belonging that Soviet modernity as project offered.

I argue that a haunting feeling is the main driver of defensive consolidation which in turn is merely the surface effect of *ressentiment*: deep-seated social frustration when collective desires are blocked. But my approach will differ fundamentally from many political analyses based on the idea of Russian *ressentiment*, themselves commonplace. These hinge on a geopolitical version of psychological projection, or scapegoating. Such resentment comes from a sense of one's own failure, the stifling of potential. The idea that a collective emotional response can light a touch-paper to political dynamite goes back to Kierkegaard and Nietzsche. As Guy Elgat interprets it (2017), Nietzschean *ressentiment* is an 'instinctive reaction' to suffering where pain is accompanied by the destructive desire for revenge for undeserved belittlement. Boris Sokolov et al. (2009), building on Greenfeld (1990), were certainly on to something when they remarked that historically, there was little unfavourable sentiment towards Americans in Russia in the 1990s. Could geopolitical ressentiment *really* take over so quickly? Could Russians *really* be duped so easily and blame others for their country's woes? Sokolov persuasively tells a story of deep generic disappointment only later exploited by elites to produce a kind of state ideology of nationalist frustration and envy. Certainly, when it comes to the elite's motivations this prognosis now seems more apt than ever. What, though, about that initial stimulus – broad 'disillusionment'?

Liah Greenfeld cast Post-Soviet Russia as a resentful 'subject' in its own right who experienced humiliation in the fallout of post-imperial decline. For Greenfeld, national identity provides the ground for individual self-esteem in a functionalist manner. Olga Malinova (2014) updates Greenfeld's argument to find Russian *ressentiment* as part of a '*repertoire of meanings* to which all speakers [of a national community] appeal'. Russian politics has increasingly become a morality play for Gulnaz Sharafutdinova (2016) where ordinary Russians are an echo chamber of managed national(ist) *ressentiment*. For historians and social scientists alike, Russian identity *is* great power mentality and inescapable as a collective disease. Hence the many treatments of the war in Ukraine that underline discourses in Russia blaming the West or Ukrainians for the conflict. Certainly, I admit such views exist and have significant purchase on the surface life of collective grievance. They come to the fore, as Sokolov and others predicted, when politicians run out of road in their domestic sources of legitimacy and compliance.

The broad 'depoliticization' of Russian people today is often coupled with an idea of delegation to elites of foreign policy. Assertive or aggressive posturing and war is then seen as a psycho-political compensation for unfulfillable desires at home: 'We can't give your kids the chance of a decent life, but we can show the West we're not to be messed with.' However, in my view the Nietzschean 'destructive' side of *ressentiment* gets too big a billing. On the contrary, French philosopher Gilles Deleuze interprets *ressentiment* as a conduit that can direct the inherent drives of persons in different directions – both destructive and creative (Jokūbas 2020). This is just as valid an interpretation of Russian frustration. Aside from a few instances of paying citizens to attend rallies, bribing the most disenfranchised to enlist, tricking or pressganging the socially marginalized, and offering a small minority of those who crave attention stickers and decals depicting 'Z' symbols, there is broad indifference to the war's aims. Foreign policy cannot really be part of an accord between regime and society, even as it buys off a small minority with blood-money. It is where the 'symbolic' satisfaction of desire falls flat. The material basis (inequality) and the 'ontological' foundations (the lost social template of inclusion) are more enduring sources of *ressentiment*. Frustration of very ordinary desires to improve one's community can be understood on any scale: at the level of the housing yard, the local region or the national (Belokurova and Vorobyev 2020).

My approach is partly inspired by Keti Chukhrov's (2020) theorization of Soviet modernity as a template for 'dealienating' political economy. Soviet people inevitably had to confront such a template alongside and in some cases as part of their sense of self. Chukhrov argues that the system, separate from its many failed attempts at re-socializing people to make them new kinds of humans, was successful in creating a potential ontological space in which individuals could – if only in some meagre and contingent way – leave behind the 'methodological individualism' of Western-type subjectivity. This was more than diffusion of individual into the mass or the temporary ecstasy of oneness with a crowd.[1] Dealienation was inseparable from deprivatization. A person could and should (try to) connect with others regardless of one's degree of ideological identification. My departure from Chukhrov is to argue that desires for self-exceeding are traceable elements using social science methods. Self-exceeding is not denial of one's individuality but reveals sincere and intensely felt attempts at connection and communication. The half-life of desires for the 'qualitative' good life of connection is not yet over. This qualitative element of feeling desire links the social to the idea of connection. Connection is driven by ends not reducible to, but also not in conflict with, individualistic wants. People in my fieldwork continuously talk about or try to reenact and reconstruct qualitative forms of sociality and connection that are templated from the 'time before' (pre-1991).[2] I argue these drives reflect a valid form of shared yet haunting identity. This should not be framed in terms of nostalgia, which is so often implicitly presented as a deficiency of individual psychology (the better-adjusted post-Soviets just 'got over it').

These haunting traces are hidden in plain sight. One purpose of this book is to shine a light on them. They are diverse and spontaneous at the same time as tracing origin in the past and having a family resemblance – they are all forms of collective purpose in pursuit of social goals. To take one banal example, forms of housing-block yard gardening among pensioner women (Vanke 2024) are a near-universal in post-Soviet countries. Another is the unconscious adaptation among today's youth of Soviet-era *subbotniki* by combining hiking as civic rubbish collection along river floodplains.[3] A phenomenological frame presupposes socially meaningful action as taking place in mundane ways not dependent on discursive

---

1. For a historicization of ideas of mass as potentially dissolving identity, see Jonsson (2013). Jonsson shows how mass psychology and social theories of the crowd in the twentieth century fail to break with the idea of separating the mass from individual rationality. In his reading of Elias Canetti in particular, Jonsson (2013: 142) helps anticipate my argument: masses consist of drives intrinsic to each human subject, and the collective experience is a situation that allows subjects to re-enact formation of identity through new identifications without depriving them of individuality.

2. Variations on the vague phrase 'the time before' were often a conversational shorthand among people to reference the Soviet period. The phrase elicits sensitivity and sometimes hurt; it responds to the frequent difficulty in verbalizing positive experience of the Soviet period because of the hegemonic sense of socialism's inevitable failure. See Morris (2016).

3. *Subbotniki* are days of 'volunteer' unpaid work. A visible political ritual in Soviet times, they continue today, as does their ambivalent meaning (of both genuine voluntarism and coercion). See Piskunov and Rakov (2020). See also Vanke (2024). In 2024 Kaluga's mayor formally reinstated *subbotniki* across the city with some buy-in from residents.

prompting or reflection.[4] In this book I tend to look at practices alongside talk. I link the reflective with what are socially meaningful 'reflexes' – repeatable actions without particularly cognitive foundation or deliberation.

In two ways then, the 'socialist period' has traction. Dealienation refers to a relation of the individual to society in which their contribution, work and positionality are always interpellated in relation to the broader aims of communism. Deprivatization goes hand in hand with dealienation. You are never outside the purview of the Soviet project, and your lifeworld's content, however quotidian, is never truly private, an object of your possession. Similarly, the broader material content of life is not privatizable as property – from the bus you ride to work, to the steel your uncle smelts, to the cacti your cousin in the research institute tends on the windowsills of her chemistry lab.[5] Even when people in practice negated deprivatization (circumstances only ever temporary and provisional – such as in treating your apartment as 'private property'), it was not possible to experience the Soviet project in terms of being outside it. Dissident actions and subversive alternative lifestyles were recuperations of various 'sincere' political positionings aimed at creating a communitarian – not an individualistic – alternative, as authors such as Alexei Yurchak (2005) have pointed out.[6] Yurchak is

4. This book clusters as 'phenomenological' those approaches emphasizing the power of social personhood over methodological individualism. I am sceptical about how far we can take psychosocial models of collective action based on a strongly discursive and cognitive framing. Like Agnes Gagyi (2017: 65–6), I seek to problematize the comparability of political mobilizations between nation-state units. One of the reasons for the narrow focus on a failure of Russians to mobilize arises out of the implication of some social movement theory that non-core struggles are a priori deficient. I return to this topic in the following chapter and Chapter 8 where I take up Gagyi's challenge to rediscover 'popular politics on the communal level' (2015: 23, see also Jacobsson 2015).

5. One could go further and propose that socialism's ontological template intensified life events of vitality and immediacy as co-experienced, rather than the object of introspection and personal reverie. Ironically, this is often borne out in the recollection of individuals in private diary form. This observation of course might be true of any society, but it remains particularly accented and noticeable among former Soviets.

6. Yurchak's definition of *svoi* as a conscious demarcation of circles of trusted sociality is contrasted by him with a sense of wider collectivity (2005: 109). However, it should be remembered that Yurchak's sample is among the relatively privileged where in-group and out-group demarcations played a key role in establishing social distinction – rather like the function of caste-like behavioural codes of elite education in Western countries. Elsewhere, Yurchak (2003: 484–5) emphasizes that despite the seeming 'duplicitous' nature of late-Soviet life where people transgressed many rules, a fundamental paradox of the period was genuine incorporation of its values into everyday life. Any attempt to understand the late Soviet period that deemphasizes socialist values works against attempts to provincialize Western master narratives about the USSR. As Yurchak goes on to note, it was perfectly possible for Soviet citizens to pragmatically work with ideology without giving it much

2. Feeling for an Absent Presence

at pains to emphasize quite sharp demarcations of social groups in late socialism. He also emphasizes how the 'moral responsibility' of group membership could be a nested phenomenon and applicable beyond his own relatively narrow purview (members of the Communist Youth League). The result was the production of 'deterritorialized' and 'open-ended [modes] of sociality' (Yurchak 2005: 116). While Soviet ethics were hierarchical (collective over individual), they did not view residual categories as in true competition with the dominant. Hence the 'stronger' values *encompassed* the others without negating them (Dumont 1986).[7] Dumont's insight about ontological incorporation is now reiterated in a broader sense in the contemporary anthropology of values (or hierarchy) by scholars such as Michael Lambek, David Graeber, and Naomi Haynes and Jason Hickel (2016). Lambek (2008: 145) argues for commensurability of values when there is operative a 'meta-value', or monist frame.

The container-like commensurability of Soviet ethical hierarchy justified the portentous term 'ontology' used by Chukhrov. Soviet modernity did propose an alternative ontology – a specific way of being (not just thinking!) – and did make it in some ways experientially 'available' to everyone, whether they liked it or not. It laid strong traces, especially in terms of enculturation and socialization. This is an uncontroversial argument, but it often leads to explanations of Soviet ways of life as characterized by dysfunction, dystopia, false consciousness and, largely since 2014, imperial-minded nostalgia. While the actual Soviet project recedes further from view into the past, all people in Russia remain in some senses 'Sovietized' through contact with family, and through the political institutions and

---

thought *at the same time* as strongly and sincerely subscribing to socialist ideals (2003: 497). Juliane Fürst (2021) argues that even counterculture movements owed their popularity to the recreation of Bolshevik values of 'selflessness' and 'collectivity'. See also Laurent Thévenot (2020) on the continuing imprint of 'grammars of commonality' in contemporary Russia.

7. Louis Dumont anticipated leftist critiques of identity politics when he argued that pluralistic 'enfranchisement' of minorities tends to negate, rather than genuinely recognize difference as a value in its own right. After 1600, ideas of human *universitas* are lost in the transition to social contract, whether in the versions of Hobbes, Locke or Rousseau (Dumont 1986: 77–86). Respectively, these represent a contract with a ruler of subjection, a contract of trust or a political contract based on equality. All three variants owe their appearance to ideas of natural law relating to individuals, not social beings. People are self-sufficient and associating through choice. The Soviet overcoming of enlightenment framings of individual and government, for all its despotism, should be considered a break which allowed a partial return to the premodern associative thinking Dumont is interested in: a hierarchy oriented to the needs of all. While Dumont did not consider USSR society an example of encompassment, he acknowledged it as a hybrid form where equality of individuals was downgraded in favour of an ideal of social justice. As Graeber points out (2001: 18), those who want to buttress an anthropological attack on methodological individualism should look to Dumont.

50 *Everyday Politics in Russia*

forms of organization which still strongly retain the stamp of 'paternalistic' or just 'socializing' ways of being.[8]

My understanding stands in contrast then to social psychology approaches which underpin the idea of collective national(ist) *ressentiment* (Sharafutdinova 2020). Social psychology proposes the power of collective identity and privileges top-down manipulation of groups, focussing particularly on individual effects. A major philosophical and methodological criticism of social psychology which I share is that it extrapolates from an individualistic empirical level (cognitive processes in a person's brain) to group processes, and that this is not only scientifically untestable, but logically untenable.[9] Nonetheless, it is understandable that researchers would make use of psychosocial frames of reference after traumatic episodes of social change – which the collapse of the Soviet Union serves as a double example of. Not only did the federal empire-state disintegrate, but the political order effectively destroyed itself. As a result, the residualization and decrepitude of the Soviet social order – what people expected as an enduring reality – came to be experienced as calamitous. Gulnaz Sharafutdinova argues that the success of Putinism lies in its usurpation of a sense of Soviet exceptionalism to redirect resentment about loss and trauma into a renewed nationalism. Jeffrey Alexander (2012) argues for the power of traumas articulated symbolically in culture to produce collectively understood meanings and influence 'common sense' in society and politics. Both approaches tend to reify collective identity through symbols and discourse, and thereby rely on a model of society as receptor, absorbing – more passively than actively – new meanings imposed from above.

In contrast to collective identity and culturalist approaches, I emphasize the intersection of lived experience with history and politics. Raymond Williams' concept of 'structures of feeling' grasps well the processes of actualization of the past in the present. It is helpful in explaining why Soviet legacies still inform imaginaries, experiences and world perceptions in contemporary Russia.[10] This is

---

8. A good example of Soviet imprinting in the most unlikely circumstances is the diverse literature on paternalistic or 'fictive kinship' within ostensibly market capitalist situations such as those described by Daria Tereshina (2019) in small businesses in Russia today.

9. There are numerous problems associated with social psychology's assumptions about the individual's place in society and the interactions between them. First, there is the widely discussed 'replication crisis'. Most studies which try to replicate social psychology findings fail. Furthermore, social psychologists cannot agree on what would count as scientific replication. Thirdly, critics point out the linguistic reductionism in such studies: language is taken out of its actual social context and interactive use. Embodiment, the material world, experience and emotion are relegated (Taylor 2017). Finally, there are both 'left' and 'right' critiques of the implicit Western liberal political bias of social psychology. The argument is that it reproduces the ethnocentric normative liberal values of the scientists who conduct it, not least the ideological commitment to individualism and an asocial focus on persons' perceptions (Wexler 1996). It is worth emphasizing that social scientists have largely unreflectively adopted a social psychology approach to 'values' and orientations in their work on Russia.

10. For an allied approach employing Williams' 'structures of feeling', see Vanke (2024).

2. Feeling for an Absent Presence

the primary meaning of 'haunting' as used in this book. A feeling haunts the post-socialist space, nowhere as strongly as in Russia.[11] Both social psychology and cultural sociology tend to neglect the immediacy of material existence, along with how it sustains legacies, via shared memory, as structuring feelings about present reality. Sharafutdinova argues that nationalism is the path of least resistance back to re-experiencing collective fulfilment in a 'Soviet' way. By contrast, I observe that 'nationalism' is less salient for the majority because widespread experiences of poverty, inequality and social injustice are much more palpable than 'the NATO threat' or 'Ukrainian fascism'. Before the war, the political 'constituency' for social justice was around twice the size of that of the 'national patriots', ironic considering the amount of research devoted to the latter dwarfs the former.[12] Furthermore, in contrast to the national, local identities and loyalties tend to have a lot of power, and this can be traced back historically to the Soviet period.

A structure of feeling about the ontological security and inclusion of the Soviet model is frequently stumbled on or intimated by scholars, but has not gained much traction – in my view because of the political implications.[13] Even in the most recent magisterial contribution to cultural history, Karl Schlögel (2023: 6)

11. 'Hauntology' of the present by the Soviet past has been deployed in various ways. Alexander Etkind (2009), drawing on Derrida, Benjamin and Freud, uses the term to refer to often unofficial cultural, memorial practices as 'specters' arising because of the difficulty in admitting publicly and adequately the crimes and 'damage' of the USSR inflicted on its own citizens. In Etkind's view, Russian memory of the USSR is infantile and characterized by 'misrepresentation' and 'apathy'. It is important to stress I am not following in the footsteps of a 'collective memory' tradition. Nor am I particularly interested in the collective 'effervescence' tradition in French sociology. Both such approaches tend towards the functional in that they posit a cohering and concrete articulation of the past. In contrast, anthropological approaches such as mine focus on experience which lies outside of, or marginal to language and cognition, in particular the way lifeworlds of the socialist past live on in the associations of people with places, their rhythms, practices and 'precognitive' dispositions.

12. The problem of salience is illustrated well by looking at long-term trends in sociological research conducted on values rather than opinions reacting to immediate events. The Russian Academy of Science published research that showed a large and growing demand for 'social justice' (60 per cent in 2018). Around a third of respondents favoured a future built on making Russia a great power, and those favouring a return to 'national traditions' were a shrinking minority (27 per cent) (Petukhov and Petukhov 2019). Elsewhere, Petukhov (2018) reports a fundamental shift of opinion away from a preoccupation with 'stability' towards support for significant political and economic change, with a majority from 2018 in favour of the latter.

13. Beyond the liberal bias of scholars against left-leaning interpretations of history and revisionism about the USSR, social, historical and cultural research carried out by scholars of Russian origin in the West may involve over-identification with a grand Western narrative of superiority and the 'deficiency' USSR thesis earlier highlighted.

feels it necessary to make special pleading for readers to accept his experiential and intersubjective study of the USSR. Anna Kruglova (2017) has argued for the salience of legacies of 'vernacular marxism' while Natalya Kozlova (2005) died before she could further develop her observations about the enduring cosmology of her 'Soviet people' into the 2000s. Kozlova's project aimed to recover the meaning of their 'slandered lives',[14] and asserted how far the values of justice and equity – freedom even – penetrated and were naturalized in everyday life. Made visible in moral economies, such values also expressed a form of vernacular socialism (Sharafutdinova 2019) helping people navigate in the present.

While I highlight how collective experience of trauma has ongoing effects, I am at pains to move away from a psychosocial model of identity as 'lack' (recall, Soviet nostalgia is usually marked as evidence of political and social 'deficiency'). Instead, I work in the tradition of social(ist) history from below. I directly or indirectly draw on Raymond Williams, E. P. Thompson and Michel de Certeau. I use the term *'feeling for an absent presence'* to emphasize how suffering can be generative of possibility and the imagination of the good life and society. The content of this haunting feeling is an urge to (re)connect in some vital yet communitarian way that goes beyond the individual. Is this remarkable? Yes and no. I argue that it is a visible trace of the desire to escape methodological individualism that exists in all societies incorporated – more or less successfully – into the highly unusual system of contemporary global capitalism.[15] The significance of Russia is that this trace remains excavatable for researchers as a fresh sedimentation, still 'damp', so to speak. In other societies it is more fossilized (but still available to social archaeologists).

Following on from the discussion of 'defensive consolidation' in the previous chapter, when we look at such tendencies in the light of a frustrated feeling for an absent presence it becomes easier to discern the contours of a different sense of *ressentiment*. Usually, this term is used to indicate deep-seated geopolitical frustrations with Ukraine and the West. However, in my view, broad feelings of *ressentiment* about the last thirty years are not mainly geopolitical in nature but about the dispossessing processes of socio-political-economic change in Russia since its transition from the Soviet era. The potential for positive or negative channelling of consolidation I link to a conceptual discussion of grievance and frustration. Drawing on Didier Fassin's anthropological interpretation of Nietzsche's idea of *ressentiment* (2013), we can differentiate the deep social foundations of frustration I find in all walks of Russian life from the geopolitical resentment of the West. *Ressentiment* is based in 'experience' and the logic of desire recognition.

14. Infamous political spin-doctor Gleb Pavlovsky wrote a blurb to Kozlova's book which uses this phrase.

15. Methodological individualism argues that individual motivations and behaviour regulate social phenomena. No one would deny the importance of individual action (self-efficacy) aimed at world-making in any society – including self-centred rational-choice and ends-directed agency. However, the social agent's freedom, while consisting in autonomous deliberation, always takes place in a particular social milieu.

2. *Feeling for an Absent Presence* 53

A large part of collective experience of life in Russia after 1991 connects to what Alexander Vorbrugg (2019) calls 'dispersed dispossession' and social suffering. An initial 'traumatic event' saw the collapse of an enduring state-political form – communist rule, as well as a large geopolitical federative formation, the USSR. Over ten years of severe socio-economic and political turmoil followed – a demographic collapse unprecedented in modern peacetime and a halving of national wealth (worse than the Great Depression). But the long span of time and both spectacular and mundane scales of dispossession make representation in scholarship hard, just as it is often difficult for those who experienced it to articulate its meaning. Just to take one example, in my fieldwork town of Izluchino the main factory went bankrupt in 1996 and stopped paying wages. This was over four years after the self-combustion of the Soviet economy and the initial effects of economic depression. The municipal hospital closed in 2018; the footbridge over the river was washed away in 2022 and only replaced by an NGO in 2024. The temporal experience is hard to comprehend, but we shouldn't discount the ability of ordinary people to reflect on and tie together these seemingly unconnected things. Even people protected from material privation partake in 'knowledge' of, and therefore experience, collective suffering and a post-traumatic disposition.[16] Fassin's work is useful in linking suffering to moral experience and the expression, often abortively, of political subjectivation. In the following chapter, I expand empirically on this hypothesis.

Some Russian leftists have made a similar assessment: that salvageable varieties of 'Soviet Patriotism' (affirmative and concrete) were discredited and discarded by Putinism.[17] This cleared the path today to expressions of chauvinistic, even fascistic

---

16. Terms like 'trauma' are criticized from the perspective that they medicalize and pathologize complex conditions of suffering. This perspective on trauma can imply a circularity: that reliving or inflicting trauma on others is inevitable or that Russia is 'culturally' prone to masochism. A related critique is that the presentation of historical events as 'traumatic' is an elite choice (Kazharski 2019) and narratives of 'humiliation' only emerge relatively late in the period since 1991. The optic of suffering and pain, with both somatic and discursive traces, is more useful. It implies the need to analyse concrete material experience. Piotr Sztompka (2004: 164) set out the case for postcommunist transformation as an emblematic example of contemporary traumatogenic social change: 'triggering factors would include unemployment, inflation, waves of crime, poverty, stretched economic conditions, overturned hierarchies of prestige, inefficiency of political elites'. It would be foolish to try to narrowly conceptualize this experience, but for the purposes of this chapter we can locate suffering in social dislocation rather than feelings of 'loss' or nostalgia per se.

17. Olga Nikonova (2010: 370–1) describes Soviet patriotism as a channelling of an ideology of 'militant statehood' containing both imperial and multinational elements in a 'semantic complex' where 'fraternity' and defence against encirclement were key motifs. David Brandenberger (1999) notes how the difficulty of associating Soviet patriotism with heroic examples gave way to russocentric etatist emphasis on a vanguard nation in the 1930s.

54   *Everyday Politics in Russia*

militarism, which nonetheless repel or confuse the majority. We need not be so pessimistic as anthropologist Serguei Oushakine (2010b), who called traumatic and vengeful responses to the Chechen wars the 'patriotism of despair'. Oushakine described those left-behind towns whose sons had been killed in the conflicts of the 1990s as a 'community of loss'. He examined how veterans' mothers responded to the state's abandonment of their own citizens. What if we extend that idea – to talk about a broader *feeling for an absent presence* and the corresponding impetus to find a replacement set of values, objects of attachment and ideas? Oushakine points to this possibility by virtue of his concern with a 'collapse of the general social context (symbolic order) within which actions and identities used to make sense' (2010b: 190).

Oushakine's insight has renewed resonance in the defensive reactions to the Ukraine war. Incomplete processes integrating different experiences, and a stunted vocabulary of disappointment and dislocation are visible in the shared reactive responses.[18] Resentment gains visibility in the actions of the security elite clique towards Ukraine which uses ideas about core nation and errant imperial subjects. But the societal roots of frustration are the loss of the overall ends-driven logic of the Soviet project and the resulting social, economic and political disorientation. Oushakine's communities of loss offer us one perspective – the negative psychosocial pole. The other – the positive pole where people overcome the temptation to give way to feelings of victimhood and vengeance – should also be given visibility. Furthermore, (chauvinist) resentment and (social) *ressentiment* can be more meaningfully disaggregated as inflecting responses to the war. We can relate them to a broadly shared sense of social suffering by a 'post-traumatic' Russian people, without over-psychologizing this argument.[19]

18. I owe this insight to a review of Oushakine by Rogers (2011). There are also limitations to Oushakine's approach. His work is strongly inflected by a Lacanian psychoanalytic frame – any desire is produced by lack. Seeing the experience of postsocialism as a fundamental 'absence' or 'loss' would ignore anthropological readings of different responses, including 'recuperative' modes that would acknowledge the difficulty of connection and moral recovery, but nonetheless see such desires as having their own logic based in universal human drives, albeit inflected by the deprivatizing experience of socialism.

19. I want to avoid recourse to psychology because it remains trapped in an individualistic framing. There is a big tension for social scientists between the terms: 'suffering' – which can be examined sociologically, and 'trauma', which many sociologists and anthropologists would be more hesitant to use. In Russia, the 'collective trauma' argument can be highly ideological – intended to present society as completely broken, which is not the case. I owe this insight to Alexandrina Vanke's generous commentary on a draft of this chapter.

2. Feeling for an Absent Presence
55

Ressentiment: A response to social disconnection and historical suffering

In the philosophical tradition, *ressentiment* is considered a state of powerless frustration. It supposedly results from suppressed feelings of envy and hatred which cannot be satisfied. The accompanying projection of a sense of one's own shortcomings onto a scapegoat has made the concept popular in psychological analyses of popular and populist geopolitics. *Ressentiment* is thought of as distinct from resentment in that it is induced by more durable and abstract sources and processes, including social structures. The classic Nietzschean definition of *ressentiment* is hostility towards an object causing frustration (Elgat 2017). Blaming the other, however, also entails denial that they are the source of frustration, instead painting them as inferior. Developed from the psychologism of the master-slave relation, Nietzsche draws on both everyday ideas about jealousy and insecurity as well as theories of the unconscious. Certainly, among those few 'true believers' in Russia's invasion, Ukrainians serve as substitute-Westerners and extreme patriotic responses like the 'Z' phenomenon map on to this destructive model (Laruelle 2022). As of 2023, there were also some who seemingly without cognitive dissonance sincerely tell me that the fight is against fascism and that Russia is the last bastion against Euro-American hegemony in the world.

Over many years I have conducted interviews with a small town 'memory' activist called Natasha who helps organize annual marches on 1st May to commemorate the fallen of the Second World War. This was part of a grassroots movement called the 'Immortal Regiment'. Scholars have debated whether this 'non-hierarchical' movement was coopted and emptied of its genuine grassroots civic content by the authorities (Fedor 2017, Gabowitsch 2018, McGlynn 2023). By attending to the talk of those who continue to take part, we get a good idea that the main motivation is the opportunity to publicly mourn and remember personal and social loss. In May 2023, Natasha gave a long monologue in answer to my question of what the Immortal Regiment means to her now:

> People like us are patriotically-minded. They are not the majority, I'm afraid. Every year they come out on the parade do it because it speaks to something inside, not because they are told to do it or how they are told to do it by the authorities. This is a shared memory of how war brought us so much pain [*gore*]. If it is the case that fascism came back over there in Ukraine, we feel it acutely because we endured it through universal suffering [*vystradali*]. I think this is why Europeans are supporting Ukraine and not Russia: Europeans did not really suffer to the same degree as people in Russia.
>
> … Simple people in Europe who really know what war is don't want this war, I think. We know there is no honour in fighting because it only brings suffering. Everyone wants to live and live well. When I talk to people in our little Immortal Regiment the point is we can come together and feel we are not alone in our memory.

56 *Everyday Politics in Russia*

The problem with the Nietzschean diagnosis is that few war supporters fit a model of vengeful *ressentiment*, even if they ambiguously repeat propaganda tropes. While we can be suspicious of the extrapolation of individual mental states to collectivities, the idea that social groups may share 'maladaptive' or destructive ideas about their group vis-à-vis another has analytic value. Nietzsche taps into the obvious observation that human needs are complex and the outcome of drives, especially frustrated ones, unpredictable and possibly destructive. This perspective leaves room for developing the idea that sentiments and desires can have a social nature which are rooted in drives 'bigger' than the individual. By attending to these we can avoid the traps of an overly narrow psychologism. *Ressentiment* can be the product of reactive forces, but its origin is not so important; it is the site of struggle between fatalistic and vital drives. However, this approach remains rather abstract.

Didier Fassin (2013) attempts really the first anthropological development of Nietzschean *ressentiment*, detaching it from social psychology. Instead, he attaches it to the material experience of social suffering of those who are 'dominated, who fruitlessly resist the sting of authority'.[20] For Fassin, '*Ressentiment* results from a historical alienation: something did happen, which had tragic consequences in the past and often causes continuing hardship in the present. Resentment amounts to an ideological alienation' (2013: 260). This is useful in differentiating the deep social foundations of frustration, found in all walks, from resentment of the West. Resentment stems from a relational sense of animosity and vindictiveness, finding psychosocial expression in projection towards others. *Ressentiment* is an 'anthropological condition' according to Fassin; it is based on 'experience' and the logic of desire is for recognition. Fassin is useful in linking suffering to moral experience and the expression, often abortive, of political subjectivation.[21] The socio-economic and political bases of post-Soviet *ressentiment* modulate frustrated desires for voice, and for social connection. 'Socio-economic' refers to the levels of economic well-being and security (not merely reducible to flattening inequality) which have not recovered from late Soviet times. 'The political' refers to the promise of *glasnost* unfulfilled: that Russians would at last be allowed meaningful participation in the political life of their country, even at the microscale. Contrast the carefully ethnographic conceptualization on Fassin's part with the abstract nationalist '*ressentiment*' of the scholars in political science, we opened the chapter with. Does the achievement of 'Great Power' status mean a better life for the majority?

Mikhail Anipkin (2018) is to my knowledge the only researcher to use *ressentiment* to capture the social specificity of the post-Soviet person. He focusses

---

20. Scheler (2003: 25–7), as quoted in Fassin (2013: 252).

21. In Jacques Rancière's terms even 'talk' about the socialist period may be 'political' because it is an imaginary transgression and a 'logical revolt' against what is the 'normal order of things', a precondition for the appearance of a (political) subject (2001: 8). I expand upon this in Chapter 7.

on a widely shared sense of the loss of social 'prospects' for those coming of age around 1990. Anipkin proposes demographic 'lostness' and political alienation as the *ressentiment* of the 1970 birth cohort, but this need not be seen as restricted to one generation. Every generation experienced direct damage to the social fabric and in many cases permanent social demotion after 1991. We can express this in terms of frustrated social mobility, in terms of lost national wealth, or in less tangible terms as many of my interlocutors have, using general ideas of fraternity and social justice. My point here is not to disagree with Greenfeld or Malinova. Certainly, Putin provides an embodied sense of national resentment *and ressentiment* with which some can strongly identify and channel anger. However, in following Fassin, it should be the task of sociologists and ethnographers to tease out from the immediacy of the international political moment the longer-term structuration of moral indignation and hurt. This is why in this chapter I have pedantically defined the structure of a *feeling for absent presences* in contrast to most existing scholarly approaches. To do that it was necessary to draw attention to the relevance of Soviet ontology as dealienated and deprivatized in the interpretation of Chukhrov. The actual experience of *ressentiment*, and whether it leads to creative or destructive action, is explored in the next chapter. Concerning the material success of resentment, we could look at those volunteering for the armed forces, allowing that financial gain, desperation at life circumstances, ignorance of reality, and social conformism and fear of stigma are equally valid explanations. We ethnographically unfold competing forms of *ressentiment* in the next chapter.

Chapter 3

ABSURD INHABITATIONS: PORTRAITS OF SUFFERING AND STRIVING

This chapter empirically unfolds the preceding conceptual discussions of dispositions towards the Russia-Ukraine war. In contrast to the idea that there is widespread support for the war's neo-imperialist aims, I proposed as explanatory concepts 'defensive consolidation' and a *feeling for absent presences*. These concepts link *ressentiment* as historical hurt to a desire for reconnection and social recovery. In this chapter, I contextualize this present conjuncture in the drawn-out experience of postsocialism – the years of dislocation and haunting after the collapse of both the Soviet project and its undoubtedly russocentric and hierarchical state. The experiences of 'losing' and being 'losers' I link to treatments in anthropology and sociology on suffering lifeworlds. In particular, I take cues from Simon Charlesworth's (2000) visceral narrative about the 'absurd inhabitation' of communities in decline in northern England in the 1990s, as well as anticipating later chapters by exploring how the loss of the possibilities of the past connects to a closing down of imagined horizons in the future. Finally, I foreground countercurrents in Russia of connection and communication that remain, in spite of all the blocking elements – political, economic, rhetorical and phenomenological – that seek to atomize, demobilize and silence. These observations of connective moments anticipate the prefigurative and active politics that emerge later in this book.

Ressentiment and consolidation present an opportunity to show anthropological aptness in drawing out the interplay of real social persons and extra-personal drives in context: a demobilized Russian society, the Ukraine invasion and the legacy of Soviet modernity. We can further this aim by introducing two ethnographic composite people who live in Kaluga region.[1] Bereft Vanya K., déclassé son of a factory worker, represents a prominent group of younger male 'losers' of postsocialism, but even here recovering of self-worth and resistance to

---

1. For the purposes of readability and economy, I make use of composites throughout this book. These are hybrid 'ethnographic characters' where I combine actual interview material from multiple real people into a single persona. I detail this ethical necessity and the compromises involved in the Introduction.

the temptations of geopolitically channelled resentment are visible. By contrast, vital Tamara G. always emphasizes her belonging to a particular community and broader sense of purpose through her connection to other significant persons. She builds her public persona as an activist in the district. Working at first on a letter writing campaign to save the local hospital from closure, by 2020 she is an elected independent municipal politician. Tamara focusses not only on the tactical and immediate moment as an opportunity to recreate meaningful socialness. She also thinks strategically and acts instinctively about building from devastation – through her myriad local 'activism' in a small Kaluga town. Her strategic disposition entails a foregrounding of collective grievance against the neglect of the Russian state and the way it serves the interests only of the powerful. The more instinctive and tactical focus is on the need to defensively consolidate society since Russia's invasion of Ukraine – which certainly seems at first glance like a version of 'my country, right or wrong'.

Consolidation can mean marshalling depleted social resources at home to help the aims of defeating Ukraine; for the vocal pro-war people there is no hesitation in donating to DIY drone builders or writing angry online comments about the perfidious West. Tamara's disposition, however, avoids projecting on the West blame for 'escalating' the war – which many 'resenters' do. Instead, she focusses on practical local efforts to work towards the recovery of Russian society without being drawn into support for the war effort. She resists this seemingly irresistible force. This brings her into conflict with the Veterans Association in the town which actively lobbies for municipal support for the war. The VA collects medicaments for troops, food and money to help individual families buy night-vision goggles for their husbands and sons. We return to active 'pro-war' groups in the final chapter of this book.

Both Tamara and Vanya's life histories show that close observation of interaction can reveal shared traces of a suffering postsocialist condition and quite different varieties of response to it. As outlined in the previous chapter, we should try to avoid the pathologizing and reductively psychologizing language of 'trauma'. Instead, social researchers have access to the analytical vocabulary of phenomenological and existential anthropology. These are better tools to get at the complexities of life in a society undergoing upheavals and dislocations. A brief justification of the philosophy behind my approach is in order prior to introducing our main ethnographic figures.

Intersubjective perspectives on suffering and striving

Following scholars such as Tim Ingold, Michael Jackson and his coauthor Albert Piette, I approach the personal experiences of people 'intersubjectively'. Vanya and Tamara live in a society characterized by widespread social suffering from the late 1980s to the present. 'Suffering' only has meaningful reality when it is recognized in a social context. The aim of phenomenological intersubjectivity is to go beyond a

3. *Absurd Inhabitations* 61

frame of self-enclosed (sometimes called 'methodologically individualist') human subjectivity. Inspired by a radical empiricism, intersubjectivity foregrounds the way immediate social experience and practical activities inform the 'objective' reality that individuals then describe to themselves or to researchers (Jackson 1996). 'Traumas' and suffering are then filtered through ongoing and subsequent *social* experiences. Reiteration in the 'afterlife' of trauma is as important as the immediate suffering caused or traced via collective events such as wars, terror and natural calamities.

Furthermore, the ethnographic method highlights – via the experience of fieldwork (living with and observing and interacting with people) – the *intersubjective* modes of shared experience: 'comparing notes, exchanging ideas, and finding common ground' (Jackson 1996: 8). The emphasis on 'lifeworlds' – after philosopher Alfred Schutz – emphasizes how intersubjective experience generates meaning, over time and definitely 'in place'. This does not mean experience is unstructured by reflection. Nor does it mean experience is 'preconceptual', since it is strongly marked by socialization, 'culture' and 'learned habits of bodily movement … spatial judgement, as well as prior knowledge' (Jackson and Piette 2015: 10). Nonetheless, emphasis is put on pre-discursive *ressentiment* as a sensory contact-point between persons and history, rather than resentment – an ideological response which tends towards the blaming of others for perceived historical injustice (McKean 2020).

This approach equally does not mean ignoring how people are strongly constrained by 'structures', the chief of which I propose as a kind of social Darwinism (discussed in detail following this chapter). This pathological ideology of relentless competition in a soulless world has strong purchase on the imaginations of almost everyone. This counter-feeling for atomization demobilizes and closes off imaginaries of a better community, forcing people to think only of their individual capacity to fulfil the immediate demands of waged labour and show themselves as 'fitter' than the 'losers' around them. The giving in to resentment and atomization can lead people to see their only individual worth in dying on the battlefield so that their relatives can collect a cheque. However, in conflict with atomizing currents, people do try intersubjectively to reshape their environment – such as through rubbish collection along a riverway while hiking in a group, or in yardwork: 'beautifying' the immediate surroundings of blocks of flats. These are very meaningful 'pastimes' for many of the people in this book.

As Ingold points out, interactions with our environments are constrained by history and particular preexisting dispositions and cultural knowledge. As such we can only 'dwell' in a way that sets actual limits on our practical activities despite our striving towards the limitlessness of our intentions (a litter-free national park, a bright yard full of flowers). Our striving towards making our environment more habitable and rewarding, even in the mundane domestic space, is still strongly intersubjective. It is interactively, reactively and proactively produced with other people as much as influenced by media or constrained by the state. In other words, even creative powers, ways of knowing things and habitual practices are generated and expended beyond the bounded individual – as Alexandrina Vanke's (2024) work on cooperative yard decoration of communal housing blocks in Russia elegantly shows. This is a topic I return to in more detail in Chapter 7 when I discuss the gestalt of crafts.

The intersubjective approach I adopt does not then dissolve in the minutiae of 'everyday life' but merely gives such experiences more prominence. Too often the study of Russian society is content with either objectivist or structural accounts (people are victims, willing accomplices or consciously powerless). It can also be too subjectivist (a few people can gain political consciousness and then connect with others to become genuine political subjects, acting on their environment). Phenomenology sees body and mind as two sides of the same coin – trying not to privilege reflection over feeling and impulse. In this approach we can try to get beyond the antimony of subjectivity and objectivity. Human experience '"vacillates" between a sense of ourselves as subjects *and* objects; in effect, making us feel sometimes that we are world-makers, sometimes that we are merely made by the world' (Jackson 1996: 21). A concern with connection is why scholars following this body of thought favour the terms 'person' and 'personhood' over individual or self. The 'person' represents an individual who is partly defined by their location in the social world – their self is expressed in *relation* to others.[2] Equally they are decentred in relation to the physical and 'natural' world. They dwell in landscapes and political-economic environments with drives and desires in common with others. Some drives (to be free of wage-labour, to dwell more in the natural world, to connect with others sincerely in service of a social cause) are modulated by those environments and historically traced pathways. Only occasionally may we witness action that has the quality of 'skilful making', reorientating material resources and time back to our immediate control – what Laura Bear calls 'poesis' in a crisis timescape (2016). Nonetheless, the intersubjective focus is well positioned to capture and record such attempts.

Vanya's absurd inhabitation

Vanya and Tamara became adults in the extended period of crisis (they are, in 2022, thirty-nine and fifty years old respectively). Their stories reveal the enduring legacy of loss, but also of social desires 'inherited' from the Soviet period which are

---

2. Seeing persons as primarily emergent through social relations sites my analysis at the intersection between convergent approaches: the relational anthropology of Marilyn Strathern and the sociology of dominated classes proposed by Bev Skeggs. A focus on the meaning of persons as revealed by their relational practices not only helps reveal the identarian bias of anglophone research (because of English's privileging of the methodological self), but also is necessary to underline my point of the influence of the communitarian ontology offered by Soviet modernity and the visibility of its traces, revealed precisely by paying due attention to relational practices as constituting personhood. See Strathern (2018: 8).

3. Absurd Inhabitations   63

strongly embedded in their lifeworlds – small-town provincial Russia. Let us make an ethnographic excursion.

Vanya was always a bright and cheery young man. I saw him off to the army in the late 1990s and took him chocolate and money to distribute to his fellow conscripts near Moscow. He was trusting, open, warm and generous. Not the kind of qualities that prepare you for being conscripted at age eighteen, though he made it through. In 2018, he's unrecognizable: in poor health, overweight and binge drinking. In short, he now resembles his factory-worker father, Lyova, who died a few years ago at age fifty-nine from a heart attack.[3] There's an apparent attenuation of that bright spark in Vanya's personality that made him universally loved in this village of Kamenka where we all have country cottages. We don't see him so often. He lost his job as a nightwatchman in a covered parking lot, and now he is making do as an informal taxi-driver, working his way between the small industrial towns of these parts, and occasionally driving fares to Kaluga, forty minutes away. Nonetheless, in the summer he is drawn to the rural family plot. Against the backdrop of poverty and lack of hope, there's something about his coming to the village that shows his 'striving-to-persevere' persists.[4]

Vanya, among others, often talks of his desires to live 'in spite of' his *prospectlessness*. Perseverance indicates this struggle. Like activist-researcher Verónica Gago, I am inspired by a particular interpretation of *striving* as revealed in the life-worlds of the marginalized. Gago sees persevering '*potencia*' in Argentina as a sign of people's capacity for autonomy (2017: 149). This autonomy is hard won, always under threat and negotiated with the structural forces of an oppressive political economic compact. This striving of Vanya's makes itself felt in the tinkering with his little wooden and cinder-block house, in the maintenance of his mother's flowerbeds even while the orchard tries to return to nature. Striving is in sitting and listening to others, including to me, in the neatness and order of his late father's garage in Izluchino where potatoes and cabbages are stored. Here in the garage, there are many half-finished mechanical projects which were once started together with Vanya when he was a child. Now they lie unfinished and gathering dust, but they still signify hope and a disposition of openness to the

---

3. There is a chapter about Lyova in my previous book (Morris 2016). Some composites and real people from that book are revisited here.

4. Some writers, after Spinoza, like to use the term *conatus* to express that 'striving-to-persevere'. Verónica Gago (2017: 231) links *conatus* to individual calculation 'from below' under neoliberal domination but also sees it constituting a collective, immanent, drive, after Laurent Bové (2009). Deleuze's version of conatus also seems to have influenced Pierre Bourdieu's concept of cultural capital: '*conatus* suggests that one may be enabled to act in particular ways, and recognized by others as possessing such capacities, even without much forethought by the agent and independent of the agent's self-declared life project' (Fuller 2014: 176). Conatus helpfully emphasizes the prediscursive, 'driven' element of striving. To reduce the amount of jargon in the main text, I stick to the word 'striving'.

world. A map of the world hangs on the wall with pins in cities – places Vanya would like to see, as he often tells me.

Because his mother no longer visits the village, the family cottage in Kamenka is starting to deteriorate. I am usually working in my yard in the village when I hear the *putt-putt-putt* of Vanya's Soviet motorbike approaching. When he's not taxiing or nightwatching, to save money he comes by motorbike to water the garden or for company. This time he wants to borrow a ladder to look at the leaking roof of his porch.

—How are you, Vanya?
—It's difficult, very difficult.[5]

While this is his usual opening of late, the one constant with Vanya is his sense of humour and wordplay. When I tell him the ladder is too heavy, he responds, 'the ladder's no more of a burden than my life!' He continues, 'the ladder's not heavy – it's fucked [*khuinya*]. It's all fucked up. I'm fucked, the country's fucked, my roof is fucked.' Soon we discover that Vanya is too overweight to climb the ladder, which really is 'fucked'; it's not a real ladder, but just planks badly nailed together by the Central Asian indentured labourers hereabouts. These are the denizens of the basement in the 'White House', a palatial mansion owned by a local bigwig in the middle of the village. He bought the place 'for a song' from a *silovik*'s wife after her husband had been put in prison for embezzlement (actually, just taking more than his 'fair' share of kick-backs). There are a number of *siloviks* in the local villages – representatives of the security ministries and agencies. They are instantly recognizable by their cars and their unpleasantly aggressive attitude towards their neighbours. When there isn't enough work on his estate, the owner lets the 'workers', mainly from Tajikistan, 'earn their keep' by day labour for the other villagers. Some of them came last year to lay a concrete foundation for a neighbour and improvised many things, including this object of discussion: the ladder.

The conversation continues as Vanya expresses regret at asking for my help and doubt as to whether it is appropriate to ask me to climb on to the damaged roof of his house. Nonetheless, I jump up the ladder and quickly diagnose the problem with the bitumen roof. Humour turns to unguarded confession. Vanya says:

It's easy for you, but even if I tried to climb up it would break. That's what my life is like. Always. I envy you. Don't ever be like me, like a loser.

Vanya uses the russified English word picked up from somewhere: '*luzer*', interchanging it with the demotic Russian term with a similar meaning: '*lokh*'.

---

5. Lit. '*tiazhelo, ochen tiazhelo*' – meaning 'burdensome, very burdensome'.

3. Absurd Inhabitations

Now, this seems too neat a metaphor. I never wanted to write about 'losers';[6] instead, I wanted to describe how ordinary Russian people become resourceful and successful in developing strategies of perseverance and resilience. I wanted to draw attention to accumulated efforts of striving and dwelling via the kind of purposeful, practical, yet life-enriching activities such as domestic crafts and decoration – represented in artefacts like home-made fishtanks (Morris 2013, see also Chapter 7). However, here we must give space to the persistent internalization of the social status of 'loser'. This is one strand of reflection and embodiment among quite different people that connects more-than-burdensome life in late-Putin's Russia with the bereft struggle experienced in the late 1980s and 1990s. I begin with Vanya because he epitomizes a person who somehow cannot escape this fate and fatalism despite all the sunniness of his personality formed in the transformative new Russia. More than anyone else I meet, Vanya cannot avoid confronting his 'failure' to achieve ordinary life, as he sees it.

Vanya projects onto my life his feeling of failure: if only he had a better job, a family, a profession and social legibility. His one dream was to have children and a 'normal' life, but that's not possible now. Maybe it was before, but it seems like life was always too precarious to attempt it. Certainly, his father – a respected factory worker – taught him that everyone could have a place and some kind of recognition. The familiar themes of the deindustrialized Soviet monotown he grew up in are rehearsed. 'I just want to talk to someone, to listen to them and so that they listen to me. But no one does.' If Vanya's marginalization is all too familiar, his themes of the desire for connection-as-recognition are common too. He has tried out all kind of jobs, both formal and informal. A sticking point, like for many men in the former monotown, is the inability to recapture a sense of worth in labour and social meaning. This, as much as loneliness or poverty, drives him to despair. He 'writes' such hurt onto his body.

Nonetheless, even his recourse to dangerous and degrading taxi-driving is not just a form of subsistence on the margins but of channelled desire:

> I can bring the shopping to the housebound lady on the edge of the village. Check on her in the snows. I like to chat to the younger guys when they go to Kaluga for a night out. Just listen to them getting ready to go clubbing. Sometimes they ask me about my time in the police and why I quit because it wasn't about doing good, being useful for society. They all know of me and it's nice like that when I can tell them how to look out for themselves.

In his increasing presence in the village, I perceive the outlines of striving. While he despairs of the cottage's disrepair, in 2021 he replanted part of the allotment

---

6. Dominic Martin makes the point that loss of social role became a 'master signifying term for post-Soviet trauma' (2021: 117). Martin cites work on marginalized groups in Russia who feel 'needed by nobody' (Höjdestrand 2009).

66 *Everyday Politics in Russia*

and with my help also raises a proper fence to the street-side of the property. Especially during and after Covid-19 and at the beginning of the 'Special Military Operation' in Ukraine, Vanya and others like him were prone to suspended animation in the unending gloom of the present – the 'prospectlessness' of waiting for the military draft. However, the tending of the garden after 2021 showed how even suffering in absurdity could be rechannelled. As war came closer, Vanya stopped drinking completely and went on a diet. He finally quit another joyless nightwatchman job in a guarded parking lot in the next town and turned again to nomadic taxi-ing in the informal economy. Vanya is emblematic not only of the category of 'loser' most susceptible to embracing military mobilization or volunteering as a way to compensate for the lack of other forms of consolidation. What 'saved' him were the remaining links in the village and town to others and to a sense of worth. We come back to this later in this chapter, and in Chapter 7.

***

On hearing so many stories of worthlessness and of being a 'loser', I was reminded of Simon Charlesworth's writing (2000) about deindustrializing Northern England. Stigmatized people often learn to internalize that stigma despite living largely decent, astute and generous lives. Charlesworth placed particular emphasis on the phenomenological approach to uncover the 'comportment' of people who inhabit such places as rustbelts.[7] Instead of looking from the privileged position of researcher who externally approaches the spaces of working-class devastation as a 'landscape', Charlesworth wanted to get at the 'practical modes of being' that are experiential. In the phenomenological tradition these modes are considered largely 'pre-epistemic', and embodied. However, in some respects Charlesworth's immersion in the field led to a failure to account for more than suffering, more than diminution of positive identity persons previously gained via work, and more than just broken bodies and habituses. While he chided researchers for their inability to see from a space within the worlds of those they studied, he was too keen to agree with his participants that the northern English rustbelt he hailed from was 'bad' – requiring a bodily submission to hopelessness. He articulated a sense of personal failure and the internalization of that failure – and the whole project of dissolution and dispossession that goes along with the late twentieth-century European experience of making rustbelts.

Anyone studying deindustrialization and dispossession in Russia would have been bound to agree with Charlesworth's diagnosis. They would have found the same listlessness and hopelessness – a sense of what he calls 'absurd' inhabitation

---

7. Charlesworth adopts the word 'comportment' from Pierre Bourdieu's sociological vocabulary.

(2000: 6) – in a world that has left many people behind.[8] Plenty have found similar things in their research on Russia and Eastern Europe. In the region's sociological literature, Sarah Ashwin tracks the endlessly suffering of factory workers' 'endurance' (1999); Charles Walker uncovers 'tedium' and 'monotony' of manual labour (2015) among self-conscious 'losers' (2016). There is an awareness of worthlessness and feelings of 'humiliation' in Tartakovskaya and Vanke (2016), a sense of 'disgrace and worthlessness' and the apathetic egoism of men in particular (Kay 2006). Finally, extending the frame to the majoritarian losers, Michael Burawoy notes 'the bewildered – silent and silenced' subordinate spectators of society's transformation (2001: 1107). Joel Robbins (2013) makes an intervention about the 'suffering slot' of anthropological research, arguing that empathy towards trauma and suffering of others is not commensurate with full anthropological understanding of others because it tends towards universalism, rather than an appreciation of difference. In addition, we can lose sight of a key value in earlier anthropology – an appreciation of cultural varieties of the 'good' that can be different from yet inform our own societies.

An openness to different ways of imagining a good life lay at the heart of my previous study of some of the same places which appear in this book. I proposed 'habitability' as a less-than-perfect, but nevertheless worthwhile aim of striving in a similarly absurd and harsh Russian rustbelt town (Morris 2016). Jon Bialecki (2016) retorts to Robbins that without a concern with the excluded and abject, reflexive critique on what constitutes the good cannot begin. I argue that the experiences of suffering and *ressentiment* go hand in hand with a feeling for striving despite prospectlessness (*bezperspektivnost*). There is disappointment that an alternative possible reality is unattainable, but this itself also generates possibilities. The suffering imagination in Vanya's world proposes a very tangible yet missing reality. This experience is acute because it can refer, through collective and personal memory, to the ontological space of deprivatized personhood outlined in the previous chapter, with reference to Chukhrov's characterization of Soviet modernity's legacy. Once more, there is nothing necessarily reflexive about this – it emerges as much in practice as it does cognitively and discursively as explanations of one's action.

Another reason why the Soviet legacy should not be characterized as provoking nostalgia is that alternative structured feelings are equally accessible, not just in memory but in material culture and practice in the present – representing a 'strategic' striving of the kind Verónica Gago articulates. Gago is inspired by Laurent Bové's work whose argument links striving against adversity to more than futile resistance. 'Strategic' striving draws attention to the inherent political

---

8. A more positive alternative to inhabitation has recently been proposed using the word 'dwelling'. My assumption is that the default for most of humanity is inhabitation, with a striving towards dwelling – that is, a situation where one is more in tune, and in harmony with one's environment (Ingold 2000). Having said that, Alexander Vorbrugg's (2022) recent work on 'slow violence' speaks to many concerns like my own.

content of mundane and semi-invisible practices which are pragmatic but more than the sum of 'coping' strategies, or rational calculation. Gago draws in turn on Gilles Deleuze's reading of Michel Foucault. She notes that attention to the meaning of 'strategy' can help overcome a reduction of action to meaninglessness in the face of blocking political or economic structures. 'Strategies exist from the point of view of micropolitics rather than structures', writes Gago (2017: 9). How can strategizing precede/avert reduction to structuration? Because a person's striving fuses her actions to collective desires, such as the connective community retrospectively projected onto an 'imagined' Soviet ontology. These desires are materialized in real practices that have no meaning as merely individualistic pursuits. They also have a pre-discursive element where a person is plunged into practices made natural. Where these practices take on a rhythm that is sustainable, they ameliorate the conscious adoption of a victim subject position, which Vanya sometimes falls into.

'What we do is make fishtanks and other nice things from scratch', said Sasha's wife Larisa (Vanya's sister-in-law). At that moment, Larisa forgets the 'rational', calculating elements that might also play into the 'competitive' or distinction-making practice of home-decoration. She and others reference the craft tradition and its importance infrequently. Most of the time, making DIY aquariums has an experiential and intersubjective logic as much as a moral economic, or social capital one. Making is not reducible to necessity, nor to 'pride in being able to do things with our hands'. To make perseverance part of ordinary existence is inherent to a more general drive or desire incorporated into experience that does not take place alone. Shared practices like making aquariums are echoes recalling the 'ontology' of deprivatization – being for a purpose in connection with others that is more than just survival or 'resistance'. Neither is this really about performing a classed identity (as self-sufficient working persons).

In my earlier work, I focussed on the agency of factory workers and ex-workers to remake their worlds over the long 'half-life of deindustrialization' which forever extended and brought new decay, injury and disappointments (Morris 2016, Linkon 2018). Three concepts emerged from the community. First, an emic term: 'habitability' – reflecting an urge to undertake practices that ameliorated the dispossessed condition – a will to flourish 'in spite of'. Secondly, habitability arose thanks to a feeling for a 'meta-occupational community' – where loyalties and interpersonal trust were maintained within a specific locale. This was true sometimes long after the (late-Soviet era) working collective that enabled those social goods had disappeared – an insight that does not only apply to close-knit small-town life. Thirdly, sitting between community and habitability are 'extended networks of practices' themselves (Morris 2013). In happier times, Vanya and his brother Sasha had talked to me of their sense of belonging to one such meta-occupational community (the town factory) despite it representing a lost object (the factory exists only as a remnant, in a few workshops). How did the community continue to haunt the present? Precisely though people like Sasha and Vanya's engagement with extended networks – iconically visible in home-made furniture, and decorative hobbycraft (fishtanks and more) – a topic I return to

3. Absurd Inhabitations

later in this book. It is worth summarizing the striving, connective side even of a seemingly dejected person like Vanya and his brother Sasha. This is visible when talk moves from the difficulty of social reproduction to activating traces of the meta-occupational community, now merely a shadow.

Vanya and men like him are emblematic of those who usually shun collective activity and visible work for the community. It is seen as something for 'fools', for show, a mockery or a trick by the local authorities to avoid their responsibilities. People appear to have thoroughly absorbed the idea that it is a dog-eat-dog world and only individualist defensive action is possible in such a tough economic environment. However, there are glimmers or reflexes of the connective impetus. In 2021 Vanya, alongside his taxiing, was mowing wealthy Muscovites' grassy cottage garden plots for cash. Usually shy of anything hinting at voluntary involvement and commitment, he was ambushed by Polina, the 'head woman' of the village Kamenka, and asked politely to help with tree pollarding along the public areas of the street in front of the houses. Elderly or disabled residents could not do it themselves. Polina was in a bad mood because the local authority was threatening to fine residents for not cutting back scrub in front of their houses beyond the property lines. She had been given an earful from one well-to-do summer resident who accused her of not warning of the impending inspection from the regional authorities. As head woman, she occupies a simultaneous real and imaginary position of authority.

Previously, Vanya had been in dispute with Polina because of what he perceived as her intransigence over bureaucratic procedures. I return to this episode later. To my surprise, Vanya and the others spontaneously began to cut up branches and limbs of an overgrown lime tree. Not only that, but they also thoughtfully cut pieces into firewood and stacked them for the elderly owner of a nearby plot who heated her house using a traditional stove. Focussed and motivated by a task greater than himself, Vanya forgot about his personal troubles. He even began to enjoy himself, going over to sit and speak to the old woman at the bench in front of her plot. As she called me in to drink tea as a 'near' neighbour, Vanya cheerfully refused hospitality, making a rare commentary on the moral economy of the village and local town: it was not for locals to expect hospitality in return for a duty of mutual aid. Vanya made a reference to the neighbour's son as a distant acquaintance: 'your Grisha worked back with my brother Sasha at the cement plant in the late 90s'. Even in these distant times and difficult circumstances, one could recognize and respond to a common member of the meta-occupational community. Later I emerged from the old woman's house to find Vanya still sitting on her bench. We talked again about raising his fence even higher; such were his fears about incursions to his plot by unwelcome visitors. At the same time, he reflected, perhaps he should reinstate a 'public' bench like the one he was sitting on? After all, in his mother's time, every cottage had a seat for neighbours and passersby to sit on in the frontage between the fence and the road. Moreover, Vanya went on, he would expand the flowerbeds in his own frontage.

A mundane and hardly visible change had occurred. Perhaps a fleeting and soon forgotten, reversed by misfortune but also one that was nevertheless striking to observers, and not just to me. Mutual aid is predictably a strong justificatory narrative in episodes like this – and they are almost a daily occurrence in the precarious lives of Russian villages, economically vulnerable towns and even cities. However, the value of long-term observation is in the ability to separate out the obvious impetus – to aid the needy and socially-near – from what can be gleaned in the experience of the encounter itself. Vanya and the other men enjoyed the activity for its own sake and as masculine consociality. Beyond that it offered a way of accessing a deeper social reflex usually denied. Meaningful ends-directed activity is combined with largely tacit social communication and submerged moral economies. Approving grunts and nods of acceptance at the positioning of tools and bodies and the bracing of branches spoke volumes. The quality of connective communication, quite fleeting, was appreciated. There were just some mundane examples and not without ambiguity – as the example of the fencing illustrates. On the one hand, there continue strong imperatives to privatize existence against the harsh 'outside', even to the extent of raising a large fence on a village plot. On the other hand, consocial practices may reemerge with just a little prompting. There were many other examples like this, usually connected to a pressing social issue, which appeal to authorities has failed to solve. These are very much 'second best' examples of communication and connection by necessity of the decaying social state infrastructure, but often they are eagerly embraced. Vanya's case is presented to show that even the most curmudgeonly, and those hiding deep wounds, are not immune from the call.

Tamara's striving to re-connect

Tamara is from a local town near Kaluga and often comes to stay in the village of Kamenka where her nephew owns a house. Older than Vanya, she was already working during the last years of the USSR. At first glance she appears the opposite kind of personality: relentlessly positive, gregarious and even steely. Like many people this age, her feelings for post-communist transition are linked to small events of suffering and humiliation, now memories that one can't get rid of. One such event for Tamara is the precipitous, calamitous social descent of her family in a short period in the early 1990s. She worked as a bookkeeper for a research lab and was soon laid off. A precipitous 'fall' ensued from comfortable middle-class existence as the well-placed child of engineers to selling newspapers with her teenage sister on Kaluga trolleybuses, risking harassment and then actual arrest by the police for hawking. This event and others like it have strong traces. People are sensitized to a feeling that their 'normal' transition into adulthood is frustrated. They are touched deeply by social change, feeling others' hurt too. For Tamara, the long-term and embodied effect of this is – in contrast to Vanya – 'merely' an overwrought anxiety in reflecting on the past and a hypersensitivity to certain triggers – particularly injustice. She passes on the experience of suffering to her children, but in ways that teach them

3. Absurd Inhabitations

the most important things about being a good person: valuing others not for who they are, but for themselves, not allowing food to be wasted, respect towards old family things and the importance of not turning away from life – your community matters, it is part of who you are, and you can't turn your back on it. What always irked me is the acceptance of injustice as part of a natural order. I guess it is a very obvious inheritance, without me really thinking about it too deeply, from the Soviet education system. People say that system had no value, but I think we can see that it instilled a particular way of thinking about social justice and responsibility, however unevenly and incompletely it may have been absorbed.

At the same time, for Tamara, suffering is sharpened by the observed and 'shared' (or perhaps, 'lived in') experience of her mother Alla (b. 1944), and her grandmother. Alla too lost her job in the sudden, and overwhelmingly female unemployment in the early 1990s. The family lost most of its stored wealth in the double confiscations of savings in 1991 and 1992.[9] They shared poverty, social exclusion and a sense of shame. Disorientation and helplessness were feelings only intensified through the mid-late 1990s. Not for nothing anthropologist Caroline Humphrey (2002) calls this period one of 'double' dispossession – people lose access to work and an economic sense of security. They are also 'no longer possessed' by inclusion in the all-encompassing domains of Soviet institutions (encompassing collectives of subsidized meals, travel vouchers). Humphrey emphasizes the dislocating feeling of being thrust out into the hard new world of marketized relations and privatized property. We can add a third element of dispossession: the ontological. Recalling Chukhov's argument, the deprivatized and dealienated world of property also had purchase on personal relations. Ironically, at the onset of unbridled entrepreneurialism (for the Komsomol insiders who divided up formerly public property) the possibility of 'self-exceeding' was abruptly curtailed. The idea of 'possession' by a collective was replaced by the well-documented and rapid phenomenon of retreat into private personal shells, sometimes literally: the reinforced steel apartment doors. Tamara's neighbours went from 'close friends' to almost strangers in less than a couple of years.

Tamara also witnessed her mother's harassment from other relatives who had better 'adapted' over this period, mainly by going into petty trade and then more legitimate businesses. The particularistic manifestation of the mother's suffering is transmitted to the daughter. She then, and now, suffers on her behalf because of the distress at the proximal cause of her mother's dislocation. Tamara suffers doubly. For her own sake and when reflecting on the meaning for herself of her partial loss

---

9. In January 1991, Gorbachev at short notice demonetized high-value banknotes in a poorly implemented anti-inflation measure which affected the least informed and most vulnerable Russians. In 1992, prices of most goods were freed from control leading to rapid hyperinflation. This particularly struck at the vulnerable who were less prepared to protect themselves by buying durable goods with savings.

72 *Everyday Politics in Russia*

of person – a 'normally' functioning mother. As she moves through life stages, the daughter's behaviour begins to mimic and echo some of the mother's practices – keeping a broken vacuum flask because it reminds her of her Soviet childhood or retrieving a worn-out (Soviet-era) dress from the rubbish because she can't bear to part with it. Loss is activated but also assuaged through her interaction with the material world from the past.

I do not present these two families of Vanya and Tamara as particularly representative of postsocialist experience, although readers from Russia and elsewhere may well recognize familiar shapes and shades of experience. However, they are emblematic of the domino effects of dispossession set in play by the abrupt disruption and long-term crisis. Such stories emphasize the 'family resemblance' of loss and its feedback. It is embodied and communicated via practice, but so too does it create bonds between different people who otherwise might have little in common.

Tamara says:

> Who showed me, an ignorant town-dweller who forgot her peasant roots, how to dig potatoes, and conserve pickles and jam? Vanya's family. Who always offered us a place stay overnight and shared food, no matter how little? It goes back another generation […] and to the Soviet times generally when my mama used to buy things for the villagers when she went to Moscow. Things that they couldn't get locally, including toys from the GDR and food. All carried by my mum on her back but thought of as an important thing to do for others. That's what needs to be said, despite the bad things.
>
> I'll never forget how my mum and I were carrying ducklings we had raised over winter in the apartment from the town to Kamenka. We had to go the long way, as the other bridge was flooded, and some people driving by came back for us, because it was so obvious that we were having a very hard time with it all. Or how Vanya's family always welcomed us with whatever they had.

Many of these aspects of her life are hidden from others, even people who know her well. Like many remarkable people characterized by *striving* rather than suffering, Tamara does not hesitate to cross class and caste-like boundaries – itself a typically dislocating experience. She 'curates' knowledge about herself in a circumspect way: she has local roots linking her family to the village where we talk. Her husband has his own business and made his way into the post-Soviet entrepreneurial class thanks to his technical education. Tamara herself has a long history working in local government and for the state in positions of increasing responsibility as a bookkeeper. Nonetheless, she is also from an unusual family of 'dissident-like' people who held critical and reflexive views of the Soviet system but were 'politically inactive', as Yurchak (2005: 107) defines them.

Despite her acute sensitivity to her post-socialist injuries linking her to Vanya, most of these aspects are hidden from him and others. People see her as one of the few confident and competent bureaucrats willing to stick up for the local town they call their 'little homeland'. This term – *malaia rodina* – is a well-worn and

3. Absurd Inhabitations

frequently deployed yet sincere expression of loyalty and attachment to place. Tamara, after growing increasingly activist in her attitudes after 2011, navigates local and regional politics without joining the United Russia party or allowing herself to be absorbed into networks of patronage. In some respects, she is typical of women of this age able to carve out political room for manoeuvre in small municipalities. In 2021 she was elected as the 'municipal head' of Izluchino, a town of 20,000, with little power but much moral authority. We will return to this story later in Chapter 5, but for now I return to her 'suffering' yet striving personhood.

Intergenerational learning and communicated memory are just as significant for Tamara's lifeworld as they are for Vanya's. Her maternal relatives contribute to her sense of moral authority, providing succour and example to Tamara. The other side of suffering, sometimes hidden, is the ability to use it to help recover moral personhood. She frequently cites the experience of her grandmother stoically having to go back to work as a result of the family losing all their savings following the monetary reform and subsequent hyperinflation of the early 1990s.[10] Tamara even now blames herself for not insisting on withdrawing and exchanging their money when there was a chance. The grandmother reassured her that 'they' would never allow ordinary people to be hurt. Today, Tamara thinks about the trusting naivety of her grandmother who believed in 'building socialism' all her life. This brings back the feelings of those suffering times – and inflects her relationships with others. These psychic effects translate into sometimes debilitating nervous conditions affecting Tamara in a variety of social roles yet ones she actively hides in her public-facing duties.

While Tamara had to start selling newspapers on local trains and trolleybuses, her mother traded in the open-air market – selling off their possessions so as to be able to afford food. Her feelings about her grandmother are compounded by the guilt she feels towards her mother:

> I'm so ashamed of not acknowledging my mother in front of my close friend when she had to sell goods in public, always on the lookout for the *militsiia*, as it was not allowed, and [because we] also couldn't afford to get her teeth fixed, so she had big gaps. I also feel ashamed that my mum and I were so busy trying to make ends meet that we didn't realize that my grandmother had to have an eye operation until it was too late and she lost her eyesight. She also refused to cash in the little savings she had for me and my brother, refusing to believe it would all be completely wasted. It's the thought of her saving up all those years for us that is so upsetting, not the actual money. It wasn't a big amount.

The point is simple, yet worth articulation. The ghostly arms of intersubjective experience reach out across time to encircle today's post-socialist people in a painful embrace. Nonetheless, this embrace is not one they are so eager to escape

---

10. Summarizing the reform from 1986 to 1991, Anders Åslund (1991: 43) notes at the beginning of his survey: 'the destruction has been successful'.

from, just as they do not wish to deny linking present to past. These drives are visible in scholarship on suffering but are usually slotted into a frame of social exclusion and pathology.[11] Once more, I resist a 'nostalgic' reading. Instead, nearly all people can articulate or, more likely, embody the sense of a missing potentiality for connection. And once again, it is the template of relations and relationality from the past that is sometimes made visible, not projections of utopian or idealized pasts. Furthermore, using the insights of recent scholarship on the anthropology of morality, I follow Cheryl Mattingly (2012: 167) in separating the deliberating ethical moment (which certainly exists in exceptional circumstance) and norm-governed morality (which is important, but overemphasized) from the ordinary as a primary site of moral work. Mattingly extends the phenomenological analysis of experience as generating moral persons. She posits the importance of a 'first-person virtue ethics' because we tend to neglect moral perspectives that emerge within actions by people in their social context. My purpose is to detach the immediacy and 'experience near' account from the particularity of individuals. This is why I emphasize how dissimilar Tamara and Vanya are yet illustrate how similar drives and connective desires can be made visible acting through them. And in turn, the striving towards, or cleaving to, such drives can reemerge as a second-order effect – in the self-interpreting and moral deliberation of real people, as shown here by Tamara.

In summer 2020 Tamara, Svetlana (a state bureaucrat from cadastral services) and I drove to see Galina – a woman Tamara had worked with in the state bureaucracy twenty-odd years ago. I had justified tagging along because this was a meeting about 'ecological civic activism'. We were semi-officially inspecting a settlement forty kilometres from Izluchino where residents had complained to a Kaluga politician about the polluting effects of a rabbit farm. Agricultural waste was being burned in the open air: a form of pollution similar to that which Tamara was battling in her town. Tipped off by the Kaluga politician – a mutual acquaintance and passive supporter of Tamara's political ambitions – we arrived on a sunny day by car to the settlement of Severinsk where 8,000 people live. Throughout the journey, along the dusty rutted road to a corner of the region time had seemingly forgot, Tamara recalled Galina and their prior working relationship. By the mid-1990s, Tamara had gone to night school and got a professional legal qualification. She had worked as a legal assistant to an advocate in the Prosecutor's (or District Attorney's) Office. Galina too had worked there. As we drove to meet her, Tamara recalled not the difficulties of the 1990s, but the nurturing environment for young lawyers, a legacy of the socialist-era institution of the Prosecutor's Office. These were educated people and the 'quality of communication and human material' was high. Everyone shared expectations of professionalism.

---

11. Recent scholarship in anthropology takes seriously social suffering as the result of the loss of the possibility of social connection. See Parsons (2014: 52) on the way Soviet order structured connections and granted them 'potency'.

You knew what was expected. You knew what you were doing. To carry out the work of the state was understood almost from the get-go. And even this was really about a common understanding of the 'greater good' [*obshchee blago*]. This was the legacy. And if something was in doubt there was always a responsiveness from colleagues. And this was not about ideological foundations which many people in any case had had to leave behind after 1991. Recall, this was the most difficult time to work in such 'organs', with the whole constitutional order in doubt and corruption and despair at every turn. But the institution had carried with it these high ethical standards of work precisely because of the quality of communication which was upheld, and the respect for the individual doing his work. But only in so far as that individual was seen as sincerely working to overcome his personal interests and foibles – again to show the quality of human material; to be engaged in a task through which the individual is more than his professional title.

Tamara spoke guardedly and haltingly at first. Then more fluently, finding her rhythm. She was careful to pre-empt the 'nostalgia' charge – turning to face me across the dusty and torn vinyl seats of the decrepit SUV. She insisted on her objectivity, noting that despite the positive qualities inherited from the social norms of the office she was later glad to leave because the structural barriers were too high: the increasingly impossible ethical dilemmas of work there and the advent of widescale corruption. Nonetheless, as we neared Severinsk, Tamara grew both enthusiastic and hopeful. She regarded the meeting with Galina as an invitation to restore the quality of the communicative relation they had once shared. It is worth digressing to interrogate further the way a notion of nostalgia has, in my view, been erroneously deployed.

In place of nostalgia – hauntings of potentiality

Dislocation and sense of absent potentiality are co-experienced in different ways. It extends through time and space and subsists, regardless of personal circumstances. It operates and assembles on two levels. It involves a sensitivity to the socially dispossessive potential of change – a cued readiness for an interpretation that is not necessarily political, analytical or even consciously categorizing. This is not nostalgia. It does not so much look back in terms of comparing loss to a superior socialist period (restorative nostalgia) – 'look what we had and have now lost'.[12]

---

12. It is striking how little concrete reference to the socialist past there is in talk. The division by Svetlana Boym (2008) of post-communist nostalgia into 'restorative' and 'reflective' may appear as salient now as ever, but there is little sign of the former. A less well-known avenue towards exploring nostalgia is discussed by Roman Abramov (2012), acknowledging how the real and imaginary pasts always exist in the tension of personal and collective experience. According to Abramov, the affective meaning of the past – of personally experienced events – drives nostalgia, a position that would support my thesis that the term is overall less useful because 'personal' experience of socialism is not directly accessible to most.

Nor is it quite a 'longing for longing' – a reflective nostalgia sensitive to the 'past structure of desire' (Nadkarni and Shevchenko 2004: 503), although this comes closest to my interpretation. Reflective nostalgia in places like Russia is said to lament the impossible recovery of a bright and naïve hopefulness that history is not yet ended. Instead, I emphasize a common feeling about the (now missing) potentiality – 'something was possible and then it was no longer possible'. However, as we will see, this sense of loss does not involve a retreat into nostalgia – but seeks meaning in the present in affective co-experience, and further, reconstructive practices. Some practices are resistant, some prefigurative, some incredibly meagre yet meaningful – as in Vanya's case.

The phrase 'something was possible ... ' reminded me of Alexei Yurchak's book title: *Everything Was Forever, Until It Was No More: The Last Soviet Generation*. Focussing on the experience of a 'break in consciousness' for Soviet people and the 'stunning shock' of the collapse in 1991, Yurchak writes that some were readied for abrupt change by their experience of alienation from the enforced ideological ritualization of life up to the late 1980s. However, even in proposing a form of oppositional identity to Sovietness: *vnye* ('outsideness'), Yurchak stresses how such countercultural poses were essentially made possible and recuperated by the system.[13] This is consistent with Yurchak's use of Deleuzian theory. 'Deterritorialization' into subcultural lifestyles anticipates a reterritorialization (2005: 128). Those same subcultures are subsumed into 'authentic' non-conformist Soviet life. This movement sets the tone for the way some think about nostalgia – a longing for the 'personal', 'innocent' and hopeful modes of thinking about the future that were possible before the 'crash'. Nostalgia would be about a reterritorialization of Sovietness – easily manipulated into the resentment we observed in the previous chapter. These affective modes seem important – surely they have an afterlife, and haunt the present even now. Yurchak is reticent in contemplating the striving potential of creativity or even 'ordinary' modes of living beyond a largely discursive, interiorized and symbolic kind. His argument is about confronting a postmodern loss of meaning. This 'loss' emerges as a political subject (a kind of post-human agent) in itself which anticipates the collapse of the Soviet project. Socially ingrained ways of living – habituses – in their *changing forms* as adaptation and evolution are less interesting to Yurchak. This prompts the question: if we accept the idea of disjuncture – or 'break' – then why not look

13. Caroline Humphrey (2007) provides an alternative perspective to that of Yurchak's ideas about freedom in being outside 'the system'. Drawing on Leonid Ionin's work, she explores how a sense of freedom is possible in a repressive society, particularly through a sense of political incorporation. This anthropologically-evidenced phenomenon is highly counter-intuitive because of the dominance of an individual rights-based notion of freedom. Viktor Voronkov and Elena Zdravomyslova (2002) also expand on the question of freedom and argue (after Oleg Yanitskii) that 'engendering environments' helped an informal public sphere emerge after the 1950s in the USSR. We could well heed this historical lesson.

3. Absurd Inhabitations

for the long-term ripple effects of that, if not in social psychology, then in more diffuse and material forms?

Everyone has a different set of interpretive cues that evoke lost potentiality and *absent presence* – as Tamara's and Vanya's stories show. My argument is that these are more frequently intersubjective effects, and are not so much aspects of identity or individual 'psychology'. They are like 'hauntings' that emerge in personal and material-world interaction. In an ethnography like this one, inevitably I privilege 'talk' between people. Dispossession and potential reconnection emerge in the sharing of a joke, a nod, an action that is as much prediscursive and 'unthought' – like Vanya's response to others in the tree-cutting episode. Tamara is an emblematic yet not an exceptional case. Just as loss is activated in the social so is the perseverance to strive. It starts with small things – marshalling her colleagues for the beautification of the front yards of housing blocks. She previously had cultivated the ground behind the institution in Kaluga where she worked for some years as a bookkeeper. Then she starts organizing collections of groceries for the parents of a child paralysed in an accident, activating those still-present transverse lines of connection from the factory identity of the town – the meta-occupational community. Grigory, now the school stationery supplies storeowner, used to work in the foundry and was an acquaintance of Tamara's husband. He has a beaten-up delivery van surplus to his needs now that the wholesalers deliver to him. Tamara connects him to the informal welding shop of her son's friend who adapts the van as a wheelchair-enabled taxi. During Covid, Tamara really came into her own. She activated another network of 'working daughters' who delivered medicines and groceries to elders using her social media account. This complemented her political career.

Only very recently could these practices qualify as 'activism' or part of developing 'civil society'. A letter-writing campaign in 2016 to save the local hospital gave Tamara wider prominence in this small-town community. Tamara put to good use her prior profession as a lawyer, linking with environmental activists to launch a legal challenge to the closure of the hospital. Despite the failure of that campaign, when the local oil refinery looked to expand, she became a one-issue independent candidate for the mayoralty election. She won and used her political capital to get planning permission for the expansion denied. A smear-campaign by the regional and district press followed. Even after this she remained committed to a strategy of

> what's possible, even now. Even if they extended the railhead to process more oil into polluting fractions, we at least forced them to acknowledge they had breached environmental standards. Just publicizing breaches of the law is now a radical action, and one still possible using legal means. The river is much cleaner now as a result of similar action on the cellulose plant. Maybe it's temporary, but they did at least install filters in the chimneys. Little-by-little. Sometimes we can't do more.

78   *Everyday Politics in Russia*

Tamara sees herself as inhabiting the civically active space in-between powerless atomization and well-networked respect and moral authority in a meta-occupational community. The relatively easy way she gained some local traction is acknowledged by her as 'absurd' yet is not so different from Vanya's expression of 'fatalism' [*pofigizm*].[14] It shows how we should avoid such a culturally essentializing interpretation. Acknowledgement of absurdity (or fatalism) does not foreclose a sense of striving. Connective action must be attempted even if the result is unknown. It is particularly in communicative action that people like Tamara unambiguously link sociality to qualitative pasts. Is this nostalgia?

> It used to be possible to make these balances, or compacts between competing demands of the state to build what is needed. I guess I am a 'socialist' in the Soviet sense, in that I would support the oil terminal if I thought it benefitted the people of Russia really. But obviously the 'power' [*vlast*] made this choice to recreate the class of oligarchs again. It is not possible to make this clear in any public talk. But you don't have to. This is why it is important to offer an alternative to United Russia, and the opposition parties unfortunately are not able to do this. Yes, we get public attacks, and personal threats. My husband has to walk with me now to the shops.
>
> They will come back and probably expand the refinery, but we showed people locally their worth and that we cared for them and so they are deserving of dignity. And this changes something in them, on some cellular level perhaps. The steps in rehabilitating society have to start at the very beginning because this society is so sick from being stifled. Rehabilitation cannot begin until they believe they can even communicate. You know I worked to save the hospital and I spent a lot of time there talking to the doctors and nurses. From that campaign they used a comparison between the sick body and society, you know? About the immune system. It needs to be stimulated at first before fighting a heavy infection.

Tamara also negotiates the spectrum of *ressentiment* responses since the war against Ukraine began. We catch up with her in late 2022. Like many other reflexive people, she talks about the war bringing to the fore half-buried traumas of the past. In some ways, she says, people would like to suffer more, for the war to become real to them. This is because the main thing that they 'grieve' about

---

14. Fatalism or, in its vernacular, *pofigizm* is important because it is often used as a kind of self-orientalizing trope by people: 'we Russians live this way because we're fatalistic'. The implication is that this is a useful aspect of political hegemony rather than a sociological reality.

3. Absurd Inhabitations

79

is how Ukrainians themselves show the power of connection and unity Russians crave.[15] In suffering, the lost community can be restored. Far from Tamara's contexts, analogous situations and dynamics can be observed. An obvious drive shared by Vanya and Tamara is the striving for overcoming social alienation in a formative dialectics of intersubjectivity. Synthesis would offer dealienation and deprivatization via restoration of broken ties.[16] A small number even find resolution in giving themselves up completely to official propaganda. So-called 'Z-patriots' celebrate the official chauvinistic militarism. However, even this is a simplification. Pecuniary gain aside (itself a major factor), if a man embraces mobilization, it may mean he does so, not out of enthusiasm for the war, but as an act of self-actualization – to overcome a sense of powerlessness.[17] For most though, 'positive' or any other social engagement with the war is not an available or legitimate source of valid connection. Most drives and searches are mundane or material – like the yard gardening Tamara started with.

Ressentiment and its parallel, chauvinist resentment, are useful in describing the possible productive and destructive channellings of connective desire at the heart of defensive consolidation. Post-Soviet affect often falls into the gap between these two ways of dealing with political emotions and ends in what Alexandra Arkhipova has called 'loneliness', and what others call atomization.[18] It is necessary to expand the analytical apparatus and political horizon of expectation and use a micropolitical lens to look at action. Otherwise, we can only focus on revanchism, powerlessness, bitterness. Discursive and symbolic hopelessness lead to an inevitable radicalization of those social groups who, given better recognition of their right to emotions and meanings, would not be so hardened. People fall prey to those who give them hope for recognition of their emotional state and moral stakes. And it is no longer so important for them that in the process of recognition the lost quality of relations is replaced by the loss of the recognition of Ukrainians as worthy of care. In December 2022, Vanya, after months of talking about the 'fucking war', without any other qualifying comments, announced he was considering signing up to be a policeman in the occupied territories. Seeing people's unease around him, he said sincerely, 'I don't want to kill any people. I just want to be of use; to help society.' Beyond the interpretations of his words as denial or naivety, we see imperatives not so far from those of Tamara. In the end, Vanya changed his mind, thanks to 'intersubjective' interventions from those around him. They have to remain nameless because of the risks to them now.

15. This finding – a kind of subconscious resenting envy of Ukrainians – could be read alongside Ishchenko and Zhuravlev's (2022) evidence of a Russian fear of Ukrainian politicization and newly found collectivism.

16. I owe this formulation, both in its abstract complexity and in its aptness, to discussions with Galina Orlova and Mikhail Svirin.

17. This insight comes from an observation made by Yakov Feygin.

18. Arkhipova made this comment in an interview on German television-sponsored YouTube in December 2022.

Success in Vanya's case was in showing him his self-worth by pointing to what he had achieved 'despite' his feelings of hopelessness in the last years. Re-planting his mother's garden. Starting to prune the overgrown fruit trees. 'You're better off alive than in that shit [meaning in the war]. You're not worth nothing, surely you can see that by the neatness of the yard, in the expectations of the old people you bring groceries. It's better not to dish out the shit or endure it too.'[19] During the second period of mobilizations in 2023 Vanya did everything possible to avoid any chance he would be called up, to the extent of hiding food and fuel in a cache in the local forest.

Tamara herself finds it difficult to openly talk since the invasion. However, in speaking to her and other 'authorities' what emerges is a 'making the best of it' response. Officials like her try to actively ignore interpellations to mobilize nationalist sentiment, focussing instead on the local. For now, this is one possibility that remains open. Life becomes even more absurd as public figures are forced into discursive dances around words like 'mobilization', 'war' and 'tragedy'. They risk very real retribution and punishment if they are misinterpreted. In early 2023 two factions emerged – the anti-war town administration which focussed on housing issues for refugees and the economic impact on the vulnerable, and the pro-war faction, led by the Veterans Association. The VA is a civil society organization backed by the regional authorities. Issues like the collection of sausage meat became hyper-politicized, with Tamara taking a risky position by publicly criticizing the Association for collecting such foods from poor pensioners: the foods were unnecessary and perishable (implying that the army should be feeding the troops). The municipality's support should be focussed on refugees: 'and we have plenty of people in need here anyway. They didn't go away because of the S-M-O'.[20] Collecting food and personal hygiene products merely impoverished further the most vulnerable locally. This was a hidden critique in plain sight of government policy.

Conclusion: Uncovering intersubjective drives towards commonality

In this chapter I have tried to illustrate and justify the advantages of intersubjective approaches and the substantively deeper historical context of post-Soviet suffering and *ressentiment* which underlie many responses to war. The deployment of

---

19. Here I condense a number of different conversations that illustrate success in persuading people not to fight. The persons reporting these conversations had set up a group to share their success, based on trial and error, to maximize the chances of people close to potential volunteers in dissuading them.

20. S-M-O – special military operation (*S-V-O* in Russian) is the 'safe' way to refer to the war. The increasing absurdity of the term, however, meant that one could use it ironically without risking retribution. A great example of how repeating propaganda terms can serve to undermine them, like 'Crimea is ours'.

3. Absurd Inhabitations

Vanya and Tamara as ethnographic composites dramatizes the contrast between, and sometimes overlap of, resentment: alignment with the state ideology of blaming the other, and *ressentiment*: a condition of dislocation which desires recognition and amelioration. Furthermore, I attempted to show how submerged or overlooked drives are often inflected by the will to communality. Drives exceed individual worries and hopes are activated, if only meagrely, in intersubjective experience. The intersubjective frame is important. People individually feel the weight of historical hurt, but *ressentiment* emerges through continual feedback with family, community and place. In fact, the biographies in this chapter are not particularly 'traumatogenic', yet both acutely reflect both biographical and more-than-personal experiences of hurt and long-durée *ressentiment*.

The Soviet system was more than just ritualized communist ideology; it was a historically specific form of modernity where the utopian, future-orientation of the whole society could not be avoided, regardless of an individual's ideas and views. However flawed the measures to 'deprivatize' the economy and society, the system had real levelling effects beyond income, access to goods and status. Chukhrov's argument (2020), as we saw in the previous chapter, is that the system presented an imaginary space of possibility that was continually held up as an ideal – an ontology. Emphasis on always building towards a 'radiant future' made references to current shortcomings, or complaints about privations irrelevant.[21] Without completely replacing desires for consumption or acquisitiveness, this form of modernity allowed people to invest themselves in the idea of production that had future meaning: the material of socialism, rather than the materialism of capitalism. More than that, Chukhrov points to the remodelling of desire *not to desire*. This is an implicit critique of social psychology focussing on the individual. The ontology of socialism was to make real and accessible the satisfaction of inclusion in this project, a project in which one no longer need to be a competing individual against the rest. Chukhrov's argument then can be extended anthropologically: against the ideal of the Western-centric methodologically individual person. It is about the directing of 'libido' – in a supra-sexual sense – that drives all humans in their shared projects and life-aims.

We don't have to completely accept Churkhov's perspective to agree with the general idea of her argument; we can supplement this perspective with a historical frame of reference, as Galina Orlova recently has. As a social archaeologist of the USSR, she emphasizes the overwhelming power of the Soviet project's rhetorical language with its focus on mobilization and acute sense of temporality (Orlova et al. 2022). Soviet citizens were always being made conscious of the historicity of their society, regardless of objective reality. They lived in a present that was experienced as simultaneously breaking from the capitalist and feudal past in the

---

21. The propaganda term 'radiant future' was frequently ridiculed by all levels of society, but that does not mean people didn't maintain a continuity in their belief in socialist modernity. Assuming somehow that people are either dupes or merely ritualistically engaged with hegemonic ideas is to ignore anthropological reality.

82   *Everyday Politics in Russia*

most radical ways and supposedly hurtling towards a future of plenitude. One might not feel up to this challenge of making history, but a person was told most insistently that she was a part of it. To live in such a society was to enter into a set of practices associated with what Marilyn Strathern (1984) has called 'partible personhood'. Soviet society strongly emphasized how community encompassed and transcended individuality.[22] The cognitive and precognitive 'relief' of knowing this not only helped individuals deal with the real privations, injustice, violence and disappointments of Soviet reality. It gave ordinary and flawed people, who may have had little understanding of the political project, permission to set aside the bigger picture and even attend to their mundane daily troubles. It did *not* allow them to develop a sense of existing outside this encompassing (monist) social system. They could not abdicate membership and identity. While some have argued that retreat into private life and cares was a statement of detachment from the system, heroic ordinariness contributed to a sense of alignment with society, and of being-in-common. After all, if I live in a society that is building communism and in which there is collective belief in its superiority to any prior form of social organization, whatever meagre contribution I make, whether serving as a nightwatchman in a Polar North construction site or cooking meals for kindergarten children, gains a sense of working with society towards a single shared aim.

Today, a keen yet often inarticulable feeling for an absent presence of ineffable 'commonality', or *obshchnost*, haunts postsocialist people. Collective memory can activate and even transmit to younger people a sense of this. In interview after interview, when interlocutors assess the current state of affairs in comparison with the Soviet order, they may begin by talking about social security and perhaps even ideological foundations, but what dominates is the sense of the possibility of social communication, reciprocity, understanding. These were imprinted in the human texture of material life.[23] These abstractions materialize in talk about workplaces, bus and train rides' social component, relationships with grade teachers, neighbours, grandparents. People are largely indifferent to the reality of the low standard of living, the Cold War, state coercion, lack of personal freedom, the technological ineffectiveness or inefficiency of the Soviet system. People in the present are jarred into mobility when the prospect of some reanimation of lost

---

22. My argument about the traces of Soviet ontology is not only indebted to Chukhrov and Marilyn Strathern. By emphasizing a particular kind of relationality of person and society under communism, I draw attention to the inherent characteristic of transcendence implicit in such relations. This relates to Pina-Cabral's (2017: 183–4) insistence on the ethnographic as revealing the centrality of personhood to a Spinozian-inspired, monist approach to anthropology. In this direction I am deeply indebted to many conversations with Anna Kruglova.

23. A less remarked aspect of Yurchak's work is his observation that a central part of Soviet life was the value given to open-ended communicative social action – *obshchenie* as an end in itself. His purview is elite intellectuals, but it would be patronizing to think of this imperative as exclusive to that particular social group (2005: 150).

formats of communication present themselves – through work relations, craft activities, volunteering, and other kinds of quasi-civicness and activism. What these modes have in common is that they can offer a substitute tinsel of connectedness. However, people want more. The thesis is simple: people suffer from the collapse of those forms of sociality that were part of the experience of the Soviet project and the near absence of any replacement of those forms. What replaced it was an explosion of practices, structures and discourses of *anti*-sociality, as we will discover in the next chapter.[24] People are ready to support anything that at least somehow promises a return to a feeling for those forms of communication and dealienated existence in the world. This is not about the 'political' in an ideological sense, not about national identity, not about empire, but about the communicative. Nonetheless, any account of the emergence of political subjecthood – whether channelling connective desires or resentment – has to account for the Soviet ontological legacy. This is the case even when we consider hegemonic discourses such as authoritarian neoliberalism and state withdrawal, as outlined in the following two chapters.

24. There are too many accounts of the humiliating and alienating aspects of social reality in the 1990s to name as antecedents for this chapter. The dismantling of sociality and its aftereffects are well described by ethnographers and others. Particularly influential were Nancy Ries (1997), Caroline Humphrey (2002), Michael Burawoy et al. (2000), Olga Shevchenko (2009) and Dale Pesmen (2000).

Part II

LINES OF CONTROL

Chapter 4

CAPITALIST REALISM: RUSSIA'S LABORATORIES OF HOPELESSNESS?

This chapter examines 'capitalist realism' as it emerges in everyday Russia. A focus on political authoritarianism and patron-client relations deflects our attention from the dominant discursive reality as experienced by most Russians: a kind of socio-economic Darwinism. This is a hegemonic 'common sense' that exhorts all to become self-governing atomized subjects – individually responsible for their success and failure in life.[1] I break capitalist realism down into two operating forms of embodied 'neoliberal' discourse. The first 'common sense' acts from above through dominant discourses and economic policies – the notorious labour code sets an example (making defending workers' rights legally almost impossible), and the paltry social protections for vulnerable groups make sure they understand their position ('the state owes you nothing'). Just as important is the response from below which internalizes and reacts – a 'neoliberalism from below'. People adapt and even partly mould themselves to the unwritten compact.

Sometimes in the literature on post-socialist transformation this internalization is tempered with a perspective that posits a more ameliorative 'domestication'. Domestication indicates varying kinds of adaptation in new national contexts, but also that ordinary people do not lack agency in the way they allow changing economic imperatives to shape them. Neoliberal subjectivity is often thought to produce strongly individualized reactions – and Russia is no exception to this. However, researchers have increasingly explored how citizens in Eastern Europe after the end of the Soviet period became active participants in incorporating

---

1. My choice of the term 'socio-economic Darwinism' is partly inspired by Olga Shevchenko's (2015) research on the psychological divestment required by individuals to pursue practical autonomy from the state. Shevchenko does not use the term 'social Darwinism' and only briefly mentions neoliberalism. Nonetheless what she describes fits well a Russian-inflected neoliberalism: a 'cult of the winner', 'moral legitimation of inequality', 'aggressive pursuit of self-interest', 'personal independence as the new ideology', 'freedom from [the state]' (Shevchenko 2015: 59, 64–5). Even here, neoliberal subjectivity is more 'defensive' and therefore in contrast to more 'positive' inflections.

neoliberal subjectivity in a negotiated, contingent manner in their everyday lives (Stenning et al. 2011: 59). What came into focus was the sphere of social reproduction and 'diverse' forms of economic management of precarity. Engagement with newly marketized realities implied not just survival but 'sustenance' in social and emotional values and relationships to enable thriving and flourishing. And this is a far cry from the template of patronal transactionalism: the idea that informal networks based on rational exchange of favours are the ultimate explanation of all political-economic reality in Russia (Hale 2015, Baglione 2016: 599). In more extreme economic and political circumstances today, the negotiation of the neoliberal compact, and what British philosopher Mark Fisher (2009) memorably called our era's 'capitalist realism', is worth revisiting.

Despite the dubious truism of Russian atomization, the imperative to stick to one's own corner (don't talk back to the boss, don't organize with co-workers, don't expect anything from politicians) comes into continual conflict with the communitarian and social drives I have described in detail. This contradiction represents a dialectical relationship in Russian society, perhaps the dominant one today. Beyond household domestication, which can include forms of solidarity within families, extended families and small communities, there are different syntheses. These include fictive kinship relations under new conditions of corporatism – explored below. There are also partial refusals of neoliberalism offered by informal off-the-books work and 'entrepreneurialism'. Only a sensitive ethnographic tracing of the working lives of real people can do justice to the way individuals are thrust into this dialectic and negotiate it. Similarly, the life-ethnographic helps avoid methodological individualism – a reduction of complexity to rational choice alone. This requires looking at people's histories of engagement with work and waged employment from within, holistically and longitudinally. Conflicts between the making of neoliberal subjects and socially immersive drives are synthesized in various ways. Once again, personal and composite portraits are presented here to represent commonly recognizable expressions of the resolution (or indefinite deferral) of conflict.

I present three case studies of men who encounter and 'live out' the neoliberal contradiction, attempting to find their own synthesis.[2] Our first subject, Izluchino resident Igor, attempts to build a career from scratch with the gas conglomerate Yamal (a state-capital formation), but finds only extreme exploitation and alienation. Like many other cases I have examined (Morris 2012), Igor incorporates neoliberal imperatives in a 'domesticated' way typical for men and not only those in a working-class milieu (he has a higher education). He uses minimal and contingent engagement with formal employment to mask and facilitate more 'entrepreneurial' informal ventures. Yet his remains a 'bare entrepreneurialism'

---

2. While this chapter is male focussed, I wrote extensively about women's neoliberal subjectivity previously (Morris 2016).

that is unwilling and unruly. In 2018 he explains why again, he's more interested in the informal economy (taxi-driving and wheeler-dealing):

> The Kaluga labour market is so narrow you know. Anyone with a decent place – with a less intense pace, regular pay, decent conditions and an understanding between management and workers – well, they hang on to their positions like there's no tomorrow. There's no growth in jobs, there's just petty trade as the only alternative. The economy got hollowed out. These jobs they offer – like a sales rep for agricultural machinery, a bookkeeper for the cement works, they all pay a ceiling of twenty-five thousand [$400 in 2018] and that's not enough to live on even after Masha goes back to work [from maternity leave]. I could get a mortgage on a flat and really put all my chips on Kaluga, but even if I got a job in sales, or as a supervisor in the Turbine plant, what would I earn? 40k, 60k? And if I get sick, I'll lose the apartment and the job and still have a massive debt. And now Masha is back at work you have to rely on the grandparents, but that's not fair in the long term. And even for Masha in the local municipal office, if she takes more than one or two days off to look after a sick child, she'd in no uncertain terms be shown the highway. I can give you any number of situations where that's happened – social protection for women is a fiction.

Tales like this are ubiquitous. Barriers to dignified social reproduction are hardly worth articulating out loud as everyone experiences them. All the costs and risks of job and employment insecurity are transferred to the individual who is then forced to 'hustle' – forever stressed out, weighing different hypothetical risks and opportunities.[3] All the while, no emotional or cognitive bandwidth is available for thinking beyond 'capitalist realism'. A measure of desperation was visible in Igor's trip to Moscow at the end of 2018 when this conversation took place. He went there for an interview with a subcontractor working for the Yamal liquified gas project. Igor stayed at my place in the big city: better than sleeping at the train station. His taking the job seemed to work against all better judgement, and he said as much. By that time, he needed a higher income because he could no longer get extra support from his parents. After 2018, Igor

---

3. 'Hustle' translates here and elsewhere in Igor's talk the word *krutitsia* (to spin around). He uses it in a negative way – people get dizzy from having to twist themselves this way and that. They literally and figuratively contort themselves to adapt to economic circumstances. Different words that mean 'hustle' have been interpreted by scholars as emblematic of the traumatizing experience of socio-economic change in Russia and the former Soviet Union. Yuri Levada's (2003) influential work on *homo sovieticus* is reliant on the term *vertetsia* (to spin) to symbolize a new adaptive yet unwilling neoliberal post-Soviet subject, while Dale Pesmen (2000) devotes a chapter to hustling (as informal fixing, wrangling in the everyday economic sphere) which remains relevant as ever, twenty-five years later.

doesn't last long in Yamal, but we pick up on that story later. Fast forward to 2022, Igor takes a night job in an oil refinery kicking back part of his pay to his boss. This allows him to pursue informal opportunities buying and selling car parts needed to replace the newly scarce spares for Western vehicles affected by the Ukraine war sanctions.

Our second biography is that of Rahimjon. Originally from Kyrgyzstan, he is a scrupulous striver, moving almost effortlessly from indentured rural servant to Moscow taxi-driver, but he also meets misfortunes. His efforts to internalize the values of neoliberal subjectivity are only possible thanks to his embedding in a traditional community network – the 'extended village' of co-ethnic Kyrgyz in Moscow. Rahimjon, despite his full-throated endorsement of social Darwinism, embraces an entrepreneurialism only possible within patronage, mutual aid and social solidarity networks. Thirdly, we meet Nikita who works for a medium-size fabricating firm in Kaluga. Through Nikita we can witness further 'domestication' of neoliberalism in Russia in the context of war and economic isolation. Enterprise paternalism, long thought decaying, is given a new lease of life but on neoliberal terms. Personal and conscious sacrifice by the worker is demanded because of the 'war footing'. In return, a curious relation of 'care' and quasi-kinship is exercised by the firm. A worker can join a corporate 'extended family' to whom one 'belongs'. This relation challenges a simple distinction between commoditized marketized sense of self (neoliberal subject) and the idea of entitlements and rights recognized by virtue of corporate identity. The latter form of 'corporatism' is a way of thinking about social incorporation going back to Soviet times (Humphrey 1983, Tereshina 2019a).[4]

Embodied engagements with forms of neoliberal discourse are inevitable for any person dependent on waged relations given the relative withdrawal of the social functions of the state. What these men have in common is that they find themselves nomadic neoliberal subjects unable to really embed fully the demands imposed on them. Furthermore, lived alienation provokes more acute searches for the recovery of social embeddedness as their working lives progress. This illustrates more materialist examples of the argument of the book presented so far: the continuing legacy of dealienated social ontologies or imaginings; the search for 'possessive domains', in the vocabulary used by Humphrey (2002). Like Daria Tereshina who has researched work hierarchies in Russia and who builds on previous work by Ferguson (2013), I argue that in each case a recombined neoliberal and re-embedding embodiment of personhood is observable. This hybrid constitutes the dominant, yet unwritten and unspoken labour compact in Russia today.

4. The question of changing paternalistic relations is one of renewed interest in studies of post-Soviet societies. See Douglas Rogers (2015), Daria Tereshina (2019a), Denys Gorbach (2024).

4. *Capitalist Realism*

What is neoliberalism and why does it need the state?

Neoliberalism is a way of thinking about social relations that emphasizes 'market competition [as] the basis of economic coordination, social distribution, and personal motivation' (Sparke 2013: 454–5).[5] In short, it is a form of market rationality. Colin Hay's (2004) general definitions are relevant in the Russian context: the 'market' as an efficient mechanism for allocation, supply-side economics, labour-market flexibility, conditionality of welfare based on incentivizing market participation, and efficient private substitution of public goods. Transformative neoliberalism concerns itself with the public and private identities of workers: how they 'understand, reflect, and act collectively upon subordination to increasingly precarious positions' within a global economy (Krinsky 2007). Neoliberal 'economism' applies market values to new spheres of social relations and institutions such as education and healthcare (Kalb 2013). This entails a 'relentless emphasis on competitiveness as a measure of all things' (Tooze 2018, see also Slobodian 2018). 'Governmentality' is a key mechanism to maintain and justify neoliberal relations; it links everyday life to the logic of what Foucault called the 'enterprise society'. Governmentality is a process whereby identity becomes increasingly dominated by discourses of self-regulation – inducing people to 'work upon themselves' to become ever more flexible to the demands of the labour market (and healthier so as not to burden residual state healthcare systems). This is not a simple top-down process of domination, however. Social control is produced though the active participation of individuals and groups in self-discipline.

Like Ilya Matveev (2019), I argue that neoliberalism in Russia entails state involvement in supporting and maintaining highly exploitative relations. More recently, even ordinary people talk about 'state capitalism' in Russia. This is a minimal and retreating state for most, and a rentier, insider division for a minority of winners. Stephen Collier (2011) adds to this perspective: rather than a focus on freeing markets per se, neoliberalism is about rethinking government according to an over-determined form of economistic reasoning. A highly truncated social state remains, but its governance 'styles' are influenced by Soviet economism. *Khoziaistvo* literally means 'management' but refers to the economic basis of any decision by the authorities. This economism is based on a narrow managerial conception of needs. For Collier, this is an example of 'formal rationality' that shows the partial evolution of Soviet ideas towards an eventual privileging of market thinking, only acknowledging the social state to a limited degree. Biopolitics (Foucault's notion of the political administration at the level of bodily autonomy) connect to Soviet planning in 'incentivization' at different scales of

---

5. A fuller discussion of theories of neoliberalism can be found in Morris (2021a), and parts of that article are adapted here in summary form.

labour and production (Bockman and Eyal 2002).[6] Collier elsewhere (2011: 190) reiterates Hilgers' (2012) argument about the potential synergy between activist states and marketized relations, underlining how *neo*liberalism as distinct from *classical* liberalism imagines a key role for governments 'in creating the conditions for diffusion of markets and market-like mechanisms'. Tobias Rupprecht (2022) reminds us that some enthusiasm for neoliberal political reform in Russia after 1991 emerged from the experience of Soviet planning (as failure). For Rupprecht, a strong element of neoliberalism in Russia is a lack of belief in the ability of state capacity to contend with complexity. In a sense, the period since 1991 can be seen as a strongly negative turn away from almost all aspects of Soviet modernity, an example almost of social nihilism.

Authoritarian neoliberalism in practice in Russia

Anastasiya Ovsyannikova (2016) is a typical critic of the application of the term neoliberalism to Russia. She believes that the social state still trumps any deregulatory momentum, citing labour protections and lack of pension reform as examples. However, empirical evidence shows that employment protection in Russia is, to put it mildly, 'poorly observed' (Gimpelson et al. 2010). In reality, 'hire and fire' is possible in many circumstances and tricking employees out of payments and entitlements is widespread. Igor's wife was only able to go on maternity thanks to a state job, in the private sector she might well have been fired. Radical pension reform did go ahead, despite opposition after 2018. Pensionable ages rose, and most people are now in a contribution-based system. Prior commitments to indexation of a basic subsistence pension were diluted; in the future universal elements will likely be replaced by means-testing and financialization of 'pension capital' (Khmelnitskaya 2017). Ovsyannikova argues that 'monetization of welfare benefits' (dilution and transformation from universality to more targeted cash payment) carried out after 2005 was overdue because of underfunding. However, this monetization closely matches patterns of welfare residualization elsewhere and key to 'austerity politics' (Wengle and Rasell 2008: 749, Trickett 2025).[7]

6. While Rupprecht (2020) agrees that Russian neoliberal thought has indigenous roots, he disagrees that the 1990s saw its implementation in any meaningful degree there. We can agree with him that there is no such thing as a 'neoliberal regime' or state. There are currents and rhetorics which shape economic relations and have material effects. The biopolitical aspects of Soviet power were traced by Sergei Prozorov (2013). Anastasia Manuilova (2022: 155), inspired by Prozorov, argues that unlike its predecessor regime, Russia is only really biopolitical in that it is interested in how people die and that such control is secondary to concern with territorial sovereignty (mineral rents). Certainly, she has a point given how much attention is paid to the monetary price of death since the invasion and little else.

7. It should be acknowledged that there is more diversity in the World Bank's thinking nowadays.

4. Capitalist Realism

Monetization also contained the logic of 'choosing' deserving groups, making them 'responsible' citizens (Kourachanis 2020). As Shields (2019: 657) notes in the case of Poland, family focussed welfare reform is a form of 'neoliberal social innovation'. It appropriates the micro-scale of social reproduction as a further space of responsibilization. It conditionally links benefits to particular forms of parenthood, upbringing, domestic work and privatization of former entitlements such as pre-school childcare.

Eleanor Bindman (2017) and others (Leykin 2019) remind us of the genealogy of responsibilization in social policy stretching back to Soviet ideas around welfare provision for the neediest only.[8] Julie Hemment (2009) points out that in the Russian case, rhetorical concessions to a social state are not matched by policy – if anything, they serve as a cover for accelerating change. While state reforms in Russia began more as performance management than marketization (Romanov 2008, Sigman 2013), the expansion of state-favoured NGOs tasked with quasi-welfare functions, who then compete for funding, has introduced market elements. Meri Kulmala and coauthors (2014) see a mixture of statism and neoliberalism in Russia's welfare policies, while Mikhail Chernysh argues that Russia is pursuing neoliberal fundamentalism (2020: 54). Inna Leykin and Michelle Rivkin-Fish (2022) argue state-directed biopolitical goals of increased fertility are compatible with marketized prenatal care, while health funding falls overall. Even a generous interpretation of the remnants of the social state reveals extreme conditionality, narrow and patchy coverage, and tokenistic provision in cases of extreme social distress.[9]

Overall, it is important to acknowledge the burden – which translates into real socio-economic, and political feedback effects – of knowing that if a person is in need the state is unlikely to provide even a bare safety net. Even in the current war, cases of refusal and avoidance of federal and regional payouts of WIA and KIA compensation are rife. This is why I bundle 'authoritarian neoliberalism' and social Darwinism together to characterize the way people confront this reality as 'capitalist realism'. However, Russia is hardly an exception. The internalization of loser-status, the visibility of surplus populations and 'reservations', and the temporal closing of horizons for betterment are all characteristic experiences of the present global conjunction, as experienced by the newly proletarianized majorities. Whether we call them 'multitude' or precariat, or in the post-Soviet case 'subproletarians' (Derluguian 2005), is less important. Similarly, the retreat of the social state is nothing new and not peculiar to post-socialist states. Regardless

---

8. See also Bockman and Eyal (2002) for a discussion of East Europe as its own 'author' of neoliberal policies.

9. One-time payments for families in 2020 during the Covid pandemic, and the varying levels of prenatal payments have not addressed Russians' unwillingness to plug the demographic gap – itself a symptom of precarization. An example of the perniciousness of the logic of means-testing is the evidence that a third of Russians do not know they are entitled to benefit payments of some kind. War-time benefits are no different.

of labels, the result in Russia is an incoherence or heterogeneity of the state bureaucratic function which we explore in the next chapter. State retreat merely underlines its punitive or delegative relations to the individual.

Responses to Covid-19 in Russia and similarities and differences to other jurisdictions are instructive. A knee-jerk authoritarian lock-down was followed by a hurry to delegate risk back to the individual and downplay both the social costs and state responsibility. Russia, in contrast to other developed economies, offered very limited income support for livelihoods, especially among the self-employed and poor. Notably, the federal centre sought to avoid almost all responsibility. This affected not only lumpenized informal workers like taxi-drivers and construction workers but also the burgeoning 'freelancer' white-collar sector. 'Gig' workers are an important category in urban Russia. As Shevchuk (2020) points out, labour processes that are negotiated via digital platforms emphasize tight algorithmic control and a loss of autonomy. This is because the platforms actually disguise incorporation of workers into 'shadow' corporations – shells for normalizing precarious work delegated to 'independent contractors' as in the Uber model (Friedman 2014). Gig work also divides up labour into small parcels, a practice which has a wider influence via spillover into other domains of work. In other words, the remote tracking of microtasks can happen to anyone, including people in the security services. One of my most frazzled interlocutors was tasked with checking online platforms for anti-regime sentiment. She worked in a call-centre type open plan office and was paid a 'piece rate', rather than hourly (according to sets of data 'approved' or not). For the purposes of our argument, work for 'shadow corporations' intensifies both punitive monitoring and self-exploitation at the point of production.

The 'everyday', biographical experience of economic relations in Russia fits with 'capitalist realism' because of what the term says about the *internalization* of economic relations and their *externalization* in bodily practices. This is a 'slowly violent' process as Vorbrugg observes (2022). Capitalist realism proposes the inevitable and inescapable internalization of economic relations typified by increasing exploitation and despair. Fisher calls the effect of this a 'preemptive formatting' (2009: 9). Formatting makes exploitation feel incorporated in everyday life; imagining an alternative is nearly impossible. Indeed, this is relevant even to the context of war mobilization and recruitment. For Fisher, 'managerial business ontology' represents a kind of 'Market Stalinism', blurring the boundaries between work and pleasure (Ewart 2023: 260). Workers, whether in former Russian monotowns, call-centres in Kaluga or plush offices in Moscow, take seriously the necessity to become flexible subjects. At the same time, the discursive dominance of the idea of the market (however abstracted or distorted) means they struggle to imagine any structural limits or remedies. This is despite them simultaneously experiencing psychic and bodily injury: *ressentiment* and humiliation. Many times, they correctly apprise that there is no object external to their 'realism' to appeal to (Morris 2016).

'Capitalist realism' plays off a word association with Soviet-era 'socialist realist' cultural ideology which perceived reality as malleable through idealist art

4. Capitalist Realism

and literature. Its projection of universalism elides a present-future distinction. Russia as a *laboratory* seems to me an equally apt metaphor. In the past, given the brutality of economic transition, other metaphors have been employed – such as Russia as a weapons-proving ground for extreme forms of exploitation (Pokrovskii and Bobylev 2003). Marianna Pavlovskaya (2018) argues that Russia is a 'state of the art' laboratory for the production of poverty under neoliberal capitalism. She further argues that international organizations and domestic agencies connive to justify high levels of poverty. Not only that, the deployment of (manipulated official) statistics *normalizes* a situation where wages are below the level required for social reproduction and where genuine social protections are absent. While not necessarily 'neoliberal', this is an example of capitalist realism as a form of structural and discursive violence. The majority are then encouraged to view the minority (two-fifths) who live on subsistence incomes as 'deservedly' poor.[10] Karin Knorr Cetina (1999) argues that the laboratory environment comes to be identified as a space of work on the malleability of objects, the refitting of pre-existing states to new orders. The laboratory does not have to 'put up with an object *as it is*'. It is an authoritarian space of material throughput with much discarded, mutated waste. Just as the laboratory metaphor proposes transformation, it also implies strategic withdrawal – of empathy and care. As Tomas Matza memorably put it, Russian neoliberalism is reliant on the normalization of the state's 'indifference' (Matza 2010: 29, discussed in Kruglova 2019). Capitalist realism emphasizes psychic despair and the closing off of the future – the 'prospectlessness' explored previously. An ethnographic approach should also be capable of emphasizing how it is also materially violent and coercive, and reproduced at different social scales

---

10. The government has long manipulated statistics to hide high levels of poverty (Pavlovskaya 2018). Unemployment benefit policy, by design and implementation, provides less support than is possible to survive on and entails humiliating conditionality. In most developed and developing countries minimal wages are calculated as at least twice 'subsistence levels'. In Russia, both are considered less than half the sum needed for actual subsistence. In 2020, Putin was forced to acknowledge that because of the way median wages of public sector workers are calculated, teacher salaries in the regions could end up being lower than those of school cleaners. In many cases this meant teachers were paid no more than the minimum wage for a region. A further complication is the component nature of pay in many professions and jobs. Many workers receive a small 'basic' pay (*oklad*) and a large discretionary element (*premiia* or *nadbavka*) over which the employer has control. In many cases this leads to most pay being 'performance'-related and received only after 'competition' with other employees for a limited pot of money. In the case of schoolteachers, 30 per cent of pay may be dependent on 'performance' which often means schools can 'ask' employees to overwork to a ridiculous degree. Since teachers do not have a detailed contract of employment, the system (common to other professions and jobs) seems designed to encourage abuse as well as self-exploitation. War-time benefits continue this logic. A 'base' is supplemented by a much larger 'premium' in the case of fulfilment of a soldier's task, which is often death.

as we shall see in the cases of Igor's work for Yamal LNG, Rahimjon's experience in the informal economy, and finally in the case of Nikita working for a local tool company whose story is more equivocal.

Ethnographic portraits: Igor's 'bad' job in the Arctic

Memorably, Karine Clément subtitled a recent book about Russia: 'how is it possible that people live so poorly in a rich country?' (Kleman 2021). For workers in State Owned Enterprises (SOEs) in strategic industries, such as liquefied gas in Yamal, exploitative and intensified labour conditions resonate with global trends. People's objections, along the lines of Clément's phrase, are acutely articulated even among SOE workers. My underemployed long-term research participant Igor reflects on his experience as a seasonal [*na vakhte*] contractor with Yamal in the far Arctic North, where 80 per cent of Russia's gas reserves are found.[11]

Most of my male research interlocutors followed their fathers as factory workers and left school as early as possible. Igor, born in the early 1980s, gained a further technical education in the oil and gas industry and spent a period working in HR departments of factory enterprises in Kaluga and Izluchino. However, his work biography differs little from working-class men. His practical negotiation of life was at the 'nexus of diverse work' (Morris 2011). He took part in informal labour driving a taxi, construction and day labouring, even working for a while as a cash-in-hand loader at a grocery warehouse. He also worked in Moscow around the time of the construction boom in 2009, sleeping on mattresses in flop houses and eating dried noodles. Despite his different class background to Vanya whom we met earlier their narratives intersect. For both men, 'social reproduction' gets increasingly precarious; work 'discipline' is brutal everywhere. In addition, Igor has an infant child when I first interview him, and a second child born in 2018; his wife experiences long periods when she is not working. Dependence on grandparents for care is the only way she can return to work. However, they, like the majority of pensioners, are also working. Igor talks of the unbearable risks, even when his wife does finally return to work as a clerk in the local municipality.

> If I could, I would go to one of the surviving factories as just a metalworker, but these professions are dying. The biggest problem our generation faces is instability. You can't plan for tomorrow. This is why I came back from the

---

11. Yamal LNG is jointly owned by Novatek, a private inheritor-firm of a Soviet pipe constructor in which the Russian state has a 9 per cent interest, China's main energy SOE, the French TNC TOTAL SE, and Volga Group, Luxembourg-registered private investment vehicle with Russian assets. Technically it is not a true SOE, but a hybrid of authoritarian state holdings and private stakes, including in Russia and abroad. Since the war, the French holding retained its stake but does not receive dividends from its investment. A ban on some Russian LNG imports to the EU was set to come into force in 2025.

4. Capitalist Realism

Moscow construction site. The work was OK, and most of the time we just managed ourselves, but when the foreman did turn up he would find ways to 'fine' us, and in the end, the charges for 'accommodation' (a dirty mattress in an unheated garage) also ate so much into the wages that it turned out I'd got my fingers burned. You notice how the bus company stopped the regular timetable to Moscow in 2015? Well, that was the year I gave up. It was just about manageable when I could come home and see the kids on the weekend. Four hours one way, and you could just turn up at the Moscow bus station and buy a ticket for peanuts. But since then, there's no service to Moscow except from Kaluga. I feel everyone more or less had the same experience, and so there's no demand for buses now.

After 2015, Igor tried to get a job as a technical worker in the turbine plant in Kaluga. He had plenty of interviews for jobs but nothing 'decent' came up. After much hesitation, Igor set off in 2018, working thirty-day shifts of up to sixty hours-a-week in the Polar North followed by a week back home. In reality, this was not technically *vakhta* but a subcontracted form of temporary labour: *kommandirovka*. As Igor went on to say:

The *vakhta* people were the lucky ones with connections that had got them longer-term contracts. They worked for 45 days but then would get 30–45 days off back home. They also got legal recognition of the 'harmfulness' of Far North labour and so a percentage, I think twenty per cent, higher pay for that. But actually, we were still not the most unlucky. There is a third class – the true 'gastarbeiters' who have no contract at all and I am confident they're treated even more like disposable diapers. So, in term of money, your true *vakhta* workers get up to 300,000 [\$4800 in 2018–9] for the 45 days and a bonus and their taxes covered. We only got 70,000 [\$1130], our travelling expenses, and a *levak* [informal untaxed bonus] of whatever we could negotiate with the foreman.

The *vakhta* people are the top – they're qualified, but they're also all people who either bought their way in or got relatives to somehow arrange it for them. And they don't do the dog's work like us.

The contract for us is also uncertain – rolling if you like, from month to month. And you're kind of locked in to the end of a building or construction project because only then will you get both a legal and *levak* bonus. You are effectively controlled by the project itself. Woe-betide you if you can't hack it until a big gas compressor plant is signed off (maybe six months), because your subcontracting manager will just abandon you – even there in the Arctic. Remember, there's no real set working day – you might get a brigade leader who gets you compensated for late working. Or you might not. There's a corporate store with everything marked up. The 'hotel' (disused freight wagons on wheels) is also useful to the employer because that's deducted from our wages but disappears into the black [economy] as undeclared income for the site manager. Many of the named expenses for workers that don't actually get paid or given us are then used to reduce the tax burden of the company.

> People started calling it 'the plantation'. I've read those books about the American South too. The difference is this is an [employment] agency that paid a bribe to get the right to exploit us. Everyone takes a cut out of us from the top guy in Gazprom, to the recruiting agent sitting in the office in Moscow who has nothing to do with it.

Many of the circumstances of Igor's work resemble the tales of military mobilization emerging in 2023. Fantastic offers entice naïve recruits, but then the reality hits. Unlike many of the initially mobilized soldiers, Igor knew what to expect. His family bought him safety boots, a helmet lining, rechargeable heat pads and cooking equipment. Apart from a helmet and padded jacket, he knew that virtually nothing would be provided on site and even the company shop, charging extortionate rates, would not be able to supply him fully. Nonetheless, Igor remained positive. He knew he could face anything. Hadn't he spent a lifetime already adapting himself? He was well used to 'working on the self' and copies of self-help books or investment and business guides were his favourite readings.

It was his father who had introduced both him and me to Abraham Maslow's *Hierarchy of Needs* – another example of the diffusion of highly individualist psychosocial models to Russia.[12] As Tomas Matza notes (2012), psychological self-work is entangled with post-Soviet class formation. Biopolitical discourses of competition, personal investment and optimization saturate public institutions, especially in education and training. This overdetermining 'realism' has overflow effects on the rest of society.[13] Igor would look down on others for their refusal of opportunities like this. They were not cut out. They were to Igor what I have called 'unruly entrepreneurs'. These are working-class men and women who baulked at what they experienced as highly exploitative and demeaning work practices and who therefore engaged only partially and on their own terms with the ethic of governmentality (Morris 2012). Almost all the brawls and shouting matches between men I observed were about 'competitive' masculine arguments over resourcefulness. Igor's experience reminds how psychic self-preparation for neoliberal imperatives meets material privation and capitalist realism. There are few defences and even homosocial relations of friendship are tainted by it.

12. It should be noted that Maslow's hierarchy of needs does include 'social' ones such as friendship and esteem from others, but these are all reflected through a prism of self-fulfilment as an autonomous and largely asocial individual.

13. Tomas Matza's work can be usefully read alongside Olga Shevchenko (2015: 56–7) on the continuous reproduction of 'social crisis' and the need for 'efficacious action' at individual levels to counter. This results in a neoliberal practical competence. As a personal attribute the imperative to become 'competent' creates a strong affinity between neoliberal political subjectivity and good and proper notions of the autonomous, anticollective, antipolitics postsocialist subject. Neoliberal dispositions may be part of a 'defensive institution' against the routinization of crisis (Shevchenko 2009).

4. *Capitalist Realism*

During his time in the North, Igor would write to me, sending photos of the barrack-room sleeping arrangements with their inadequate protection from the cold and elements. I received a photo of him sitting near a massive compressor with multi-coloured pipes he and his colleagues had constructed 'like Lego, not using our skills, just following instructions'. The turbocompressor turned extracted gas into liquid to be pumped into megatankers and sailed to meet 15 per cent of the world's natural gas demand. Yamal is 50.1 per cent owned by Novatek, the second-largest gas producer behind Gazprom. Like many large enterprises, Novatek shares are held by state-capital corporations like Gazprom and are traded and held by international investors, though Russian billionaires are the majority owners. Since the war, some of its shareholders are now sanctioned, but as of 2024, the EU has balked at a genuine embargo of Russian LNG. Predictably, Igor quickly grew tired not just of the compact he had agreed to, but also to the way labour was treated and isolated:

> We weren't people even to them, just *inventar* – a material resource that had a rapid depreciation. Any hint of grumbling or even asking too many questions, taking too long and it was clear we'd be in trouble. People kept their heads down. The isolation meant there was nothing we could do, and no one to turn to.

Political-economic reflection like Igor's is generated by experience and reinforced through sharing talk. Over time, Igor's analysis (often discussed in a circle of acquaintances) became more and more 'structural' – linking his misfortunes to the 'bigger picture'. At the same time, he also became more critical of the imperative towards an entrepreneurial spirit he had formerly extolled. He talked about 'burn out', about how having to 'hustle' meant he had no time or energy for his family life. Sometimes he talked about his 'depression' at the lack of 'any alternatives'. He tried all kinds of desperate endeavours including pyramid selling and even cryptocurrency trading. In 2022 we talked for a long time about how the wartime conditions in Russia reminded him of his early childhood.

> It's like perestroika again. The kids ask me for pocket money, and I say – 'there's nothing'. And they say they'll soon start some rationing, and it will be like people trading privatization vouchers. I remember Dad getting two leather coats for his vouchers in the 1990s but they were fake leather and disintegrated in a month. They'll no doubt start withholding wages soon. Again, migration will become a matter of force and not choice. People will once more experience the shock when they're naked and others are in furs. We live in a place where there's an absence of normal life. 'All for the front' but also some profiteering for the nomenklatura! Groundhog Day again!

Like his working-class compatriots, Igor makes ready use of the mnemonic resource of the Soviet and perestroika periods. He has considerably more resources than Vanya: education, family support, savings and property, and some 'social capital'. By 2018 however, Igor becomes increasingly politicized thanks to the work of Alexei Navalny's group who publicized corruption. Igor's talk mirrors the turn that Navalny takes towards more 'socially populist' topics of justice and equality. Igor refers to the lack of resources in his children's school, and how the poor pay for the 'yachts of the rich'.

Igor has also taken the long road to a social position not unlike the most marginalized in Izluchino. By 2023 he has become an unruly entrepreneur himself, using minimal engagement with formal employment to mask his main reliance on informal ventures beyond the purview of the state. After the oil refinery (out of action because of a lack of parts and air attacks), Igor makes use of the shift pattern in another local firm, operating a machine turning raw limestone into powders for the building and agricultural industry. This job gives him a full two days off between his long arduous shifts – the typical regime in industry is a regimen of two twelve-hour shifts over forty-eight hours, followed by a rest period of forty-eight hours. Between the shifts he works on a large village plot he bought some years ago, slowly constructing wooden cabins using his own labour and that of people who owe him favours. He eventually wants a 'passive income' from tourism, 'especially now there will be a boom in domestic tourism'. The oil refinery job was supposed to 'protect' him from the military draft, but now he takes his chances. Like others, he trusts to the incompetence of the state to overlook him – or find other victims first. However, his politics change too: initially appalled at the invasion of Ukraine, he becomes a hardcore defensive consolidator – highly critical of the 'collective West', the Ukrainian leadership, but also his own government.

Igor's dream is a 'passive income' he has read about in self-help books for entrepreneurs. This is one reason he likes talking to me: as a person who comes from a 'normal country', I can apparently tell him all about how to become a true entrepreneur 'honestly'. However, Igor has a much more active sideline in illegal activities.[14] This income stream helps sustain the capital investment needed to keep his building project alive. Reflecting further, Igor often talks about 'meeting the system halfway', critically analysing 'the system stacked against people' [*ulozheno vsyo protiv liudei*] as he understands it. In 2024 he is 'relieved' to vote for Putin. 'I'm glad I understand there is no choice. It's liberating not to think about politics.' His feeling for how to get by and get ahead needs no particular reflexivity because it is based on the highly embedded meta-occupational community he grew up in. Despite saying he feels liberated in not thinking about the war or politics anymore, he makes a point to articulate how 'violence' from the state-capital compact creates dilemmas that provoke an active, negotiated response from individuals.

> The job market is like this form of violence [*nasilie*] – it's as much psychological and anything else. You try to meet it half-way, but whatever you do it's like trying to negotiate with a crazy, a psycho. Look at the way job descriptions are advertised in this country. Before my job at the Powders Plant, I interviewed at

14. This is a good example of where I have to pull back from full description, for obvious reasons.

the aluminium plant. I know people don't approve of it because of the pollution, but there you go. Look, I can show you on my phone: 'Will have to undertake a period of probation without pay'. The advertised pay is about twice the local average. But this ad is for work that is unambiguously for tricking losers [*razvod dlia lokhov*] …

Other interlocutors would frequently share similar job descriptions for all kinds of work, not just manual and technical. They were often shocked and disgusted by the requirements, especially as Russia moved to a war footing and the rhetoric of sacrifice for the greater good appeared to intensify the exploitative logics of subordination. 'William', a young Moscow-based transgender man, struggled to find work after his transition in 2021.[15] We would often send each other job descriptions and discuss them. In early 2023, we discussed an office job vacancy that offered the following:

The worker will not be subject to delays in payment of salary. Worker will have a contract that conforms to the legislation of the Labour Code. Key personality traits of the successful candidate: stress-resilience [*stressoustoichivost*], adherence to subordination [*sobliudenie subordinatsii*].

William commented sarcastically:

They start off by selling you the job based on the fact they obey the law and pay wages on time as if to say it's quite normal to cheat employees in general. And then immediately follow up with something really nasty in case you got your hopes up: 'come to us but know that we'll just immediately shout at you and let loose on you [*sryvatsia*], but make sure you know how to shut up and not react'.

Igor also reflected at length on the meaning of the labour 'market' gaslighting people. By this he referred to how people ended up embracing their own exploitation and self-exploitation. Here Igor touches on the difficulty of thinking outside the accepted 'realism'. He doesn't call it that; he uses the term 'resignation' [*smirenie*] – illustrating the penetration of helplessness, if not consent to change. The politics of resignation have been proposed as contributing to the dominant 'structure of feeling' in Western societies (Benson and Kirsch 2010). In a recent intervention, Søren Mau (2023) links economic and social domination to explain the 'mute compulsion' of contemporary capitalism. Capitalist realism, as a handmaiden to objective economic compulsion, naturalizes the effects of neoliberalism from above and below. That realism is palpable indicates how such resignation and helplessness operate at different scales. But this is not the end of the story.

Workers learn to accept *bezperspektivnost* [prospectlessness] and incorporate it into a worldview, normalizing the idea that they will work for peanuts and

---

15. Some trans people choose non-Slavic sounding names after transition.

then may be discarded or defrauded anyway at the end of the probationary period. Igor is characteristic of that significant subset who do not so much 'domesticate' neoliberal material and rhetorical imperatives unwillingly from below as to 'hack them'. Once again, researchers working in the tradition of Raymond Williams argue that while a dominant structure of feeling may overall produce resignation, it can also reveal a disjunction. Resignation is not always disempowering even if what it generates is a reluctant discontented response (Benson and Kirsch 2010: 468).

Denys Gorbach, writing on Ukrainian deindustrializing cities, discusses how an 'ability to self-exploit and apply constant efforts in juggling various forms of capital one possesses to prevent its devaluation' is manifest in the widely understood specific uses of the verbs 'to spin' and 'to twist' [*krutitsia, vertetsia*] (Gorbach 2024). Igor is a self-defining 'spinner', a word he frequently uses when talking about his tactics for social reproduction in an environment where strategy is impossible but tactics, including illegal ones are necessary. His 'hacking' does not preclude partial internalization of entrepreneurial imperatives that align with neoliberal governmentalization. Igor's trajectory is significant: from accommodation to a position much closer to the déclassé peers he initially looked down on.

Christina Scharff's feminist research on the psychic life of neoliberal subjectivity is relevant here (2016). Scharff foregrounds concrete effects of self-training that recall the emic terms 'spinning' and 'twisting' that we find in the Russian and Ukrainian contexts. Noteworthy too are her categories of domesticating dispositions: hiding injuries, constant action, anxiety, pathologizing others, surviving difficulties. However, some other contours she identifies are resisted by people like Igor. He does not 'disavow inequalities', nor does he fully embrace risk. Russian capitalist realism increasingly politicizes him. Recalling Giorgio Agamben's version of biopolitics (1998), we could call Igor's positioning one of 'bare entrepreneurialism'. It is bare because it speaks of diminished citizenship based on exclusion and inclusion at the same time and on the most unappealing terms, yet which are dictated by the state-capital compact. Igor falls short of domestication at the level of psyche suggested by Scharff, partly because deterritorialized lines of flight are available away from formal economic compulsion: informal and illegal practices that partly substitute social reproductive capacity and provide psychic satisfaction.[16]

16. Agamben is best known for his employment of two terms. 'Homo sacer' is the citizen without citizenship subject to a 'state of exception', a term adapted from Carl Schmitt based on the idea that regimes may diminish citizenship rights in times of crisis. Neoliberal governmentality as experienced in Russia is a making of the exceptional, something normalized and internalized. Agamben's 'bare life' refers to the classical Greek distinction *zoe-bios* that separates citizens as political beings from animal bodies.

4. Capitalist Realism 103

The taxi driver and the metal turner: Problematizing concepts

In this section we take a brief look at Rahimjon's experience in the informal economy, and Nikita's work for a local Kaluga metal component company.[17] Rahimjon came to Russia in 2012 at about the age of twenty through a revolving door of co-ethnic recruitment. The Russian sponsor – in this case a local economic elite with substantial property assets – would recruit Kyrgyz groundsmen to tend his country 'estate' in the village of Kamenka, satellite to the town of Izluchino. Kamenka is a place many well-to-do Kalugans have their country houses, known as 'dachas'.[18] When the groundsman wanted to leave – either to better prospects in Moscow or to go home – he had to reproduce himself by recruiting a co-ethnic – almost always from his extended village back home in Kyrgyzstan. Those recruited varied significantly in their skills and experience. Rahimjon was young and not up to the physical and other demands of the job in the large and unfamiliar gardens. In the summer of 2012, he was replaced by an Uzbek who had more experience.

Kyrgyz have fewer immigration hoops to jump than other Central Asians for historical-legal reasons. Rahimjon took pride in his 'preparedness' prior to coming to Russia. He would show me his document and talk in great detail about how authoritative figures in his home village had helped him get ready, partly echoing Igor's experience. However, as Malika Bahovadinova argues (2023: 318–9), as much as migrants 'prepare' themselves, Russian bureaucracy is designed to extort and produce opportunities for repeated dispossession – even in things like forcing migrants to buy insurance at an artificially inflated rate. Quickly falling out with his 'employer' made Rahimjon's situation highly precarious. Without patronage of a well-connected ethnic Russian, he could only locally work as a day labourer and lived in an unheated cattle-shed in the village. Nonetheless, he sought out opportunities to work on rural building sites in the Kaluga area. He was even excited by the risks of getting challenged by the police over his *'patent'* (work permit), seeing it as a game, an opportunity to show he was more resourceful and had more 'smarts'. However, that summer his 'ethnic price' became increasingly evident to him – there was no way he could earn enough on a low day-labour rate to save money to see him through the winter. He would come to my plot and, like an exchange trader, relate to me how much his stock price that day was. 'Highly undervalued', he would say, 'only 180 Rubles [$6] today', with humour but a serious undertone. He looked with envy on the Uzbeks doing much better paid work in the village and town who at that time could earn $30 a day cash-in-hand doing relatively untaxing labour. Then, calamity. Despite believing in the power of

---

17. Nikita's life as a younger man is described and analysed in previous work (Morris 2016).

18. I tend to avoid the term 'dacha' as it can describe any kind of rural second properties: from a one-room shack to a palatial building.

Figure 2 Uzbek workers in the village.

his relatively well-documented basis for working and living in Russia, at the first contact with the police he was extorted of all his saved money.[19]

Crisis provoked Rahimjon to leave the area, putting his trust in connections – via intermediary Uzbek workers who represent a sort of local manual worker aristocracy – with co-ethnic Kyrgyz in Moscow who worked in high-rise construction. However, after two seasons of this work again he was cheated of much of his savings, this time by the Kyrgyz 'money holder' of the group. Convinced that returning home to Kyrgyzstan would result in neither recompense nor would be accepted by his family, Rahimjon got a loan from other countrymen to pay for the rent of a taxicab in Moscow. However, when I caught up with him in 2020, he described himself as 'king of the world': Russia's version of Uber (Yandex) had 'saved his life'.

> Everything is alright now. Yandex solved all my problems. I just work and work and work. I can earn so much this way. And the system allows me to learn how to earn more. I want to drive to all the cities around Moscow because that way, I can make more money. The app makes it flexible [*gibko*], the hours, I mean. And

---

19. Rustamjon Urinboyev (2021) describes how even with entirely correct migration documents, Central Asians may remain 'semilegal' because of police and migration service corruption.

I am flexible. If I start to fall asleep, I stop. But this way I can work for maybe 36 hours before I feel dangerous. Then a short sleep and my protector [*kum*] will wake me up. He will also tell me if I should stop, where I shouldn't drive because of lots of police [taking bribes]. Here, look at my rating: 4.6 stars. Soon I will change the floor mats from fabric to real rubber as they are easier to clean. I am aiming for 4.9 because then I will get more out-of-town rides and airport trips when the app shows high demand.

Rahimjon's relationship with the taxi app Yandex would be familiar to many observers of the gig economy. It purportedly allows workers to become ultra-adaptable masters of their entrepreneurial inner spirit. However, this hides the extreme levels of (self)-exploitation involved. Sleeping, eating and peeing in a rented car. As Andrei Shevchuk argues (2020), the success and ubiquity of platform labour in Russia are a continuation of the neoliberal deregulatory drive. The driver takes the risk yet pays around 60 per cent of income to the car's actual owner. He pays Yandex all kinds of fees. He pays the Moscow traffic police bribes daily (Rahimjon and I calculated this could be 10 per cent or more of income). The police find it easier to target ethnic minority taxi drivers than 'civilians', and Yandex drivers are so visible because of their cars' livery. Rahimjon was still in his early twenties and revelled in the adventure offered. He also got a kick out of the competitive model of governmentality offered by the app: he quit smoking, dressed smart and was even more polite than necessity demanded – all in the pursuit of the cherished fraction of a star.

When I was in Moscow I would message Rahimjon to work as my driver offering him a premium on the Yandex quote for journeys. Yandex, like Uber, offers tiers of service and Rahimjon started to call me his 'comfort plus' client. His relationship to a marketized self was playful and deadly serious at the same time. When I suggested a trip to Kaluga from Moscow (200km) he thought not only of the high fare, but that this would increase his 'authority' within the world of the app, and more so *beyond* the app among his co-ethnic network. He had to ask permission of the car's owner (a Kyrgyz 'elder' in his co-ethnic group). Rahimjon had, in 2019, never driven beyond the Moscow ring road. I was worried about him being overconfident. However, he also calculated the risk in relation to reward. I had anticipated this and updated him as to the better quality of the rural roads since the last time he had lived in the 'provinces'. Next, we negotiated about times. I wanted to leave at 6 am, but Rahimjon argued that this would artificially suppress the price of the trip because of low demand (a strange logic showing how the app had 'captured' his mind; after all, I was paying him partly *outside* the Yandex system). 'Pay me what I'm worth' was his frequent refrain. If neoliberal economism as an embodiment could have an individual's name, that name might be Rahimjon. This was not the 'bare' entrepreneurialism but a tenaciousness, almost obsessively internalized kind.

What was missing from this story was an essential dependency, and not on me. Ironically, his success was thanks to his embedding in a traditional community – the extended quasi-kinship network in Moscow. Aksana Ismailbekova (2025) notes that the transplantation of kinship hierarchies from Kyrgyzstan to Russia involves 'deterritorialization' of territorial relations back 'home'. But this process also dilutes or at least transforms the relation. Essentially, exploitation in Moscow is made permissible to support the continuity of 'moral' relations at home (supporting kinship coherence with remittance payments). This is the dark side of 'deterritorialized' kinship – what happens in Moscow to 'sustain' the traditional structures in Kyrgyzstan can amount to trickery, betrayal and exploitative dependence, as much as mutual aid, support and mentoring. Moreover, in time it is likely Rahimjon will start to experience some of Vanya's feelings for dispossession. As Elena Borisova argues (2023), the long-term toll of obligations of care that migrants take on leads to premature ageing and health problems. What young Central Asian men think of as temporally delimited opportunities to grow rich trap them in endless cycles of return and exploitation in Russia.

Rahimjon, despite his full-throated endorsement of social Darwinism, embraces an entrepreneurialism only possible thanks to co-ethnic patronage and trust – and even that is not so dependable, as seen from the times he could not fully rely on his countrymen. We could call it a variant of patronal-client entrepreneurialism. The risks of car ownership (insurance, repayment schedule, maintenance) are borne by an elder who is backed by capital from the group. From the outside, the Uber model resembles extreme individualization and governmentalization of the marketized self, but in Russia that is not the case. Most Russian and non-Russian drivers alike work according to the model Rahimjon used. Nonetheless, ultimate risk of capital loss is devolved to the individual – both from Yandex and the ethnic sponsor. If Rahimjon had a serious accident, insurance would not cover the full costs and his debt 'peonage' would become much worse. His relationship with his relatives back in Central Asia is financialized as they are the ultimate guarantor should he fail. This extreme devolution, even in a patron-client relationship based on ethnic and regional ties (recall that trust is built on the fact the group originates from the same group of villages in Kyrgyzstan), means we can call this arrangement another example of capitalist realism: the 'logic' of market relations trumps all else, even if forms of embedding and alternative ways of establishing trust exist.

***

Finally, we shift focus to Nikita, whom I have known since he was in his early twenties in 2009. Initially, Nikita's labour biography resembled Igor's. He kicked against the pricks, leaving badly paid and precarious work in local Izluchino factories for the informal economy. He worked for a few years in an underground cooperative factory making double-glazed windows (Morris 2016). However, as we catch up with him in 2018, he has moved to Kaluga city and works for a metal fastenings factory in an enormous Special Economic Zone (SEZ) set up by the governor in the 2000s. The SEZ served multinational automotive firms including Volvo, Mitsubishi, Peugeot, VW and many other suppliers, almost all of which shut up shop after the beginning of the Ukraine war. In the period 2009–18, Nikita also looked to 'hack' the neoliberal compact, changing his job as frequently as his car (i.e. every six months). On the one hand he uneasily put up with privations and humiliations in pursuit of foreign car ownership – a levelling status achievement. On the other hand, unlike Igor, Nikita showed quasi-acceptance of capitalist realism at the same time as greater willingness to turn to full 'exit' – a paradox illustrated by his years in the underground cooperative and a marked tendency towards autonomy. He would never call himself a 'spinner', and denied experiencing precarity, exploitation and 'work on the self'.

Now, Nikita works at the metal fasteners Zastezhka. Since 2018, he worked his way up to quality control and responsibility for a few metal turners. The firm has expanded and quickly replaced the lost foreign clients with new buyers for its wares, essential for the building of new 'big-box' sites which facilitate 're-shoring' lower-tech production initiated by the war. It is tempting to see Zastezhka as representing an example of 'decaying paternalism'. It offers a few discretionary benefits that resemble the old Soviet-era 'social wage' system in return for much more naked exploitation and self-exploitation (Morris and Hinz 2017, Gorbach 2020). 'Bad jobs' are ameliorated just enough by offering an absence of those 'negatives' associated with the worst of the 1990s, and token 'positives': no wage arrears,[20] pension contributions, and things like a clean shower room, subsidized canteen and free work clothes. Benefits in kind were historically important in the Soviet era and are called in the literature 'social wages'. At the height of their availability in the 1980s, they added up to 25 per cent in value of the actual cash wage – things like good quality subsidized meals at work and kindergarten places. Even in the present, they have significant cash-equivalent value.

On one level, paternalism attempts to stabilize labour 'churn' in small, medium and even large enterprises in Russia today.[21] Workshop relations are highly personalized *and* individualized. Immediate bosses exercise patron-client power and everything depends on being in the good books of a supervisor. At the same time, impersonal yet individual performance on the job is measured by output. On the one hand this looks like a manual control reinforcement of neoliberal rationality: if you are unwilling to not only outproduce others as well as exhibit reflexivity *and* deference, then you're out. Capitalist realism is written into the most personalized of labour relations. Elsewhere, I have argued that SEZs in Russia are laboratories for diffusing further neoliberal economism (Morris 2021a). SEZs (like their deterritorialized counterpart, gig-economy apps such as Yandex) are literal states of exception where foreign (and since 2022, state appropriated and redistributed) capital is granted much leeway in labour relations as well as

20. The fear of wage arrears, a near-universal experience in 1990s industry, never disappeared and neither did the phenomenon itself. In 2022 arrears was still an issue provoking labour protest. The patriotic argument that in wartime workers should accept labour discipline does not have much purchase.

21. It should be remembered that demographic change means that 'exit' strategies of labour 'churn' (workers frequently changing job) are still viable, despite the universality of highly exploitative relations.

108   *Everyday Politics in Russia*

sovereignty.[22] Despite the war, both capital and state formations would like this compact to continue, and there are signs that such zones will thrive, albeit under partial Chinese tutelage. By 2024, the VW plant where many of my interlocutors had worked in the 2010s was being prepared for retooling, potentially for Chinese automotive. The greater 'laboratory' is of course the Russian state itself, where almost uniquely in Europe, workers have no real right to representation or legal recourse. However, domestication puts a twist on this.

Even in the SEZs, which are now morphing into a hybrid militarized regime under wartime conditions, things are not so simple as they seem. There is still the structural power of workers just quitting, eking out a living in the informal economy. They can also leave the country, go into 'internal emigration' in the empty interior, or just downgrade employment – taking nightwatchman jobs, as Vanya was seen to do earlier. Enterprise paternalism is given a new lease of life, but on militarized neoliberal terms. Personal and conscious sacrifice by the worker is demanded because of the 'war footing', and in return a novel 'care'-relation emerges at the firm level. This partly occurs by necessity – there are increasing demands to hold on to labour and coercion is insufficient to do this. Secondly, firms suddenly have a strong retention instrument in the form of protecting workers bureaucratically from wartime mobilization.[23] In the longer term, this allows them to ask for more sacrifices and further efforts by employees to 'work on themselves'. Nikita is a case in point: a person highly valuing autonomy who might well be tempted to become a more unruly entrepreneur like Igor. Evidence, however, points to a new emergent strand of paternalism based on fictious kinship,

---

22. SEZs' success has been in work intensification, the socialization of blue-collar locals in accepting downgraded labour terms and conditions *and* training white-collar workers in more effective coercive surveillance-managerialist methods. In terms of transnational state-capital collaboration to increase productivity, global connectivity (notably with the Silk Road rail system), and in providing a relatively low-tech domestic manufacturing base, SEZs are an outstanding success. These effects are not contained by the zonal boundary – they 'scale' via further expansion of 'lean' enterprises beyond the zone as TNC infrastructure and human capital investment have an effect on the whole region. The 'zone' is not a spatially contained territory but an elastic administrative state of exception that has expanded throughout the region to encompass many clusters containing dozens of diverse foreign and domestic firms in urban, brownfield and greenfield sites. In terms of 'register' too, the SEZs exercise a strong discursive effect, making new working relations 'common sense' beyond the zones themselves, affecting local politicians, employers and workers in other enterprises. Overall, the 'register' effect multiplier is more important than any administrative-legal deregulation and should be seen as part of neoliberal scaling itself.

23. The recent argument that Russia will be forced into some kind of fiscal stimulus or 'military Keynesianism' has not found many supporters (Trickett 2023). In any case there is little sign of opportunities outside manufacturing that helps the war effort or replaces lost imports.

4. Capitalist Realism

109

buttressed by the war. Protection is offered, and loyalty given to the firm, in lieu of patriotic sacrifice at the real frontline in Ukraine.

Nikita invites me and co-workers to a dinner party in late 2022. No one likes to mention the war, as I've learned throughout this visit. I also talk to Nikita later alone:

> You saw what it's like. They're family to me. You worked with me at the plastic workshop.[24] That doesn't compare, even though there we were all school friends. Here it is tougher, but you know what you're giving yourself for. All the benefits and pay are 'white' [transparent to tax and pension authorities] and that itself might be enough. Unlike a lot of the places in Izluchino, you can feel this is Kaluga because the big boss takes real responsibility for everything. And even though times are never easy, the place is doing well because of the human relations between the management and us workers. I mean, they didn't just fire me when I was slow at the beginning, you know. The main thing was as long as you looked sharp about yourself, there was time to get used to each other. How does it differ? Well in some ways it doesn't: there's still the expectation to work a lot of unpaid overtime. But then you can get that back as leave.

Knowing Nikita for over fifteen years and his previous life as 'flitter' between formal and informal work, I was shocked, but also persuaded. Such a turn around on the way he'd talked about work relations before was no act. Furthermore, because his sister, Katya, and her husband were also my long-term research interlocutors I was able to carefully triangulate Nikita's talk. Katya's husband, who worked in middle-management of the firm, at another occasion sat with me and Boris over some corporate tea event. Boris works in the marketing department and takes up the story:

> The funny thing is, we barely do any marketing. Eighty per cent of our work and budget is … parties. Feel-good shit. I mean, I trained in audio-visual studies and wanted to be a filmmaker. And in this job, I can do that! We make all kinds of goofy spoofs of Hollywood movies for the firm with workers as actors. It's not just for morale, and it's not just because the owner is eccentric. It's because, well, it does kind of represent what the firm is … there is a cohesion. I'm not saying we're unique in the region. We do also do stuff for the Governor: like shoot serious videos. And then there is also the corporate social responsibility angle. We beautified the square in the Kirov district, and it gave us good PR and the Governor got some of that too. And you know what's funniest? We were taught that 'voluntary weekend work' in the USSR was a myth, that it was coerced. But

24. As part of fieldwork in 2010, I spent a short period working with Nikita and co-workers in the underground window workshop. Workers were nearly all known to one another, and the enterprise was partly run on cooperative lines with a share of profits.

in our firm at least people do respond to a feeling of being valued [*chuvstvuiut, chto ikh tseniat*] and come out after their shift to do such 'work'.

Writing on large-scale corporate social responsibility (CSR), Douglas Rogers (2015) is circumspect about the applicability of the term 'neoliberalism' to his research materials on the oil industry in Russia. His hesitation is based on how the Russian case reveals corporate paternalism. However, the activities of his oil companies could be seen as another example of domesticated neoliberalism. Corporations take over paternalistic functions of the local state and become major social sponsors. Simultaneously, social provision becomes disembedded from the local population. Subsequently, Rogers observes that CSR tends towards encouraging narratives of entrepreneurialism, even in the cultural sphere. CSR also entails technocratic responsibilizing of social problems devolved to individuals and small groups on the basis of competitive tender. Social programmes are 'sponsored' by a corporate 'client'. In Rogers' view they serve state building as much as the development of an entrepreneurial reality because projects are integrated with regional administration and governance.

In the case of Zastezhka and Nikita, we have a further development of a hybrid corporatist type of neoliberalism, in a partly naturalizing form, and which subsequently aligns with the particular capitalist realism of Russia today, even in wartime. Nikita and others genuinely feel thankful to the firm for protecting them from military mobilization. They inscribe 'sincerity' into their self-governmentalizing efforts to 'pay back' the firm loyally. We could call this third type: fictive 'corporatist entrepreneurialism'. 'I'm fast, I give myself to the work. But I can get faster', Nikita told me in 2018 when he had just started working at the firm. I had asked him to take time out to watch the football World Cup, taking place in Russia. Instead, he went to bed early because he had a shift the next day, which was unlike him.

Fictitious kinship is extended by the firm as a corporate 'extended family' to whom one 'belongs'. Whether this is 'cynically' calculated by employers and HR departments is beside the point. Both employees and managers have a 'feel' for this relation, as Boris points out, expressing surprise at its success, despite his embeddedness in this process. Similarly, the actual degree of incorporation into the 'worldview' of Nikita is not so important because he has learned to be his own best surveyor, or *nadzor*, regardless of his instincts towards autonomy. Fictive incorporation is one possible future for the so-far failed 'defensive consolidation' to find a point of purchase in people's lives. However, I would not underestimate the continuing attraction of both unruly entrepreneurialism: kicking back with 'weapons of the weak' against the hurtful world of waged labour, nor bare entrepreneurialism, which represents a kind of partial self-exclusion from the 'market' of labour relations.

In Zastezhka, while people are encouraged to goof off in videos parodying the latest blockbuster (despite the war, all Hollywood cultural products), the competition to become a funny worker and a character is itself the other side of the coin of neoliberal subjectivation. Emotional labour invested in acting a

4. Capitalist Realism   111

part for the marketing department is evidence of the intensity of commitment elsewhere. It also contributes to continual feedback into the fictious kinship model the firm promotes. Despite their difference in social class, Boris and Nikita were able to become good friends. This relation challenges a simple distinction between commoditized marketized self (neoliberal subject) and the idea of entitlements and rights recognized by and reified within a neo-collectivist corporatism. Even here we see an elective affinity between 'atavistic' collectivist drives and neoliberal yet paternalist relations which sustain the state-capital compact in Russia today.

Conclusions

Diffusion of the market-as-common-sense into ever more domains of public and private life coupled with the erosion of the welfare state has been implemented by a professional political class in allegiance with powerful sections of capital. Since 2000, a capital-state nexus has entrenched and extended to new social realms: from pensions, public-sector pay, domestic utilities, anchoring the perspective most Russians have on work relations. However ubiquitous though, as in most of western Europe, this project never commanded widespread public support, and anger and frustration at its long-term implications now inform every shade of everyday politics.

In this chapter, I observed different domestications and adaptations to capitalist realism. Rahimjon's engagement represents an extreme, but one available to ethnic Russians too. His seemingly complete effacement of any subjecthood apart from self-exploitation is tempered by the continuation of non-marketized relations in other spheres – in co-ethnic trust networks. Rahimjon represents the microproletarianization of workers such as food couriers and taxi-drivers in patronal entrepreneurialism. They are subject to algorithmic control for maximum extraction of surplus value within shadow corporations. This happens of their own 'volition', via internalization of the demands of maximal self-exploitation and the delegation of all externalities to the individual and wider society by the platforms themselves (health costs, accidents, insurance, pollution). However, we observe the imbrication of state (which owns bonds in such companies, allows them to operate as quasi-monopolies and sustains anti-labour legal environments) and financial and political elites who own such companies. The scaling effect of microproletarianization of swathes of economic activity in Russia via concentration of market share is unprecedented outside of China, facilitated by what some observers call 'hybrid surveillance capitalism' (Østbø 2021).[25] Others argue that Russia moves towards a digital 'control society'. The always-imperfect arrangement of such assemblages, evidenced by failure of technocratic governance during

---

25. The most popular search engine in Russia (Yandex) also owns the main social network and the most popular email service, and controls both the main ride-hailing app and an increasing share of the food courier business.

Covid lockdowns, gives rise to re-routing of digital technology and resistance via 'disassembly' (Orlova and Morris 2021).

Should we view Russia as another 'normal' country, as Andrei Shleifer and Daniel Treisman (2005) once proposed? In their view, Russia was well on the way to becoming a middle-income country facing typical developmental challenges. Instead, I would contend that Russia is 'normal' in ways that reflect its championing of authoritarian neoliberalism (Bruff 2014). Its characteristics are the dominant politics of 'austerity': a continuously residualizing social state. This is accompanied by the other disciplining factor of real incomes falling over protracted time periods; limited social mobility and the privatizing of educational opportunity maintain a small plutocratic class or caste; there is continuous and seemingly limitless expansion of indebtedness and precarity; social reproduction is largely responsibilized and privatized; a rentier alliance between state and capital interests sustains itself even through partial elite turnover. Finally, multinational corporations' clout and the intensification of their role in the economy were not checked by war in Ukraine, merely transformed. Corporations, whether foreign-owned or the domestic assets of weakly supportive elites, were transferred to existing loyalists and lower-tier elites.[26] All watched over by the nascent digital control society.

The recourse to domestication should give us pause for thought. As Kangas and Salmenniemi argue (2016), domestication should not be a term that merely indicates the localization of neoliberalism – a further adaptation of the passive postsocialist subject. Drawing on Bakhtinian ideas, they posit a dialogical relationship between neoliberalism and postsocialism. My point is to show how the most vulnerable and seemingly 'marginal', such as the three composite people in this chapter, enact and embody such dialogic movement in their striving towards less precarious social reproduction. They take seriously, yet reflexively, offers of *care*-ful corporate neoliberalism precisely because they are incoherent and contradictory. A dialogue implies evenness and equality, but people understand that traps await them everywhere. Where I differ from Kangas and Salmenniemi is that this process involves active re-working on the part of folk that is carried out beyond the symbolic or discursive sphere (hence it is more than 'dialogic'): it involves material and bodily struggle and repeated 'submission' or fights with the mutely, and not so mutely compulsive effects of capitalism.

Douglas Rogers (2015: 15) cautions against 'uniting things under the theoretical sign of the "neoliberal"', but at the same time his proposals chime with the core aim of this chapter: the necessity of a more serious ethnographic examination of how flexible labour regimes, SOEs and the state are linked. As I argued, these linkages intensify the politics of resignation on the part of ordinary people as they are further incorporated into neoliberal (self)governmentality. Rogers (2015) noted in his study of the oil and gas industry in the Urals that capitalist

---

26. Before 2022, it was argued that sanctions had strengthening effects in the market position of leading MNCs, see Gurkov and Saidov (2017).

4. Capitalist Realism 113

'incorporation' via privatization after communism does not necessarily mean coherence or coordination in governance and corporate identity. In addition, the term 'incoherence' is distinct from 'hybrid assemblages' (Ong 2006) or 'parasitical co-presences' (Peck 2004). 'Deregulatory' governance (in the sense that it lacks finality or fixity) inevitably, and often unintentionally, opens holes in the fabric of economic and social relations.

Eeva Kesküla argues that instead of paternalism, the post-Soviet company as a total social institution cedes ground to the privatization of social reproduction. Her reiteration of the classic Polanyian argument which sees kin relations as disembedded from the company (2014: 59) may only be part of the picture (her fieldwork concerns traditional extractive industry). The actions of the firm Zastezhka seem like a novel form of neo-paternalistic corporatism, but it would be foolish to predict their effects. Don Kalb (2013) argues that anthropologists examining the local effects of neoliberalism have to choose between Weber and Marx. There are echoes of this in the general debates on Russia – Simon Kordonsky's neofeudal estate hierarchies (2016) versus Matveev's state-capital alliance (2019). The 'capitalization' of social relationships is visible in the cases in this chapter (the Weberian pole), but material necessity and social reproduction mean all interlocutors express their class positioning and engage with hegemonic narratives about their marginalization. They do this by embracing social Darwinism as 'strivers' or rejecting it in 'bare entrepreneurialism' – sometimes both, as in 'unruly' modes. However, corporatist entrepreneurialism as a zombie relation just keeps coming back. As Kalb goes on to say, what's missing from the Weberian position are 'rational collectivist claims on states'. I earlier argued that these are extractable phenomenologically, but we can also detect the traces in the ersatz corporatist relations of Zastezhka. I explore the care and kinship metaphors more fully in the next chapter, where we discuss citizen's demands of state bureaucracy and its agents.

Chapter 5

INCOHERENT STATE: ON CO-PRODUCING GOVERNANCE FROM BELOW

There are many abandoned industrial sites on the road into Izluchino. On approach, a traveller spies numerals patterned in white inset bricks on each dusty-red chimney telling of their year of construction: '1961', says the first one, and then on even larger stacks: '1971', '1981'. There is no further continuation of this sequence. The stacks and workshops are largely silent or derelict. Closer to town though, a twin metal stack with spiral veins in the tricolor of the Russian flag reassuringly belches steam. We've reached the Kotelnaya – heating plant № 1. Emblematic of the survival and fragility of small settlements throughout Russia, the Kotelnaya is critical infrastructure and viewed as part of the state by locals. The truth however is different. This heating plant was built in 2004 by a private Moscow communal infrastructure company. This allowed the Soviet industrial plant (which heated both factories and town and was ten-times larger) to be decommissioned, its parent enterprise already defunct. The municipality therefore owned neither the plant, nor the land or equipment. It paid for heating to a holding company set up in Kaluga. However, the Soviet-era underground piping that stretched from the plant to the housing stock remained in municipal hands. This is a typical yet unsustainable situation throughout Russia because these pipes are 80 per cent 'beyond usable exploitation' due to age. In 2014, the building and land were transferred to the municipality, but the gas boilers themselves are leased from the energy holding company to a private 'supply' company owned by enterprising local elites. Frequently, the municipality is notionally in arrears to the 'supply' because of non-payment by households of their energy bills. This doesn't hinder the 'supply' company taking on debt to expand its services to other districts while enriching the elite and 'blackmailing' the municipality. This typically confusing 'Russian-doll' structure of part-privatized utilities and legalized extortion of locals causes frequent outages and legal disputes.

'The thing is, I'm completely alone. I can't retire, even with this damn diabetes, even though my eyes are failing. Someone has to keep the place going.' This was among our first conversations when in 2010 I sat with the portly and wheezing chief engineer of the Kotelnaya Nikolai Viktorovich. His was a familiar refrain of many tropes about the 'absent state' and loss of human and infrastructural capacity since 1991. In my second period in the town of Izluchino, I had little to do during

116   *Everyday Politics in Russia*

the day when everyone was at the factories. And so, for a long stretch of time I would follow the fifty-something man around, from the heating plant on the edge of town, to the offices of the municipality manager's office, to the satellite stations and gas mains in other settlements where blue flames burn brightly through a thick inspection window, heating water, pumping water. This is the lifeline of almost all towns and cities in Russia, where blocks of flats rely on remotely supplied central heating during the 'season' between October and mid-April. In part thanks to his poor eyesight, I became Nikolai Viktorovich's personal driver as well as part of his family. I was fortunate to be intimately connected with the Kotelnaya until the 'Chief', as locals called him, retired in the late 2010s.

As I trudged through the mud, snow and then slush, following the Chief, I discovered that despite his words he was anything but isolated. Everyone knew him, and most importantly, deferred in most matters relating to the vital infrastructure of the town – well beyond the purview of the heating infrastructure. Yes, it was true that he no longer had eight *slesary* (all-purpose workmen) to monitor and fix the creaking heating network – the partly buried, and by turns, very visible surface hot-water pipes around twenty kilometres in length. Polya and Tanya – two warm and good-humoured technicians – were on shift for eight hours a day at the main plant. They would arrive on bicycle whatever the weather. In the spring and summer, they tended a vegetable and flower garden at the back of the building. As municipal employees they were a constant source of information about the politics of the town and barometers of local networks of rent-seeking:

> Polya: Kartovsky [the owner of the 'supply' company] has a new car – worth a million [$35,000 in 2010]! And we only get 7000 a month [$250]! … Did you hear about the armed robbery in Toskino? They robbed the French-owned dairy for the payroll – an inside job for sure. I know because they cordoned off the main road to Kaluga and my man couldn't get home from the Sixty-Eighth settlement. You know, at quarry number Fifteen … Before Kartovsky we had Yampolov, who also 'got' a car immediately. That was a Landcruiser, and this one is a Lexus. They say he won't last long as only the Customs and Excise guy has a Lexus here-abouts. They won't allow such petty bourgeoisie [*meshchanstvo*] behaviour from the utility lot. It's reserved for *them lot* alone. I reckon he gets 100,000 a month [$3500]. What do you think, Tanya?
>
> Tanya: I think he'll get in a prang, or someone from the prison Zone will get his outside friends to steal it. There's only one road in and out so he's an obvious target. What's it like in more favourable [*blagopoluchnye*] places, like in your country? [she turns to me]. I bet people don't go around showing off with cars like us. They're above that. And there's less crime, right? You don't have oligarchs, and our brand of petty tyrants [*samodury*] in Lexus cars, I'm sure!
>
> Polya: I think you said enough, Tanya! We shouldn't talk about politics in front of people, especially foreigners. Watch out it doesn't get back to the Chief!

In private, the Chief was inclined to agree with them. I would sit waiting for him with his 'girls' (the women were in their late forties) and they would gossip as in any office. Soon he would return from inspecting the plant, and we would leave. In thirty minutes (after stopping to see what meat had arrived at the surviving collective farm market) we would be sitting in the mayor's office as the Chief pedantically instructed water treatment staff about pipes and pressure. 'What does that have to do with heating?', I naively asked him. 'Oh, nothing, of course'. We would drive out to the municipal vehicle park where Nikolai would find different reasons to persuade Boris, the full-time excavator driver to 'follow, just follow me, will you? I need you for half-an-hour. And how's the wife, did she like the cake?' Most episodes were unrelated to the heating supply – an autumn storm had blocked the main road into town with fallen branches; a lorry had shed a load of gravel on the technical bypass to the town; 'auntie Tanya' who worked in the new monastery complex needed some ground levelled for the kitchen garden laid out by the new priest from Moscow.

The Chief was initially not an employee of the municipality but of the 'supply' company until 2014 when the plant was municipalized. He was informally tasked with working between the supplier, the energy company who owned the boilers, and the municipality itself which owned the town heating pipes. On the face of it, the muddle-through the Chief faced daily was a classic case of deregulation moderated by good-old paternalistic governance. Without ever articulating it, he

Figure 3 The Chief and his workers fix a leak.

118   *Everyday Politics in Russia*

acted as a microscale, self-appointed 'plenipotentiary' of the capital-state nexus. He mixed formal authority with charismatic and informal practical leadership – usually backed up by local politicians. He had had two Soviet and post-Soviet professional lives already, rather like Tamara. He had been director of a diesel engine repair plant in Kazakhstan until 1995, and then the chief engineer of a large collective farm near Moscow until around 2005. His main job in Izluchino was – despite the part-privatization of heating itself – to keep the public network of pipes pumping hot water through the taps and radiators of thousands of flats and homes. He and other technical 'bureaucrats' were left to pick up the pieces when conflicts over property and responsibility inevitably arose.

The subordination of formerly public goods and utilities to the market is never complete. Susanne Wengle notes the opposition yet resignation of mid-level bureaucrats in the face of the extensive liberalization of energy in Russia (2012). Stephen Collier, writing on similar contexts of inherited Soviet infrastructure management outside the metropolises, points out that these legacies represent a hybrid assemblage with neither the market nor state able to adequately govern the biopolitical 'conditions of existence' of a population (Collier 2011: 3). For Collier, like Xenia Cherkaev (2023), governance cannot be understood without adjusting for the different historical understanding of property rights. The 'substantive economy' of the socialist urban space was *khoziaistvo* – managed and marshalled property aimed towards a redistributive equilibrium of resources, albeit under conditions of generalized shortage and a militarized state. Neoliberal reform since the 1990s aims to undo, or 'unbundle' this, in Collier's words. This leads to the micro-scale governmentality we discussed in the previous chapter. In the context of utilities this is best exemplified by the mass roll-out of water and gas meters since the 2010s where previously most public goods were provided at a fraction of their economic cost, let alone with thought of profit. However, as Collier notes, while Soviet-era infrastructure remains, unbundling is incomplete, and this is nowhere as true as in (often buried or poorly accessible) heating pipe infrastructure. District heating with minimal consumer control as to temperature level or water throughput remains the socialist model of the *teploset* – or heat network. Shutting it off to consumers who don't or can't pay is not an option, and metering does not deter many people from intentionally or unintentionally falling behind on their bills.[1] Here we are interested in the incomplete unbundling of social relations which continue to modify that blandest word: 'governance'.

No doubt what seems like erstatz governance by devolved actors like the Chief appears as one cog in a local network of 'neopatrimonialism' (Gel'man 2016). The bureaucratic structures of the state are supplanted by patrons and clients exchanging resources and loyalty beyond an unwritten rules-based system.

---

1. While some authorities do resort to blocking apartment sewerage for non-payment of water bills, it is harder if not impossible to cut off individual apartments from district heating supplies. Enter any less fashionable or well-to-do apartment hallway and you will be greeted by an itemized list of apartments in arrears on their various utility payments.

5. Incoherent State

Changes since the 1990s have resulted in a 'vicious circle of socially inefficient changes which served privileged private interests' (Gel'man 2016: 4). Russia is, by various accounts, a deficient 'network state' (Kononenko 2011), or a 'dyadic constitutional order' in eternal conflict with an administrative regime 'destructive of effective governance in its entirely' (Sakwa 2010: 197). Some critiques see the external imposition of Western governance models as the only option to break the cycle. Alternatively, critics propose the cultivation of oases of 'good governance' from within (again, based on Western models). These might then propagate more widely. But what if such observed co-production of governance from below was already a socially embedded form of in(co)herent stateness that normative governance models cannot really measure or evaluate?

In this chapter, we start from the perspective of the incoherent management of Izluchino's heating system to show how, at different levels of governance, meaningful 'devolved' co-production of the state takes place. Even after large parts of it are no longer 'public' ownership. I argue that co-production is more than about 'niches' of autonomy, proactive citizenship or state responsiveness – observed at regional and municipal level (see respectively, Moliarenko 2016, Fondahl et al. 2019). There also exists a 'substantive economy' – one of time, emotional labour and active listening. This is documented in recent ethnographies of Russian bureaucracies like that of Aleksandra Zakharova who aims at drawing a 'moral cartography' of state-work (2023) and in the research of Tatiana Kuksa (forthcoming) on how clients and gatekeepers of medical care together make 'documents-in-action' work for both of them. I argue, building on such examples, for a generally emergent co-production of state-work, and not only between individuals and state bureaucracies; it emerges in the intersubjective relations of groups of people; consciously or not they work together to reroute – like leaky heating pipes – the vital lines of responsibility, processes and rules. People like the Chief complain about lack of funding, and conflicting lines of authority but are drawn into taking responsibility for making the state real – as an 'actor' legible to people. So, for technician Polya, the local 'state' was not to be found in the substantial charismatic authority of her boss, but in his network of responsibility and kin-like ties with others working nearly as 'equals' for the 'common good'.

While there remain many 'petty tyrants', what state capacity existed was activated through work in concert between people 'like' her boss. They were legible to her as 'Soviet people'. This was similar to Tamara, who sought to uphold the 'quality of communication' in public service. This is a specific form of state-making aimed at maintaining life and sustaining the well-being of citizens. It speaks to the socialist themes of 'care' and kinship-beyond-kin in the circumstances of ongoing multiple insecurities. I focus on a small village and town here as the examples of governance from 'below', but really the point is the diversity of micro-scale interactions that gain the quality of co-produced state-making. State-making is space-making – carving out room to manoeuvre, but also to imagine forms of bureaucratic action that cannot be reduced to clientelism or command. While it is hard to imagine 'theorizing up' to national scales, the state as a morally inflected relation deserves more exploration beyond the existing accounts of specific instances of negotiated

120 *Everyday Politics in Russia*

law (Hendley 2017), informal enforcement and security (Volkov 2002), or state-corporation and other state-society interactions, including private companies undertaking 'social' governance (Rogers 2015).

The Chief is emblematic of a widely operative moral, as much as patronal economy: a continuing legacy of *khoziaistvo*.[2] Nikolai Ssorin-Chaikov (2003: 21) identified the productive meaning of state incoherence in his study of communities in the Far North after 1991. Marketized transformation reproduces, reinvigorates even, local identities and relations to the state, even as it seeks to undo them. Ssorin-Chaikov found the state's 'social' life was reenergized by incoherence. Just as citizens 'resist' individualization of responsibility of heating costs, refusing to pay bills or hacking in various ways the supply of utilities,[3] the state too may work to 'rebundle' the communal logic of the utility network. The Chief's role sat outside of the usual patron-client relation observers impute to Russian governance, and the main sustainer of corruption and incompetence.

> You saw the 'representative' from the region centre [euphemistically referring to the Procuracy] come yesterday with the gas company man? He was trying to find an instrument out of order in the *Kotelnaya* so as to meet his 'target' for fines – it's twenty thousand rubles per infraction. Sometimes, inevitably we get large fines because of the aging plant we have. He pays some of it 'upwards' to his boss, and eventually, a man in Moscow, you know the one. But this system of *otkat* [informal institutional tribute] has to have a reverse side. A mirror, if you like. Not everything can be made into a source of business, though that is the hidden purpose of most 'checking' … It's also true that half my staff are not up to the job – the 'smart' [*soobrazitelnye*] ones went into business long ago. But that at least left me some conscientious ones [*sovestnykh*]. But that too has to be compartmentalized [*razdeleny*] – you have to let them do their second and third jobs and put up with absenteeism.

Today it is a truism that Soviet legacies of 'paternalist' and clientelist relations have straightforward purchase on the present – particularly where the relationship between state and society is concerned. It would be easy, given the pressures of war, to agree that a defensive consolidation around the leader and state institutions would be accompanied by renewed corporatism. But the will of the political elite and regime is not so easily transmitted through the cogs of bureaucracy. Instead, I argue for stateness as an 'organism' in an uneasy symbiosis with the 'environment' that is Russian society and the overlaid rentier economy of private holding companies and corporations. I propose stateness as co-produced at different levels with the active engagement of citizens. Characterizations about 'state withdrawal'

---

2. As with the previous chapter, I admit a distinction, and a significant one, between patronal (embedded) and paternalist (disembedded) relations.

3. Water as a utility is routinely 'hacked' both in rural areas by secretly connecting one's property to the mains, but so is electricity, albeit less permanently.

5. Incoherent State

and poor bureaucratic capacity, while objectively true, are symptomatic of two biases – that the centre is always strong at the expense of the periphery, and that bureaucracies are coercive and distant. Why does this matter? Because whether scholars adopt the line that the current Russian state is powerful and coercive, or that it is weak and ineffective, they reproduce a caricature of what stateness really feels like to the average person.

Tatjana Thelen argues (2011, 2018) that the study of (post)socialist bureaucratic institutions remains 'orientalizing'. Scholars see 'personalist' network structures which overlap lines of governance as inherently inferior to an idealized Weberian notion of impersonal legal authority. However, extra-legal solutions to governance problems, the ongoing lack of clearly delineated property rights and civic responsibilities, as well as the incoherent fuzziness of state institutions deserve analysis beyond normative framing.[4] Such frames express real experience and genuine failure on one level, but also reveal biases.[5] My approach uncovers how co-produced governance represents an enduring continuity in how things get done. In addition, such governance (re)activates ideas about care and kinship.[6] A logic of care is not reducible to 'paternalism' nor clientelism. It does not reveal locals duped by nostalgic ideas of community solidarity into papering over the state's failings. Instead, governance as care stems from a social(ist) logic of interdependency and collective responsibility – even when actors are themselves turned into corporate employees in opaque holding companies, or resort to network-like structures of responsibility.[7] In this chapter, I also take a multi-scalar view, circling back frequently to the micro-level where most citizen-state interaction takes place. To illustrate, I present short vignettes illustrating three levels of interaction between

---

4. My use of 'incoherence' is indebted to Joel Migdal's work (2004) in criticizing implicit ideal-type scholarship on the state. In Migdal, the state is integrated and interacting with parts of society to a transformative degree (on bureaucracy). Society and state are a 'melange', not pyramid structure with rule-making mechanisms at the apex. Migdal asks scholars to shift attention to 'local control' of the periphery, the power of (often local) social forces to thwart state agendas.

5. The aim is not to act as an apologist for the real and endless failure of institutions to protect and support citizens, but to contextualize Russian governance as not nearly so different from the dysfunctions we may observe in our own Western bureaucracies (which have more than a modicum of corruption and personalism themselves) at the same time as trying to cut through to genuine differences: kinship and care frames and fuzzy property regimes, without resorting to orientalizing cliches.

6. My approach is indebted to recent work on reconnecting state and kinship (Thelen and Alber 2017).

7. 'Collective responsibility' has often been studied for its pernicious and 'anti-developmental' effects in Russia (e.g. Ledeneva 2013a, 2013b). On the more sociological side, connective ideas about responsibility have been frequently seen as a cohesive, even positive social forces – whether in relation to youth associations or therapeutic communities, to give just two notable examples (Stephenson 2015, Raikhel 2016).

122 *Everyday Politics in Russia*

'state' and 'society'. We first return to unlucky Vanya, as he struggles to deal with the most elementary bureaucratic issues relating to his village plot. Then we take a snapshot of the longstanding district-level trouble with rubbish collection. Finally, we look at responses to the national military mobilization which started in 2022. Each moment here is highly specific yet typical of experience throughout much of Russia.

A logic beyond human understanding: Microscale troubles with bureaucracy

Vanya, recall, was busy making good his neglected village plot in a small settlement called Kamenka within easy reach of the town Izluchino. The village lies within a designated national park, complicating legal and cadastral rules. This village – because of its picturesque locale and easily accessible from Moscow – is inhabited by a broad socio-economic mix: impoverished ex-collective farm workers living in ramshackle smallholdings of up to a hectare, factory workers with 'ancestral' plots dating to the post-1945 period or before – usually an acre or less, and middle- and upper-class *dachniki*: owners of leisure plots from Kaluga and Moscow. Vanya banged on my door in summer 2021, and his face was a picture of anger and frustration. He was at his wits' end.

> I've been to see Frolova, that pen-pushing bitch, and she won't sign the paper, she says 'your proforma that you're not registered there in the village and live in the town is insufficient. You need this and that paper'. I said, you must be joking! I don't have all day, it's not like I'm some Muscovite who can spare the time and money!! You let those tourists and rich folk pay water rates for the summer only, but ordinary citizens get treated with prejudice! There's just no logic to it. Or only a logic that's beyond human understanding![8]

Vanya takes an hour and several cups of tea to explain how he was trying to put his affairs in order after his mother's death. 'Order', however, implies multiple contingent aims and operations.

First, he had to get his cadastral documents legible to the state to not only pay a reduced 'summer' rate for his water but also 'gasify' his property (get a state subsidy to connect his shack to the gas mains). Before banging on my door, he had travelled to the next village where the rural administration is located. It's

---

8. Later, Vanya normalized his relationship with Frolova without her agreeing to his demand. This normalization was possible because of their mutual recognition of 'fictive kinship' – hers, on the basis of her longstanding responsibility to the village, and his, on the basis of his family's ancestral ties. In this case we have an example of (fictive) kinship relations as expressing differences in power, but these are hardly different from the 'respect' demanded of disinterested bureaucrats elsewhere.

known by all as 'Frolova's' because that is the surname of the village administrator, unchanging over three decades as its thankless function passed from mother to daughter. Vanya, in his words, had 'an altercation that got me worked up into a right snot', a not uncommon frustration among locals. His botched 'application', or *obrashchenie* to the village administrator, was just the beginning of his Kafkaesque trial and error to get a foot in the correct 'door of the law'.[9] He was trying to establish the status of his plot as 'uninhabited' except in summer and therefore entitled to a lower water and rubbish collection tariff. The sought-after document was a *spravka* – basically a stamped piece of paper with some lines about his living arrangement which would have been sufficient proof that the village authorities recognized his temporary habitation. In turn, this *spravka* would make his further applications to the water and other authorities legible. However, a *spravka* is itself a material example of state incoherence and co-production. As Vladimir Kozlov has pointed out (1996), a *spravka* is a special form of documentary improvisation and amendment – best translated as 'reference material', with an etymological root in the word 'rectify', or 'redress'. A *spravka* is supplementary to other evidence and only works in concert with other proofs to co-produce a bureaucratic truth.

Vanya's trials lasted a long time even after I had helped him get his *spravka* by going back to the administration in the company of the village elder. A few days later he came to me again. He'd been sent from pillar to post and travelled many dozens of kilometres to different *instantsii*, or official points of contact between citizen and bureau. Now, he had given up. The 'absurdity', as he put it, didn't end with a *spravka* in hand. Vanya admitted that he couldn't communicate in a language that made his request legible. His story indicated how class stratification intersected strongly with successful access to bureaucracy.

In contrast to his situation, many of the village's middle-class residents were able to ignore bureaucratic requirement such as the rubbish collection tariffs: the penalty was insignificant. Vanya's neighbour, who had a large smallholding and a swimming pool, didn't even receive a water bill because he had illegally connected his property to the watermain years ago and was 'invisible' to the authorities, pretending to get all his water from a pumped well. Our so-called watermain was a set of pipes pumping untreated water from a spring (on land owned by nobody) into a tower (built 1987), the electrical motor of which would burn out at least once a month. In late autumn and winter the power would also frequently cut out sometimes for days, due to storms and snow.

Further incoherence was illustrated by the rubbish-collection schedule. In early summer and autumn when few people were around, the rubbish collection tender holder would skip our village if he thought he could get away with it. Memorably, the district press would write in its Soviet officialese about the 'non-observance of the schedule of rubbish collection as a near universal experience' and the municipal environmental manager would provide a quote such as:

---

9. In Kafka's parable, the protagonist cannot pass the gatekeeper of the 'door of the law' and the reason for his failure is never explained to him.

124   *Everyday Politics in Russia*

[T]he rubbish strewn throughout the town and highways is evidence of the sluggishness [*nerastoropnosti*] of those services and organizations of the district Housing and Communal Services who are responsible. They need to be whipped into line [*podstegnut*], and we will definitely do that.[10]

Every year the same promises; every year a new municipal manager and still serious environmental problems due to uncollected rubbish remain visible everywhere. While people were quick to complain, the legal mechanisms for forcing households to pay rubbish dues were inadequate, mirroring the situation of widespread 'utility debt' in city apartments.

Fifteen kilometres away in Izluchino, Vanya lives in a roomy flat he inherited from his parents.[11] For years the town has, like the village, had unreliable rubbish collections. They broke down completely in the 1990s as the town-forming enterprise responsible for utilities had gone bankrupt. Only towards the end of the first decade of the 2000s did the municipality instil a semblance of regulated, frequent collections from all housing blocks. A new disposal site away from the inhabited part of the municipality was opened in 2011. However, in the 2010s matters again deteriorated mirroring the situation with the Kotelnaya. The municipality concluded contract after contract with waste management companies as part of reforms meant to institutionalize the provision of services on a market basis and put a legal firewall between private provider and municipality.

These contracts, however, were little more than legal fictions for a convenient continuation of provisions based on cronyism to members of the local micro-elite – just like with the heating supply. Sometimes 'contractors' (little more than a one-man band) stole a little and the collection continued as before. Sometimes they stole a lot and got caught, even imprisoned for fraud. Not because of effective law enforcement, but according to the principle that one must always share illicit rent-extraction upwards, according to the informal institution of kick-back: *otkat* (Kordonsky 2012). Legislative changes at the national and regional level also played a part. The need to actually dispose of waste in a way that meant it did not remain exposed in some disused quarry; the need to lease specialist lifting vehicles and matching dumpsters – these and other issues came to a head in 2018 and collection of rubbish actually ceased for weeks with local municipal workers and citizens alike resorting to burning the piles of plastic bags, making air pollution in the town even worse (recall that at the same time the district was in an undeclared political war over the expansion of the oil refinery).

10. From a district newspaper in 2013. For obvious reasons, here and elsewhere I obscure the actual identity of the locales, though all quotes are unchanged and most administrative organizations are described without alteration.

11. Much of the life of this town, including the lives of Vanya and his brother, are detailed in Morris (2016).

5. Incoherent State

At that time, my friend Olga was a citizen journalist and documented the new rubbish wars with her camera and blog. It was easy for the district elites to blame this 'backward' town's leadership for political point-scoring, even though these issues are universal throughout Russian municipalities of small and medium size. Olga summarized the situation in 2020:

Politicians perform this double-cynicism: They think on the one hand: Russians always wallowed in their own shit, they'll find a solution on the individual or yard-level – call it 'muddle-through from below'. On the other hand, the politicians themselves are part of the 'mass' and they know how to exploit the basest psychological foundations of humanity: suspicion and slander. They blame the previous director of the Housing and Communal Services company and they blame the citizens themselves for not being willing to walk downstairs and deposit the trash in the new containers, instead continuing to use the internal chutes. Or they say that people at night are dumping waste building material, or it's Muscovites paying bandits to secretly ship waste to the town.

And they know people will half-believe one of these lies. Now in reality it's simply that the company leasing the trucks with the lifting gear suddenly 'ran out of money' and the financial director 'emigrated' to Dubai. The trucks sit idly in a yard in Kaluga, but because the dumpsters were upgraded the municipality can't just manually load them onto ordinary trucks. And in any case, there are few yard-workers left for such work. Most of the Central Asians, if they do such work, would rather do it in Moscow. It's a kind of perfect storm, but it's not the municipality lacks the possibility, it's as if these conflicts were created by design to screw us over.

Our final ethnographic moment finds us in October 2022 in the kitchen of Kirill, a factory worker pondering the likelihood of being mobilized for the 'Special Military Operation', as everyone is careful to call it to avoid unpleasant consequences such as a jail term. This time it is me tearing out my hair trying to get Kirill to take action to avoid the draft: run away to India (he's a bit of a hippy), go back to Moscow to work a construction crane where he can lie low anonymously with an unofficial work contract. There are other options I put to him over coffee and Turkish delights. Kirill is sanguine:

At the end of the day, they won't get to me. Remember, these are paper records, I think my military ticket is actually registered with my mum's apartment address. This is my wife's flat, God bless her. In any case, I'd be in something like the third group for priority because I've got flat feet. Maybe I'll get that job at the aluminium smelter in Obninsk? By the time of spring [2023], we'll have either taken Kiev again or we'll all be dead. Don't call me fatalistic, it's just you have to fight the sluggishness [*vialost*] that is the Russian state with sluggishness sometimes. It's the only way to stay sane.

Actually, my wife works for 'My Documents' [the onestop state-citizen service] and there they are actively sharing the lists of occupations that are now safe and others which will likely be safe in the future. It's an unspoken thing. You go there and if you're military age and just look like you might not really understand how things are going, they will take you aside for a private chat.

Kirill waivers in our many conversations but is certainly capable of resolute action; at one point in 2020 he had taken his extended family for 'a long holiday', as he called it, to Bali (via Istanbul, hence the sweet treats) to avoid Covid-19 lockdowns, using up his savings in the process. Regarding metallurgy, Kirill's job prospect in the city of Obninsk close to Moscow is viewed as providing 'protection' [*bron*] from mobilization as a kind of 'reserved occupation' according to the conflicting and confusing rules around military service. Later, in 2023, Kirill noted with some smugness that his 'instincts' had been correct: his partial inaction and avoidance of panic had been justified. He noted the continual back-peddling by politicians on the question of digitizing military records, reminding me of the unlikeliness that competing agencies of the state could ever coordinate their work enough to include pension and work records, educational achievements and other personal data in a single military register.[12] Kirill then is a vivid example of a 'structure of feeling' for state incoherence in Russia that is by no means entirely reflective of dissatisfaction with its incompetence.

These snippets of Russia's state-society relations serve as the entry point into further discussion in this chapter. I will return to each of the three contexts in turn, as well as the heating chief, and illustrate how Russian citizens exhibit a keen 'feel' for a particular incoherence in the bureaucratic function which is both by accident and design. The Russian state is designed as incoherent to aid illicit enrichment via rent-seeking at every level. It also delegates (but not only in neoliberal fashion) many issues of governance down and down the ladder until they reach the individual citizen such as Vanya. Is community burning rubbish in one's back yard, whether in a village or town, the final unfortunate statement of individual responsibilizing I started exploring in the previous chapter?

State in society: Mutually transformative relations between bureaucracy and citizens

A 'state-in-society' approach recognizes the mutually transformative nature of relations between bureaucracy and citizens. Agents' autonomy should be taken as read, regardless of the well-documented KPI-ization of Russian

---

12. On the insurmountable barriers to creating a digitized security state to aid mobilization in Russia, see Komin (2023). The Russian press reported in late 2023 that despite assurances that a single-digitized register of citizens subject to potential mobilization was supposed to have been ready by autumn of that year, the project was being pushed back to 2025 at the earliest. IT experts are pessimistic about even this date.

bureaucracy – where quantitative indicators of 'key' performance are applied to ever-new levels of governance.[13] The Russian state is like any other: no unitary actor but a 'melange of social organizations' (Migdal 2004: 49) where imperatives other than implementation of policy are operative. Bureaucrats, even in seemingly least responsive modes (such as military mobilization), can find it useful to align themselves with, or make implicit concessions to ordinary citizens for many reasons, including moral ones. It is true that often difficulties and obstacles make citizens dependent on the patronage or indulgence of officials. In turn, bureaucrats are often in an invidious relationship of dependence themselves to powerful and corrupt higher-ups. This results in opportunities for rent-seeking at all but the lowest level.

To get documents in order, as Vanya attempted to do, you need a cadastral plan. The plan may need to be created from scratch because rural property was only formalized, and then only nominally, post-1991. In the local context of Izluchino and surrounding villages, a district prosecutor's family 'captured' and monopolized the real estate market through various patron-client alliances. This did not (usually) involve open corruption, but the 'family's' lawyer and land agents could charge high fees for their service because they knew their documents and advice, including the quasi-legal *spravka*, were 'better quality', as they sometimes put it, than others. In any legal dispute, courts and state agencies would side with person in possession of these plans, and not others.

Dependency, while it is relevant in many cases, should not mislead us to think of state-society relations as always and necessarily entailing power gradients leading to rent-seeking or exploitation of the vulnerable (which was certainly the case in military mobilization in 2022). Without exaggerating the ineffectiveness and poor quality of state services in Russia, their overall *incoherence* – the keyword of this chapter – means that bureaucrats daily exit their designated roles as

---

13. Pavel Romanov (2008: 19) notes the awkward imposition of new public management performance-based targets in Russian social services. In environments where informal and personalized forms of organizational culture remain, such innovations can promote more corruption and poor capacity than already existed. The use of commercial-application key performance indicators is taken to an extreme in Russian state agencies. For example, in 2019, twenty-four indicators of performance were applied to regional-level government from measuring the average time necessary for a family to get private housing, to income ratios of the population and access to basic goods. Almost all public sector employees encounter forms of KPI rating of their work. As Bogatyreva and Matveev (2018) note, KPI in the Russian public sector is a 'market surrogate'. The few anthropologists, such as Serebrennikov (forthcoming), who have studied KPI-ization in action, see it as essentially undoing itself through collusion from below in 'fiddling' the meeting of targets.

crooked Weberians.[14] Not only do they 'lean across the desk' in a gesture that co-produces the state with the citizen because of the contractions of the law and its enforcement, they also step into a moral relationship with the citizen – acting in a compromise 'best fit' for the circumstances, to 'help' the citizen in what are absurd and impossible situations. This is more than the 'sympathetic communication', that Zakharova (forthcoming) describes as a universal necessity for the local bureaucrat. Co-production problematizes a dependency or clientelist perspective. Bureaucratic agency is not just about making their own lives easier, getting a slice of some corrupt pie, or placating citizens in the face of a Byzantine system of paperwork. Nor is it about meeting internal targets of technocratic KPI that regulate encounters. Nor is it about eliciting gratitude in the form of post-hoc bribes or gifts (Morris and Polese 2016).

Ironically, the nurturing of a non-disinterested relationship brings people back around towards an ideal of the state – acting via moral and often personalized imperatives. In place of paternalism or patronage, we find practices of accommodation, 'devolved' co-production of governance, and a shared feeling for stateness. As I argued earlier in this book, we can trace this to an ontology of Soviet social(ist)ness. Regardless of the coverage and inconsistencies of the workings of Soviet bureaucracies, the mental image, and more importantly, the feeling for the Soviet state, implies ends-orientated notions of care (which can go hand in hand with a rather callous or unfeeling position towards the non-compliant individual), quality of communication and, of course, purposive state action. Here we get ahead of ourselves. First, a short discussion of what I mean and do not mean by 'state' and the literature underpinning this.

The missing citizen-bureaucrat encounter

Despite well-documented rent-seeking and clientelism, there is no reason to argue that Russian bureaucracies do not meet Weberian criteria in the day-to-day execution of their tasks: specialization by expertise, referral to regulations, adherence to organizational hierarchy and impersonal application of rules. Observers often draw attention to the technocratic effectiveness of some institutions – such as the Prime Minister's office under Mishustin (2020–), the Moscow government under Sobyanin (2010–), and aspects of the financial machinery of state – such as the Central Bank, tax authorities and economic development ministries. On the back of the 1990s, where the Russian Federation faced multiple threats to its very existence in the form of insurgencies, economic collapse and potential political fragmentation, 'bringing the state back in' after 2000 was a way for scholars to emphasize the challenges of building state capacity

---

14. Max Weber not only bequeathed the idea of an elective affinity between capitalism and religion, but also gave political scientists an ideal type of the clerk applying impersonal rules of bureaucracy which facilitated the rise of the modern state.

from a perceived low and the response to a 'crisis of governance' (Roberts and Sherlock 1999). No-one would deny the effects of the trifecta of elite conflicts over property rights, 'transition' to a market economy, and the mothballing of much industry, as well as the continuing legacy of Soviet institutions. These meant that Russian governments and society alike faced almost insurmountable challenges.

Characterizations such as the 'enfeebled and profoundly dysfunctional state' (Roberts and Sherlock 1999: 478) quickly gave way to a literature on corruption and rent-seeking as a 'feature' not a bug (Ledeneva 2013a). The retreat of the social and planning state was also part of (neoliberal) policy design. Less remarked on was the fact that historically much governance had in any case been devolved – to collective farms and enterprises in the late Soviet era. This devolution continues to this day. A quasi-elder in the village of Kamenka takes decisions in consultation with residents, and informal political leaders are visible in the town of Izluchino. In practice, scholars tend not to pursue the logics of informal governance to their conclusions. Instead, it is taken as read that personalized and informal hybrids of governance undermine state effectiveness and lead to deprofessionalization of services (Moliarenko 2016); organization through interpersonal relations is dysfunctional and incompatible with healthy institutional development (Flikke 2021).

While Helmke and Levitsky (2004: 727) discussed the complementarity of informal institutions to governance which may entail organized corruption and privatized violence, they did not make a judgement about dysfunction. They pointed out that informal decision-making was not the same as weak institutions or abuse of authority. Their innovation was to point to the power of 'socially-shared rules … enforced outside of officially sanctioned channels' as enduring and self-perpetuating. Furthermore, these are not 'cultural' phenomena, but institutionalized forms of mutual social expectations. Helmke and Levitsky (2004) observe that unwritten rules of the game can serve convergent, competing, ameliorative or substitutive roles in relation to formal rules, depending on the context. All at the same time as the formal institutions and rule-systems continue to exist and operate.

Invariably there is simplification of Russia's 'state' and 'state capacity/ effectiveness', respectively.[15] Either the state is incorrigibly dysfunctional because of poor formal governance, or its strong coercive state capacity results in equally poor 'effective' governance. As Richard Sakwa put it: 'control' or 'chaos' (2021).[16]

---

15. Anthropology was an exception. There are numerous micro-level studies of the local state that complicate the picture.

16. Interestingly, Sakwa (2021) also sees rhizomatic elements to Russian political reality and so his argument anticipates my own. My thesis is that Russian society as a whole illustrates quite vividly elements of Deleuzian thinking on the state and libidinal drives at work in social groups. Unlike Sakwa, I do not see 'disaggregation' of governance as 'de-institutionalized', but that this disaggregation implies the operation of alternative institutions which are informal but nonetheless rule-bound.

Where resources are marshalled for politics – the so-called *adminresurs* – they serve to strengthen the so-called neopatrimonial 'power vertical'. Citizens are rewarded for political support, redefining entitlement to public goods as conditional on loyalty (Allina-Pisano 2010). But *adminresurs* is not just activated during elections by patrons. It has a mind of its own – as we saw in the person of the Chief.[17] As Natalia Forrat (2018) puts it, the focus on pure conditionality and corruption in the use of *adminresurs* to pursue narrow political aims ignores an equally relevant socially embedded aspect. The relational and balancing logic provided by Helmke and Levitsky was not fully incorporated into scholarship on post-Soviet governance.[18] All states may be both locally efficient and dysfunctional in equal measures. They can be deceptive and deaf-blind to citizen supplication. Depending on circumstances, they can be 'present' and interventionist in a way that garners social approval. The dominant view is of the Russian state as a poorly functioning authoritarian technocratic model (Gel'man 2018), underlined by the evidence of its failure to cope with the challenges of pandemic, economic stagnation and war. However, this falls short of the full picture. The mismatch between the field of bureaucratic coverage expected by citizens and its reality gives birth to informal institutions operative within the bureaucratic encounter itself.[19] Institutions may be 'dysfunctional', fostering unequal access, at the same time as ameliorative and substitutive. Any four of Helmke and Levitsky's informal institutions can be operative simultaneously (convergent, competing, ameliorative or substitutive).

A return to 'stability' after 2000 was strongly associated with a return to 'state capacity'. David White links regime legitimation and survival to better state functioning (2018). In Natalia Forrat's (2018) extension of this argument,

---

17. A major interest for political scientists is the wielding of state capacity to manipulate elections. See Smyth (2002) for an example. Elections though should be seen as exceptional events in the signalling of patronage and the potential for rewarding clients with resources. As Harvey (2020) notes, patronage networks, even at election time when signalling of future resources to be distributed to loyal clients, are not always clearly consolidated and subject to local variation.

18. Gel'man (2004) provides an example of how a research agenda that took seriously the balancing role of informal institutions might have arisen. Ledeneva (2013a) applies such insights to a system-level (macro) context. Examples of scholarship that take seriously and provide evidence for state capacity via the interaction between formal and informal institutions are Schenk (2021) and Lazarev (2023). Even so, more work is needed on how state organizations themselves may contain durable forms of informality, or formal-informal institutional symbiosis (Barsukova and Ledeneva 2018).

19. In sociology, practices deriving from a mismatch between state capacity and citizen's expectations could be called 'hysteresis effects', after the work of Pierre Bourdieu. However, hysteresis also generates the hybrid governance forms observed here.

infrastructural resources, such as a better funded and staffed educational sector, support authoritarian resilience. However, White allows that strengthening capacity does not necessarily mean expectations of economic opportunity, let alone access to basic welfare, are met. He also hints at my main critique: 'capacity' and effectiveness beyond the ability to collect taxes is a 'slippery concept to define' (White 2018: 131).[20] The massive and growing size of the informal economy, largely invisible to bureaucracies, should give pause to any argument that because of growing tax receipts and technical modernization of bureaucracy the overall reach of the state increased (Morris 2019b).

A few short conversations with research interlocutors on issues like rubbish collection, continuity of heating supply, access to hospital care and the state of roads suffice to undo many of the statistical artefacts about increasing state capacity, and the reign of 'stability'. We zoom in on the creaky, yet purposeful negotiation between different forms of governance where 'the state' emerges as a moral relation and is (de)regulated in a particular way. *De-regulated* governance is not an absence of regulation, but the application of 'law as social process' (Roy 2009).[21] This is both regularly improvisational, but also, by necessity, predictably relational in the Russian context. Tatjana Thelen and her collaborators see an opportunity for researchers to fill an 'analytical gap between state images and practices' through what she calls 'stategraphy'. Observing the state up-close would allow analysis of 'relational modalities, boundary work and embeddedness of actors' (Thelen et al. 2018: 2).[22] What is often missing from our perspective is the dramaturgy of the encounter between citizen and state-worker.

20. Even on fiscal issues, one can argue that the move to a low flat income tax in the early 2000s did not really reflect a rise in 'capacity' in a meaningful way. It merely increased tax revenues by focussing on large resource companies such as Gazprom and Rosneft, not the individual or entrepreneur.

21. To make clear the meaning, throughout this chapter I spell this term 'de-regulation', when refereeing to Roy's (2009) specific meaning of informalized governance as 'open-ended and subject to multiple interpretations and interest' (2009: 80).

22. Thelen (2011) critiques the dominance of neo-institutionalist theories of post-socialist societies. Informality contributes to theorizing association and embeddedness that accompanies economic relations. In turn, this helps overcome normative assumptions around informality (a deficiency perspective). The 'deficiency' debate between Thelen and others can be reduced to an acceptance or rejection of the validity of socialism as an 'alternative form of modernity'. Similarly, the justification of the term 'post-socialism' is an extension of that debate. As informality persists, is ingrained, embedded and insinuated in practices, it supports a theorization of social relations as hybridized and therefore post-socialist societies themselves as expressing ongoing difference from places that did not experience state socialism.

Relational approaches: From bureaucratic proceduralism to the anti-state machine

Anthropology has often inquired how states emerge primarily in everyday encounters between the bottom rung of 'street-level' bureaucrats and citizens and that therefore institutions are 'hollow'. They should be approached in historical context and using micro-level empirical work. Within political science, Timothy Mitchell argued that the state as a concept is weakly defined and should be studied as a 'sociocultural phenomenon' (1991: 77). To usefully research the state, scholars should focus on its effects as emanating from both ends of the spectrum: organizational configurations which make it appear divided from society, but also microprocesses where it is always peopled – with bureaucrats who have their own ideas as well as material and moral interests. Individual state agents reproduce organizational behaviour. But they also act, unconsciously, through learned preference, in a way that gives specific character and purpose to those organizations that then become more than the sum of the whole (Bendix et al. 1992: 1012).

The shift towards looking for state effects in political science occurred at the same time as a parallel process in anthropology. Drawing on Foucault, scholars like Sharma and Gupta (2006) argued that it was the encounter between citizens and state actors that made the state real within a drama of 'bureaucratic proceduralism'. Others, however, find that micro focus brings its own problems. A focus on encounters may downplay questions of how bureaucracies maintain social and political order in specific ways which benefit the powerful and reinforce existing stratification. It is in the differential way it treats citizens that the state can remerge as a 'thing', which is undeniably how it is understood in Russia. The state may be incoherent overall as an agent of social order, but it does cohere at times when clear divisions of caste and class need to be made for the purposes of furthering accumulation and dispossession – as in the example of Izluchino's elite in matters of property rights, Vanya's travails with his utility bills, and Kirill's musings on military mobilization and informational asymmetries deriving from interactions regularized with the state.

Bob Jessop's work exemplifies the post-Marxian theorization of the state. For him, the 'state is a social relation'. What that means is that states are made up of an 'ensemble of socially embedded, socially regularized, and strategically selective institutions and organizations' (Jessop 2016: 49). This kind of approach makes space for the unequal contestation of governance by interest groups. Institutional integration is frustrated from within, and requires diverse micropolitical practices dispersed throughout society. Jessop also brings in the question of temporal sovereignty. This fits well with thinking relationally about Russian stateness. Time matters – from the temporal burden in visiting offices of state (Vanya spent a day to merely find something out) to the way control is ceded by state officers depending on the time of day when their supervisors are absent. So many times we were told 'best to come after 4pm … ', or, 'come in the morning when the others are on their rounds'. Furthermore, state governance is spatiotemporally compressed. A vivid example is in the garage spaces of urban Russia – the times and specific areas of urban Russia that are policed have a regularity that citizens incorporate into their routines of avoiding the state's gaze. I return to those spaces in the following chapter.

Beyond political economic debates, state-society relations manage, as much as reinforce, inequalities. The parlous situation around governance inevitably induces a co-production of the state, and this necessitates a set of moral recognitions which may or may not undo structuring effects that favour the powerful. Furthermore, it is worth considering the patchy spatial coverage of state institutions in Russia, even the police, tax and local government. Bruce Kapferer and Christopher Taylor (2012) refocus the study of the state by applying the Deleuzian dynamic of territorialization-deterritorialization, an approach I will shortly turn to. For the purposes of this chapter, the Deleuzian approach thinks of state-like logics as driven by a territorializing impetus – pinning down land and people into mappable and subordinating objects of ground rent. At the same time, an opposing dynamic operates – a kind of counter-systemic, 'rhizomatic' force which opposes the mapping effects of states. In Kapferer and Taylor's reading, power, coercion and the effects of governance do not disappear, but they meet an equally vital force – in a dialectic that is never resolved. In the rest of this chapter, I revisit the various scales of co-produced governance introduced at the beginning – the village scene, beset with the problems of deterritorialized governance because of the historical legacy of undefined property rights. I also look at the municipal level, where the issues of supply and demand of governing capacity are played out most acutely.[23]

How ordinary people lay claim to care by propertizing the state

Vanya, in our opening vignette, had seen the Kafkaesque side of the incoherent state with his failure to get his water bill adjusted to reflect seasonal residence. The unfinalized nature of property rights and the resulting necessity to engage with local and regional bureaucracy were a carefully chosen example. Like urban garage blocks, many rural plots – owned by tens of millions of Russians – lack full legibility as private ownership. This is also true for things like critical, yet mundane infrastructure – the roofs of housing blocks, waterlines between housing, even gas and powerlines as they cross the vast terrain of incoherent property rights. It is not that the final owner of the property is necessarily in doubt. The powerlines belong to 'efficiently' privatized companies in Russia.

---

23. Due to limits of space, I do not expand scope to the 'national' level; I do not see much analytical use in doing so. The third vignette on mobilization shows the near impossibility of coordinating bureaucratic capacity at levels above the district. Even in taxation and 'biopolitical' management, one could put forward an argument – as I have elsewhere (Morris 2019b) – that the state remains relatively weak in making itself legible, and populations legible to its agencies.

As Xenia Cherkaev notes (2023), over the course of the Soviet period, a sophisticated yet incomplete property regime became established where use and benefit were accepted short of the notion of ownership. This situation carried over to the present and is one reason for the relatively lax legislation restricting use of property (until the 2010s) where one could often find shops in residential flats and businesses in private garages. The neglect of private property as final ownership also contributes to the continuing incompleteness of state records pertaining to land and real estate. Cherkaev also notes that disaggregation of the understanding of property into 'use', 'benefit' and 'ownership' had a moral quality connected to socialist ideals of the collective purpose of property. Absolute possession and even formal possession can be foregone for the sake of *cooperative* benefit – hence the well-known examples presented by Alena Ledeneva of *blat* (1998), where socialist property is improperly yet advantageously enjoyed by in-groups.

Such informal and collusive alternatives to Western ideas of property rights mean that the bureaucracies lack coherence in their response and may be seen as deficient by outsiders. Regulatory 'ambiguities' and unintentional deregulatory situations may be 'the basis of state authority and serve as modes of sovereignty and discipline' (Roy 2009: 83).[24] Scholars tend to emphasize the current era as a period of super-charged recentralization in which even regional governors were transformed into mere 'functionaries' completely dependent on the centre (Busygina 2018: 7). At the same time, horizontal networking of subnational political and business elites continues, as well as real processes of governance from below (in multiple senses).[25]

But there is a less deterministic perspective on such governmentalizing effects. Instead of the conclusion that ambiguity indicates the vulnerability of the individual to bureaucratic power or rapacious privatization, a more realistic picture is one of co-production and cooperation, a bureaucratically self-contained 'cultural tradition' even, in conflict with the system of rewards, command and organization an institution presents to the outside world as its modus operandi.[26] Let us return to the micro-level situation of Vanya – like many he wants to make use of a state subsidy to get a gas connection to a domestic property that had never previously been grid connected. This was until recently the status of the majority of Russian single family-occupancy houses and connection requires

---

24. Part of this section appeared in a different format in Morris (2019c).

25. The drawbacks of relying too much on interpretations of politics via the lens of the super-presidency and centralization were made clear in the response to Covid-19 where most Covid governance was devolved to regional authorities (Chaisty et al. 2022).

26. On the relation of actual bureaucratic work to its management and presentation, I am indebted to Tom Dwyer's classic theorization of industrial accidents (1991: 95–6, 126). He uses the term 'cultural tradition' to refer broadly to the development of knowledge, values and even power among workers to control processes at work and their peers at odds with that of their bosses. In the bureaucratic case, external inputs can also become 'transformed social relations'.

5. Incoherent State 135

the work to be signed off in person by the local authority's gas engineer. For a private householder this might take weeks, many trips out of town (to the District centre) and 'significant' paperwork.[27] However, an 'emergent organisational form' of bureaucracy (Thelen et al. 2017: 6) streamlines this process by making use of informal co-production. A retired engineer now deals with the paperwork for a small fee, informally, of course. The utility office openly advises but does not insist customers apply to this neighbouring *kontora* [an unspecified office] to shorten and simplify the application process. The retiree allocates the installation and inspection to a qualified person who provides the necessary safety documentation. The *kontora* is a spatial version of the *spravka* we saw earlier – operating as an indeterminate and informal part of the bureaucratic assemblage.

This processual informality shows the embedded social relations of actors – plumbers, utility clerks, building inspectors, local authority cadastral officers (gas lines need to be accurately recorded on maps) and heating engineers. They recreate and change the state through their semi-formal, partly informal relational modalities. This is not 'resistance', nor is it 'corruption', or even clientelism. At the simplest level it illustrates the agency of bureaucracy to effect 'devolved' solutions that become semi-formalized practices through time and are cemented through recurrent street-level bureaucrat encounters. As Plueckhahn (2017) notes in a similar context, 'adaptive' or 'creative negotiation of bureaucracy' is possible because all parties agree to the non-final status or 'fixity' of documents and ownership alike. At the micro-level there is continuity in who you have to deal with. This allows fictive kinship to arise and endure over time – as we saw in the case of the village administration and Vanya. Fictive kinship offers a route back to quality of communication and even some efficacy, at the cost of overly familial relations.[28] The Weberian notion of legal-rational authority is replaced by the scolding, then soothing and confident tones of the utility office 'lady', whose name and patronymic we – for it makes sense to make these visits in the safety of

27. At an online portal for the 'Presidential programme', no-fee gasification of rural houses (in accordance with Government Order №1152-r) has a neat infographic that potential beneficiaries are presented with. An orange gas pipe runs straight from a substation, dips under a tree and across a property line to emerge in a home and connect to a stove, boiling a smart-looking hob kettle. In reality, most people will need to do much leg-work to collect six documents to access what is presented as a 'single window' process. In addition, a consumer would need around two-months' average salary to complete the internal work to an official standard inside their home.

28. The literature on fictive kinship notes its political potential: both acting as a cover for what are unequal power relationships at the same time as allowing the weaker party to make claims on the stronger. Fictive kinship is alive and well in the most 'modernized' contexts, such as tech companies' tribal appeals for loyalty among their workers on the basis that they are all of a special elect, to online communities in support of Ukraine on the basis that they are kin in the North Atlantic Fellas Organization.

136   *Everyday Politics in Russia*

numbers – quickly learn to intone sonorously: 'Galina Borisovna! Tell us what we need to do to make the paperwork easier for you?'

Moving the lens thirty kilometres north to *Rosreestr* offices (the Federal Service for State Registration, Cadastre and Cartography), the bureaucrat in charge here is more schoolmarm. Svetlana Sergeevna pushes a single sheet of paper silently across the desk allowing us to read the 'Material Inspection No. 2565' carried out in the name of the State Land Inspectorate. This document is over 500 words of bureaucratese stating that our grass verge is too unkempt. Pausing for effect, she then mildly chides us for our failure to keep our grass short during the fire season. Here too there is a moral element to the fictive kinship relation we enter. We are not intimidated because we are used to an internally consistent bureaucratic cultural tradition of accommodation. This is at odds with the conventional image of clientelist corruption. We promise to get the grass and scrub cleared from our own and our neighbours' frontage, and she in turn promises to retroactively cancel the summons – something she's not technically authorized to do.

Later, we meet a different member of the cadastral staff at a seasonal street market; she works with Svetlana but is more forthcoming because she is an acquaintance of ours. It turns out that, due to informal connivance between different district branches, all the cases of fire-risk have been 'closed', and no one need worry about fines for fire-risk 'at least this year'. Over some tea in a local café, our cadastral informer talks more about micro-level KPI-ization of work – known in Russian as 'the stick system'.[29] Such quota-systems of workload management could be countered by manipulation of documents – constituting an informal 'institution' within the formal cadastral organization.[30] The informalized management from below of unrealistic expectations about recording 'cases' is evidenced even in the case of police investigation of serious crimes (Serebrennikov forthcoming). In the work of the mundane cadastral bureaucracies, the undoing of 'the stick' is made visible: the non-transference of cases from paper to digital records is a way of 'slowing down' or even eliminating work; then there is 'mining', or salami-slicing existing cases to create multiple cases when a quarterly target is due; paperwork dungeons: physical spaces where unfinished cases are conveniently abandoned, never to be found again; and most importantly, 'collective' interagency and interdistrict agreements to under-report and align statistical reality to suit the

---

29. 'Stick system' translates *palochnaia sistema*. Best known within the police force in Russia in the 2000s and formally now abandoned, the system was essentially a quota target of cases to be processed. The 'stick' comes from the word for a vertical pen-stroke on paper.

30. The effective use of informality and informal institutional rules to resist and re-make KPI-zation of bureaucracy should not be underestimated. In *Rosreestr*'s case, the requirement to carry out on-site inspections of rural villages was utilized to temporally fill Svetlana's job with bureaucratically dead time where she was supposedly collecting evidence for reports but was in fact making her work invisible to the higher offices of state, instead, co-producing state work in a complementary institution of dialogue with citizens – as we saw in the example in Chapter 3 where Svetlana visited a 'fieldsite' to check pollution.

5. Incoherent State

municipal/district agenda. Our village's temporary reprieve was an example of the latter; however, unless the documents were 'filed' in a metaphorical paper dungeon, they may yet come back to haunt us. Having said that, the unrealistic demands of the stick system are regularly revealed. The regional water agency forced all rural properties in 2018 to install meters at the expense of consumers. However, due to non-compliance and the cost of sending out staff to the physical locations of meters (sometimes over two metres underground), the policy was abandoned within a year. A local water agency staff member personally (and rather triumphantly) told me to just 'throw away the meter'.

Martha Lampland (2010), looking at communist-era experience, has argued that the production of 'false numbers' (and not just provisional ones) as a routine process may be tolerated by both street-level bureaucrats and managers and auditors alike for practical, institutional or moral reasons. We saw in the example of the gas-connection arrangement, and here too in Svetlana's work, the active capacity of state workers and citizens to go beyond 'accounting realism' in pursuit of shared goods. As Elena Bogdanova has argued, 'care' relates kinship to politics (2005). In other words, there was usually a meaningful 'function' to the input of fake data into a system. Legal order, even semi-privatized, in Russia cannot do without relations of compromise and social interaction where duty is realized towards citizens at the same time as to the hierarchical relations of rent-seeking. As Bogdanova argues, the intervention via care as a political duty towards citizens contains the traces of the Soviet-era universalization of an ideological imperative. Care may mask hierarchies and lead to fuzzy justice, but it should not be dismissed in favour of a conclusion about 'dysfunctional' law.[31] In a sense partly articulated by Bogdanova, fictive kinship and clientelistic 'corruption' are two sides of the same (in)coherent governance form.[32]

More broadly, the episode on grass-cutting is just one mundane example of many official amnesties that temporarily solve unresolved legal ambiguities. These relate to property ownership and capital assets and affect both rich and

---

31. Even in the law proper, the operations of courts, Kathryn Hendley (2017: 13) argues that despite Russia languishing at the bottom of indexes measuring the rule of law, reality reveals a 'functional' everyday experience of justice at odds with 'the common wisdom about Russian courts as incompetent and corrupt'. My not infrequent chaperoning of research participants as litigants in Russian courts supports Hendley's findings.

32. Timothy Frye (2017: 18), drawing on Hendley (2013) and others, uses a rational choice frame to come to similar conclusions to mine: for 'revisionist' property-rights scholars, Russia is characterized by 'legal dualism' – some parts of the justice system work to the benefit of citizens and others not according to an overall logic of autocratic governance that balances economic and political interests. I propose a reflexive, moral set of reasonings and historical impetus for such dualism. Furthermore, my approach differs from the 'unrule of law' lens of scholars like Vladimir Gel'man who impute poor governance to the dominance of personalized and informal rules over formal institutions (2004).

poor (Limonov and Vakhrusheva 2010).[33] Rather than processes of permanent formalization we should view them as lacking finality – as examples of Ananya Roy's 'de-regulation'. This set of processes, while reinforcing inequalities, also has a palpable moral quality – one may get one's gas connection another, more formal way. However, it is strongly implied that a more 'humane' way is preferable, both for the sanity of the supplicant, and because it also closes the bureaucratic loop in a way that benefits the local community. At each step, the participants communicate, often verbally, the superior and also *licit*, rather than illegal or improper logic of this de-regulated coproduced governance.

This is exactly as I predicted it would be as I led Vanya, almost by the hand, to the local office to finally get a gas supply for his mother's little cottage. This was a more positive experience for him than the case of the water-rates *spravka* and other aspects of the cadastral services, where capture by local elites leads to detrimental outcomes for citizens and the functioning of property rights alike. Here, in the tripartite image of 'state capacity' according to Melville (2022), coercive and extractive components of efficiency undermine the administrative. However, it is unhelpful to look at a concept like 'capacity' as if there were strands of competing 'good' administrative, and 'bad', corrupt forms. While my master concept of 'incoherence' resituates things from the perspective of the average citizen who is bewildered by the seeming cross-purposes of governance, the overall system conforms to the organic metaphor. Each component interacts with the others in a way that overly rationalist or structuralist approaches fail to capture. Egregious examples of clientelist rent-seeking push the social organism to develop practices of 'inoculation' against such parasitic diseases.

***

Let us come back to the perennial issue of waste management and utility services at municipal and district level, to illustrate how the incoherent state serves as a long-term politicizing issue for Russians, as they learn, sometimes over decades, to reflect on and use their feelings for the socialist past to critique it and become nascent political subjects.

As we saw earlier, in Izluchino and the wider district of 50,000 people, local elites competed for control of the rubbish collection business in the town because it was ripe for siphoning off municipal funds for private gain via tendering companies (recalling the age-old Russian tradition of tax 'feeding' as an informal institution).[34] The competition for control by leveraging informal ties higher up led to the involvement of the District Procuracy – (allied with the ascendant district elite), and then Regional FSB (who saw municipalities as potential 'clients'

33. As mentioned earlier, one example of an amnesty relates to the belated opportunity to legalize incomplete ownership of automobile garages, but there are numerous others.

34. On 'feeding' (*kormlenie*) and other institutionalized forms of informal governance, see Ledeneva (2013b).

5. Incoherent State

against their competitors, the Procuracy).[35] The first 'formal' result in 2013 was the imprisonment of a local politician for making a private loan to himself from ringfenced municipal funds to buy an automobile. Another court annulled the existing waste contract – recalling the gossip of our Kotelnaya technicians at the beginning of this chapter. The bigger picture was the continuation of the blurry line between insufficiently formalized aspects of state procurement, contracting out and provision: overlapping or obscure delineations of jurisdictions, legally incoherent contracts, opaque 'holding companies'.

While Russian courts can be effective for individuals seeking redress, the outcome of cases for local businesses is like rolling loaded dice. Memorably, when one autumn the entire town temporarily lost its electricity connection (and therefore heating supply) due to a property dispute about where the substation happened to be situated, the Court decided on a technicality against the plaintiff (the electricity supplier) on the grounds that the electricity substation in question was not the property of the supplier and had been legally shut down by a third party. 'Trash' wars between elites, interruptions to heating supplies, the way different elites opposed or supported the oil refinery and these legal battles over substations are just a few illustrations of governance fatigue the local community experienced over the incoherence of the 'state'.

Tendering practices around waste, maintenance of quasi-public housing, heating supply and even minutiae such as subletting of public buildings to help the parlous local budget were disrupted and renegotiated by new constellations of elites, and micro-level conflicts were continually elevated to a meso-level informal competition between different *siloviki* (state security) organizations to the detriment of whole communities' well-being and confidence in the state's ability to get even little things done. Despite the picture often presented of Russians'

---

35. The Procuracy Service is a fifth wheel of the Russian security state. As a balancing and disciplining agency with high status it can intervene and 'overrule' the Interior Ministry Police and other agencies. This is because it has the authority to refer all kinds of cases directly to the courts based on its own investigative capacities. A US near-equivalent would be the District Attorney's Office, or on a national level, Attorneys-General. Unlike in the United States or other jurisdictions, the Procuracy is a federal-level office which is not answerable to any branch of government (including the Ministry of Justice – which can only supervise the courts), unelected and de facto a paramilitary force. By design its duties partially overlap with the Investigative Committee of the Russian Federation (a kind of weaker FBI-equivalent) which is supposed to undertake preliminary scoping of potential criminal cases. Dating back to the time of Peter the Great, the Procuracy has been a highly politicized institution whose purpose is as a meta-level monitor within the state (*nadzor*) and to serve as 'the eyes of the tsar'. As such, in the eyes of many citizens, it is imagined as part of the state that acts as an ultimate check on local power as much as a coercive organization acting in its own interests. In Izluchino, it is inevitably called in as an arbiter in all kinds of disputes, even over the quality of road repairs and the intentional debt-loading of utility companies.

140   *Everyday Politics in Russia*

exclusive consumption of federal TV, all these cases were covered in detail by the local press and regional TV. While in each case the journalists were affected by their own links via patronage and access to politicians, and also the need to self-censor, even today in 2023 it would be a mistake to say there is no diversity in coverage. Just like the image of the 1990s where on a national level oligarchic interests used media for competing political ends, Izluchino residents have access, via internet, print media and regional TV, to jarringly different versions of the same events: whether about non-collection of rubbish, or whether the oil refinery expansion is good for the town.

***

Sometime after the episode where the town's electricity was cut off, I was back sitting in the gas boiler hall with the Chief. One November in Izluchino in the early 2010s, the heating season had already begun, but as often happened, on Lenin Street the underground pipes burst. The Chief, his *slesar* Vitya and I drove out to the site and met the municipal manager (the deputy of the municipal mayor we met in Chapter 3). The unitary service company for communal services was de facto bankrupt and, as we saw with the fate of the rubbish collectors' lorry park, its technical equipment was idle due to non-payment of its contract. Pressure was being applied to get the region authorities to pay off the municipal debts. Yet the private company that was sitting on some of the excavating equipment had in turn sublet this plant out to a firm operating locally in a limestone quarry.

While the owners of this enterprise represent Moscow-based finance capital, the local manager quickly agrees to send out the moveable plant to dig up Lenin Street as we stare him down in the slanting rain. The municipal manager runs to the post office, where, in a backroom, the former engineer of a steel fabricating company has worked as a simple clerk since he was pensioned out of his main job.[36] This clerk gets on the phone. By the next day, the Chief, Vitya and I are standing in a trench watching the municipal plumbing service weld enormous hot-water pipes together (which is also not their job – they're only supposed to work inside housing) supplied by the local company at cost to the town (reimbursed using funds invisible to the District). We have an example of 'spectacular infrastructure and its breakdown' in action and commensurate 'innovation and improvisation' by the incoherent state and 'community' in response (Schwekel 2015).

In the 2010s as I followed the Chief around, I observed and was privy to many analogous examples of stateness as a product of informal institutional agreement and neo-*khoziaistvo* coordination.[37] A major national project renovating and

---

36. I describe the plastic and steel fabricating companies in detail in Morris (2016).

37. Douglas Rogers (2015) argues that in oil regions, corporations 'stretch out' and act as meta-coordinators with regional state agencies across diverse fields of social interaction via 'corporate social responsibility'. My point is that such action is multiscale and comes packaged with assumptions about morality.

5. Incoherent State

141

replacing the decrepit Soviet-era Sport and Leisure centres was only possible in Izluchino thanks to the co-mobilization of local businesses – both for funding (provided both transparently and via back-channels) and labour and material as contributions in kind. After the failure of rubbish collection, systemic clean-up of the town was achieved by marshalling capacity in a similar manner. Even immovable state infrastructure, such as an unadopted road (formerly owned by a defunct collective farm), could be upgraded using a hybrid coordination of community resources ('voluntary' money contributions), informal management by key businesspersons, and the approval of multi-layered state agencies (district cadastral agency, procuracy, rural administration) to asphalt three kilometres of rural track connecting two settlements.[38]

Typically, these practices are viewed through the lens of coercive and socially deleterious networks, but recently scholars such as Olga Moliarenko have shown the possibility of examining these as durable forms of 'shadow governance' (2016). Her account helps us bridge political clientelism and state as co-constructed. Moliarenko avoids essentializing the Russian experience as political indifference and unresponsiveness by design. She shows how 'mobile financing funds' invisible to the centre are important to the functioning of the state. Considered an anachronism (Desai et al. 2005), these shadow funds nonetheless remain significant at the municipal level. Shadow governance implies connivance between different agencies: the infamous Procuracy, other levels of government and citizens. It extends to shielding the locale from the central organs of state by falsifying tax records and adjusting census returns while municipalities keep secret and more accurate 'books' on economic activities. But such connivance is not just about necessity or subterfuge. Moliarenko draws attention to the proactive coordination from below as derived from shared assumptions and ideals about the 'good of the territory' [*na blago territorii*]. Moliarenko is careful to point out that this coordination needs to be disaggregated from corrupt enterprises and clientelism because it fulfils needs via leveraging the 'network state' (2016: 129).

More recently, researchers have started documenting and theorizing informal governance at more than just a macro or regional level. Fadeeva and Nefedkin (2018) argue that reciprocity and symmetry are as conceptually valid as patronage and clientelism in examining low-level governance. Babintsev and Iurkova (2016) extend Moliarenko's insights in their examination of micro-level processes, arguing that such 'informal practices in municipal governance' express a dialectical tension between ends-directed (common justice) and means-based (client-network justification). The regularization of such payments to fuzzy institutions like the

---

38. Moliarenko (2016) sees the emergence of hybrid forms of coordination from below as filling a gap to replace the role of the Communist Party as a state institution before 1991. From my own observation, I would prefer to think of such coordination as a carryover from the Soviet period of the moral authority and rational ideals of the allocative, modernizing and redistributive *khoziaistvo*-matrix. On ownerless roads and property, see Moliarenko (2018).

142 *Everyday Politics in Russia*

watermain connection office is a good example of co-production of the state via shared and pervasive understandings of the licitness of informal practices. Davide Torsello cites as 'social empowering' the discursive function of corruption in relation to governmentality (2018: 3). If everyone knows about 'it', this information fosters social equilibrium because petty forms of informal payments and favours are institutionalized. Furthermore, the dramaturgical and spectacular aspect of state failures invites the corresponding improvised yet also publicly scripted response that even tends to cliché in the local press where we can frequently read:

> resources of the municipality were rallied in conjunction with the input of the leading enterprises of the district and the voluntary efforts of citizens to eliminate the problem.

What sound like euphemisms for failure and arse-covering are as often a reflection of the incoherent state caught in the act of 'shadow' public works.

Conclusions

While citizens negotiate with a bewildering set of bureaucratic cross-purposes, state-making goes on. The term 'in(co)here' expresses a legacy of contesting vested rights to act on behalf of society. Still operative are ontological assumptions about communal property regimes, social responsibility, the sharing of risk in the face of uncertainty, social embeddedness and fuzzy authority. Authority is as much claimed on the basis of collective agreement as imposed from above. This was true of the Chief – on paper just the manager of the heating station. In reality he was recognized by all and sundry as 'responsible' for the town's water and gas infrastructure as well as unrelated issues and even the overseeing of funding for the new 'FOK' (physical fitness-health complex: the federal rebuilding of sports infrastructure). This situation is typical too in villages around Izluchino where an 'elder' has as much clout as the appointed administrator. These examples coexist with genuine and acute socio-economic problems of poverty, underfunding, unequal access and rapacious corruption. The state is incoherent, and yet a structural feeling for it emerges which may result in meaningful innovative action. The more we look ethnographically at the Izluchino heating and rubbish crisis – very typical tests of state capacity – the less it conforms neatly to neopatrimonial models alone.[39]

---

39. Nor does it look entirely like the (neo)liberal devolvement of risk onto individuals as a cynical plan by the authorities to forestall collective action in the face of social problems (Henry 2012). Laura Henry and others focus on the visibility of complaint-making and its officialization under Putin and Medvedev. They correctly see it as a minimal, individualizing and depoliticizing process.

5. Incoherent State

In no way, however, do I wish to underplay the terrible performance of all levels of state provision in Russia. In September 2022, with the onset of the first autumn frosts, several sewage pipes from communal housing in Izluchino failed simultaneously. The war has exacerbated the enormous shortage of labour, especially in the sphere of poorly paid municipal work. An equally predictable cycle of deflection, buck-passing and desperate calls to the district prosecutor's office ensued and it took over eight weeks to fix the problem of human effluent pooling in the back yards of blocks housing hundreds of people. The Municipal Enterprise of Communal Economy, or more recently, the Municipal Unitary Enterprise for Communal Economy (*MPKKh, MUPKKh*), is contracted by the municipality and on the latter's behalf collects resident payments for 'the improvement of public services'. Such 'improvement' – in Russian, *blagoustroistvo* – is the *raison d'être* of municipal governance. Everyone has good and bad to say about this contracted-out service and the torturous abbreviations like *MUPKKh*. The magical incantation *blagoustroistvo* is on everyone's lips, including Tamara's:

> The *MPKKh* said the problem was on land *between* the building and main sewer. The sewerage company said the leak was in the basements of the blocks. In the end I drove to the Prosecutor's office to get someone to come out, but they referred me to the telephone number of the *GZhI* [the State Housing Inspectorate] – this is now the algorithm of how to solve our problems. There is authority/power [*vlast*] everywhere and its duty is to help its population. It's a never-ending task and the citizen has to take on his load. You know in advance you have to do the rounds, but eventually you'll find a responsive authority (*instantsiia*) that feels it has a moral duty to you.

This is a typical conversation. Issues like the sewer leakage were never downplayed in the media; on the contrary, they were constantly used as wedges to discipline municipal heads like Tamara – who was ousted at the end of 2022 as a result of media pressure about the rubbish collections. Just as often as the appearance of collective substitutional-state action, residents despaired of stonewalling, subterfuge, buck-passing and inaction.[40] As with the example of rubbish collection and disposal, living with a majorly dysfunctional local and district administration could last

---

40. Beyond the scope of this chapter is the widespread falsification of records by state-workers, not in the interests of citizens, but to hide what seem like insurmountable issues caused by underinvestment. In the neighbouring district of Kaluga region, it is common knowledge that water safety records are falsified by lab workers. By the same token, medical staff felt 'obliged' to massively falsify Covid certificates without any expectation of payment by citizens.

years. As Brian Taylor memorably showed, the Russian state in aggregate does very little for its citizens, very badly. And despite cosmetic and patchwork trickledown of oil wealth from the centre, little has changed since his research. According to Taylor's own calculations, in 2007 at the height of economic recovery, Russian state capacity was the second lowest in the world among middle-income countries (Taylor 2011: 191).

When the state becomes fully legible to Russians, it is in violent disputes over property rights and naked political coercion. At the local and district level too, there is a daily and acutely felt incoherence. This is partly the result of the stubborn persistence of normative ideas about care, collective development and fictive kinship. Such norms amounted to a 'moral economy' of care; when the state-society contract broke down in the 1980s and 1990s, the experience was one of loss and dislocation (Sharafutdinova 2023: 61). Gulnaz Sharafutdinova makes a powerful critique of the still-dominant paradigms in Russian sociology of atomization and individualization. Powerful because she shows how out of kilter the study of Russian society is in relation to the advances made in scholarship of the state as a social relation. Thelen and Alber (2017) show that the view of 'too much kinship in the wrong place' is not about 'resisting' rational bureaucracy but neither is it an atavistic holdover in undeveloped institutions. The 'sincere' performance of non-disinterested relations between state workers and citizens is merely a return to an integrated study of how things get done in complex societies. This is as much a matter of bureaucratic logic as the disinterested, rule-bound professional of the Weberian ideal.

Expectations about a particular way of state-caring derive from norms more than rights-based ideas of duty. They are 'structures of feeling' that relate to collectivist notions of relation between state and citizen. The resolution of problems in the bureaucratic sphere entails competencies of recognizing relatedness. This, as Bogdanova showed (2005), is because legal 'rights' to protection under socialist collectivism did not exist, instead replaced by a framework of 'protection' and care [*zabota*][41] – leading to discourses and practices marked by recognition of vulnerable personhood, ironic given how often scholars point to the dehumanizing 'ends-driven' logic of Soviet socialism. The reality is a paradox that remains to this day – a state logic where 'human' rights are not legible, but where at every step the 'human', or rather 'social personhood' of the other, has

---

41. Bogdanova (2005) also draws attention to the ends-driven, yet parental logic of 'care' contained in the word *opeka*. *Opeka* in contemporary Russian relates to wardship and guardianship, most commonly encountered in the phrase *organy opeki*, i.e. child social services. This word is borrowed from Polish and relates to the Latin *procurare*, 'to take care of', from which we get the verb 'curate'. Bogdanova convincingly shows how 'care'-as-relation became so enshrined in ideology that it had quasi-legal ramifications.

some purchase.[42] Such feelings are not fully explained by (Soviet-era) paternalism or patronage. As Morgan Liu puts it (2005), writing about hybrid governance in Central Asia: what sounds like paternalist supplication is a way citizens invite state-people to acknowledge and enter into a moral relation with governance: the state as responsible from the position of paternal discipline and responsibility for the greater good of human development. This 'legacy' is in coexistence with a liberal-individualist rights-based way of thinking about social goods and the strong society-wide rhetoric of (self-enriching) neoliberalism more generally. In Ssorin-Chaikov's (2003) chronicle of precarious rural life in the Far North, state failure in the 1990s was itself 'productive' of local identity and new relations towards stateness and state people. The more it is felt as an absence, the stronger the attempts at re-enchantment among people, echoing the Soviet logic of creating an 'etatization' of the everyday, including work and leisure.

A further paradox is overlaid: citizens are faced with a dilemma – they continually express frustration, outrage and hurt at the uncaringness of state agencies and bureaucrats, at the same time as harbouring healthy suspicion, doubt and even fear of state workers, fully aware of the fickle, dangerous and coercive capacities (Morris and Garibyan 2021). Citizens must be continually reflexive in their encounters, both along axes of Liu's collectivist-individualist interpellations of the state, as much as the 'distance-nearness' ones. Incoherence does not just equate to the expectation of frustration (as in Vanya's experience). Bureaucracies harbour actors with multiple identities at once. They are moral persons who are receptive and helpful and who bear the traces of an ends-orientated development model. There are state workers with their own cultural traditions and informal institutions of accommodation, and also clients and patrons in networks of licit and illicit exchange.[43] It is in the next chapter, in expanding on the relevance of the micropolitical, that we unpack the way people enact mobility vis-à-vis the manifestations of the state, along with their active distancing from, and engagement with, visible forms of the market economy. Co-producing the state should be seen in the context of continual processes of negotiation elsewhere – across the whole spectrum of social reproduction.

42. As Thelen and Alber note (2017: 16), 'belonging' as a category to use to interrogate citizenship may seem nebulous but is frequently deployed by Weberian-type bureaucracies in apportioning rights (think of how one must prove 'ties' to a country to help define residency where a person has more than one citizenship). A relation of care in state-citizen encounters in Russia expresses a trace of the 'belonging' that collectivism imposed in the Soviet ontology we explored earlier in this book. Whether you liked it or not you were incorporated into a logic of deprivatized relationality with others and that included the state.

43. Here on the meaning of incoherence my argument has resonance with Migdal's (2004) agenda: state-in-society as research open to what he calls the 'culturalist' turn: cohesive and organizational capacity at odds with a Weberian perspective. He contrasts this agenda with a system-dominant structural perspective, a rationalist perspective and with historical institutionalism. This is not a 'state autonomy' argument but a bureaucratic autonomy and reflexive (to local society) feedback system.

Part III

LINES OF FLIGHT

Chapter 6

NOMADS: AN INTERMEZZO ON GARAGES AND OTHER NONPLACES

There are nearly six million individual vehicle garages in Russia according to the State Cadastral Register Service. These garages are not attached to people's homes; they are usually in single-story contiguous blocks some distance from apartment housing. Forty per cent of these garages are not registered with the state. As we saw in the previous chapter, governance and the state in Russia must contend with institutional forms that do not fit Western perceptions of effective and impersonal bureaucracy. There are economically rational reasons why people do not register their garages – taxation, red tape and so on. As a result, agencies like the Cadastral Service offer nearly open-ended 'amnesties' to encourage people to make them visible to the state. At the same time, the amnesty represents an 'institutional' standoff between state and society: many owners do not see any advantage in making their property more visible to the state and assess risks of expropriation under the status quo as minimal.[1] Cooperative management companies may be responsible for the garage blocks without owning the land itself. 'Economic' activities in garages, particularly in smaller cities, are significant. Sergei Seleev and Aleksandr Pavlov estimate that of the 30 to 50 per cent of untaxed self-employment in Russia a significant portion relies on access to garage spaces. Some garage work resembles that described in the current chapter: individual mastery of in-demand skills such as vehicle spray-painting. However, in general, garage work bears a family resemblance to the tradition Russian *artel* – a community of craftsmen working to order and self-organizing. Flexible self-exploitation may involve furniture production, meat processing, in fact, almost anything you can

---

1. Expropriation is certainly a real phenomenon with regards to unregistered/incompletely documented property. The point here is about how people make calculations about the relative risk depending on many factors, including structured 'feeling' for the state.

150   *Everyday Politics in Russia*

imagine taking place there (Seleev and Pavlov 2016, Morris 2023b, Vanke 2024).[2] We should also recognize the overwhelmingly gendered quality of garage life and work, though in my journeys to garage blocks I have encountered numerous examples of women using them for more than just parking cars.

Resisting the eye of the state almost always has a 'moral' foundation, as James C. Scott (1976) memorably noted in his work on peasants in Southeast Asia. Like the 'economy' of the village, the Russian garage and the larger moral economy it represents form a system where all kinds of practices take place according to a logic that is not reducible to the market society, even while garages freely interact with that market. The profit principle and hierarchical work-relations may be less important than other aims such as building social ties or reciprocity. Like the bureaucracy we encountered in the previous chapter, the garage block represents a space and community of co-creation – production, consumption, education, reflection. 'Leisure' includes sexual recreation, just hanging out, being in a place alone and contemplation, or in studied intense activity. Time can be compressed, suspended. Often what draws people here is the absence of 'bossing around' and fewer clear disparities in power.[3] Elements from 'normal' life can be transplanted. Just two examples from recent experience in the 2020s are a barbeque selling meat and a motorcycle repair business specializing in American marques – both in the tiny town of Izluchino. These archipelagos of life, urban yet detached from the town, are vividly depicted in the 2020 documentary film 'Garage People' by Natalija Yefimkina. Promotional material for the film depicts a club of weightlifters in a metal shell-like structure. The text entices the viewer to come to

2. The scale of unregistered property for storing automobiles is thought to be around 3.5 million units. The fact that the current property amnesty where owners can legalize their garages with the cadastral register lasts five years gives an indication of the difficulty of retrospective legalization and the long backlog. Often permission for the erection of a brick garage was given in the late Soviet period by a now-defunct enterprise. However, many garages were built without permission after that. Furthermore, the land may have belonged to one enterprise, and the building to a private owner. Sometimes documents dating back to the initial permission do not exist, making legal registration today difficult if the garage does not have records of an account with a utilities provider – another way of retrospectively registering. Even without documents, local municipalities have the authority to allow legalization due to the amnesty law. The amnesty is aimed at increasing the number of taxable properties visible to the state.

3. Throughout this paragraph I am indirectly referring to those elements Scott (see in particular Chapter Six, 1976) found noteworthy in the moral economy of the village he studied which aimed at reducing unjust exploitation by landlords and expressed norms of fairness via reciprocal aid and minimal social rights. Scott was indebted to E. P. Thompson's deployment of the term 'moral economy'. Moral economy was both simple but radical notion: to take seriously the holistic interaction of culture, reflection, shared rationality and agency among dominated groups.

6. Nomads: An Intermezzo on Garages   151

'Russia's unwelcoming north, [where] garages stretch out into endlessness. Behind rusty doors everything can be found, except cars. They are a refuge.'

The idea of particular spaces in Russia as 'islands' or 'cells' marked by boundaries is not original. Finn Sivert Nielsen (1986/2006) memorably wrote of Soviet towns and factories as island-like identities. Belonging to such an island guaranteed one's welfare because such place-based attachment provided entitlement to goods like healthcare and other elements of the 'social wage': the non-cash benefits of significant importance in these societies (Morris 2016). Caroline Humphrey's memorable phrase about 'possessive domains' refers to such places apart (2002). By contrast, Alexei Golubev (2020: 103) notes the official Soviet disquiet about the 'negative social agency' provided by interstitial spaces such as stairways and basements in the urban environment. 'Agency' meant things like people having sex, listening to popular American music, or smoking and drinking.

Nielsen's island approach was based on the idea of economic rationality as centrifugal. To escape the extractive-re-allocative logic of the Soviet centre, islands became fortresses, not from the Cold War threat, but from each other. Enterprises sought to distance themselves as an act of self-protection from the central Plan which tried to control and monitor them.[4] To 'seek out a sheltered Place and entrench' (Nielsen 1986/2006: n.p.). The desire for autonomy may have an economic rationale, but as Scott showed, a host of non-economic values drive it. In Golubev's account of stairwells, he too notes the idea of protection and shelter from the gaze of the state.

The garage space transplants aspects of 'normal' life without adhering to rules about the payment of taxation, food safety, hierarchy, clocking-in at work. These are absent, or at least fundamentally challenged. But this is neither anarchy nor a state of nature. After all, the brick-built blocks are clearly demarcated property; they can be bought and sold, and the police will, reluctantly, come along if things get too rowdy or worse. Furthermore, there is a legally visible 'cooperative' nominally in charge.[5] In wealthy areas there are gated garage blocks, some dating back to the Soviet period, with guards and fences and boom gates and 24-hour lighting. These

---

4. In a similar spatial metaphor, Nikita Pokrovksii and Sergei Bobylev (2003) have written of the infrastructural, employment and bureaucratic gradient in Russia as producing 'cellular globalization' with enormous spaces emptied of all three trappings of the modern state.

5. Garage cooperatives were often formed in the 1980s but due to so many changes in the procedure for registering them, some exist only as bureaucratic relics with no actual paperwork remaining. As a result, individual garage users may even lack legal documents of ownership – sometimes the only document linking a legal person to the garage is an individual contract for electricity supply. Furthermore, in the same land plot of perhaps twenty to thirty hectares (hundreds of garages), there may be different 'shades' of legalized possession and legal governance – from 'black', through 'grey', to 'white' (all documents lodged with various state organs). Legal disputes over the ownership status of garage plots have even been heard by the Supreme Court of the Russian Federation.

Figure 4 A garage block in Izluchino.

are uninviting, lonely places. They are hardly worth talking about. But in the small town of Izluchino there are three enormous hives (or warrens? – both organic metaphors are apt) of self-built brick garages, each with heavy steel-plated doors just beyond the edge of town. None of them are guarded and few are lit at night. You can lose your way easily because the rows, each with a sloping sandy track, are not numbered, even if the garages are. You might have to orient yourself to the rather distant high-rises to the south, over the no-man's-land of scrub.

(De)territorialization against the state form

Gilles Deleuze and Félix Guattari see the state as engaged in a never-complete task of 'crystalizing' relations and networks through 'territorialization' (1984: 145–53, 2017: 502–5). However, modern administration takes a step further towards abrogating socially 'coded flows' of kinship alliances which served as a basis of the political and economic in 'primitive' societies. Modern states require 'deterritorialized' fixing of people's relational identities in abstract documents. With the development of proto-capitalism and even before, economic 'deterritorialization' (the money form as a 'decoded flow') proceeds in parallel with state-formation. At first it is through the mobility of merchants' credit notes in the Mediterranean and Arab worlds and later in the abstract determination of

6. Nomads: An Intermezzo on Garages

ownership and power via increasingly sophisticated techniques of governance. Eventually, the capitalist state (and the socialist one too) becomes the ultimate regulator. It is 'immanent to the field of social forces' (1983: 252). Decoding, in its Deleuzian framing, is political. It literally 'evacuates the meaning out of all existing social codes' in favour of a 'substitution of economics for politics' (Buchanan 2008: 31–2). The tension inherent to such processes of state formation and modern capitalism gives rise to 'collective mechanisms' that ward off such tendences. 'Micropolitics' – whether in the nomadic impulse of historical peoples to escape sedentary life, or the everyday tensions inherent in modern societies between emancipatory and repressive tendencies – are then expressed 'pragmatically' and appear immanent to everyday practice.[6]

Where do desire and libido come into this? Deleuze and Guattari assume that gregariousness as an impetus – the desire for society or community – is a basic drive for human beings (Buchanan 2008: 19). People are 'libidinally invested' in the 'production' of such relations.[7] Desire is about reproducing connective (coded) social relations.[8] Micropolitics are Deleuze and Guattari's attempt to rethink 'resistance' as a vitalist impetus that – counterintuitively – *precedes* domination and which inheres within an overall model of 'flows' not located within individuals but comprising forces acting in micrological associations. This differentiates the Deleuzian micropolitical from postmodern notions of radical democracy (Krause and Rolli 2008). The micropolitical is not the sum of 'politics in miniature', or Scott's 'little acts of sabotage or resistance', but about 'retaining desire as a primordial "micro" essence or' disposition (Gilliam 2017: 131). Drives include 'fascistic' ones

6. Micropolitics see Deleuze and Guattari attempt to grapple with Foucault's idea that power recuperates any resistance because it pervades the social field. They do this by proposing a biosocial model (which is intended idiosyncratically to serve as both metaphor and also literal description) of 'desire' and 'drives' that are emancipatory and precede the occupation of the social field by structuring power. They use the work of Pierre Clastres who saw war in so-called primitive societies as an endless mechanism to ward off the institutionalization of authority. Deleuze and Guattari coin the 'war machine' to describe processes and practices immanent to societies aimed at retarding the sedimentation of state-like hierarchies. Theirs is not a romantic appropriation of anthropology, however. They are deadly serious in rescuing a psycho-social idea of human drives that goes back to Spinoza from the clutches of modern psychoanalysis at the same time as responding to the structuralism of social sciences in the postwar period and addressing what seemed to be a failure of the emancipatory potential of 1968 and Marxism in general.

7. The use of 'production' is important to get away from the idea of libido being concerned with compensating over some lack – as in Freudianism and Lacanianism.

8. Deleuze and Guattari write simultaneously about how psychoanalytical models such as the Oedipus complex are not primordial elements but derive from modern institutions, but also in response to Foucault. Their 'solution' is ingenious – a kind of reworking of Spinoza via Nietzsche by recourse to anthropology while famously 'remaining' Marxist by 'forgetting' Marx. On the relation to Marxism, see Garo (2008: 66–7).

along with 'lines of flight'. Both are part of the repressed 'infrastructure of society itself' (Read 2008). In this way, human beings are always and everywhere in a 'situation-ready' attitude: anticipating co-assembly of autonomy, rather than re-acting towards some external source of power. While revolutionary politics tends historically to be recuperated by the state-form, Deleuze and Guattari anticipate contemporary ideas about social struggles through their emphasis of 'minoritarian' critiques of institutional politics (Braidotti 2006).

The minor mode of the political entails looking to how subaltern group practices can be grasped and appreciated, as forms of alternative, or subversive politics, performed seemingly within the major key of the dominant, yet subverting it in 'refusals and reworking' (Katz 1996: 491, Filc 2020). Let us go back to the earlier examples in this book: the dislocating experience of forced labour migration to Moscow by unemployed Izluchino men, and the similar dispossession of Moscow middle-class women in new, seemingly unwelcome care roles, can become a source of critique and subversion. Deterritorialization is disruptive of former subjectivities but prompts a politicizing response. The experience of relocating to Moscow to literally enter a chthonic space – underground and occupying the position of a demon – was profound for many men.[9] This movement looks like a coping tactic, but it can be reassembled as a sequence: D-R-D. Deterritorialization: uprooting completely from a former identity and place and insertion as invisible workers into Moscow's new capitalism. Re-territorialization via money savings to buy rural property back in what they call their 'small homeland' of the village. Deterritorialization occurs again, as many men disappear into the informal economy undertaking forms of 'unruly' or 'bare' entrepreneurialism after their long experience of wage labour exploitation (Morris 2012). Educated women, valued more by the state in the socialist period than today, are cast into unemployment in the 1990s. Their best years irretrievably lost, a minor refrain is to impart a strong ethic of holistic care to their wards. In this way they try to get back recognition and to promote an idealized and Sovietized notion of whole-person *vospitanie*, or 'upbringing' (Morris and Garibyan 2021). A third example: young people also take a *line of flight* from the starting point of the organized Soviet practice of 'voluntary labour'. They repeat it, but differently, by collecting rubbish while hiking in the countryside and refusing the organizational control of this practice by a state-like entity.[10]

9. One of the major politicizing experiences for many men in Izluchino was the realization that Muscovites were afraid of them and saw them as 'genetically different', as one local put it. When (ethnically white) migrant workers emerged furtively from the Moscow building sites at night to buy alcohol, people would shy away from them.

10. While feminist readings of Deleuze and Guattari emphasize the usefulness of the 'minor' mode, this should be carefully contextualized. The minor is not an alternative to the major but a differentiation – a splitting off from an existing form or structure.

6. Nomads: An Intermezzo on Garages

These are some lines of flight that emerge when established mass-society forms of political struggle and even 'newer' social movement forms seem to be ebbing. This change from majoritarian to minor modes of the political accompanies the parallel shift from Foucault's disciplinary societies to the micro-scale control society (Deleuze 1990, Garo 2008: 64–5). Deleuze here is in direct conversation with Foucault: the latter's notion of power is one that internalizes to the body and also depersonalizes through 'governmentality'. This is met by Deleuze's proposition: desire as a flow of political forces 'that exist below the thresholds of conscious communication and intent' (Colebrook 2008: 127). Micropolitics presuppose mundane and less visible practices because they assume the political can be located in everyday life. This doesn't mean people are bereft of other so-called 'higher' forms of political agency, association or reflection; instead, it recognizes that the political itself emerges initially and primarily as a form of pre-organizational social assemblage before deliberation in a public sphere. Leftist attempts to incorporate Deleuze and Guattari are sometimes guilty of a revolutionary romanticism by ending the sequence prematurely: D-R – envisaging a final concrete space of 'refuge' beyond capitalism or outside the state. Scholars aim at undercovering practices aimed against the coalescence of state sovereignty over life (Robinson 2010).[11] But the 'nomad' figure is not meant to be read in this way.

The nomads may move, surreptitiously within the state form, hiding the location of caches for their reproduction while still 're-territorializing' themselves at particular advantageous times, such as during a census thanks to which social funds may subsequently be disbursed. However, the metaphor (of the crafty nomad) is not fully satisfactory as it implies conscious design and action. We could also see it as romanticized orientalism. By contrast, a phenomenological frame proposes purposive action at the intersubjective, not individual level. My recourse to a famously allusive and oxymoronic thinker such as Deleuze is in no way meant to detract from the naturalistic and empirically driven approach of this book. Thinking with Deleuze about proactively emancipatory drives is essential. Not only because the micropolitical is largely absent in an appreciation of postmodern-type 'authoritarian' societies such as China and Russia, but because these societies very obviously prefigure our own post-democratic degeneration. Deleuze was engaged in a serious debate with Foucault about power. The 'ideal' for him was a literal force in human life which entered 'actual experience without being contained by it … that cannot but be felt but always escapes' (Massumi 1996: 395). Deleuze remains a paradoxical thinker who rejected empirical representation for the sake of transcendental experience – desire for him is a force prior to the

---

11. Andrew Culp (2016) takes readers of Deleuze and Guattari to task for their persistent readings of revolutionary romanticism. More careful readers heed their warning against equating their terminology with emancipatory rebellion. Equally, darker forces may arise from the imperative to become contrary under capitalism and the control society.

social.[12] I anthropologize his ideas to put desire back into the social world. I phenomenalize Deleuze; I show that desire emerges in intersubjective experience of actual minds and bodies. I offer a reading in the spirit of his understanding that there is a socioeconomic and political dimension to libidinal investment. Desire allows a political 'subject' to emerge as a result of an encounter between conflicting imperatives – productive and antiproductive. The former is socially and collectivizingly creative. The latter privileges consumption, policing in place of freedom, politics as depoliticization or as fascism, progress as individualized neoliberalism in place of the commons.[13]

Capitalism entails deterritorialization, or 'de-coding'; consider in history the maritime trading town which belonged neither to the backcountry nor fully to the empire (Deleuze's example). The ultimate logic of deterritorialization is the digitization of biomaterial – DNA and iris scans are appended to credit files. Pertinently to the Russian context, the physical presence of individuals can be extracted from the world in the form of face-recognition software and then distributed between the remote terminals of the security state. Even before the Ukraine war, in 2021 at a protest against Alexei Navalny's arrest, the unassuming husband of a prominent political commentator was arrested off the street using this software. Deleuze predicted the rise of this 'control society' (1990). However, the social person, or rather the libidinal drive for emancipation, is always tracing this same fluctuation between flighty deterritorialization and (re)territorialization. We have already seen many examples in this book without naming them as such. In a strictly spatial sense, the upending of former industrial workers makes them 'deterritorialized' (because they are anonymous and interchangeable to the state and capital) material. They are out of place in Moscow. Deterritorializations, while not necessarily escaping the logic of a social system, can be improvisational and creative, and trace the 'lines of flight' of the nomad.[14]

The nomad is a figure representing the 'warding off' of the state apparatus and of extricating thinking from the state model (Deleuze and Guattari 2017: 416, 436). This does not intend a romanticization of the 'primitive' against a perniciously

---

12. For the purposes of readability, I reduce the complexity of Deleuze and Guattari's thought to a few of their many evocative terms. In doing so inevitably I simplify, and this is why I see my work as thinking with them rather than as my taking a 'Deleuzian' position. This is similar to Deleuze's approach himself towards canonical philosophers such as David Hume and Spinoza.

13. Here I am indebted to Gilliam's (2017) reading of the micropolitical.

14. Lines of flight are linked to the better-known trope of the 'rhizome'. For readability, I stick to the figure of the nomad. 'Lines of flight' are a motif for connection rhizomatically and transversely, not in a tree-, or root-like structure. In a different biological metaphor (the evolutionary symbiosis or mutualism of orchids and wasps), lines of flight also imply a continual process of de-and-re-territorialization. For Deleuze and Guattari, the aim is to accelerate de-territorialization to its absolute degree. De-territorialization would be a way of overcoming the subject-object division and achieving 'immanence'.

civilizing state-form. Instead, the extent of territorialization (indexation, demarcation – such as in a tax code, census return or cadastral register) is always met with nomadic counterforces. Similarly, deterritorialization – such as the erasure of place-based identity (the national over the local) – meets nomadic limits, such as when a community suddenly finds its voice in opposing the cutting of a forest or the polluting of a river and articulates 'our' connection to a particular expression of territory. Some forms of the predisposition for animals and humans to territorialize are evolutionary and contribute to a sense of place through the making of art and creativity, as we will see in the next chapter.[15] However, Deleuze and Guattari propose desire as a force that is productive and social, not instinctual nor aimed at repairing a traumatic separation. Whether we take these thinkers literally as offering an anthropologically-grounded analysis of objective psychosocial reality is not so important. We can, once again, think with them to offer a usefully perpendicular angle of attack in exploring and uncovering tectonic social processes writ large (but minoritarian!). We can uncover the nomadic in everyday practices of the lifeworld and social reproduction – whether tinkering in garages with sparkplugs, or three-dimensional embroidery crafts depicting utopian local landscapes and rooted identities (explored in the next chapter).

Contemporary nomadism in wartime: The limits of the state

'Nomadism' is not an identity and is employed to avoid binarism. It is not 'opposed' to the state-form; it exists alongside and interacts and undermines it at the same time. Nomadism is a particular relation of wariness and limitational exposure – something we saw in the examples of bare or unruly entrepreneurialism in Chapter 4. Izluchino district's denizens express a strong 'territorializing' attachment to place. They, like many Russians, talk more about a 'small homeland' than a national identity. This is especially true now, as the war effort is territorialized (identifying quotas based on territory for mobilization) by the Russian state itself. This explains why and where military mobilization was effective: in those areas where local loyalties could be cynically leveraged through tricking people into thinking they were taking up arms to defend their locality or community in a 'territorial defence unit'. Not so in Kaluga Region. By contrast, voluntary enlistment occurs sometimes because of the social pressures and stigmas of local communities. Of course, there are relatively poor people for whom the monetary gain seems worth it. Often standards of hegemonic masculinity also manipulate people in their relationship to the war. Social and economic marginalization plays a role in pushing some towards embracing a romanticized idea about deterritorialization that comes with volunteering (you think you can become someone else in a space apart from the state). But in Izluchino there are many nomads who at best pity the mobilized,

---

15. Similarly, the affective bonds of persons territorially can shape political discourse – inarticulately, and incoherently – and produce 'microfascisms'.

158   *Everyday Politics in Russia*

and at worst see them as motivated by greed or by the cupidity of relatives. Being mobilized or volunteering is, ironically, the end of the nomad's unrestricted movement across space 'smoothy', as Deleuze and Guattari put it. The sharp edges of the striated state funnel you to the frontline instead.

> The nomad has a territory; he follows customary paths; he goes from one point to another [...] But the nomad [unlike the migrant] goes from point to point only as a consequence and as a factual necessity; in principle points for him are relays. [...] even though the nomadic trajectory may follow trains or customary routes, it does not fulfil the function of the sedentary road, which is to *parcel out a closed space to people*, assigning each person a share and regulating the communication between shares. The nomadic trajectory does the opposite: it *distributes people (or animals) in an open space*, one that is indefinite.
>
> (Deleuze and Guattari 2017: 443)

Here we get a taste of what the authors are trying to do with the figure of the nomad. Elsewhere, Deleuze and Guattari talk of a particular jurisprudence of nomadism based on an experience and 'institution' ever slipping away from the state apparatus (Marneros 2021). This is the line of flight that entails both deterritorialization in the face of the state, and reterritorialization upon a trajectory away from it (Deleuze and Guattari 2017: 444–5).

The garage is not a space to 'make money' in labour, but it is one where people are always tinkering in a way that might be work. There are no set hours, but there is a rhythm one might even set one's watch by. Valera is usually here spray-painting cars for a good living. Sometimes Zhenya comes over and the work is suspended. For days at a time. They open up a kind of 'café-club', as they call it, replete with exotic alcohols, dance music and disco lighting.[16] You know that when your spray job is nearly complete, the work will be interrupted as Valera invites other tinkerers and connoisseurs of the Soviet-Russian automobile to come over and admire his work, to figure out a problem, to mix paint and chew the fat. Valera lives with his elderly parents and is socially awkward. He went to live in Ukraine for a while with relatives. He then got a job in Germany in a supermarket because he is of Volga German colonial stock, and those same Ukrainian relatives had moved to Germany in the late 1990s and got passports.

After earning some money, Valera came back and began obsessively fixing old Russian cars, sometimes for free. He 'pimped' my ride with velour seats, new rims and chrome. When I used to drive into Moscow people would stop me and ask me to sell them my very incongruous 1999 Lada station wagon. Valera loves his work. He loves doing everything one normally does in a flat at his garage instead. He cooks and he washes his clothes in his garage; he reads books and watches television in his garage. He fails to make enough money to really cover his living

---

16. I wrote about the garage space as refuge from everyday cares at length in Morris (2016).

6. Nomads: An Intermezzo on Garages

expenses in his garage (in the back of the story there are still the state and his parents' pension and apartment). He woos girls and fist-fights their older brothers in his garage. Valera is that nomad who does not move. Or rather, he moves while seated at his work bench, peering through a welding helmet like a spaceman. Valera knows how to wait. As he is 'awkward', how did he work in Germany, we wonder? People there thought he was mentally 'subnormal', and he would just wait for them to pick up their shopping and leave. He waited out their prejudice and refused to gain any proficiency in German. Even now, when he has status as an 'authority' on old cars, he is strangely immobile but in a way that speaks to his line of flight into the deterritorialized territory of the garages.

We make an agreement over the phone to meet him at the underground double-glazing workshop in the vast half-abandoned industrial 'village' island known as 'Sixty-Fourth', a name that does not appear on any maps but refers to the numbering of passing-places on the freight rail line. The workshop there now has access to an impressive space in which he can finally work on an old German Opal hatchback. When I first started visiting the workshop – hidden in plain sight among two-storey industrial buildings in various states of abandonment and disrepair – I thought: this must be a freak occurrence. In subsequent years the island within the island kept reappearing in different places – back in the garages or in a half-abandoned village building. Even in wartime, work goes on making windows as Ukrainian jet-engine drones fall nearby, programmed to attack the oil refinery in the neighbouring 'island'.

Valera doesn't turn up. He has a different sense of time and has got lost reading up on the technical specs of motorcycle accumulators. I have to borrow Katya's jeep and collect him. He reluctantly comes along, but on the way he asks to call in to the pet shop for cat food. I buy him the cat food to hurry things along. He explains he had forgotten to feed his parents' animals (they are too infirm to do it themselves). Everyone is frustrated, but Valera is oblivious. We take him home and after a few hours when we drive past the garages, we see he has walked back there, and he is now soaking the back of his neck from a rain-water barrel. The welding on the Opal is done months later by another person, in contrast to the strict observation of spray job orders.

***

The roads beyond the regional highway are a projection of the garage spaces. Automobility expresses a kind of general grammar of (in)security. For many there is a mantra on how to build habitability out of compartmentalized existence: 'car-apartment-village-plot'.[17] This sees achieving automobility as the

---

17. Simon Kordonsky and his fellow researchers in the Khamovniki group popularized the term 'distributed lifestyle' over twenty years ago to draw attention to the continuing salience of agriculture and mobility as survival tactics. Subsequently this term has been used to argue for a type of alternate, or even retarded, modernity for Russians in a socio-political environment characterized by universal insecurity. See Moliarenko (2013) for an overview.

160   *Everyday Politics in Russia*

predicate to autonomous self-protection against the threats of capitalist realism and the state combined. The agents of the state (in the guise of the Road Police), mobile bandits and nouveaux riches' armour-plated SUVs, are all equal dangers in the symbolic and real road network of Russia's car culture. However, densely populated European Russia is still only a state-archipelago. There are oceans of smooth space where the necessity of driving licence, insurance and documentation can be refused. These are the customary paths – on a relay that describe lines of flight. Valera would not come with us as we, for no good reason, retraced the journey to Severinsk I had taken with Tamara in Chapter 3 to investigate potential allies in her environmental campaign.

Anna Kruglova's research (2019) on drivers and passengers in the Russian Urals region shows how road spaces between towns exemplify the stretched-out, flattened and contingent rule of the Russian state. Similarly, my passengers (I'm driving Katya's jeep) now express their interstitial understanding of the road, street and highway. Beyond the safety of the garage, they encounter a number of 'others' who are nomadic. We stop off at Olga the citizen journalist's country cottage. It's just been robbed and we race off in a new direction to search for the culprits. Olga has a gas blowback pistol for personal protection. And a drunk passenger fires it out of the car window in frustration. After a while we realize the regional authority ran out of money even more quickly than usual this year: the asphalt on this stretch is so bad it makes no sense to continue. We will only be able to make twenty kilometres an hour and suddenly this crawling along sobers everyone up. A local (where? Most houses near the road are abandoned) has tried to fill potholes with limestone chippings. A typical fix where the state runs out of state-ness. Here again it peters out into clumps of broken asphalt. We feel safely exterior. We stop the car in the centre of the highway and someone goes to explore an abandoned village. At least a third of villages on official maps are uninhabited now. Even I, an outsider, know every possible route of the lonely patrolman here and so I relax. The deterritorialized policed state only exists in so far as it has enforcement cameras linked to digitized database, the bane of the Muscovite driver's existence. While Moscow city has more cameras than most European countries, here they end about halfway between Kaluga city and Izluchino. Izluchino is hardly where the backcountry begins, but even so it feels almost invisible to Moscow. From Izluchino to Severinsk, the patrolman rarely ventures. And now we are another thirty kilometres beyond the former. And yet only four hours to the biggest and yet most unequal capital city in Europe.[18]

The nomad's impulse is not instinctive but based on a shared social logic. It is not well grasped in 'cognitive' rationalizing terms either. This is why in this chapter

---

18. There are some good reasons to consider Moscow's exceptionalism further. Despite lower standards of living than in the other large centres of Europe like London, Paris and Berlin, Moscow has a significantly higher municipal budget whether in real terms or, for that matter, per head of population in comparison to the rest of the country. The cliché that Moscow 'is not Russia' is accurate.

6. Nomads: An Intermezzo on Garages 161

there has been little 'talk' among interlocutors. Nonetheless, there certainly is a political subtext of emancipation through nomad practices which emerges sometimes on the surface of talk and reflection. This is why desire as a political drive towards undermining control and governance requires a humanizing influence. For Deleuze, humanity is nameless and impersonal. Deleuze rejects the relevance of lived experience and the interplay between that experience, knowledge and intersubjective understandings of the world. However, we can turn to the work of social historian of subaltern subjects Jacques Rancière to 'humanize' the nomadic impulse. Like cultural historian E. P. Thompson, Rancière's philosophical project can be summed up as privileging 'thought from below'. His project aims to underline, not only to the intellectual equality of all, but to foreground the significance of modes of expression and comportment of those that historically were considered mute or intentionally silenced – in particular, the 'plebian' figure from, or of, the demos. Rancière insists that politics emerge when those who are 'unaccounted for' express dissensus on the basis of rejecting hierarchical constraint – particularly from 'policing' state bodies. As a consequence, democracy and politics can only be renewed by turning attention to those excluded from the 'normal' purview of the political.

Following Rancière, to give specificity to Deleuzian politics we need to look at practices where 'self-declaration' is evident: where a person is in a context where she gains representative form before another person without presuppositions of inequality. This is part of a 'method of equality' (Rancière 2016). Rancière sees the mode of occupation in contemporary social struggles as symbolizing a claim to equality on the basis of autonomy. Various 'occupy' movements are important, not for their particular demands or political strategy, but because they both materialize and symbolize what for him is 'the political': secession in a place *aside*. His transverse view of politics is, then, not completely unlike Deleuze's. This asideness can then aspire to reconstruct the commons (Rancière 2017). To summarize, Rancière is indispensable in thinking about counter-state democratic politics from below. These politics are actions emerging from a presupposition of equality and a capacity of ordinary people to undertake transformative mental and physical actions in spite of their double dispossession – lacking genuine rights of political participation and being seen as mute.[19] The original site of micropolitics is where society begins this process in quite mundane ways but which contain this idea of verification of the potential for equality. Anna Secor and Jess Linz (2017) return the image of the squatter and those who are drawn to 'no man's land' to

---

19. Rancière, in his insistence on the a priori ability of the 'demos' to speak and claim equality, must be seen as a reference point for sociologists looking to uncover the political content of ordinary action. As Bosteels argues (2010), Rancière's ideas about the politics of the demos can be seen as a response to social scientists and political philosophers frustrated with the disorderliness of subjects even as they sympathize with them – the 'republican' legacy visible in the emancipatory-democratic thought of Chantelle Mouffe and Pierre Bourdieu.

162   *Everyday Politics in Russia*

the Deleuzian frame. 'Holding open' spaces that do not conform to the normal hierarchies is the beginning of politics.

Following the key movements of Deleuze and Rancière's ideas, we can plot them as points overlaid on the spaces of the garages and underground workshops. First there is the counter-state nomadic imperative. Then there is the political significance of how this imperative already assumes a way of thinking and acting from below. These occupations are improvisational – the small workshop making plastic windows moves around. It starts in a garage and then squats in the sub-basement of a company making steel cable. That company itself is imperfectly visible to the state as well as to shareholder owners in Moscow. The workshop artisans pay a peppercorn rent to the foreman of the cable turners' brigade. For the foreman too, this is a line of flight. The Moscow company is none the wiser. Metaoccupational alliances facilitate this smooth movement from one place to another. One metalworker always knows, vaguely, faintly, another. The occupational genealogical and space intersect through a kind of socialist haunting.

In 'the time before' (before 1991), their respective families were embedded in a community of ranked workers. Now, the community does not exist as such, but the trace remains – it is 'meta-occupational' because the factories and Soviet ontology in which it was formed no longer exist. Assumption of equality as welders or sons of welders enables and articulates the flow of labour and workers – invisible to the state – through the industrial zones and garages. This articulates Rancière's distinction between community and *demos*. The micropolitical challenge to the state can emerge only from a demos – a category of people deterritorialized as a result of their superfluity. Under socialism they were a fully particularized body of a community. Ironically, they speak of that 'time before' as an era of real political rights. While they had no genuine union representation, they enjoyed symbolic value (in Soviet public culture) and wielded structural power to leave the job or go slow, as well as a certain quasi-feudal leverage with the lord – the right to an audience with the enterprise director who was tasked with personalized management of disputes (Morris and Hinz 2017).

In my first foray into Izluchino in 2009–10, I tinkered at the workshop for a short time. Despite my externality – foreigner, researcher – it is easy to acquire a kind of temporary and contingent acceptance because the principle of equality is an entry requirement. It takes me a while to persuade them to let in a 'professor' – after all, we are an ignorant and arrogant class. Everyone working here at the workshop has left the old factories, or even the new German and French ones, because they understand that equality is only possible through autonomy. Now, a certain sleight of hand is required here because there is an external agent who reinserts the products (high-quality window frames and glazing) back into the 'white' and visible-to-the-state market economy. However, he remains at a distance to the true concern and in any case, he isn't paying taxes himself. The discursive content of the workshop group shows manifestations at every step of this urge to autonomy via 'asidedness' from the state and the freedom through nomadicity of the artisans. The setting strongly resembles how we imagine the historical *artel* – or peasant cooperative of semi-formal artisans. There is a strict democratic principle. Seleev

6. Nomads: An Intermezzo on Garages

and Pavlov (2016) in their book-length sociology of garages make frequent note of the moral economy they encounter: profit 'sharing' and proportionality, allergy to wage-based and time-delimited labour, autonomy and political expression of garage work, cooperative learning and delegation. This assumption of equality combines the sphere of talk and the material.

Kolya, the 'junior' aluminium turner, has to be listened to as an equal, even if his conversation seems puerile to the older men. My dexterous ability in fixing spacer widgets between the glass and the frames grants me temporary recognition as an equal worker, and aspects of my class and cultural difference can be attenuated for a time. Even though everything about this nomadic space is fragile and temporary, I reencounter the stubborn persistence of the workshop over the years as my own interlocutors move on to some other form of nomad existence – in taxi-driving, informal plumbing services and day labouring. Of my original interlocutors, only Sasha remains. But even in 2018, I am able to visit him there. Now I am an outsider again to the group of half a dozen men working the same electric Turkish lathes. Something of a continuity in their perpetual line of flight from the state remains.

That such a vital force as nomadism in the garage spaces and underground workshop sustains itself barely below the surface illustrates a general problem with socio-political research on Russia. In the years I have told these stories from my research, inevitably these phenomena are repackaged for the scholarly world as part of understanding 'informal economy'. The response has always been to see these ways of life as curious exceptions. Or they are atavisms dying away as Russia further converges with global north forms – whether tight state governance of 'economic' activities, or of the superiority of the wage-labour arrangement. Similarly, the frame of economic rationality means these practices are at best seen as defensive attempts to carve out autonomy in shrinking spaces salvaged from socialism, and at worse fateful forms of internalization of neoliberal subjecthood – after all, some of these practices do resemble entrepreneurial resurgence of the craft worker and entail 'hard' work. Worse, even anthropological accounts may revert to a classed language to express disquiet with such spaces – Alexei Golubev takes earlier observers to task for their disgust at yards and stairwells of apartment blocks as 'spaces of alienation', dehumanizing the users of this space and belittling their motives (2020: 111). In reality, even in my own experience, stairwells were also understood as places of leisure and freedom. Most problematically, because these practices can only be grasped in their full meaning using micro-level methods of ethnographic engagement, the automatic assumption on the part of mainstream economists is to dismiss them as irrelevant. They are seen as 'anecdotal' or anachronistic in the greater scheme of things. After all, if garage tinkering were truly significant, surely the Russian government would get a hold of it and economists find a way of gauging it. For me this shows how partial and unsatisfactory is the projection of knowledge about Russian society.

The fact is, we *do* get very telling glimpses of the way nomadicity acts as a major constraint on the 'big' politics of the Russian regime. Almost like clockwork, year after year one of the technocratic 'liberal' elite will come out with a speech or proposal to 'make white' (make visible and legal) the enormously dynamic 'minor' part of the economy that the taxman and census taker and even local municipality has little idea of (Morris 2019b). Far from being 'minor', it is certainly a substantial part of the money income of tens of millions of individuals. For every technological/technocratic solution, the nomads find a way of 'hacking' the system. As the macro-political logic of rentier state capitalism faltered in Russia, even before the war on Ukraine, people began to notice a turn from hydro-carbon extraction as its *raison d'être* to neo-feudal expropriation. For a while, observers began to talk of 'people as the new oil' – after all, the informal economy did seem ripe for 'whitening' and Russians still received subsidized or low-cost utilities, petrol, housing and other benefits. Seasoned economists and pundits like Vladislav Inozemtsev and Valerii Solovei aligned their analyses with the common sense of political science on Russia: people are supposedly atomized, passive and unable to recognize common interest; therefore, their ability to resist the extractive state machine was broken.

The 'lines of flight' framing I have used here underlines the irresistible counter-current to extraction and state agencies' efforts to fix people in place. As mobilization of military personnel for the war in Ukraine continues, we see the imperfect application of the digital control society brought to bear in a relatively ineffectual way reminiscent of the battle with Covid-19. The state-formation resorts to ambushing young men in the street and even using face-recognition software to find runaways at the apartments of their grandmothers. This should be seen as a sign of weakness overall in terms of capacity, not strength. As I write this chapter in 2023, some of my interlocutors are snared in the wildest of circumstances. Even then, they have ingenious tricks up their sleeves, like wearing a 'Scream' mask at the shared entry-way where the cameras are. However, the majority of people's mobility describes the nomadic trajectory – deterritorialization to re-territorialization. Recamping – whether physically, or in employment from the locale where they are most likely to be snared. Rematerialization on some smooth yet reassuring surface where mobilization for the war is less likely. As we saw earlier, for those with more of a footing in the formal economy this is also possible. One can quit a job as a lathe operator in a fixings firm for a 'better' (safer) job in aluminium extrusion. The Obninsk-based metallurgical enterprise is not on the list for military mobilization of workers. For the nomadic, a line of flight away from the war is about remaining in place so as better to anticipate where the next blow will come from.

The Deleuzian frame, together with the micropolitical idea of voices-from-below that Rancière inspires, is something I have always had in mind when reflecting on deterritorial-reterritorial practices together with their initiators and participants. People of course generally don't like to think of themselves as 'nomads' because of the connotations of the word. However, the 'flight' to autonomy (which not-so-paradoxically requires social embedding) and the idea of a reflexive and intersubjective movement are articulated widely (Morris 2016). For many, the imperative and – dare I say it – even desire to remove oneself remain. To keep a distance from certain eyes of the state for the cause of social reproduction (a dignified life for oneself and one's children). To enable an element of self-

6. Nomads: An Intermezzo on Garages

regulation without the same forms of hierarchical oversight in the harsh labour market, we encountered earlier. These imperatives emerge as strongly shared values and desiderata. Nomadic spaces, whether economically determined or not, question by their existence the 'proper' social order of Russia's political economy. The presupposition to much nomadic space in Russia is of equality. This equality is not distributed from above but actively made from below. According to the challenge to the liberal sense of the political, this nomadic dissensus is the essence of politics. In Rancièrian terms: where the partition of the sensible according to notions of 'the police' is not manifest, the political may arise.

The political implications of the 'informal economy' have a history stretching through the whole of the Soviet period (the retreat of the Soviet state during the 1920s New Economic Policy, to name just one episode) and beyond, as the *Khamovniki* researchers at the Moscow Higher School of Economics have shown in a series of projects, but particularly in their work on Russian 'seasonal labour migration' – an unstoppable and almost invisible force of human nature (Plusnin et al. 2015). The refusal of police-ordered 'allotment' aligns Rancière's ideas (2001: 10) of the political with Deleuzian notions of movement through space in contradistinction to the state. What is distributed in nomadic spaces in Russia – whether people, materials, money, knowledge – is allotted at the outside, while still in contact with state-ordering.

In this chapter, in sketching out the hazy outlines of the nomad spaces I am guilty of emphasizing the masculine dominated and also reinforcing an undeserved picture that after all, nomads are essentially a re-feudalized *homo economicus*. Nothing could be further from the truth, but it requires another chapter – on craft, production as pleasure, and a less gendered form of 'tinkering' – to do full justice to this movement away from capture and towards a newly socialized striving that is so important in Russia today.

Chapter 7

CRAFT AS POLITICS: FROM SALVAGE ECONOMIES TO MENDING THE WORLD

From the perspective of the last chapter, the reader could be forgiven for assuming that the only source of micropolitical association is in masculine garages and workshops, or 'escape' into the informal economy. They may reasonably object that the nomadic lines of flight depicted are only available to a relatively déclassé type of small-town (once again: male) denizen. He is youngish, with little to lose and a long-standing embeddedness within a particular type of classed community. In this chapter, I trace equally important underground currents. These express a striving towards autonomy in the 'mundane' practices of craft, creativity and other seemingly innocuous intersubjective practices.

From learning to cross-stitch imaginary local landscapes of wool and cotton, to the fad of Soviet furniture restoration among the Muscovite lower-middle class, a commonwealth of crafty things emerges. People take salvage, repair and mending seriously, even embodying an entrepreneurial 'craft revival' in Russia (Krupets and Epanova 2023). One day in 2015, I was sent out in a taxi to scour Moscow for a particular Scandinavian furniture oil for my restorer acquaintances. Even in the village of Kamenka I was entangled in craft: could I bring a particular metal part from Britain (the titanium must be better there) for a worker to repair a tool?

These practices help people recapture various values they perceive as missing-in-the-present, yet attainable markers of sociality in pursuit of the good. While sometimes private and personal, many activities can be traced back to the Soviet values of culture-as-volition encompassed by the term *samodeiatelnost*. This term most often translates as 'amateur dramatics' and refers to the corresponding tradition in many thousands of Soviet cultural circles and clubs at their height in the 1960s. However, the root of this word, 'self-action', highlights an inherent tension. Soviet 'culture' was intended to be carefully channelled and controlled from above. The reality – also observable today in conditions of paranoid wartime surveillance – was that individual and collective pursuits were more likely to be spontaneous, at odds with the aims of the state, and emanating from inherent needs and desires from below. An alternative, perhaps more common meaning of the word *samodeiatelnost* [unsanctioned initiative], refers to disapproved actions that occur in conflict with the norms or plans of an authority.

168 *Everyday Politics in Russia*

Homemaking is political because so many practices blur the distinction between productive workplaces, garages and the domestic sphere. Susan Reid (2006) wrote on the open-ended ideologizations of domestic decoration and arrangement in the USSR. Throughout the Soviet period of mass-housing, to be authentically socialist was to display autonomy and resourcefulness in 'personalizing' the domestic space, with an assumption of various forms of repair, mending and making to complete the home (Smith 2010). And this 'feeling' for the socialist home was thoroughly internalized and eventually conceded by state ideology as normal and even desirable. The achievement of an authentic 'homely' space within a socially mixed housing block was key to socialist legitimacy because it allowed large numbers of people to experience a sense of dignity (Smith 2010: 128–30). This dignity derived not only from new access to privacy, but from semi-autonomous making and mending. But homecrafting was always held in tension with the official sphere, and therefore potentially disruptive.

Today, because of their social nature linked to broader questions of recognition, practices as diverse as DIY repair and making, gardening, as well as semi-public crafts have a potentially deviant quality, and may be interpreted or articulated as elements of the micropolitical.[1] *Craft* in multiple intersubjective modalities, scales and in utopian yet embedded circumstances is part of a 'form of life' as emancipation. This is the proposition of variegated thinkers loosely grouped as 'new materialist', and 'more-than-social movement' theorists of 'craftivism' (Hawkins and Price 2018, Papadopoulos 2018, Pellizzoni 2022, Tacchetti et al. 2022). Craft as an affirmative moment links to the micropolitical as developed by both Rancière and Deleuze (Checchi 2021) unfolded in the previous chapter. Micropolitics are implicated with prefigurative and materially focussed reworldings. This is valid even on a tiny scale: 'a "form-of-life" as a doing tailored to being' (Pellizzoni 2022: 157).

Crafty activity speaks to 'transverse' ethics because it presupposes connectivity (with the material of the world, and with others in similar pursuits) prior to institutional capture or affirmation. Practices are political because they develop new regimes of perception. Craft is also related to reterritorialization because it is invariably 'woven into the fabric of landscapes and lives' (Hawkins and Price 2018:2). It sticks stubbornly in place so as to connect with material to be worked on and with others in a common pursuit. Recall the fishtanks discussed earlier. Making DIY aquariums was equally political as it was social. It meant scavenging in the ruins of Soviet factories – acknowledging the value of socialist production-scapes even as they were dying. Making fishtanks required collaboration and

---

1. On the historical tension in the USSR between the control of culture and its more 'cosmopolitan' expression, including in amateur dramatics, see Tsipursky on 'socialist fun' (2016). 'Self-action' is not the same word as 'DIY' craft or activity which is *samodelnyi*, deriving from the verb 'to make'. *Samodel* (self-made) as a noun can have the flavour of an inferior, improvisational quality. The term for craft is of a different root: *remeslo*, but often has a narrower meaning than in English.

7. Craft as Politics

169

'socialist' competition – complex forms of recognition. Fishtanks 'domesticate' industrial production to crafts beyond the consumption economy, where scrap material like acrylic and plastics could be worked on in leisure time and usually at home. Fishtanking links deindustrialization as a resource (gleaning) to the 'natural' environment – fusing them in craft: river pebbles and hardwood stumps (the aquatic biome) sit in a container of waste hydrocarbon (acrylic glass is essentially a plastic). Fishtanking makes visible the community as engaged in a minor kind of utopianism – making biomes capable of withstanding the catastrophe their builders live through. For Papadopoulos (2018) 'compositional politics' emerge as part of a Rancièreian shift towards (re)generative changes in the conditions of life. These are 'more than social movements' because they are not prescriptive, and the primacy of resistance is to be found in the creation and experimentation over opposition, and 'aesthetic' intertwining of creativity and politics (Checchi 2021: 148, 137).

In many cases of making and mending in this chapter, any impetus that might stem from expressing class distinction through craft is detuned by the necessity of cooperation. Here I will focus mainly on the small town of Izluchino, but what is remarkable is how different strata in this sharply unequal society have much in common – as if mending a small part of the world with an eye to the past and future was a common expression of micropolitical desire. Even in the small town itself there are strongly marked economic differences, with the emergence of a new middle class of bureaucratic functionaries – better rewarded than others by a new social compact whereby state workers are supposedly better paid and protected. Nonetheless, the new middle classes are just as likely to lust after a new crotchet stitch, share harvested flower seeds for yard plantings, or attend Claymation classes in the Soviet-style House of Culture facilities – historically a site of the institutionalized collective cultivation of arts and entertainment.[2]

My first encounter with how seriously people treat craft was when I documented in Izluchino what we might now call a viral pastime: home-made tropical fishtanks (Morris 2013). The fruit of networking and skill-exchange, hand-made decorative elements were given pride of place in people's modest, and sometimes rundown homes. People like forklift driver Sasha were keen to replace manufactured and shop-bought elements essential to the functioning of the aquariums with their own, including filters and heating elements. But framing this as cultural 'capital'- building and distinction-making was inadequate. The practice of building a biosphere capable of sustaining tropical fish (not shop-bought, but home-bred and

---

2. The 'House of Culture', *dom kultury*, is a holdover from Soviet times. A community arts centre with many activities traditionally served urban settlements of varying size and funded, like many facilities, by enterprise subsidy. Falling into disrepair in the 1990s and 2000s, many Houses have been partially renovated recently to reinforce the Soviet-era normative ideal of culture: traditional entertainments and crafts of 'improving' quality on communal life (Donahoe and Habeck 2011) staged in a specific site of control and supervision by the state (White 1990).

170 *Everyday Politics in Russia*

swapped between friends and neighbours) was dependent on cooperation between members of an extended social network – in particular the meta-occupational community I have frequently elaborated in this book. Exchange and learning to make the not-unsophisticated items required embedding in a peer-network characterized by recognition of equality.

In my time in Izluchino, I remained 'outside' the mutual-recognizing network of families' dark arts of cutting acrylic, painting pebbles, making carbon filters and the like. The practice was specific to making precarious lives more habitable; a defiance against the absurd inhabitation we encountered earlier. It was compensatory in some ways: providing a kind of productive autonomous outlet and skill co-recognition. As an outsider, I could not give or receive recognition because I did not display the *techne* of the maker. Showing skill was complementary to lifeways (or, 'forms-of-life') in the face of severe want. Fishtanking was aligned with other practices of *salvage as provisioning*. Tanks were made from surplus, stolen, 'obtained' or found materials, often related to industrial processes, themselves 'surplus' or precarious. The specialist metalworking plant and plastic extrusion factory from my initial fieldwork are now defunct (Morris 2016). Alongside the crafty pastime of fishtanks, such phenomena provided 'practical' provisioning elements such as furniture, food and the means of further self-production and a modicum of independence from the consumer economy.[3] Activities were incorporated into a moral economy of the poor (who remain the majority in Russia). This economy comprised men and women as practical self-sufficient subjects who saw themselves as superior to middle-class people. So there admittedly was a 'negative' element of class distinction. More importantly, there was competition in making a bigger and better aquarium *within* a particular social milieu, but as a 'game-like' process it required cooperation, help and mutual recognition of the 'rules'. Few thought of the resulting objects as the result of single individuals.

This 'extended network of practice' harked back to the brigade-team relationship in Soviet times within the compressed social geography of the factory. It produced its own 'socialist feeling' of equality and mutual respect deriving from useful labouring personhood – a reality that of course may not have existed for more than fleeting moments and spaces in the Soviet period itself. In this chapter, I revisit the practice of fishtanking, but shift the perspective from salvage as provisioning – a type of gleaning in the ruins of postsocialism – to creative making and mending as political categories. Xenia Cherkaev's work (2023) centres on gleaning as the work of collecting, reusing and making in an economy of remainders. The origins of gleaning lie in biblical injunctions to leave behind the remainder of a harvest for the poor. In medieval and even modern Europe, gleaning was considered at different times and places to be a right enshrined in

---

3. Alexandrina Vanke notes (2024: 186), alongside Petr Jehlička (2021: 9–10), that food self-provisioning and gardening in Eastern Europe should not be seen as merely a survival strategy of the poor, instead emphasizing such practices as creative, enjoyable and at least partly political, along the lines of the moral economy model.

7. Craft as Politics

social relations. Cherkaev describes how the famous Stalinist death penalty for gleaning during famine gave way to a kind of unwritten right-to-remainder under later socialism. Under conditions of shortage in the consumer economy, gleaning materials for personal use became just as acceptable as the better-documented relations of *blat* (delayed reciprocal favour exchange). Uncovering more diverse and durable practices like the aquarium crafts I described in detail ten years ago, I focus here on three ethnographic moments and their political meaning: family woodworking, a network of embroiders and oil painters, and thirdly, a complex constellation of people connected with metalworking within the House of Culture facilities. The latter includes children's craft groups within a different facility, yard gardening and decoration. In a final coda-section, I describe street stickering and graffiti – a more overtly political practice that allows us to transition to the book's final empirical chapter on 'open' political activism.

What communitarian philosophers tell us about 'good' craft

I watched from the sidelines in Izluchino as acquaintances would visit each other to help work on the aquariums, bringing bits of scrap material, tools or even hand-made contraptions such as specialized acrylic clamps and moulds.

> It's nice when people come to you outside work for help – they phone you up and check on how you're doing … don't be afraid, someone will see and try to help you. We just spend time together like normal people … get satisfaction from it – that they did it themselves. I suppose it's a kind of inner happiness. You've just got to try to do it!

Sasha, my very nomadic and later unemployed forklift driver, said this to me over his shoulder as he and two others fixed some aluminium foil to the lid of his aquarium. The extended conversation this quotation is taken from served as a neat summary of my previous book about making the precarious habitable in the ruins of postsocialism (Morris 2016). Frequent articulation, as well as observation, of 'inner happiness' in engaging in shared pursuit of this and other craft-hobbies led me to explore these practices as productive of a self-sufficient 'good'.

To escape the frame of necessity, compensation or mere complementarity to a salvage life-world, I looked to the work of neo-Aristotelean and communitarian philosopher Alasdair MacIntyre (1981). This strand of communitarian thinking rescues forms of sociality where practices result in an 'internal good' – i.e. recognition of the excellence of that practice that cannot be reduced to material advantage or even superior status (Knight 2008).[4] The MacIntyrian concern with

---

4. My own reading of MacIntyre, like Andrew Sayer's, is indebted to the work of Russel Keat (2008). Keat makes it clear that there is a slippage between notions of 'good', and goods as products of practice. He notes that external goods might be thought of as instrumental

moral development by the marginalized sees it as a precondition to participatory politics that escape a liberal-individualist frame.[5] 'Practices' describe activities which are ends-in-themselves, not means to an end. Most importantly, building on this communitarian tradition, 'practices' require embedding in a particular mutually recognizing social setting.

The desire for recognition as a mark of equality is central to Andrew Sayer's (2005: 55) notion of the moral significance of particularized identity, explicitly building on MacIntyrian concepts. Sayer's (and my) interest in communitarian philosophy was prompted by a concern with the social geography of dispossessed moral communities. However, a craft focus concerned with a recovery of an ideal of the (internal) good allows us to build out of that frame to a more universalist proposal. It also moves beyond Pierre Bourdieu's famous relational notion of dialectical competition (cultural capital as distinction). Thinking back to Rancière's primarily symbolic language-based approach, 'dissensus' is limited to proletarian speech. Using craft and other shared pastimes we can shift attention to the political content of cultural work. From Bourdieu's cultural consumption, we can move the focus back to a (socialized) desire for production.

Like Sayer, I build on Macintyre's communitarian politics, making use of his idea of 'goods internal to practice'. This is an intersubjective frame where 'practitioners themselves take the lead in defining their internal goods, though this does not rule out contestation of their definitions and identifications, indeed debate may be intrinsic to the vigour of the practice' (Sayer 2005: 112, Morris 2013). Internal goods generally rest on the skills and excellences developed through participating in activities and practices. Most importantly, they cannot be alienated through exchange. Here, Sayer's reading recalls discussion of the traces of Soviet propertizing of use-value we referred to earlier. Furthermore, the materialization of internal goods reminds us of anthropological proposals like Michael Lambek's. For Lambek (2010: 3), means-focussed activities are an example of Aristotle's 'actuality', and show how the 'ordinary is intrinsically ethical and ethics intrinsically ordinary'.

As we saw in Chapter 5, Cherkaev (2023) highlights the distinctions in Soviet property cosmologies between 'use', 'benefit' and 'ownership'. These distinctions allowed ethical justifications by people to re-appropriate material resources for

---

ones and of course have a place in any discussion of human flourishing. Furthermore, Keat advances the discussion of goods in relation to the market economy and consumption. He points out that although marketized items of private property are acquired through transactions facilitated by external goods like money, they are often enjoyed in the context of non-market activities and relationships. In other words, consumer goods often have an important role in non-market *practices* (Keat 2008: 5–6). This is a useful jumping off point into the world of craft. Can production become a form of practice and what does it say about people's valuing of the internal goods resulting from it?

5. This is somewhat in contrast to Jacques Rancière's work where a movement via morality to political consciousness is less visible.

'non-public' use. Elsewhere in *Gleaning for the Common Good*, Cherkaev illustrates the intersection between craft as more than salvage and the concerns of the previous chapter – the desire for autonomous production beyond hierarchies. 'Gleaning' is a less familiar term that fits the creative salvage of material and personhood which emerge as a result of the imperfect allocative and 'market' economies of socialism and postsocialism respectively. In Cherkaev's study for example, a loose Soviet collective of mountaineering enthusiasts creates light-weight kayaks in 'communal' production from scrounged and stolen materials. The actual crafting is surreptitiously carried out in workplaces or at home. Cherkaev's ethnography observes how political morality emerges through collectivist use-right. Waste from military-industrial lightbulb manufacture serves to facilitate making decorative glassware such as flowers and plates – this is *gleaning in common* and links the Soviet with the contemporary period. For the practitioners, they were engaged in Soviet self-making, collective labour and ethical obtaining but 'not a state thing, now receding into memory' (Cherkaev 2023: 45, 48).

Cherkaev's research is exceptional because most studies of such practices see the expression of a genuine commitment to collectivist thinking as an impossibility. The interpretation of practices remains wedded to methodological individualism. For Alexey Golubev and Olga Smolyak (2013), creative hobbies produce the acceptable face of individualism in the USSR. They are influenced by Vera Dunham's now canonical tracing of the promotion under Stalin of middle-class values. Golubev and Smolyak make the nuanced point that consumption desires were incorporated into acceptable communist practices via DIY. Practical skills could be applied in a way that improved the Soviet gendered self – enculturing them appropriately – decorum in dressmaking for women, practical mechanics and engineering as male mastery of matter and space. However, not much attention is paid to how many of these practices were carried out intersubjectively. As a result, DIY and *blat* are usually interpreted as redirected libidinal desires of frustrated consumers and an 'essential technique of individualization in a culture which had always officially emphasized and prioritized collectivity' (Golubev and Smolyak 2013). No one would deny the importance of individual action (self-efficacy) aimed at world-making in any society – including self-centred ends-directed agency. However, the agent's freedom, while consisting in autonomous deliberation, takes place in a particular social milieu. In reality, the skills of Soviet DIY, like those of today, were taught and exchanged within family and friendship groups and gendered fantasies of individual mastery were less important. The sociality of such milieux helps us understand gleaning, or salvage as a micropolitical practice – utopian, intersubjective, practical and other-regarding.

Many examples of co-production in crafts, hobbies and pastimes resonate with a particular social intensity because of the meta-occupational community in which they take place. Metalwork hobbies require skills that men acquired working together in a collective work environment. As Tatjana Thelen (2011) has pointed out, the way workplace relations stimulated strong social ties and even emotionally intense relationships in the socialist period remains a blindspot to scholarship. This is partly due to the carrying over from Western sociology

174   *Everyday Politics in Russia*

assumptions about Fordism and post-Fordism that may not be applicable outside the core global north. From Fordist experience, work-relations are seen as inferior, non-voluntary, 'weak tie' associative forms. In Soviet-type societies, the opposite was frequently true. Alexandrina Vanke, in her book-length study of working-class creativity, has also argued that 'ordinary culture' of craft, arts and gardening stimulates the political and ethical in various ways: promoting a 'national imaginary [...] a sense of attachment to the nation' through parochial and mundane practices of occupying space – in particular, through housing block yard-tending and cultivation (2024: 39). This can give rise to a popular nationalism and local patriotism that is by degrees politically prefigurative or insularly xenophobic. Taking Vanke's focus on handicraft and creativity as a cue, we dive into the worlds of making and mending. First up, the intergenerational communication of craft as skill – in turning wood.

Woodcraft as a shared imaginary accessing the past

I was surprised to encounter an electric lathe in the dingy yet spacious flat of a retired railroad engineer in Izluchino's five-storey brick apartment buildings. Once on the insulated balcony, the smell of woodshavings and the dust was unmistakable. Denis Grigorievich had worked on the railways but like his father had always turned wood, making figurines from pictures or his own invention. His father had taught himself this art after suffering an industrial accident and becoming permanently disabled. Denis strongly articulated the importance of a locus of control. Derived from his father's battle with adversity – in the late Soviet period, this striving for autonomy in making stemmed from precarity: it was hardly possible to survive on a disability pension, let alone in the 1990s. But Denis also made woodworking into a kind of double-virtue – a practice where as a 'good' it was valued internally with many unique pieces not offered for sale, but others were made to order for profit.

As a kind of baseline, this woodworking is quite a typical case of highly skilled home-production valued for its own sake but also a reminder of the necessity of self-resourcefulness. In anthropologically emic categories, this was expressed as the need for an ability 'to make things' not only to get money, but to become an ethical person of worth. Denis reflected on how after the collapse of the USSR, this intergenerationally transferred skill was one of the few things that allowed him to derive value as a person while not losing himself to fatalism. He was anxious his daughter, now in her forties, develop her own creative impulses and interests. Katya, who had married a Muscovite and lived in the capital in modest circumstances, made jewellery, painted in oils and ran an afterschool group where children made their own toys from recycled and 'gleaned' (usually surplus and 'worthlessly' discarded) materials. Of interest here is the conscious and unconscious valuing of crafts for various 'political', and politically sensitizing reasons, in an intersubjective and intergenerational expression. We come back to Katya in a short while.

7. Craft as Politics

Figure 5 The folk craft fair in Izluchino.

Olga Gurova (2009) builds on the idea that objects have a 'cultural biography' and applies this frame to the lifespan of clothing in Soviet society. In the Soviet period, the 'social demise' of things could be indefinitely delayed by reuse and repurposing. In the present, the memory of a culture of preservation in an economy of shortage persists. This trace of a cultural biography can generate a moral economy less sympathetic to consumption via money-wealth. An alternative to 'fast fashion' and disposable clothing, the cultural biography of Soviet garments foregrounds the intersection of things, mending and making, and values that resonate politically with 'dissensus'. The realization of Soviet people as active crafters of clothing and other things led to the creation of uniquely salvaged materials that were 'sad to throw out' (Gurova 2009: 55). Both creation and preservation were – according to Gurova – politically charged with discontent and resistance. However, with time, the durability of Soviet-remade garments itself becomes a source of political propertizing. The 'thing' is recognized as containing a staying power that allows the insertion of the owner into its 'cultural biography' – primarily via repurposing.

Denis' woodworking and his daughter Katya's subsequent incorporation of his figurines into her own practice in various ways gave 'things' – and the connection they represented between generations – a political flavour. In one example, she created a photocollage of her fathers' figurines inspired by Soviet film characters. The figurines were placed within incongruous settings – such as a lavish shopping mall with high-end shops, a run-down abandoned factory setting,

176 *Everyday Politics in Russia*

or an ultra-modern, Chinese-built metro station. Children in her afterschool club were tasked with trying to insert the past into the present in a way not to underline its incongruity, but to highlight its value against transience. This also 'salvaged' one of the few memories available to many people of (self)-production from a lost time. Many middle-class children did not have any such artefacts at their disposal and were instead asked to find Soviet-era packaging (usually a retro version of it) or clothing instead. One child remarked on the durability of her grandparent's acrylic pullover and its retention of a bright green colour, provoking a conversation about the disposability of contemporary consumption. Like the fishtanking, while I was not a participant in craft, as an observer I sensed these practices came to prefigure what Schechner calls the 'actual' (1988): 'change, creativity, and future making not in the realm of presumably shared imaginaries [...] but as something actualized in the event by concrete articulations of things and processes' (Halse 2018: 183).

Knitting not cruel optimism, but visualized utopias

In 2018, Lena and her sisters sit in their clean and bright family apartment in the Komsomolsky microdistrict of Izluchino. Their mother is still putting in her shifts at the factory and their father poots around on his electric scooter to their vegetable allotments. Youngest sister in her late twenties, Yulia, has a nail-painting business operated from the home and she earns more than the rest. The other two, a bit older, have 'bad' jobs they don't like to talk about. The insidious nature of their art and craft catches me out. I spend many years focussing on their parents, and the children's day-jobs, but the most important thing in their lives is staring me in the face. Yes, I went on hikes to collect litter with them when they were in a 'scene'.[6] That was when they were both newly married and now both are divorced.

The then-twenty-somethings would all load up with sacks and spend a couple of nights camping along the river and collecting in bales rubbish left by the anglers and the tourists. Then, a brother-in-law would come in a flatbed and collect it. And the barbeques and night swimming would continue. At home they obsessively learn new techniques, from watercolours they move to oil painting. This was prior to the advent of YouTube videos and so they learned from others and from books. The result was passable landscapes and still lifes. More recently, they learn cross stitch. Some of their social circle just knit patterns of teddy bears and kitschy templates from magazines, but the sisters and a few friends knit landscapes 'of the

---

6. 'Scene' here translates *tusovka* – a loose-knit group of young friends who often have a common interest. While many loose-knit groups no longer use this Soviet-era word, the word retains utility sociologically to define youth-group identities. See Pilkington (2002) and Narvselius (2016).

7. *Craft as Politics*

river as we'd like it to be', and of an idealized Izluchino – with a restored monastery complex (no one knows if such a thing really existed – all we can find are cellars). The Children's House of Culture is miraculously restored from its near-derelict state. In the bright wools of the stitching there is no obscene graffiti or leaking roofs. Pride of place in the apartment is a cross-stitch map of the locality with imagined, exotic sounding places – an ice-cream parlour in the factory complex, a merry-go-round at the back of the tyre shop.

The rise of cross-stitch is no doubt a global phenomenon and the majority of practitioners make modern-day kitschy samples from templates. Like elsewhere, cross-stitch communities have sprung up in Izluchino that both express local 'territorialized' realities and link people online. Similarly, in Russia there is a mix of the progressive and conservative potential to craft communities. The act of making things together with others is a form of 'being at home in the world' that feminists have proposed as politically empowering (Fisk 2012). Certainly, in the sisters' case this was unambiguously articulated as an anchoring activity expressing their feeling for their 'small motherland' in a situation of acknowledged crisis. Many women readily take up nostalgic or conservative themes, including patriotic ones since the war in Ukraine began. Lena's extended network showed a more utopian territorialized bent – creating real and imaginary versions, and not just pastoral, of their familiar places without looking backwards too much. The ordinary cares might be an impasse, but this is not the 'cruel optimism' described by Lauren Berlant (2011). The production of crafts is utopian and reflects the deep traumas of the past and present, even to the extent of many completely disavowing the present and reality. However, 'flourishing' and actualization are visible in the practice itself, which is often a shared and communal one. Berlant says that cruel optimism results from desiring despite the unattainability of an object. The good life dreamt of comes up against the 'compromised conditions of possibility' (2011: 24). Lena gave away the stitch map to her sister when she left to live north of St Petersburg. Just like that. It hangs in the hallway of their Svetogorsk apartment rather modestly. However, Lena kept the oil paintings for her parents.

Berlant prompts us to think about 'crisis ordinariness' and the 'intimate public sphere'. Her findings on US neoliberalism are not news to denizens of postsocialist countries, as Katařina Kolářová has argued (2017). The desired good is articulated in both the crafted item and the practice itself. The affective reworking of the 'false consciousness' argument by post-structuralist writers like Berlant deserves critique. She makes the charge that by clinging to optimism and fantasy, people's 'affective attachment' means they endure and inure themselves to failing systems and mounting injustice. Like the philosophers who inspire it, 'cruel optimism' largely ignores the insights of phenomenology. What is missing is that the intersubjective experience and the realization that we can undertake action in a kind of rhythm and responsiveness with others (whether in stitching or not) offer a way beyond thinking about individual subjectivities trapped by their own fantasies and

178   *Everyday Politics in Russia*

nightmares in a container of the self.[7] Where Berlant (2011: 99–100) is more supportive of my argument is in her tantalizing suggestion that in overcoming the false lure of cruel optimism, spaces of ordinariness can help articulate and 'agency can be an activity of maintenance, not making'. This recalls Veena Das' (2007: 7) memorable phrase about the capacity for all kinds of structural and real violence to 'seep in to the ordinary' but which by the same token provoke a 'descent' into that 'ordinary' to rediscover sources of agency.[8]

In the House of Culture salvagers and menders meet

Within the same 'scene' as Lena and her sisters moves a mixed-gender constellation of makers, menders and salvagers, all revolving about access to the enormous brick House of Culture (*Dom kultury*) in Izluchino. The *DeKa*, as it is known, is owned and run by the municipality. Built in the 1980s and falling into disrepair throughout the 1990s and 2000s, it contains a warren of rooms and performance spaces. Housing private businesses and the municipal offices, it also served as a nomadic refuge for employed 'cultural workers' (such as community artists and performers), technicians and maintenance workers doing work unrelated to the arts, and an extended network of – often underemployed – young friends. It was through a local librarian there that I originally met the 'scene' in 2009. Lena and her sisters were there along with the male electricians Vasya and Yasha (then in their late twenties). Still paid a bare subsistence wage, they now supplement their income with a mobile disco, but their main source of activity aside serving the municipality's needs is welding decorative window grills, and fashioning DIY metal and wood objects, from hunting knives to recasting lead as shot for anglers. They learned part of their trade from a professional repair workshop in the same building run by an older man who fixes garden tools and refrigerators.[9] In a separate building

7. For Berlant, the intersubjective frame is relatively neglected for the affective, bodily orientation of a subject, albeit alienated and perhaps split from herself. To Berlant, intersubjectivity is a fantasy or fake (2011: 197, 250). Even affect is hardly a force to be reckoned with being always 'mediated' by a pre-exiting identity and bracketed off from cognition.

8. Penelope Deutscher (2016: 190–1) reads Das as responding to Foucault's work constructively, to suggest that 'forms of death are understood to combine with forms of life'. As part of the recovery of agency within a renewed emphasis on the 'philosophy of the ordinary', it is useful to think of many materialist everyday approaches as responding in some way to Foucauldian biopolitical thinking.

9. The 'trade' in fixing electrical appliances expanded after the beginning of the Russo-Ukraine war in 2022 as appliances became more expensive and spare parts harder to find. Some elements of the appliance repair economy resemble that described in India by Badami (2018). 'Repair' is inadequate to the understanding of creative repurposing, 'upgrading' and innovation entailed in this informal work. Similarly to Badami's findings, Russian practitioners make similar critiques of the Western idea of proprietary rights that seek to prevent DIY repairs of electronic and other products.

7. Craft as Politics

(the children's House of Culture), the older Svetlana Grigorievna (a senior cultural worker) undertakes an endless roster of children's craft circles, rather like Katya in Moscow. Here she offers no less than six forms of decorative and applied art classes, all for a small contribution from parents. She is employed by the municipality. Her real passion, however, is Slavic-pagan-inspired (*rodnoverie*) craft from natural materials. At the annual town fair, she and her husband sell exquisitely crafted items, from dream catchers (another globalized phenomenon) to soul-protectors – a kind of bark pouch with a leather strap containing dried peas. Through Svetlana I was introduced to the indomitable Tanya from Chapter 5, who comes to the Children's House of Culture to lead classes on decorative DIY arts from found objects. This is also the main stimulus behind a women's movement for yard gardening. *Rodnoverie* is often focussed on expressing placed-based belonging and may veer into the political as much as the spiritual realm.[10]

As an honorary member of the main *DeKa* 'scene' into the late 2010s, I had unfettered access to what was nominally a non-public municipal space. In fact, given its size, it was, de facto, an extension of the spaces 'aside' the state that we observed in the previous chapter. One could even think of it as an aggressive form of the nomadic line of flight – daring to take up camp right next to the source of local authority. Beyond the Houses of Culture, I was also frequently shown around the home of Svetlana's main assistant Tanya. Tanya had a workshop at the Children's House of Culture but preferred to work at home. There she displayed intricate metal models of ordinary objects: birds, cars, buildings. All made with surplus wire from the moribund factory up the road. Her favourite 'classes' instructed children in carving wooden flotsam from the river into faces and animals. There were many other 'production lines' to this salvage art and bricolage. By the mid-2010s however, she was devoting most of her time to the yard 'improvement' (the *blagoustroistvo* phenomenon recounted in Chapter 5). Tanya was engaged, with the help of political figure Tamara whom we met earlier in this book, in a *guerrilla* war with the municipality over her *guerrilla* gardening initiative.

Tanya lived in one of the most rundown blocks in Izluchino with a granddaughter and disabled son. The roof leaked and flooded the basement. She was involved for a time with the recent phenomenon of maintenance self-management by residents of apartment blocks (Smyth et al. 2023). After 2015, she had sought to semi-formalize her long-standing efforts with a group of residents to improve the one part of the local world that required little resource: the front yards. Imagine a semi-enclosed rectangular space 100 metres long by 150 metres wide. On each side is a five-storey brick block of around one hundred apartments split between four or five entry-ways. There are no lifts in the blocks and inadequate space for parking. In the spring and autumn, the yard is churned up into mud. In the summer, dust forces people to close windows. There are a few crude benches in

---

10. In Russia *rodnoverie* is sometimes simultaneously nationalistic and anti-establishment, with the potential to ally with racist ideologies (Saunders 2013).

front of the houses, an overly high pavement around the perimeter, gaps between the houses and tracks worn into the ground where people take the shortest paths. Where there is asphalt, in inadequate parking areas it gets annually broken into chunks and is haphazardly replaced, just like the children's play equipment. The only thing of permanence is the strip of neglected scrub between the pavement and the grilled ground-floor windows of the apartments.

At first, improvement of this strip of yard was entirely spontaneous. People everywhere in the former Soviet Union are probably familiar with this phenomenon: people plant saplings, vegetables and flowers under or close to their apartment windows. However, given the density of residents and the fact that the 'care' of these plots falls under the purview of either a block housing committee or local municipality, the strip-gardening is a good example of how individualized and atomized actions are always quickly entangled in necessary social intercourse and intersubjective interaction. Along with gardening, many residents undertake 'beautification' – adorning spaces with painted fences (also useful to stop trampling), and animal and other figures made from scrap materials like plastic bottles and car tyres (Vanke 2024: 65). Alexandrina Vanke showed that such 'co-creativity' activates collective and social feelings, as well as maintaining a kind of symbolic order in a disordered and unloved space. It evokes both a yearning-like 'salvage' mentality and more utopian potential. Practices of beautification may or may not have political meaning for participants, but sooner or later they result in engagement with the relevant state authority – even if at the lowest possible level, as we observed earlier in our discussion of bureaucracy. While Vanke (2024: 63) sees such practices as examples of 'everyday resistance' and politicized, other observers in Russia belittle them as 'shitsville aesthetics'.[11] This term has become an internet meme, with photographic examples of such craft published on an eponymous social media page of nearly half-a-million followers for the purposes (mainly) of ridicule. Just the name alone ('shitsville' – which sounds ruder in Russian) evokes how politicized is the interpretation of the Soviet and post-socialist urban remainder, and unappreciated attempts to salvage it.

Tanya, like many yard-carers, was aware of the resistance she faced, both on the grounds that her work was 'kitsch' and 'Soviet-nostalgic', and on the basis that these spaces were the purview of the state and so it was ridiculous to try to

---

11. There are two terms to bear in mind: *Estetika ebenia* (lit. 'aesthetics of fucked-up-far-away-place') and *'mukhosransk'* – 'flyshit-ville': an unpleasant far-away place. DIY activities are denoted only by the first phrase: *'estetika ebenia'*. I have asked Russia-based colleagues why they don't write about such aesthetics in their research. Mostly, I get a negative response as if such naïvely kitsch yard-work were beneath the attention of urban studies and sociology. I would go as far to say there is an inbuilt political bias in scholarship to invisibilize the 'wrong kind' of craft and active communal work as political because of connotations with 'lower classes' or Soviet nostalgic practices.

tend them. However, as with Cherkaev's (2023) argument about propertizing, the trace of the blurry meaning of use/ownership can be extended. Any 'use', appropriation or marking of these neglected spaces can take on a political meaning because of the strong bifurcation of attitudes towards property in the last forty years. As Olga Shevchenko (2009) illustrates in her book about coping with the long crisis, many post-Soviet denizens turned sharply inward to a fetishization of personal property and a militant, even religious defence of it that becomes visible in the 'fortress' mentality in urban spaces: heavy steel doors and gratings protect apartments, gated communities of car owners take over yards, people rig garages and vehicles with traps, or arm themselves to defend their property. However, equally important is the communal caring aesthetic exemplified by the thousands of Tanyas who inhabit a space stretching from Riga to Vladivostok.

Later in the 2010s, Tanya enlisted my help with many small errands and tasks; I was but one small cog in her mobilization. From a small beginning, she began regularizing what had been informal favours and begged help: the delivery by truck of sand for paths and black earth for plantings became an annual timetable. Eventually, she gained the blessing of the municipality and the formal-informal yardwork was incorporated into the local plan with newspaper columns written about it. When she was offered a part-time job however, she declined as she wanted to exclusively focus on the daily tending of the local yard with her block neighbours:

> The thing is, this can all fall apart as soon as you turn your back. It's better to keep some distance too as if the municipality thinks they can take it for granted they will just as soon stop helping. Also, there is my responsibility to the older people here in this block. It's a kind of necessary patronage – I know how that sounds but it is true.
>
> Am I a social worker too, you ask? Well, I guess so, even I am just as lonely as anyone. As for the 'local improvement services' as they call it, they talk about how everything is privatized and how now everyone is responsible for their own upkeep in their flats. Well, if they want it that way, they can just leave us alone to get on with the yard. We'll only ask for a little help with deliveries.

Forms-of-life in craft as prefigurative politics

Sceptics might see this chapter as a narrow foray into 'lifestyle'-as-politics which assumes that traditional forms of struggle and organization are impossible or doomed to failure (Pellizzoni 2022). More broadly, craftism as a form-of-life ought to be evaluated within the context of progressive prefigurative politics (Monticelli 2021). This evaluation revolves not so much around the question of whether the embodying of alternatives genuinely critiques the status quo, 'refuses' it in some way, or not. Instead, this chapter proposes that processes originating as responses to precarious social reproduction coalesce over time. They link to creative, socially connecting and means-rather-than-ends practices in pursuit of an internal good. Some of these, if not all of them, genealogically trace back to 'ancestors' in Soviet times. Salvage and gleaning on the ruins of postsocialism and the leftovers of capitalism do comprise a folk politics: they acknowledge dispossession and the new barriers towards the good life without giving in to 'cruel optimism' about overcoming them. They are pragmatic and practical in a way that means they are often misunderstood and ignored by our logocentric scholarly focus on social movement manifestos.[12]

Prefiguration is often opposed in the post-Marxist literature to accelerationism. We need to anticipate a future liberated form of society, any way we can. Key concepts are embodiment, connectivity with like-minded, envisioning without deterministic templates, affirmation-as-representation (in minor, mundane ways) of ideals despite the backdrop of continuing inequality, want and exploitation (Monticelli 2021). The focus in this literature is still logocentric and self-conscious – what Monticelli calls the creation of '*intentional* communities' which may or may not be openly oppositional (2021: 108–9). We will turn in the next chapter to these self-consciously activist groupings. Prefigurative political thinking is strongest when it acknowledges how mundane practices may powerfully actualize a desired future in the present, be it horizontal decision-making (in the yard gardening, in the *subbotnik* rubbish collecting) and immediate results in the material world of utopian imaginings. A common critique of prefiguration is that it is rooted in the privilege of the global north middle class. This is illustrated with empirical examples of 'failure' such as Occupy or Assemblist movements, sometimes criticized as 'exclusionary', individualistic and a luxury (Monticelli 2021: 111).

My point in this chapter is to show that 'politics' in the sense I have been using throughout this book, after Rancière and Deleuze, exists along different points on a line of flight. Mundane and seemingly innocuous practices of crocheting and painting are not exclusive of other more activist ones. They do not compensate for atomization but work up the same desiring selves that push along the line of flight towards actualizing a life of community *and* autonomy, and a productivist one at that. Not only that, recalling E. P. Thompson and Raymond Williams, practices expose pre-existing substrata of emancipatory models of culture and feeling. Many modes of utopian craftism trace their origin to ways of bringing to fruition an autonomy-in-common in the Soviet period. Next, practices reveal 'ordinary ethics' as embedded in the social side of making, craft and production. This is what Michael Lambek calls the ethical as 'a modality of social action or of being in the world' (2010: 10).

We see this modality at work in the interaction between experience, sociality and growing self-awareness of the power of making together. Yard caring, seed

12. On logocentrism, see discussion in Lefebvre (1991: 16) on the need to go beyond a 'priority-of-language thesis' that privileges logocentricity over practices in social space and body-world interactions.

7. Craft as Politics

183

planting, letter writing to the municipality and town-hall meetings are not circular or truncated. In a smaller settlement than Izluchino called Demidovo, processes of 'local initiative' as they were called, evolved out of yard care and similar problems into a successful ecological activist movement. Locals reached out to the seasoned 'interlocutors' with the state like Tanya and Tamara, and Izluchino supplied bodies and experience to the Demidovo cause.

Demidovo's case was similar in some ways to Izluchino – an ecologically sensitive site selected for exploitation by Moscow – this time for rubbish burial. Julia was a died-in-the-wool ecoactivist who had protested all over Russia in the 2010s. Through her, I was introduced to a similarly seasoned 'Navalnyite' – a young Kalugan man who had been important in building organizational capacity in the region and who had ties to Demidovo. With some help, a local pensioner in the settlement was put in touch with Greencity, a group of semi-commercial NGO 'civil society' trainers. They coached those wishing to win government grant money, but in this case their work was gratis and 'activist'. It was possible because it was carried out quietly and from a base in another regional city. They provided some legal training and slowly, local pensioner Gennady transformed himself from a concerned citizen, who had had experience only in acting like Tanya as a conduit and unpaid volunteer, to a lynchpin in collecting signatures. He drafted information *spravka* requests and reviewed court decisions and financial documents. In interview with another local activist in 2021, at which I was an observer, he said the following:

> Everywhere it turned out there were documents that could prove almost all the processes of siting the disposal dump here were in breach of law. In essence, we had to go through the motions as if we were prepared to go to the courts. This pressure and initiative are sometimes enough. The higher authorities are terribly afraid of the term 'social movement', but these tricks from below only work if you can back them up with genuinely affected people from the community itself.
>
> If we actually went to court, we'd probably lose and the financial burden would split the group. But we don't have to go that far to ward off the developers. It's like applying for a job, you set up the documentation as best you can and kind of 'dance' between authorities [*raznye instantsii*] with the paperwork. Eventually someone will feel obliged to respond. Look at this sea of document files I have in my desk – [Gennady spoke from a bedroom in his house that had been converted into a home office with a large desk covered in papers].
>
> It worked for us because Demidovo was an active place before the rubbish dump. And though we couldn't have managed without the help of Greencity and the others, there was human capacity to do something. And even state capacity to respond. It's a weird situation that the law 'works' to a certain degree if you are prepared by interaction with it. Keyed in [*podkliuchennyi*] to how it can be used to indirectly force concessions. We had the paramilitary police sent out here to intimidate, but they still backed off and re-sited the dump.

Figure 6 Collecting signatures opposing a planned rubbish dump in Kaluga region.

Gennady was making a concession to his audience because at least one of the activists present was partly affiliated with a 'systemic' opposition party (i.e. a party unwilling to directly oppose the regime). However, his comments relate to what some call the 'opportunity structure' of the fractured, overweening and overworked local bureaucracies. The 'experiential' entanglement of activists as energizing and sustaining them is explored in the following chapter. Here we should emphasize the way people can build on experiences of yard tidying to become legal experts in environmental zoning practices and the drafting of documents.

When I read accounts of prefiguration along the lines of self-conscious logocentrism, I think of these sometimes-intense practices in Izluchino and elsewhere in Russia. I reflect that emancipatory and utopian practices can 'just happen', especially when people become attuned to their common purpose in craft which connects to care for their locales. This is the value of the intersubjective framing of desire that this book foregrounds. And essentially, this frame is arguably part of the Russian intellectual tradition of mutual aid going back to Peter Kropotkin. For him, the political defence of community was as hard-wired into humans as evolutionary processes. Pellizzoni (2022: 164) writes that the risk of recuperation of 'new materialist practices' is obvious. Think about how consumption at farmers' markets becomes a new form of status competition. However, it is still worth thinking in terms of the 'how, not the what', i.e. the emancipatory practice-frame I have emphasized here: from fishtanking to yard-gardening. Furthermore, 'recuperative' critiques that argue that capitalism will always incorporate resistant practices neglect that in the contexts I am describing, the emphasis on salvage and the absent presence are already given. People use craft to show they are 'position-ready' to reembrace potential reconnection. Could these Russian craftists be far less susceptible to commodification than we usually assume about such practices? So much of what I have inadequately described with words emphasizes the practice itself for the purposes of an internal good (though many are clearly utopian too). In some cases, craftism recognizes its imbrication in commodity forms without relinquishing its parallel form-of-life: a socially embedded aspect. A case in point were the items Svetlana sold – once a year – at the town fair.

Pellizzoni (2022) writes of 'second order' emancipation after Giorgio Agamben (1996) in terms of 'doing what one is' – a merging of identity and practice – but this neglects the more powerful intersubjective aspect that is required for an 'ontology' to emerge. As Pellizzoni critically notes, Agamben's form-of-life concept relies on a monadic, individualistic subject, and is incomplete for thinking in genuinely socially utopian terms about emancipation. Reeves-Evison and Rainey, writing on repair studies, discuss the metaphorical power of crafting/mending things to represent a 'superior' social order. Henke (2000) writes of mending as a political act of foregrounding the existence of 'material' within the symbolic, and how repair extends to relational modalities between people without necessarily requiring strong discursive involvement (such as admonition, encouragement, or rhetorical justification). These currents are made visible in the relations Tanya, Svetlana and others try to build and are not untypical in community work around housing in postsocialist spaces, as numerous studies have shown (Clément and Zhelnina 2020, Smyth 2023, Zhelnina 2023). In these cases, as we shall explore further in the next chapter, 'involvement' was transformative on people prior, or independently of a logocentric-cognitive inclination to action. Finally, Kirstin Munroe (2019) reminds us that in thinking about social reproduction, we tend to forget that 'work' or 'production' at home is necessary in transforming even the most mundane of consumer goods – typically in cooking and cleaning. In my reading, household production is itself labour; one that can be mending, repair, in a cycle that – as we saw in the previous chapter – exists *aside* the consumer economy. The cycle of provisioning labour does not fully integrate with traditional consumption. In a relation of autonomy, gleaning, salvage and even creative practice, social reproduction salvage practices detune clear distinctions of property.

Conclusion

Anna Tsing relates the more-than human relationship of mushrooms and foraging people to the devastation of capitalism. She uses the assemblage concept to describe multispecies 'livable collaborations' (Tsing 2015: 28) and 'co-dependency' to survive a precarious and devastated environment (cf. Jasarevic 2015). When I first read her book, I was reminded strongly of the actual gleaning, foraging and DIY-making projects of Izluchino. I also related to Tsing's book because some people in Izluchino collect, eat and sell large quantities of mushrooms. Sometimes they sell enough in a season to buy a car with the proceeds! They forage also in the devastation of the industrial forest – the decaying and even not-so-decaying factories. In summer 2021, my friend Vanya and I carried a 25 kg roll of linoleum out of a small foreign-owned mill housed in an enormous Soviet factory complex. This was 'gleaning'. A slightly damaged roll could not be sold. The Russian manager was told to destroy it; instead, he gave it to Vanya – who worked as a night watchman at the mill. We unrolled it at his summer house in Kamenka near the industrial town. The house was built in the 1970s on a plot 'gifted' by the Soviet industrial enterprise, but it has never been entered into the cadastral register. We cut the linoleum using a hand-crafted hunting knife into fence panels and tied it to the fence posts around his vegetable plot using discarded electrical wire gleaned from some other half-life deindustrializing space. The posts are made of plastic tubing – thick black tubes for the gas industry – similarly gleaned by Vanya's brother ten years ago when he too was working in a decaying enterprise. The lack of screening of the vegetable plot from the road meant that the crops were vulnerable to both animals and passing humans – who might treat the plot as one more place to glean. Vanya's brother had given up on the plot. He suggested selling it to Moscow developers who already are turning the place into an 'eco-village' tourist site. Vanya was keen to try to avoid this fate for his 'ancestral' home.

Tsing's mushroom gatherers create a non-scalable economy in the ruins of scalable industry (exhausted commercial monoculture forestry). She calls this 'salvage' – value produced without capitalist control (2015: 63). Tsing also sees them as projects of freedom. She argues that latent commons, like the economies of mushrooms in the United States and Japan, are not exclusive human enclaves. In Russia there are improvised and nomadic connections forged by human agents between natural and deindustrializing commons. Commons of any kind presuppose a social resource of value, and an ecology of social reproduction. They remain a human-orientated construct, despite posthumanist intimations in writing such as Tsing's. Yes, they entail mutual relations between human and non-human, but as Marilyn Strathern argues, interpersonal ('social') relations are a 'special case'. They require both interaction *and* recognition (2020: 8), rather than the mushroom-human assemblage based on mere mutual 'affordances'. Furthermore, mutuality implies 'co-presence' or 'participation' in salvaging the commons (Pina-Cabral 2013). Finally, salvage and making find common roots in the humanizing of the socialist project – an experience even young people can vicariously experience, and which is transferred to them through intergenerational learning.

Galina Orlova (2004) wrote on the efforts of Soviet citizens to effect 'smoothing' of the systemic flaws of socialism through 'little tricks' of hacking the immediate environment. She argued that the ontology of Soviet personhood aimed at breaking down the division of human and material. In a vernacular set of relations, this entailed endless improvisation as the Soviet person became a unique kind of *homo faber*. In the economy of shortage and incompleteness, these little tricks were compensatory (fixing a new TV which had shorted out; protecting the inadequately lubricated door-hinges in a Soviet automobile). Learning tricks also transformed the 'domestic craftsman' into an active practitioner who saw the defectiveness of things as an illusion. Through intersubjective effort, flaws could be overcome, just as the tyranny of the object over the person was possible to tame (at the heart of Soviet Marxism's materialism). Likewise, the tyranny of the individual was possible to escape as a Soviet(ized) person. As Vanya and I pinned the linoleum to the posts, he said, 'this is our fence! We made it. We're not losers!', making explicit reference to the question of *ressentiment* described earlier in this book. The anthropology of relations proposed by Strathern and the examination of 'mutuality' by Pina Cabral are both examples of an attempt to balance subject-object structure-agency explanations by way of intersubjective, co-present and experiential understandings of the social.

'New materialist' approaches to politics give half an explanation for the politics of craft. Papadopoulos (2018) writes of creative practices in terms of 'politics as power with'. Forms-of-life are shared which reorder the practice of existing arrangements as 'alternative ecologies'. Papadopoulos, inspired by Rancière, sees as possible the emergence of a 'processural justice', a 'thick justice', even if it cannot prefigure more than its own existence. His conceptualization of craft comes close to my own when he writes that 'Craft at its core is not about making things or producing relations but about leaving yourself aside for the sake of viably coexisting

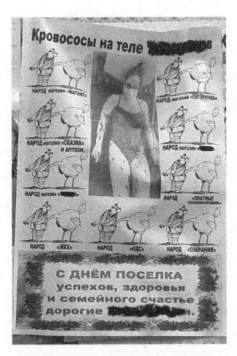

Figure 7 Political postering in Izluchino, 2019: 'Leeches on the body of the Town.'

with other things and beings' (2018: 23). He sees this as an 'imperceptible' but not invisible politics. We can transition from the politics of creative activities to activist politics by briefly mentioning how one element in the '*DeKa* scene' in Izluchino evolved over time. The same lighting technicians making hunting knives and other items soon discovered the internet, as well as stickering, and later, 3D printing to express their creativity and identity. With the help of a computer-savvy friend they contributed to the nascent local website about Izluchino 'from below' by making 'branded' stickers for their own web project called 'We Are Izluchino: this belongs to us'. Using the *DeKa* facilities they made templates: a kind of yellow triangle with the slogan overlaid. They then printed these off as sticky-backed decals and distributed them to friends and peers to be stuck on beloved places and objects in the town. Over time, this project even took on a marked political character, as pollution, violent corporate raiding, political corruption and then Russo-Ukraine war proceeded to exercise local people. Eventually they teamed up with Tamara and put up political pamphlets on her behalf. Like myriad examples from across Russia today, stencilling, stickering and old-fashioned graffiti is a major political act in social and physical spaces from whence other forms of political expression and dissent have been progressively driven out.

Chapter 8

'THIS THING WE DO': WARTIME ENTANGLEMENT OF PEOPLE IN POLITICS

This final empirical chapter focusses on reflexive political subjectivity and the emergence of 'the political' in settings of activism. It looks at people who self-identify as activists or 'active'. However, in no way should the penultimate position of this chapter indicate some kind of implicit hierarchy; that finally we come to 'real' activism – out in the open and having 'real' effects on Russian society – for good or ill. My purpose throughout has been analytical holism. The micropolitical includes different kinds of subject positions, practices and activities. The point is that however diverse the political, and whatever its direction, the relational, in-practice and grounded aspects are usually key. In this chapter, I use 'community-scale' case studies to illustrate the broader context of politicized involvement, networking and activism in the increasingly difficult domestic environment in Russia.[1] I bring out the interactions of people with their immediate social environment and how it affects trajectories into activism. I am inspired by scholars such as Karine Clément (2015), Samuel Greene (2019) and others who have foregrounded the local roots of 'unlikely mobilizations' and political activation. However, situatedness is more than a concern for locality, or intellectual and other resources that make for 'critical mass'. A key question is how people undergo transformation from 'desubjectivation' to a revival of social consciousness (Clément 2019: 9; see also Gabowitsch 2017). Here, Clément is responding to the paradigmatic presentation of Russians as atomized and unable to think of themselves as part of politics.

To help answer the question of transformation, I focus on the intersubjective experiences of activists – the social and emotional impetus for them.[2] This requires

---

1. Part of this chapter's conceptual apparatus is derived and updated from Morris (2023c). I am indebted to Mack Tubridy for discussions about 'prowar' activism and access to his interviews with such groups.

2. While my aim is to illustrate intersubjectivity as a politically activating experience, the war in Ukraine severely curtailed my ability to observe research interlocutors. Therefore, as elsewhere in this book, my evidence must remain unsatisfactorily 'logocentric' – focussed on second-hand recounts of experience and my own textual summaries of what were intense and fruitful interactions.

190   *Everyday Politics in Russia*

attention to the way a 'new social imaginary' emerges at the micro level (Clément 2019: 9) – not one person at a time, but in the interactions between people. Without this, it will be harder to give a full account of the 'bigger' questions like histories of politicization, matters of organization, as well as capacity building and migration between sites and causes of contention. I contrast the political and activist trajectories of two composite neighbours, Polina and Felix.[3] Polina 'represents' environmental activism before and since the war and its relation to anti-war actions. Felix in turn gives a flavour of another facet of defensive consolidation in Russian society which supports 'victims' in the occupied part of Ukraine but stops short of open 'pro-war' action sponsored by or aligned with the state.[4]

Drawing together strands which show how different forms of activism arise thanks to similar intersubjective resources, I examine the questions of how and in what way decentralized activism survives alienated formal political contexts, general distrust towards politics, and significant risks for organization. Russia is an exemplary case of a post-modern authoritarian society, but the point should be laboured that this book is about seeing Russia as just one part of the spectrum of regime-promoted anti-politics (alienating people from action) that exist in all societies. This chapter is a story of continually transformative activism: it is hard to define single causes or coherent groups. One week, a group works together on flyers highlighting the illegal burial of rubbish in a national park. The next week a single activist 'affiliated' to the environmentalists undertakes covert anti-war vandalism. A month later, a smaller core of collaborators funds legal advice for an elected politician to deny a planning license to a polluting plant. By the same token, solidarity in work collectives activates motivation and reflection among people who want to 'do something for Donbas', whether in the form of lethal or humanitarian aid.

Felix, who works for a local entrepreneur, is spurred on by interactions with his colleagues and boss to collect resources to be sent to Donbas since 2014. However, he couches his ethics in 'apolitical' language and discursively pivots away from prescribed scripts. After February 2022, through a process of deliberation within this charity group, a collective decision is arrived at to supply Russian soldiers with non-lethal aid. This political trajectory can be linked back to the original activities of the group and those like it. In 2022, members had felt disillusioned by their experience (in 2015) with a pro-regime sponsor, and now they wanted to distance themselves from it. Some similar groups expanded in 2023, supplying resources to aid more explicitly in fighting (ballistic vests, night-vision goggles, quadcopters). Felix's group was in an intermediate position – continuing to focus on 'humanitarian' aid. The 'whys' of this related to the genealogy of the group – its 'bitter taste in the mouth' after regime sponsorship versus its 'happier' later

---

3. Once again, it's necessary to remind readers that because of ethical concerns I am obliged to obscure more about the cases than I would like to.

4. I try to limit the use of scare-quotes, but here they are essential to indicate the one-sided view some have of who are victims in the war, but also that the terms 'anti-war' and 'pro-war' have become harder to define over time.

Figure 8 Donbas aid collectors in 2014.

association with a local business. Later, organization morphed into an informal association with Felix's motorcycle chapter – an avowedly 'non-regime' group that looked askance at what they felt were unseemly antics of well-known regime-friendly biker groups like the Night Wolves.[5] While explicitly 'pro-war' groups are much more visible since 2022, they are not the focus of this chapter, though they are discussed later in contrast to the discursive and practical distancing undertaken by Felix and company.

From Arendt's vita activa *to infectious pragmatism*

Two seemingly contrasting cases illustrate how similar the genealogy of transformative activism can be – whether it is consolidating, or 'anti' war. Nomadic and transverse activism should provoke analysis of the micropolitical

---

5. A lot of op-ed ink has been spilled about the Night Wolves, and even casual observers admit they are not representative of biker culture in Russia or elsewhere. A sociology of bikers, including Night Wolves, would probably reveal agendas that run transverse to regime aims and politics by any measure. The politics of many actual groups would be masculine mutual aid, and 'political' aims based on recreating the conditions of Soviet supra-national community. As one said to me, the Ukraine war is a 'temporary affair', and they looked forward to returning to meet with Ukrainian clubs.

192   *Everyday Politics in Russia*

foundations of contentious or substitutive politics. In a sense, this strand in political phenomenology can be traced back both to Hannah Arendt's pathbreaking work on totalitarianism and to a dissatisfaction with it. On the one hand Arendt emphasized the importance of horizontal relations between people 'in the public' prior to institutional formation. This is what totalitarian atomization aimed to destroy. On the other hand she set up a hierarchy whereby the Aristotelian ideal of *vita activa* (active rather than contemplative life) remained at the pinnacle of human behaviour associated with the individual's autonomy. For neo-republican Arendt, individuals are active when they surpass 'behaviour' or 'norm', whereas the idea of political activity as 'craft' or 'making' (highly social activities, as this book has argued) is relegated to beyond the polis (Canovan 1998, Topolski 2015).

Despite Arendt's asocial shadow cast over the active life, scholars have recently shown how emotion, co-present solidarity and creativity affect the understanding of forms of resistance written into everyday life and not reducible to intentionality (e.g. Hughes 2016, Pottinger 2017). Activists, despite their dispersal in Russia and in exile, especially since 2022, draw on the shared experience of political collaboration in concrete actions and overlapping and uninterrupted lines of communication (particularly online) to intensify their sense of solidarity and cause. In this chapter, I pay closer attention to intersubjective mobilization and the concrete micro dynamics of the social setting. Despite what is now a rich literature on political contestation in everyday life, the dynamics of activist 'culture' and 'network' often remain something of an afterthought. I turn to 'experience' as a way for participants to share transformative feelings. As Cheryl Mattingly argues (2019: 419), the 'phenomenological point is not that social categories and conditions should be disregarded but that experience cannot be reduced to what they encompass or call attention to'. In the words of Polina, a long-standing anti-regime and now anti-war activist:

> This [political activism] was such a thing [*takaia shtuka*] we were occupied with [*zanimalis*] since 2011. Just because many of the people who I shared it with [*s kotorymi uchastvovali*] are not here anymore doesn't mean it ends. We continue to do it together even if we're apart.

Ways of thinking and acting in common emerge as a consequence of, and not prior to, entangled experience. This 'thingness', to ground discussion in the language of activists, persists and binds after the event. This is the phenomenological challenge to framings of agentic intentionality, Arendtian beings of action, or structural accounts of networks. Shared causes are actualized by the lived experience, as well as encounters with others. As Clément and Zhelnina argue (2020), shared experience in activism can bridge local and bigger worlds. Pragmatism can be infectious, particularly concerning social politics grounded in local inequalities. Entanglement in common experiences which are 'micropolitical' or just part of the everyday means the horizons of contention and entanglement never disappear. These everyday experiences might include working as a food courier with exploited

8. Wartime Entanglement of People in Politics

co-ethnics, participating in a protest picket among mixed generations, or just hanging out in a YouTube livestream among politicals and responding in the chat.

Writing on 'everyday politics', Benedict Kerkvliet (2009: 240) makes the point that for many, there's no 'going into' or 'leaving' of contentious contexts. Even if on the back burner at times, because so many live in precarious circumstances which continually manifest themselves in everyday life, one is immersed in the political and forced to confront it. In Kerkvliet's study of the relatively powerless, conformity, evasion, 'modification' and resistance exist on a spectrum of subjectivation alongside 'formal politics'. Subjectivation, however, is not possible without people coming to relate common experience to shared visions of a 'common good'. As I have consistently argued in this book, this relates to long-standing feelings structured around 'socialism' in the vernacular sense: one's sense of being an equal part of a bigger community serves as a starting point for exploring ideas of recovering a broad egalitarianism and articulating demands for social justice.

Defensive consolidator activism

While no doubt many readers are most interested in oppositional groups, a social feeling for action is equally true of 'defensive consolidators' like Felix who are neither 'supporters' nor active 'objectors' of the Ukraine war. They want to come together with others and exercise social action and activate their frustrated desires for connectivity. Essentially, my argument is that much so-called 'pro-war' activity is a redirection of this social drive. It is revealing that many people like Felix are exercised to contribute because of the 'lack of care' by the state for Russian soldiers. Without ethnography it is impossible to differentiate between those who genuinely support military aims (though it is unclear what these aims are, even to propagandists) and those who contribute because of the 'defensive' idea of care for Russian soldiers and others as deserving of 'protection'.[6]

This form of consolidation driving engagement would not be unusual in the history of citizen reactions to a state's foreign policies, regardless of whether they support them or not. This concern for one's 'compatriot' and not for the 'other' is entirely within the character of just and unjust wars alike.[7] What is of interest

---

6. When I reviewed my fieldnotes alongside the transcripts of interviews conducted by colleagues among unequivocal pro-war volunteers, I was struck by the similarities in the almost obsessive concern with the care for basic needs and the projection of an almost domestic, familial care. To some pro-war organizers of groups, the preoccupation among contributors of things like cooked food and trench candles was a source of significant annoyance because in their view they hindered a focus on more pressing needs that would help the war aims.

7. It also seems to me the Russo-Ukrainian war might be worth studying for the exceptional sociological (not moral) phenomena of Russian nationals donating significant sums to the Ukrainian army.

here are the specifics of the social motivation: the hapless mobilized, the Donbas resident or displaced person can equally be an object of care and thereby bridge the gap in two ways. Help for them represents a contribution by the local world to the national-social imagined whole (and here we should still note ambiguity even among supporters as to the place of Donbas in their world). Of his 'personal history of involvement with the Donbas' as he calls it, Felix has the following to say in 2022, looking back all the way to 2014:

> It's not 'personal' as you put the question, but part of who I am within the town. Or rather, perhaps, I mean, among those people here, particularly, at work, who want to lead by one's authoritative example. Maybe it's partly from parents, who knows? Upbringing makes a difference. So many were indifferent about the Donbas, and maybe even I was a bit at first. But who would help if not me? It's kind of fast and slow [realization] at the same time. It came from knowing people in my work team with relatives in Donbas, and elsewhere in the Ukraine [*sic*] and knowing from my own similar family history experiences.[8] Slowly you become aware of the similarities – not immediately. And little things you could suddenly do – like we have so much stuff lying around that we don't need and then someone says, 'bring it to Griboyedov Street' [a collection point]. And you're like: why not! Is it so hard?

Felix, like many defensive consolidators, linked his own feelings of hurt to the projected victim status of Donbas residents. In some cases, this developed into political alignment with the Russian regime's talking points about a Kyiv government of 'nazis and drug-addicts' holding the 'good Ukrainians' hostage. In most cases, however, the picture is more ambiguous. Certainly, in Felix's case and that of most of the working-class 'blokes' in my research, he never subscribed to any regime discourse beyond a 'vernacular' patriotism at odds with nationalism or jingoism (Goode 2018: 269). He was not unusual either in a wider circle and this should give pause for thought about the penetration of the extreme rhetoric of TV mouthpieces. As Dekalchuk and her coauthors agree (2025), there remains a significant political distance between 'die-hard' conservatives and the rest of society.

Numerous sociological studies find 'die hard' conservatives a marginal (15 per cent) yet vocal (because their views align with the TV propagandists) minority, with extreme views in comparison with others. Yet they are unlikely to be active because of their deferral to authorities. In talk with them, they shy away from involving themselves even with pro-war patriotic activists because this would conflict with their contingent loyalist view on the adequacy of the authorities ('they know what they're doing'). Contingent because even they are aware of widespread corruption and incompetence. As Goode (2018) argues, much more

---

8. This is a good example where I cannot comment on the family history resemblance for ethical reasons, except to say they involved displacement.

prevalent are 'everyday patriots', but within this large group I would distinguish further between critical realists, like Felix, and the 'reactives'. The latter work their way from the resentment and shock, which we observed at the beginning of the war, to a position that essentially ends in alignment with the war aims of the state. The best we can say is that in the future these people would soon forget the war and the 'reasons' for it. These 'reactives' are the ones sometimes ingeniously making home-assembled drones and flak-jackets. The former – Felix's group – are the conscientious middle ground: critical realists. Having said that, it is not meaningful to try to quantify and clearly delineate patriotic groups, in my view, despite the best efforts of many scholars since the war began. However, we can say of 'moderates' that they have the potential to draw the majority to their position depending on the social dynamics of a political situation (such as more obvious regime infighting or economic problems).

The rest of this chapter is organized as follows: The next section develops my concept of entanglements. Then, in the case sections, I look at the migration of activists from electoral politics to ecological and anti-war activism as the public space of possible protest and opposition has shrunk rapidly since 2021 and even further since 2022. In line with the experience of other people in this book, formerly prominent activists are forced to rediscover both micropolitical scales (in small, seemingly invisible actions and dispositions), as well as contend with exile, dispersion and the rise of competing pro-war activism. Thirdly, in contrast to the view that only the latter form of voluntaristic activity is now possible – particularly in support of 'our boys in Donbas' – I end the chapter with Felix's example of ambiguous grassroots activities that are neither oppositional, nor co-opted.

Conceptualizing Entanglements: Rediscovering the socialization process in activism

In a recent overview of civil society development, Susan Stewart and Jan Matti Dollbaum (2017) argue that despite some differences, Russian and Ukrainian civic organization retains important commonalities. Their broader point is that instead of looking at structures *per se*, it is more instructive to focus on processes and results. War underlines this insight, with 'hobbyist' semi-informal small groups in both countries arguably bearing the brunt of supporting service personnel, under-equipped by their respective states. Fundamentally, the war brings home how important Charles Tilly's central question remains about the 'illusion of the actor' in social change and political contention. From both the Ukrainian and Russian perspectives we can fall into the trap of taking for granted the image of 'determined, unified, self-motivated political actors' (McAdam et al. 2001: 159). Yet networks are composed of contingent assemblages of individuals and diverse social agents. That action occurs at all is a wonder, and in both countries much organization and coalescence of interests and purposes take place in contexts

196   *Everyday Politics in Russia*

that are hardly conducive to study or observation – they remain the 'thing' that emerges in shared experience.

If social ties are the basis of movement recruitment, we should take seriously the task of tracing how networks develop, change and geographically move over time. The alternative, as Doug McAdam argues, is to leave activism in a black box. Mischa Gabowitsch (2017, cf. Bikbov 2017) also complains that the 'black box' of scholarship on protest in Russia tends to overlook fundamental moments of transformation experienced by participants and which have very long-term effects. Similarly, despite a putative focus on change, there is a tendency to imply a kind of unchanging quality to the beliefs and positions of opponents and supporters of the regime. What sometimes follows is a deterministic explanation of movements' recruitment (McAdam 2003: 286). Following McAdam (and his sometime-co-author Tilly), I take seriously the task of mapping experiential density and shared commitment in activist networks. In addition, I want to get beyond too static or container-like conceptions of identity and network.

My argument is that it is necessary to look at experience and practices as intersubjective phenomena – 'within relationships and between persons' (Jackson 1996: 26) – to chart a course between overly subjectivist (agency-based, or ideological-focussed) and objectivist (structural) accounts of activism. Essentially, this is the main task of phenomenologically inspired scholarship. As McAdam (2003: 283) notes, a network approach comes with its own blinders. Beyond structuring variables, one needs to search for relational mechanisms and processes without assuming an 'oversocialized conception of the individual' (McAdam 2003: 287).[9] In other words, the dynamics of the social setting where activists interact matter a lot, but thinking of people as passive containers of ideology is as simplistic as a rational choice model of motivation. And this is clear from talks and observations of my 'anti' and 'pro' war people: neither fit neat divisions, many had points of contact in their worldviews (even towards Ukraine and the 'collective West').

McAdam reflects on the limits of structuralist approaches to social movements and proposes more of a role for agency. We should enquire as to *how* and by *what process* of socialization people come to think of themselves as part of a movement. What does it really mean to have a particular politicized identity, to actively choose participatory action? Geography and anthropology have recently made important contributions to how emotion, (co-present forms of) solidarity and creativity affect the understanding of new and hybrid forms of resistance. These scholars also show how studying activism can move beyond intentionality (Hughes 2016, Pottinger 2017). One of the aims of this chapter is to make such an approach more visible and viable to those studying non-democratic contexts.

---

9. By 'culture' here, McAdam does not refer to differences in national or ethnic setting, but to the quality of interaction in a specific social milieu. Elsewhere McAdam criticizes the deterministic approach to organizational culture, arguing that 'culture' is built from the relational nature of interaction in activism.

And Russia is a great illustration of post-democratic social citizenship despite the odds. Whether we look at alternative unions, environmentalists or anti-war groups, people are typically more loosely institutionalized and less hierarchical. As Laura Henry notes, changes in information technology mean that the term 'organization' is increasingly plastic. Small groups or even individuals can be effective in seeding activism once transplanted from one site to another, perhaps especially so in the febrile environment of niche activism in a wider social field where action is politically constrained (Henry 2006: 109, 102). They may lack the permanent copresence and density of netness that institutions and traditional workplaces provide, but instead are entangled in a wider web of looser affinities and contingent alliances. Indeed, this was already described by Russian sociologists who uncovered informal public spheres in the USSR period that were permeable to the private and which provided an alternative political locus to classical 'social movements' (Zdravomyslova and Voronkov 2002). Activists, despite their dispersal, draw on the shared experience of political collaboration in concrete actions and overlapping and uninterrupted lines of (particularly online) communication to intensify their sense of solidarity and cause. This is not unambiguously 'affective' because the mechanism involves overcoming an individual-psychological sense of incorporation into a cause. As I have argued earlier in this book, entanglement is as much about overcoming a sense of self and emotions connected with a personal response to injustice, as it is about activating such emotions in common. For sure, there's something of both at work here, but drives to connect are, in the phenomenological frame, not the same as emotions. We come back to the key difference this book proposes between structured 'feeling for' and emotion.

I call this process with regard to activism, *experiential entanglement*. Ironically, my main finding is that this entanglement has a long half-life, with commitment and purpose not decaying nearly as much as one might expect due to increasingly febrile formal political atmosphere in Russia. Furthermore, experiential entanglement facilitates activism that remains grassrooted and resists cooption by the state, even if one views some types of activism as (in)directly supportive of the Russian army. 'Entanglement' overcomes a subject-object division, where purposive action is delegated to the individual (and their cognition or emotional attachment) or the movement according to rules of hierarchy. Experience is a way for participants to share transformation via contention. Ways of thinking and acting in common emerge as a consequence of entangled experience. This is the phenomenological challenge to agentic intentionality or structural accounts of networks (Jackson 1996: 22, Mattingly 2019: 423).

Peripatetic anti-regime activism before and since the war on Ukraine

I sit in the kitchen of Polina, twice convicted under anti-protest laws brought in after 2014. She jokes that she's in 'temporary retirement' until 'someone has died'. It is 2022 and nostalgically we look through her computer files of ecological protests going back to the Khimki forest actions in 2010. 'But you know, I can't retire. There's still too much demand for my work, you know?' she smirks. Later when I leave Russia, she sends me photographs by encrypted messenger of her latest anti-war graffiti. She's particularly proud of stencils which show a heart shape next to the word 'Ukraine'. She and her elderly mother (taken along to lessen suspicion) use these stencils on garages, children's play areas and pavements. Polina is just an ordinary office worker from a city, but much of her activism is focussed outside her home town. Polina's case underlines the main argument of this chapter – the inherent elasticity of networks and political engagement. These are inevitable results of the decimation of the public political sphere but also ensure the continuation of micropolitical action even during war and ever-narrowing public sphere. Furthermore, co-experience and personal entanglement

Figure 9 Anti-war sticker saying 'no to military invasion of Ukraine. Peace to the nations, fight the rulers.'

8. Wartime Entanglement of People in Politics

of activists with each other through peripatetic attachment to causes make for coherence and familiarity, not atomization or despair. It is because of people like Polina that 'ordinary' Russians know their compatriots oppose the war. It is long-term peripatetic 'refusers' like Polina who inspire a new generation to find their own ways to resist, even though they will never meet each other.

I had originally talked to Polina because of her involvement with organizers of protests and leafletting against the siting of a rubbish dump in the village of Gvozdovo, a similar case to that described in the previous chapter.[10] Just to illustrate the loose yet capacious network of activism, Polina knew people like Tamara (the politician-activist we met in Chapter 3) through her ecology work, as well as a prominent oppositional electoral organizer who had also got involved in the dump opposition. I had – independently of Polina – also met these same activists (though before the war). A fourth activist, Dmitry, was a younger environmental socialist who had made videos of the progress of the groups in countering the dump site. They all knew Polina and each other, but only very rarely had met – usually when actions such as roadblocks, demonstrations and the like were occurring. The research process of encountering these interlocutors illustrated both the exceptional and ordinary entanglement of these activists. In my search for environmental protestors, I would inevitably uncover preexisting links between them and yet they all hailed from very different places, backgrounds and were hardly 'professionalized'. Even Dmitry, who had got involved with Navalny in a reverse process of politicization, was initially concerned with pollution in a local city. He had migrated to the cause of electing Navalny nationally as a way of advancing the ecological cause locally. Polina takes up the story of network formation:

> Despite its reputation as a place where the Chekists monitor your every post, we always used VKontakte to talk until around 2019–2020. This is where I had my initial talks about the Kaluga dump with Dmitry and 'met' him. It's clear if you have a common interest no one is afraid of 'provocateurs' because they are obvious in their speech (they get bored) and because they don't know how to have a conversation.
>
> On the contrary, it is ordinary folk in Gvozdovo who thought we were provocateurs. There was a pensioner from Moscow with a dacha there, and also a couple of retired women who had lived there all their lives. It took some persuading that we were not from the security services, sent to stymie their efforts. But this is where our own experience comes in. Prior organizing. You know what to do: how to collect signatures in a legal way and account for crowdfunding, set out and phrase leaflets. And in doing these things together with the local folk – sitting them down at the computer and showing them how to make up a leaflet – that you win their trust. Even so, later on the movement

---

10. For obvious reasons of security, I have heavily obscured various aspects of her case, creating a composite of various interviews with different activists in different locales.

probably did collapse because of real provocateurs from the anti-extremism police sent in to cast doubt on the funding arrangements.[11]

Like to you now, I showed examples of my work of previous ecological protests – posters, leaflets. After, I had a lot of posters made up in Moscow by a 'friendly' print shop. That's how I got my second conviction according to Article 212.2. We even 'celebrate' my arrest anniversary by having drinks and toasting it every year. After the second conviction everyone knows you must go into semi-retirement. There's still a YouTube video of my first arrest online and we watch that and think about how we could never imagine the country turning to fascism. What? You don't agree? Well, I guess it's a pretty limp fascism as no one here [in the locale] has denounced me yet, even though most people do know about me. And, no, it wasn't me who cut down the Saint George ribbons from the lampposts on 9 May [Victory Day]. I did get a visit from the beat police officer after that. But he's not stupid either. We just sat and drank tea while he complained about the busy-bodies in the Veterans' Association sending him after the fifth column.

***

Shies[12] [the action in the far North to prevent trash dumping in 2021] was a kind of watershed for many – either their first action because nothing else was possible anymore after restrictions on picketing in Moscow, or a final stand in solidarity when it was still possible to undertake mass actions and actually confront the criminals – it had resonance particularly to me because we were standing up to Sobyanin, the acceptable face for many of the regime. You know, it was like Maidan in Ukraine for me, I mean, us. At least how I imagine it. We felt a connection with Ukrainians. And I don't mean that in terms of the political effect or anything. Just the experience of being together with old and new people. After that they all became like friends to me, even though most of them I haven't seen since then. And I won't probably ever see Petr [Navalny organizer], or Dmitry [eco-socialist] again. Especially not now that both of them left Russia permanently. On the other hand, it feels like new people will come to learn they can still do things, and the point is to encourage them that

11. By triangulating with other participants and viewing public material pertaining to the case it seems clear that a relatively concerted effort was made by representatives of the security services to discredit the campaign.

12. Shiyes, or sometimes transliterated as Shies, was an encampment protest. See Tereshina (2019b), Slabinski (2022) and Kuzmina (2023) for details on how important it was in terms of rethinking activism and contention in Russia. Tereshina emphasizes the shift towards moral solidarity and worth, and Slabinski argues Shiyes indicates a shift towards emotion as a mobilizational imperative drawing a broader group of activists to the cause. Kuzmina noted the ideological diversity of Shiyes participants and the eclectic incorporation of different narratives.

8. Wartime Entanglement of People in Politics

they are not alone. There's no better way than graffiti and stencilling, and I can still use the abilities I had from before.

In later talks with activists, an acquaintance of Polina discusses other avenues to continue 'doing something' about making the environment better. Masha, another woman in her forties, was involved with an activity frequently the focus of middle-class urbanites looking for the 'good life' in the country. She was part of a group setting up 'eco-settlements' where inhabitants pooled money resources, tried to reduce hierarchies in communal organization, and embraced an ecological lifestyle. While beyond the scope of this chapter, and not wishing to go into too many details for ethical reasons, this area is in fact a relatively socially levelling practice that is not so 'classed' as it might appear. And in entering more fully this world of practical prefiguring work – one we discussed in the previous chapter – Polina and Masha appear willing and able to connect with more 'ordinary' locals they perhaps previously had considered impossible to reach. We often quarrelled about questions of loyalty, propaganda-effects and 'patriotism', recalling the earlier themes of this book.

Blurring the picture between work, subculture and Donbas charity

Remarkably, in 2023 Polina (openly anti-war in her public speech) was still able to converse with Kaluga neighbour, Felix, who was part of the local motorcycle 'chapter'.[13] Felix had got involved in collecting medical and food supplies for Donbas displaced people in 2014 before he had become a biker. I had travelled with him by van to deliver them to a dispersal point in Rostov-on-Don in 2015. Felix stayed in touch with this group called 'Help for Donbas' and independent of any national effort. He was encouraged by his boss – a local entrepreneur – who allowed him to collect food and provisions locally and store them in the firm's garage. Later, the company expanded its activities with Felix as the main organizer. I was present at social events where the 'collective' discussed their motivations and the framing of their charity work. In some respects, these narratives resembled those used to embody the missing state capacity to care we discussed in Chapter 5. It is worth returning to a perhaps controversial point made at the beginning of the book: my criticism of a Crimean consensus wholly positive about annexation. Part of the reason Felix got involved in aid to Donbas was because of the frequently dismissive and distrustful attitude of people around him to this 'cause' and a widespread fatigue with Ukraine topics once it became clear that the economic costs for return of the peninsula would be borne by the poorest. However, Felix's

13. Here I must comment that for readability I have transposed Felix (also a composite of three different interlocutors) for an actual neighbour of Polina's to avoid any possibility of her being identified. Nonetheless her interactions with defensive consolidators were real and frequent.

positive experience in the workplace was meaningful and spurred him to propose similar work among his motorcycle brethren. After all, bikers are 'kin' to each other, he surmised. They are a model community of diverse people yet connected to each other.

As we saw from the opening comments, Felix had come to activism through what he insisted was an 'apolitical' sense of duty to help others – particularly vulnerable people. Like many working-class men he was very critical of the Russian government, but generally avoided talk about political figures. He and I kept on good terms and sometimes discussed politics. As of 2023, his group expanded their work in what he was careful to describe as 'humanitarian' aid. Unlike some other grassroots organizations in the Kaluga region, the biker chapter and Felix made a conscious decision to remain, as they put it, 'outside politics': not seeking, and refusing contact and patronage from political figures, but also not posting or saying anything to express a position on the war. This was unusual (of public organizations, not of bikers) but is revealing. There are numerous 'civic' positions with members able to think of a Russia after conflict, though hardly with a different kind of regime, and who more than passively oppose the war. We saw examples of this earlier. It is not incongruous for them, just as much as others, to consider activities and practices that support Russian service personnel with non-lethal aid (flak jackets, toiletries, food) while also acknowledging, privately or even publicly, the present and future catastrophe for Russia and Ukraine of the war. In their neighbourhood's WhatsApp group there was continuous sparring, with people like Masha and Polina posting provocative messages against the war, while others pushed back. At one point, some implored anti-war people to stop posting because they were certainly breaking criminal laws against speech criticizing the war.[14]

Felix never responded one way or another, but over tea one day, the topic of the WhatsApp group arose. He commented on one anti-war poster, 'well it's good she expresses her opinion. At least she's got a brain, unlike the "Z" idiots in the yard'. I had witnessed Felix, while parking up his bike, remonstrate with a common neighbour who had a 'Z' decal on his jeep. 'Do you even know what that stands for?' Like numerous interlocutors, Felix expressed a complex set of intense feelings: unhappiness at the militaristic symbolism of the war which tended to attract 'the idiots who don't know history'. On this, he and his bikers were relatively consistent – they were active in commemorating the Second World War as 'sacrifice' and tragedy. Biker 'politics' also has a supra-national 'Soviet' element to it. Certainly, we can speculate that the obvious yet uncomfortable parallels unfolding in 2022 of a war of aggression made it psychically more pressing to wall off the commemorative activities from the present.

The biker chapter itself had strict rules on conduct and the display of symbols. In some respects, it felt more like a cross between a religious organization and a

14. Here it is worth adding a methodological and ethical point that I decided to leave this WhatsApp group to protect its members from unforeseeable problems connected with my membership. Later a member of the group would forward to me screenshots.

tourist club.[15] Undoubtedly, within the group there were strong differences over the invasion as they met for one of their first big *slety* [outings] in March 2022. Nina Eliasoph (1997), in her work on 'small-mindedness' in the United States, emphasized the inordinate amount of cognitive labour that goes into avoiding couching one's cares as broader political concerns. The language of self-interest made topics 'safe' enough for Americans to activate a sense of the political. However, in the Russian case, for Felix it was a sense of scale, not reducible to patriotic flag-waving or nationalism, that produced action in the local. And the 'good' Soviet project was a part of this. When he joined the motorcycle club, one of his first suggestions was that during the 'outings' they made to different Russian cities they should always visit the local museum or historical site (particularly the ubiquitous Great Patriotic War commemorations) and bring something (perhaps just a fridge magnet) from their own local museums. Later the club got their own stickers expressing their deterritorialized yet grounded identity. Felix's ideas about regional ambassadorship then gained momentum among like-minded people. It fed on a feeling for history that went hand in hand with a reclaiming of public spaces for a subcultural group. This is another Russian domestication from the biker cultures in the West from whom such values are borrowed: 'righteousness' on two wheels (Piano 2018), conformism within non-conformism. In Russia this is a heavily 'sanitized' scene in comparison to the original. There are no racist or white-supremacist symbols in Russian groups. Nor is there criminality. Bikers are no exception to the mainstreaming of many older subcultures:

> So, the most important thing is showing we are from different places, but we are together, when we all go on a 'tour' together. I will have the Kaluga badge, but others will have Gatchina, Tiumen, and others from Belarus, Germany. For some people, it's a national 'Russian' community [*russkoe soobshchestvo*], for sure ... there's some from the club that are part of the Donbas group, and others that just post patriotic stuff on VK. But these are pretty different kinds of people. The point is it's about something which connects people and is bigger than a single country. We don't just have ethnic Russians [*russkie*] in our groups.

Overall, it would be foolish to suggest Felix's position was more visible than the performative 'Z' patriotism on evidence in public (although that has severely waned since 2023). However, his 'quiet' politics of local-transnational scale are certainly not the minority. And given how so much pro-war patriotic action fell short of real 'activism', it is worth considering how effective it really is. One of the most vocal 'pro-war' groups in the locality was complaining vociferously

---

15. I am not the first to note the 'secular sect' characteristics of biker culture. Ennio Piano (2017) discusses how the public nature of affiliation (club leathers) acts like the membership of a religious sect and produces significant coordination of activities. In turn, motorcycle clubs produce mutual-aid goods while discouraging free-riding, particularly in contexts where they are populated mainly from people on the margins of society.

already in mid-2023 of a lack of volunteers to collect supplies and money. With a sarcastic tone, Alexander, the organizer of a group called 'Everything for the Front', published a video in VKontakte berating his audience by saying,

you must have so many more problems at home now than those freezing their arses off in the trenches. Mortgages are more important than the death there? Stop saying 'it's not my war', are you a man or what? It is your war. Just like it's your land ... If you don't want to feed your own army, you'll end up feeding the enemy.

'Well', said Felix, after watching the video with me, 'he gets a lot of views, but not so many likes, it appears'. And continued:

Elena there in the chat – you and I both know her [most online groups are very locally situated]. She talks about how angry she is and is happy to write a long tract about how 'every soldier is a relative [*rodnoi*] but I never realized our society is so full of morally lost [*moral'noe propashchee*] and egoists'. But the fact is, she wouldn't even chip in for the diapers we collect [to use as first aid], let alone the quadcopters this Alexander bloke is raising money for. This extreme reaction is understandable, but look at it for a moment. It's like an uncontrollable 'death wobble' on a motorbike. You fight a movement one way and end up pushing the bike further the other way until you get into the ongoing traffic. She's about unlimited connection to the soldiers and then suddenly she's generalizing about the whole of society being 'human beasts' [*skotstvo chelovecheskoe*]. Though here she's probably correct when she says herself that only ten percent of those who say they contribute to this Alexander are telling the truth.

Stepping back from the ethnographic moments with Felix as a biker, I had known him for many years before his induction into the club-chapter. Certainly, his interest in being 'righteous' and 'nomadic' at the same time made for a neat fit between his personality and the philosophy of the club. Righteousness, in the literature on bikers, is associated with the way the social group makes individuals 'whole persons' by making them more than themselves. Writers on the spiritual community theme even note the likeness of biker culture to Ferdinand Tönnies' idea of *Gemeinschaft* – traditional community ties. In the biker context, this provides 'closeness, love and solidarity' to members (Grundvall 2018: 207). The gravitation of Felix to the club seems like one more expression of frustrated desires for social connection and entanglement. One which was at least partially fulfilled experientially and bringing with it a feedback loop of more involvement in the 'politics' of mutual aid and volunteering.

Returning to Polina, I learn that alongside expanding her collaboration with the eco-settlement, she has found a new 'friendly' print shop willing to break criminal laws and turn out hundreds of anti-war stickers for her to share with others and use herself on street furniture. Activism, severely disrupted, continues in the micropolitical ruts and hollows left in the fabric of Russian society. Co-experiences

8. Wartime Entanglement of People in Politics

of anti-war stenciling and stickering make a new generation of activists. They move peripatetically through the disaster around them and even combine politics with prefigurative practices like growing organic crops and making compost. This, like the nomadic garage people of Chapter 6, involves reterritorializing the often deterritorialized 'lifestyle' politics learned online.

The paradox of entanglement: Loose networks yet binding politicization

In this summarizing discussion, I reflect on points of connection between the fuzzy 'fields' of activism described in this chapter. I also develop the concept of entanglement and the role of technology that are important to the field of activism in Russia today. I then reflect on their relationship to some of the classic ideas about contention outlined earlier.

The horizontal networking between relatively diverse individuals, groups and loose affiliations is important. In a sense the cliché – 'It's the taking part that counts' – really does say it. In both cases, what is most sustaining of the movements are the co-experienced elements: reciprocity among activists, their long-standing yet loose social relations, which allow easy diffusion (transfer of information and personnel) and collaboration, facilitated by technology that allows them to be geographically or physically dispersed but still closely connected. Even in Polina's case, she is sustained by a flow of little micro-feedbacks. This is both online and offline. She always returns to the scenes of her 'crimes' and looks for signs of responses to her graffiti in public places. Sometimes her stencils and words get responses in kind.

Anthropologists inspired by Actor-Network Theory have called 'netness' a form of entanglement because of its potential to change the reflection of the individual about the meaning of their personhood (Case 2011). Charles Tilly's use of netness is a separate coining that emphasizes membership and density of connecting points and only indirectly indicates the importance of social embeddedness. My adoption of the term 'entanglement' allows me to emphasize that shared or lived experiences contribute to network relations. Technopolitical entanglement entails a looser, yet also somehow more sturdy knitting of quasi-public political identity and the personal, than was possible before the internet. Take Polina again. Sometimes for long periods she is not directly involved with anti-war or eco-activism and has major political differences with others, but technology allows a 'nodding' acquaintance to continue, and she still feels part of an invisible community – she cannot leave it because she is 'entangled'.

Jan Matti Dollbaum, Andrei Semenov and Elena Sirotkina (2023) recently evaluate the success of the Navalny 2017–18 mobilization campaigns for political rights. They stress activist experience and genealogy as factors. Seasoning in prior experiences of campaigning and generating informal networks were important. Networks were sustained online in fallow periods. Activists gravitated towards the Navalny campaign not just because of a strong commitment to the cause of 'fair elections', but because of diverse and cumulative grievances (see also Bikbov 2017). Anna Zhelnina (2023) emphasizes processes of trust-building, collaboration and horizontal networking as a kind of experiential learning about how not to be powerless. These are long-term processes with origins in other grievances or moments of contention. I also wish to emphasize the 'processual' development of activist potential through both cognitive and 'unconscious' experiential learning.

The focus on process aligns with Clément and Zhelnina's recent (2020) emphasis of more phenomenologically inflected perspectives on how activism, pragmatic politics and networks are mutually constituted and 'grounded' in everyday experience, practices and routines. These are neither cognitive, affective, nor structuralizing arguments. Linguistic bias (logocentrism) in some ethnographic work makes it hard to communicate how 'natural' their activities felt to all my interlocutors. They lived in the 'clothes' of their activism, often *without* much emotional intensity, and I could certainly feel and observe this without the need of any words.

While my 'sample' here is composed of self-selecting 'actives', Polina's meta-reflection on the success or failure of different campaigns and approaches is worthy of note. After all, reflection also frames activism as sensitive to the meaning of the 'experiential' side. The cases give us an insight into the long-term problem of a lack of coalescence among antisystem groups, long seen as a barrier to a more unified opposition (Smyth 2006, Kolstø 2016, Semenov 2017). However, despite the pragmatic rhetoric of triangulation between causes and groups, their story is really one of a post-coalescence, post-social movements perspective, another example of activist learning. As Samuel Greene has argued (2013: 41), activism develops in Russia after 2011 by 'frame bridging' (a concept familiar from social movement studies), but increasingly depends on politicization. Terms like 'movement' or 'migration' are inadequate for what is essentially rhizomic, horizontal and 'nomadic', as I argued in Chapter 6 when attempting to characterize the vectors of micropolitics more generally. At the same time, the Russian cases are hardly like the polycentric civic networks we might find in 'democratic' countries (Greene 2013: 43).

The 2011–12 Bolotnaia protests against Putin's return to the Presidency – an abortive social movement – are a watershed event after which these activists, more or less disillusioned with electoral politics, turn to the base, to grassroots causes, and to micropolitical antiregime 'propaganda' and 'agitation' (the former term they use repeatedly). This is a tendency shared by very different activists, even 'journeymen' who were not strongly politically 'left', such as Polina (Morris 2023c). A surprisingly outward-looking stance was shared by Polina and all my interlocutors. Their 'politics' are still resolutely based on the primacy of lived experience and even self-transformation through action. Focus on action was clearly so important to some activists that as an internalized disposition it threatened my ability as researcher to win their trust and connect with them. The suspicion and 'vetting' that I was subject to only underline this; a professor lacks the capacity to adequately speak with, or for, left and other oppositional groups until he has entangled himself in struggle or lived injustice. Here again we encounter a paradox of this mode of activism: while globally aware, peripatetic activists present themselves as not embedded in a particular ideology and not shaped by a common history of struggle. Their sense of network is loose and their political subjectivity opportunistic or even pluralistic and intersectional.

In their choice of action, connection and articulation of grievances, they attempt to escape easy incorporation into any of the well-known or visible vehicles of opposition in Russia today – be it nationalism, the co-opted 'system' political parties, the so-called liberal intelligentsia opposition (as the former Navalnyite says, 'perhaps we were always naïve to think Navalny had a chance'). They would likely think of Tilly's brokerage as too static a conceptualization because it presupposes a fixity of positions, rather than their experience of a more contingent, uncertain politics. This is a version of nomadic activism that evokes the resistance to state-forms we discussed in Chapter 6. As for Deleuze and Guattari, for Paolo Virno, movement and mobility – characterized as the potential for 'defection' – become more important as tactics of resistance than are traditional modes of activism bundled as openly oppositional protest (2004: 76).

Conclusion: Experiential origins of everyday politicization

Combining objective and subjective accounts of actors with phenomenological perspectives strikes me as important. In the 1980s, new social movement theories began grappling with the problem of the individual and collective action, cognition and emotion. This resulted in a new political science pioneered by Alberto Melucci (1989) that would not reduce movements to coherent groups with a structural integrity or imperative. Instead, Melucci highlighted intermediate processes between the levels of individual and movement. In a sense, this was a parallel approach to that undertaken by Tilly in sociology's turn towards relational modes of inquiry. The 'latent' politicization of everyday life as inspired by Melucci is visible in more and more research on the post-Soviet area (for an explicit call back, see Jacobsson 2015).

Both Melucci's and Tilly's approaches offer points of departure into what I have called the experiential approach to activism. Melucci (1989) writes of the importance of attending to the 'submerged' reality of movements to avoid the abstraction of 'networks'. McAdam, Tarrow and Tilly (2001) write about the 'integration of cognitive, relational and environmental'.[16] In this chapter, I have argued that while shared cognitive motivation is important to networks, the experiential or 'felt' entanglement of activism is also worthy of consideration. I describe the experiential side of activism as phenomenological because this emphasizes the importance of intersubjective lifeworlds inhabited by

---

16. Both Melucci and Tilly are accused by some of remaining culturally reductionist (Bartholomew and Mayer 1992, Brubaker 2010).

activists.[17] These might have reflexive surfaces in 'talk', and sometimes they are overtly 'ideological', but they also have prediscursive, prerational foundations (Charlesworth 2000: 4) in the unarticulated embodiment of injustice. Consider the experience of the weight of the courier's backpack, the long-term injuries of class from the auto assembly line, the sensation of the placard-photo of a political prisoner ripped away by the police officer, as well as in the shared experience of being in a march, picket or contentious action.

Activism is considered the first step in building institutionalization and scaling up movements. I argue for closer enquiry into the mechanisms of struggle – the micropolitical 'being in the world' that produces potentiality, commitment. This isn't a restatement of the age-old question of agency versus structure in phenomenological clothing.[18] Instead, I challenge the deterministic interpretation that favours consciousness and intentionality over transformations through social activity. 'Pragmatism' may denote human interrelationships with the world that are not necessarily cognitive. In the poststructuralist tradition this has returned as 'affect': articulation of 'sticky' intensities (Ahmed 2004: 66) against a backdrop of the ever-present threat of frustration and disengagement (Clément and Zhelnina 2020). Activism and micropolitical struggle are often thought of as the beginning of 'building' institutionalization and scaling up movements. Often this is not possible or even desirable. Instead, in building entanglements activists create a gravitational logic of organizing, network-extension, and further shared experiential struggle. This is also in contrast to encountering the world of contention only at the discursive level – the rebuke of the activist to the professor. The chasm between saying and doing is where most people falter. On this point, Felix the vernacular patriot and Polina the anti-war activist can agree.[19]

17. The term *lifeworld* (after Alfred Schütz and the phenomenological tradition more generally) emphasizes the domain of the everyday, immediate social experience and practical activity. See Jackson (1996).

18. James Jasper's work has emphasized the cultural context of social movements and individual agency, as well as emotion (see Jasper 2004, 2007, 2018, respectively). My approach is grounded in phenomenological anthropology, which has points of contact with such cultural turns in social movement research but remains suspicious of unqualified terms such as culture, subjectivity and identity as points of entry into explaining social phenomena.

19. I owe this insight to an informal discussion in spring 2020 started by Gregory Afinogenov on Trump-era activism in the United States.

Chapter 9

PEOPLING THE EVERYDAY POLITICS OF POSTSOCIALISM

The aim of this book was to peel back the curtain on place-specific examples of the ever-present desire for connective freedom that I believe can be found in any society. The result is what might appear an anachronistically hopeful ethnography, conducted among people living despite prospectlessness by design and now exacerbated by war. This is a landscape where 'politics' is mainly reduced to compliance and atomization even among those people who wish to mildly improve their immediate social, economic and environmental experience. No doubt to some the book's purpose is a futile task. Not only is an ethno*graphy* like this book biased towards the written logocentric presentation of reality, but also the locale chosen to reveal the more-than-glimmers of micropolitical desire appears to be undergoing a profound catastrophe. There seem few places to hide, let alone oppose and refuse. Serendipitously, the search for signs of a will-to-a-better-world is sometimes more fruitful in the worst of circumstances. Many new ethnographies of resistance, empowerment and political voice are emerging from anthropologists working in Ukraine. But just as interesting a society which serves as a test of everyday politics is Russia. Many also think 'we' in the nominally democratic West are very different, but trajectories are surely shared, however inoculated one considers 'our' societies. Criminalization of oppositional speech, the incarceration of 'dangerous' others without due process, extreme 'capitalist realism' via endless competition, the almost complete residualization of what used to be a universalist welfare state. These are, after all, tendencies many states share. Even if we haven't quite woken up to them yet.

'Eye-level' yet in-depth empirical approaches avoid the idea of political economy as a statistical abstraction of data points – the 'surface effect' of traditional PE (Cameron and Palan 2009). In this book, my 'everyday' politics approach has incorporated human narratives, material culture and practices, values and imaginings into a description of a social reality as valid empirical objects. 'Scale reduction' as a research tool in the political economy tradition of US anthropology proposes local sites of research as a 'window onto wider and evolving landscapes of power […] to get at critical junctures' – which neither traditional ethnography, nor macro historical study can offer alone (Kalb and Tak 2005: 4, 13). At the same time, feminist social reproduction scholars (SRP) have drawn attention to the

210 *Everyday Politics in Russia*

invisibility of numerous activities in 'everyday life' that have long remained invisible to mainstream scholarship, but which are important to maintain capitalist relations of exploitation (Katz 2001) and violence. SRP focusses on social relations between capital and labour at points of production beyond the workplace to explore economic 'value' in multiple domains – particularly paracapitalist activities (recall the garages), social networks as vectors, and further hegemonic processes at ground zero (Mitchell et al. 2004). To adopt Katz's memorable phrase, the 'messy, fleshy' (2001) matter of a peopled political economy does not mean making the individual a primary unit of analysis – but rather to better reveal how the person is entangled in 'innumerable flows that intersect everyday life' (Barlott et al. 2017: 532). For Katz (1996), this is the meaning of 'small' or 'minor' theory from which a new generation of feminist scholars have developed 'everyday political economy' to better integrate 'autonomous agency' with landscapes of structural violence (Elias and Ria 2019: 218). In the context of this book, a dominant capitalist realism confronts nomadic forms of flight towards connective autonomy and a *vita activa*, despite all the obstacles and the hidden injuries of postsocialism.

Defensive consolidation and ressentiment

In Chapters 2 and 3, I spent time considering Russian responses to war as defensive consolidation, and it is worth reiterating that position. Prompted by the immediate disaster of war, defensive consolidation, while expressing fears of punishment and collapse, also attunes people to the long-term decline and aporia the political compact represents – that there has been neither socio-economic renewal, nor even purpose. As Karine Clément argued in her book on 'patriotism from below' (Kleman 2021), consolidating feelings arise thanks to the perceived shortcomings of the social compact – and these are the 'fault' of both elites and 'the collective West' in the popular imagination. Polina the activist and Felix the patriotic biker continue a conversation about the active life and practical agency even after February 2022.

In other cases, consolidation 'cleaves' to an empty and silent authority – illustrated in contrasting responses to Prigozhin's 'mutiny' in June 2023. While security services seemingly panicked and passed the buck, ordinary people helped marshall excavators to block highways preventing paramilitaries marching on Moscow. Events related to the war – small or large examples of state ineptitude, or downright callous disregard for basic needs of civilians and soldiers alike – brought home to many that social renewal was even more necessary, and that they themselves had to begin to consider a future meaning of the nation. Attempts to rechannel frustrated desires for social action echo emptily in the hollow drum of governance. Nevertheless, people act connectively, one step at a time, as seen by Tanya the yard gardener, Polina the activist, and Felix the biker. While understandably many observers now focus on neo-imperial resentment, the vast iceberg of social *ressentiment* lies just beneath the waterline – the contact-point of

9. Peopling the Everyday Politics of Postsocialism   211

feeling between persons and history. Disappointment and dislocation are powerful movers of this sense of lost opportunities in the long crisis-transition from 1991.

It was important to reject the term 'nostalgia' for a number of reasons. Andrew Gilbert (2019: 297), while making a recent case to positively reevaluate the term, admits that the way 'nostalgia' is discussed invariably forecloses any critical potential in the term. Nadkarni and Shevchenko (2004) are close to my argument when they trace in the present the past structure of desire: a 'longing for longing' that they believe the Soviet utopian project sustained – that the 'best' was ahead. I emphasized the persistence of a common feeling for potentiality – 'something was possible and then it was no longer possible'. I used the term 'absent presence' to talk about how vernacular feelings for 'socialism' and communalism represent a postsocialist *haunting*, even among people who think of themselves as 'anti-communist', or as paragons of methodological individualism. I used a phenomenological tool-kit – looking at interactions in situ and intersubjectively. I tried to build on the theories of scholars like Alexei Yurchak and Sergei Oushakine who have proposed the experience of disjuncture and loss at the end of the Soviet project to get at the social trace of how that loss might be recuperated. People say and do all kinds of things that pull them apart, that set them on tracks of debilitating subordination to the state, to the 'market'. I have tried to attune myself and the reader to moments that reveal the intersubjective searches for 'commonality' or *obshchnost*.

People, sometimes drawing on mnemonic resources of the Soviet period, are jarred into mobility when the prospect of some reanimation of apparently lost formats of communication and connection present themselves – through work relations, craft activities, volunteering, and other kinds of quasi-civicness and 'activism'. My point in this book is not to propose the exceptionalism of Russian society, but to show that the Soviet ontological legacy is merely conducive to rediscovering alternatives to capitalist realism and neoliberal authoritarianism. No doubt other societies have their own resources to do this, but it strikes me that there is a general allergy among some scholars towards seriously considering the socialist project as a deprivatized and monist, yet incorporative ontology, as scholars such as Chukhrov, Cherkaev, Kozlova, Kruglova and Orlova do. Submerged or overlooked drives in the present are often inflected by the will to communality. These are activated in intersubjective experience.

The intersubjective frame is important. People feel individually the weight of historical hurt, but *ressentiment* emerges through continual feedback with family, community and place. I made an active choice in this ethnography not to focus so much on the enormous social and human destruction that the end of the Soviet project brought. The biographies in this book are not particularly 'traumatogenic', yet they reflect both biographical and more-than-personal experiences of acute hurt in the postsocialist span of history. The point is not that a particular person suffered destitution or social death. It is that every living person has the potential to experience a 'structured' feeling that is partly dislocated. Aspects of the socialist experience that proposed universality and incorporation were available and now are denied as even having existed in the first place. In a sense, *ressentiment* is the feeling of being gaslit by history, even if it is not fully cognized.

The structuring feelings of inclusion, purpose and supra-individualism are 'available' to all, as a vernacular sensing of injustice about the present. This sensing is bound up with another – of striving *potencia* – communal action was once possible and incorporation into a greater task was part of the really existing ontological space. The irony is that this is very far from the common readings of 'nostalgia'. In fact, to experience such communal *potencia* requires no awareness, memory or connection with the USSR itself on the part of Russians or anyone else. Nonetheless, intergenerational communication is a much under-researched phenomenon in Russia and former Soviet places. Today, people might well have internalized positive feelings for the utopian potential offered by 'the time before', despite areas of material dysfunction in the provision of goods or colonialist legacy.

The focus in anthropology has been on 'shortage' and the influence of the economistic frame has been highly damaging to understanding, as Thelen points out (2011). The USSR comparatively lacked certain things but was also a place of 'abundance' – particularly of communication, feelings of connection and sincere relations based on the idea that persons can be more than individuals. My contention is that, while normalized from above and below, the long crisis since 1991 has never really abated. It makes more acute the responses, whether defensively consolidating around narratives of encirclement and threat, or, more significantly, the searches for absent presences of connection and qualitative communication of the possible good. *Ressentiment* expresses the desire for social reparation above all. This is both present and absent at the same time; Soviet-era ontology leaves a trace, but there is a strong effect of the regime's promotion of its irreplaceableness and scare tactics of capitalist realism's 'There is No Alternative'. The result is a social(ist) reflex that still kicks out when triggered the appropriate way.

The neoliberal-corporatist nexus: Quasi-kinship and state devolution

Conflicts between the making of neoliberal subjects and socially immersive drives are synthesized in various ways in the everyday politics explored in this book. They are 'domesticated', 'corporatist', 'unruly', as well as 'bare' forms of governmentalized entrepreneurial selves. Building on my previous theorization of postsocialist refusals of capitalist realism, I followed three distinct examples, exploring their convergence in the wartime economy of Russia in 2023. Anticipating the Deleuzian 'lines of flight' into the garage economies, when persons are incorporated into the new gig-work precarity or the corporatist forms of industry, capital is forced into contortions that present cracks to further exploit for labour. Partly as a result of state withdrawal, loyalty and conscious sacrifice by the worker are demanded because of the 'war footing', and in return a strange relation of 'care' and quasi-kindship emerges. It offers 'belonging'. This relation challenges a simple distinction between commoditized neoliberal subject and the idea of entitlements and rights recognized by virtue of corporate identity. Is

9. Peopling the Everyday Politics of Postsocialism   213

this a retreat of neoliberalism or an easy concession recuperated by further self-exploitation? It is unclear.

Ironically, it was military mobilization for the war in Ukraine that revealed how precarious the neoliberal compact remains. Drawing on Christina Scharff's feminist framing of the psychic responses to neoliberalism (2016), I showed how 'hacking' the compact becomes ever more visible against the threat of pressganging (different forms of military mobilization). While the most vulnerable communities are subject to social and economic pressures conducive to making them accept (and even then, unenthusiastically) mobilization, these should be seen as the exception they represent. Observers have talked about Russia as a necrospace, but it is truer to say that 'death-price' has become a key biopolitical criterion for incorporating surplus populations. Nonetheless, military volunteering and contract service are uncommon choices and frequently stigmatized – a far cry from the picture some paint of a pro-war consensus. Most people seek lines of flight away from mobilization or actively make use of the incoherence of the state and corporatist offerings of 'care' to protect themselves. Even here we see an elective affinity between 'atavistic' collectivist drives and neo-paternalist relations which sustain the state-capital compact in Russia today. Sustain the war they do not. Contrary to some perspectives, capitalist realism is not conducive to waging wars of aggression. While Russia moves ever further in its vanguard role towards a Deleuzian digital 'control society', the techno-authoritarian assemblage gives rise to hacking and resistance via 'disassembly' (Orlova and Morris 2021), a topic explored in the second part of the book.

Projections onto Russia of the inherent political biases of observers inadvertently lead to a simplistic reification and simplification of 'state' and 'state capacity/effectiveness', respectively. The fuzzy incoherence of state institutions deserves analysis without recourse to normative frames of 'institutional failure', 'endemic corruption' or 'state withdrawal'. Without ignoring the ineffectiveness and poor quality of state services in Russia, their overall *incoherence* means that bureaucrats must exit their designated roles. They more often 'lean across the desk' in a gesture that *coproduces* the state with the citizen because of the contradictions of the law and its enforcement. At the same time, they reproduce a moral relationship with the citizen in what are absurd and impossible situations. This problematizes an unambiguous dependency or clientelist perspective.

In place of models of Russian state-mindedness as overwhelmingly paternalist we find practices of accommodation, 'devolved' co-production of governance, and a shared feeling for stateness. This traces back to the socialist era's ontology of incorporation and deprivatization. It implies ends-orientated notions of care and purposive action. 'Care' can be equally *callous* as it is person-centric and other-regarding. It is a mistake to see society as a passive receptor of the actions of state institutions and bureaucratic organizations. Especially in the Russian case, these pitfalls lead to overestimating the state's coercive and biopolitical power and underestimating both bureaucracy and *community* capacity. In an uneasy concert, they contest or reshape regime goals. Scholars such as Olga Moliarenko have shown the possibility of examining durable forms of 'shadow governance' (2016). Like

214   *Everyday Politics in Russia*

her, I try to build a bridge away from politically determinist accounts. The observed co-production of governance from below is not a 'third way', but a practical, self-reproducing and socially embedded form of in(co)herent stateness. State agencies undertaking shadow public works are ever present. Even the Prigozhin mutiny of 2023 showed this. Bulldozers sent to dig ditches without clear orders and with the ready involvement of citizens. Building on the exceptionally detailed scholarship on the workings of Russian courts and on property rights by Kathryn Hendley (2017) and Timothy Frye (2017) respectively, I propose a reflexive, moral set of reasonings and historical impetus for state workers-citizen interactions in co-making the incoherent state.

Desiring nomads and micropolitics

In the middle part of the book, I laid out a model of political-economic libido indebted to Gilles Deleuze, and a political activization drawn from Jacques Rancière. Deleuze and Guattari assume desire is a basic drive for human beings towards the social. People are 'libidinally invested' in the 'production' of such relations, but the despotic and then capitalist 'socius' are spoilers – social bodies that usurp 'production': they elbow out the inherently cooperative and altruistic elements of community building. The use of 'production' is important to get away from the idea of libido being concerned with compensating over some lack – as in various psychoanalytic theories. Desire is *a priori* about reproducing connective (coded) social relations. Micropolitics are Deleuze and Guattari's attempt to rethink 'resistance' as a vitalist impetus that anticipates rather than reacts to domination. 'Lines of flight' inhere within an overall model of 'flows' that are more than individualistic. Despite his reputation as an elusive thinker, revisiting Deleuze's ideas about proactively emancipatory drives is essential. Not only because the micropolitical is largely absent in treatments of postmodern-type 'authoritarian' societies such as China and Russia, but because these societies very obviously prefigure our own post-democratic trajectories.

Rancière's radical rethinking of the political proposes that – contra models such as those of Chantelle Mouffe and Jurgen Habermas – the essence of the political is the expression of dissensus by the 'uncounted for' on the basis of rejecting hierarchical constraint by the 'police'. Politics can only be renewed by turning attention to those excluded from the 'normal' purview of political studies. Refusals and occupations materialize and symbolize what for Rancière is 'the political': secession in a place *aside* that then aspires to reconstruct the commons (Rancière 2017). This repositioning towards a politics from below is indispensable in thinking about counter-state democratic politics. Anna Secor and Jess Linz (2017) use the image of squatter in the same way I turn to the image of the garage nomad: those who are drawn to 'no man's land' – to the Deleuzian centrifugal lines of flight. Movement along familiar lines is akin to keeping access to viable spaces that do not conform to the normal hierarchies. This is the beginning of *demos* politics. The micropolitical gambit can emerge only from a *demos* – a category of people deterritorialized as a result of their superfluity.

A vital force, nomadism in the garage spaces and underground workshop sustains itself below the surface but is everywhere tangible and visible to people with eyes and ears. Instead of seeing these ways of life as viable and widespread, researchers generally find them too troublesome to take time over. Similarly, economistic frames see these practices as at best defensive attempts at carving out autonomy in shrinking spaces of refuge against neoliberalism. Most problematically, because these practices can only be grasped in their full meaning using micro-level methods of ethnographic engagement, the automatic assumption is to dismiss them as irrelevant. War shows how the model of social reproduction remains the nomadic improviser, willing to put distance between herself and the state even while remaining receptive to potential concessions and loopholes.

Figure 10 Cakes decorated with 'fuck the war' and an ambiguous Eastertime abbreviation, 2024.

216   *Everyday Politics in Russia*

While I emphasize the male-dominated garage spaces, in craft and production as pleasure, I open the perspective to a less gendered form of making and mending. This does justice to the broad movement away from capture and towards a newly socialized *striving*. Furthermore, the micropolitics of other-regarding creativity can coexist with strongly intersubjective experience of political activism, whether in oppositional protest, labour organizing or anti-war actions. The partly emotional, partly experiential entanglement of activists has a long half-life, with commitment and purpose not decaying nearly as much as one might expect due to the impact of war and domestic political constriction. Furthermore, experiential entanglement facilitates activism that remains grassrooted and resists cooption by the Russian state. The micropolitical struggle continues, even if only in a minor mode; this is important in prefiguring a space for an alternative way of thinking – without wars of aggression and without alienation from politics.

The new history of (post)socialism and its ontological traces

A tough task in this book has been to draw on the new historical writings about the 'socialist' period and connect them to lived experience in today's Russia, more than thirty years on. This is timely; many scholars are currently focussed on efforts to get at the complexity, and even normality of life in the late USSR. How is it possible to maintain belief and desire in an atomizing space? What links people in this book is a sense of *striving*: purposive desire and imagination – a social instinct made more acute by the experience of the communist experiment but one we could uncover in any place. This can be based on mnemonic resources of the 'real Soviet' past, or a trace of the ontology of socialism. Regardless of ideology, both evoke a make-believe space of quality communication. Not only that, but this space of communication and common activity – in work and also in leisure – transcended the means-end distinction. The 'end' of a better, more humane socialist society was taken for granted, even while it was not naively thought of as generally realizable. The memorable contribution of Keti Chukhrov, to which I give ethnographic treatment, is that dealienation in the USSR cleared space for the emergence, however fleetingly of a new ontology – a new way of being – if only in an idealized and deferred form. I also owe a debt to Natalya Kozlova for her recuperative model of the meaningfulness of Soviet values, especially in her introduction and reinterpretation for a new audience by Gulnaz Sharafutdinova (2019). Most importantly though, I have, as in recent work by Alexandrina Vanke (2024), tried to work in the tradition of Raymond Williams and phenomenology. I use the term *'feeling for an absent presence'* to emphasize how suffering and loss can be generative of possibility and the imagination of the good life and better society. The content of this haunting feeling is an urge to (re)connect in some vital yet communitarian way that goes beyond the individual.

This is thrown into sharp relief against the relentless precarity of existence in contemporary Russia and the course of destructive transformations of the last thirty years, I draw together in the materials, people and reflections of the book. Russia is a 'crisis heterotopia' – a time-space containing what look like the most dysfunctional elements of contemporary capitalism and the authoritarian tendencies of the modern state. But Russia as heterotopia is merely one world within our world. Current crises there are played out in no greater relative dramaturgical intensity than in our own societies. Like the crisis heterotopias Foucault and Miskowiec describe (1986), Russia's is both banal, taken for granted, but also delimited – we can trace its edges. Similarly, heterotopias contain dual meanings; they are mirrored. They reflect crisis but also give glimpses of resolution. They have room for several tendencies and subregions of dwelling that try to escape along lines of flight. Provisioning, informal and delegated governance, everyday politics, activism and solidarity show us how the small (and often quiet) theories of everyday political economy link up into the form of small lifeboats for the people whose lives I trace out, inadequately on these pages. DIY Lifeboats are more than just a striking image. As metaphor they encapsulate both flight and stuckness; inconspicuously they wait for us on deck. As DIY projects they come from craft, improvision, refuge and solidarity. But they require people to work together at the oars; an individual can hardly manage alone. The lifeboat as a meagre yet ultimately delivering heterotopia is the closest we can get in our times to imagining how to make our own rescue.

REFERENCES

Abramov, R. (2012), 'Vremia i prostranstvo nostal'gii' [Time and place of nostalgia], *Sotsiologicheskii zhurnal*, 4: 5–23.

Agamben, G. (1996), *Means without End: Notes on Politics*, trans. V. Binetti and C. Casarino, Minneapolis: University of Minnesota Press.

Agamben, G. (1998), *Homo Sacer: Sovereign Power and Bare Life*, trans. D. Heller-Roazen, Stanford: Stanford University Press.

Ahmed, S. (2004), *The Cultural Politics of Emotion*, Edinburgh: Edinburgh University Press.

Alexander, J. (2012), *Trauma: A Social Theory*, Cambridge and Malden: Polity Press.

Alexseev, M. and H. Hale (2016), 'Rallying Round the Leader More than the Flag: Changes in Russian Nationalist Public Opinion 2013–14', in P. Kolstø and H. Blakkisrud (eds), *The New Russian Nationalism: Imperialism, Ethnicity and Authoritarianism 2000–2015*, 192–220, Edinburgh: Edinburgh University Press.

Allen, I. (2021), *Dirty Coal. Industrial Populism as Purification in Poland's Mining Heartland*. Unpublished PhD diss., KTH Royal Institute of Technology, Stockholm.

Allina-Pisano, J. (2010), 'Social contracts and authoritarian projects in post-Soviet space: The use of administrative resource', *Communist and Post-Communist Studies*, 43(4): 373–82.

Anipkin, M. (2018), 'Pokolenie "lishnikh liudei": antropologicheskii portret poslednego sovetskogo pokoleniia' [The generation of 'superfluous people': an anthropological portrait of the last Soviet generation], *Neprikosnovennyi zapas*, 117(1): 290–308.

Arendt, H. (1958 [1998]), *The Human Condition* (Second Edition), Chicago and London: University of Chicago Press.

Arutunyan, A. (2015), *The Putin Mystique: Inside Russia's Power Cult*, Northampton, MA: Olive Branch Press.

Ashwin, S. (1999), *Russian Workers: The Anatomy of Patience*, Manchester: Manchester University Press.

Åslund, A. (1991), 'Prospects for economic reform in the U.S.S.R', *The World Bank Economic Review*, 5(1): 43–66.

Babintsev, V. and O. Iurkova (2016), 'Neformal'nye praktiki v munitsipal'nom upravlenii' [Informal practices in municipal governance], *Vestnik gosudarstvennogo i munitsipal'nogo upravleniia*, 1(20): 69–75.

Badami, N. (2018), 'Informality as fix', *Third Text*, 32(1): 46–54.

Baglione, L. (2016), 'Post-Soviet Russia at twenty-five: Understanding the dynamics and consequences of its authoritarianism', *Polity*, 48(4): 580–611.

Bahovadinova, M. (2023), 'Before the Law: Policy, Practice and the Search for the "Prepared Migrant Worker" in the Transnational Migration Bureaucracy', in J. de la Croix and M. Reeves (eds), *The Central Asian World*, 318–33, Abingdon and New York: Routledge.

Barlott, T., L. Shevellar and M. Turpin (2017), 'Becoming Minor: Mapping New Territories in Occupational Science', *Journal of Occupational Science*, 24(4): 524–34.

Barsukova, S. and A. Ledeneva (2018), 'Concluding Remarks to Volume 2: Are Some Countries More Informal than Others? The Case of Russia', in A. Ledeneva (ed.),

Global Encyclopaedia of Informality, Volume 2: Understanding Social and Cultural Complexity, 487–92, London: UCL Press.

Bartholomew, A. and M. Mayer (1992), 'Nomads of the present: Melucci's contribution to "New social movement" theory', *Theory, Culture and Society*, 9(4): 141–59.

Bassin, M. (2011), 'Eurasian Vision of the Russian Nationhood in Space', in K. Schlögel and E. Müller-Luckner (eds), *Mastering Russian Spaces: Raum und Raumbewältigung als Probleme der russischen* Geschichte, 47–64, München: R Oldenbourg Verlag.

Bear, L. (2016), 'Time as technique', *Annual Review of Anthropology*, 45: 487–502.

Belokurova, E. and D. Vorobyev (2020), 'Overcoming depoliticization: The 2014 local electoral campaign in St. Petersburg', *International Journal of Politics, Culture and Society*, 33: 203–20.

Bendix, J., B. Sparrow, B. Ollman and T. Mitchell (1992), 'Going beyond the state?', *American Political Science Review*, 86(4): 1007–21.

Benson, P. and S. Kirsch (2010), 'Capitalism and the politics of resignation', *Current Anthropology*, 51(4): 459–86.

Berlant, L. (2011), *Cruel Optimism*, Durham, NC: Duke University Press.

Bialecki, J. (2016), 'Getting beyond arguing over "getting beyond the suffering slot"', *Jon Bialecki*, 15 September. Available online: https://jonbialecki.com/2016/09/15/getting-beyond-arguing-over-getting-beyond-the-suffering-slot/ (Accessed 2 May 2024).

Bikbov, A. (2017), 'Representation and self-empowerment: Russian street protests, 2011–2012', *Russian Journal of Philosophy and Humanities*, 1(1): 43–54.

Bindman, E. (2017), *Social Rights in Russia: From Imperfect Past to Uncertain Future*, Abingdon and New York: Routledge.

Blackburn, M. (2021), 'Mainstream Russian nationalism and the "State-Civilization" identity: Perspectives from below', *Nationalities Papers*, 49(1): 89–107.

Bockman, J. and G. Eyal (2002), 'Eastern Europe as a laboratory for economic knowledge: The transnational roots of neoliberalism', *The American Journal of Sociology*, 108(2): 310–52.

Bogatyreva, M. and N. Matveev (2018), 'KPI as market surrogate', *Research Paradigms Transformation in Social Sciences*, Proceedings of the International Conference on Research Paradigms Transformation in Social Sciences (RPTSS 2018), 26–28 April, Irkutsk National Research Technical University, Russia, 230–8.

Bogdanova, E. (2005), 'Sovetskaia traditsiia pravovoi zashchity, ili v ozhidanii zaboty' [Soviet tradition of legal defence, or in expectation of care], *Neprikosnovennyi zapas*, 1(39): 76–83.

Borisova, E. (2023), 'Ambivalences of care: Movement, masculinity and presence in Tajikistan', *Ethnos*, 1–20.

Bosteels, B. (2010), 'Archipolitics, Parapolitics, Metapolitics', in J.-P. Deranty (ed.), *Jacques Rancière: Key Concepts*, 80–92, Durham: Acumen.

Bové, L. (2009), *La estrategia del conatus: Afirmación y resistencia en Spinoza*, Madrid: Tierra de Nadie.

Boym, S. (1995), 'From the Russian soul to post-communist nostalgia', *Representations*, 49: 133–66.

Boym, S. (2008), *The Future of Nostalgia*, New York: Basic Books.

Braidotti, R. (2006), 'The Becoming-Minoritarian of Europe', in I. Buchanan and A. Parr (eds), *Deleuze and the Contemporary World*, 79–94, Edinburgh: Edinburgh University Press.

Brandenberger, D. (1999), 'Proletarian internationalism, "Soviet Patriotism" and the rise of Russocentric Etatism during the stalinist 1930s', *Left History*, 6(5): 80–100.

Broome, A. (2009), 'Money for nothing: Everyday actors and monetary crises', *Journal of International Relations and Development*, 12(1): 3–30.

Brubaker, R. (2010), 'Charles Tilly as a theorist of nationalism', *American Sociology*, 41: 375–81.

Brubaker, R. and F. Cooper (2000), 'Beyond "identity"', *Theory and Society*, 29(1): 1–47.

Bruff, I. (2014), 'The Rise of authoritarian neoliberalism', *Rethinking Marxism*, 26(1): 113–29.

Buchanan, I. (2008), 'Power, Theory and Praxis', in I. Buchanan and N. Thoburn (eds), *Deleuze and Politics*, 13–35, Edinburgh: Edinburgh University Press.

Burawoy, M. (2001), 'Neoclassical sociology: From the end of communism to the end of classes', *American Journal of Sociology*, 106(4): 1099–120.

Burawoy, M., P. Krotov and T. Lytkina (2000), 'Involution and destitution in capitalist Russia', *Ethnography*, 1(1): 43–65.

Burawoy, M., A. Burton, A. Ferguson, K. Fox, J. Gamson, N. Gartrell, L. Hurst, C. Kurzman, L. Salzinger, J. Schiffman and S. Ui (1991), *Ethnography Unbound*, Berkeley: University of California Press.

Busygina, I. (2018), 'Zachem i kak reformiruiut Rossiiski federalism' [Why and how are they reforming Russian federalism], *Kontrapunkt*, 11: 1–8.

Caffee, N. (2013), *Russophonia: Towards a Transnational Conception of Russian-Language Literature* (Doctoral dissertation, UCLA).

Callinicos, A. (2005), 'Epoch and conjuncture in Marxist political economy', *International Politics*, 42: 353–63.

Cameron, A. and R. Palan (2009), 'Empiricism and Objectivity: Reflexive Theory Construction in a Complex World', in M. Blyth (ed.), *Routledge Handbook of International Political Economy (IPE): IPE as a Global Conversation*, 112–25, London and New York: Routledge.

Canovan, M. (1998), 'Introduction', in, H. Arendt (1958), *The Human Condition* (Second Edition), vii–xx, Chicago and London: University of Chicago Press.

Cetina, K. (1999), *Epistemic Cultures: How the Sciences Make Knowledge*, Cambridge, MA and London: Harvard University Press.

Chaisty, P., C. Gerry and S. Whitefield (2022), 'The buck stops elsewhere: Authoritarian resilience and the politics of responsibility for COVID-19 in Russia', *Post-Soviet Affairs*, 38(5): 366–85.

Charlesworth, S. (2000), *A Phenomenology of Working-class Experience*, Cambridge and London: Cambridge University Press.

Checchi, M. (2021), *The Primacy of Resistance: Power, Opposition and Becoming*, London and New York: Bloomsbury.

Cherkaev, X. (2023), *Gleaning for Communism*, Ithaca: Cornell University Press.

Chernysh, M. (2020), 'The Structure of the Russian Middle Class', in J. Nikula and M. Chernysh (eds), *Social Distinctions in Contemporary Russia Waiting for the Middle-Class Society?*, 51–64, Abingdon and New York: Routledge.

Chukhrov, K. (2020), *Practicing the Good: Desire and Boredom in Soviet Socialism*, Minneapolis: University of Minnesota Press.

Clarke, S. (1995), *Management and Industry in Russia: Formal and Informal Relations in the Period of Transition*, Cheltenham: Edward Elgar.

Clastres, P. (1977 [1974]), *Society against the State*, New York: Urizen Books.

Clément, K. (2015), 'Unlikely mobilisations: How ordinary Russian people become involved in collective action', *European Journal of Cultural and Political Sociology*, 2(3–4): 211–40.

References

Clément, K. (2018), 'V chem problema s avtoritarizmom?' [What's the problem with authoritarianism?], *Neprikosnovennyi zapas*, 121: 76–88.

Clément, K. (2019), 'Social mobilizations and the question of social justice in contemporary Russia', *Globalizations*, 16(2): 155–69.

Clément, K. and A. Zhelnina (2020), 'Beyond loyalty and dissent: Pragmatic everyday politics in contemporary Russia', *International Journal of Politics, Culture, and Society*, 33(7/8): 143–62.

Cohen, S. (2001), *States of Denial: Knowing about Atrocities and Suffering*, Cambridge and Malden: Polity.

Colebrook, C. (2008), 'Bourgeois Thermodynamics', in I. Buchanan and N. Thoburn (eds), *Deleuze and Politics*, 121–38, Edinburgh: Edinburgh University Press.

Collier, S. (2011), *Post-Soviet Social: Biopolitics, Neoliberalism, Social Modernity*, Princeton, NJ: Princeton University Press.

Culp, A. (2016), *Dark Deleuze*, Minneapolis: University of Minnesota Press.

Das, V. (2007), *Life and Words: Violence and the Descent into the Ordinary*, Berkeley: University of California Press.

Dekalchuk, A., I. Grigoriev and R. Smyth (2025), 'What Russian popular conservatism is made of? A Multi-Dimensional Mosaic of Values and Social Groups,' *Post-Soviet Affairs*.

Deleuze, G. (1990), 'Society of control', *L'autre journal*, 1: 177–82.

Deleuze, G. and F. Guattari ([1972] 1984), *Anti-Oedipus: Capitalism and Schizophrenia*, trans. R. Hurley, M. Seem and H. Lane, London: The Althone Press.

Deleuze, G. and F. Guattari ([1987] 2017), *A Thousand Plateaus: Capitalism and Schizophrenia*, trans. B. Massumi, London and Oxford: Bloomsbury.

Derluguian, G. (2005), *Bourdieu's Secret Admirer in the Caucasus*, Chicago: Chicago University Press.

Desai, R., L. Freinkman and I. Goldberg (2005), 'Fiscal Federalism in rentier regions: Evidence from Russia', *Journal of Comparative Economics*, 33: 814–34.

Deutscher, P. (2016), '"On the whole we don't:" Michel Foucault, Veena Das and sexual violence', *Critical Horizons*, 17(2): 186–206.

Djagalov, R. (2021), 'Racism, the highest stage of anti-communism', *Slavic Review*, 80(2): 290–8.

Dollbaum, J., A. Semenov and E. Sirotkina (2023), 'Active Urbanites in an Authoritarian Regime: Aleksei Navalny's Presidential Campaign', in J. Morris, A. Semenov and R. Smyth (eds), *Varieties of Russian Activism: State-Society Contestation in Everyday Life*, 256–78, Bloomington: Indiana University Press.

Donahoe, B. and J. Habeck, eds (2011), *Reconstructing the House of Culture: Community, Self, and the Makings of Culture in Russia and Beyond*, Oxford and New York: Berghahn.

Dumont, L. (1986), *Essays in Individualism: Modern Ideology in Anthropological Perspectives*, Chicago: University of Chicago Press.

Dwyer, T. (1991), *Life and Death at Work: Industrial Accidents as a Case of Socially Produced Error*, New York: Springer Sciences.

Elgat, G. (2017), *Nietzsche's Psychology of Ressentiment: Revenge and Justice in On the Geneaology of Morals*, Abingdon and New York: Routledge.

Elias, J. and S. Rai (2019), 'Feminist everyday political economy: Space, time, and violence', *Review of International Studies*, 45(2): 201–20.

Elias, J. and L. Rethel, eds (2016), *The Everyday Political Economy of Southeast Asia*, Cambridge: Cambridge University Press.

Eliasoph, N. (1997), '"Close to home": The work of avoiding politics', *Theory and Society*, 26(5): 605–47.

Eliasoph, N. and P. Lichterman (1999), '"We begin with our favorite theory … ": Reconstructing the extended case method', *Sociological Theory*, 17(2): 228–334.

Erpyleva, S. and S. Kappinen (2023), 'Resigning themselves to inevitability how Russians justified the military invasion of Ukraine', *Public Sociology Lab* report with *The Russia Program at GW*, 23 November 2023. Available online: https://therussiaprogram.org/ps_lab_1 (Accessed 2 May 2024).

Etkind, A. (2009), 'Post-Soviet hauntology: Cultural memory of the Soviet terror', *Constellations*, 16(1): 182–200.

Ewart, P. (2023), 'Towards a Post-capital Horizon of Possibility. Mark Fisher, the Renewal of Critical Theory for the Twenty-First Century', in D. Bosseau and T. Bunyard (eds), *Critical Theory Today: On the Limits and Relevance of an Intellectual Tradition*, 257–79, Cham: Palgrave Macmillan.

Fadeeva, O. and V. Nefedkin (2018), '"Regional'nyi dirizhism" i sel'skaia samoorganizatsiia v Tatarstane' ['Regional dirigisme' and rural self-organization in Tatarstan], *Krest'ianovedenie*, 3(3): 95–114.

Fassin, D. (2013), 'On resentment and ressentiment: The politics and ethics of moral emotions', *Current Anthropology*, 54(3): 249–67.

Fedor, J. (2017), 'Memory, Kinship, and the Mobilization of the Dead: The Russian State and the "Immortal Regiment" Movement', in J. Fedor, M. Kangaspuro, J. Lassila and T. Zhurzhenko (eds), *War and Memory in Russia, Ukraine and Belarus*, 307–46, Cham: Palgrave Macmillan.

Ferguson, J. (2013), 'Declarations of dependence: Labour, personhood, and welfare in Southern Africa', *Journal of the Royal Anthropological Institute*, 19(2): 223–42.

Filc, D. (2020), 'Is resistance always counter-hegemonic?', *Journal of Political Ideologies*, 26(1): 23–38.

Fisher, M. (2009), *Capitalist Realism: Is There No Alternative?*, Ropley: John Hunt Publishing.

Fishwick, A. (2014), 'Beyond and beneath the hierarchical market economy: Global production and working-class conflict in Argentina's automobile industry', *Capital & Class*, 38(1): 115–27.

Fisk, A. (2012), '"To make, and make again": Feminism, craft and spirituality', *Feminist Theology*, 20(2): 160–74.

Flikke, G. (2021), 'Dysfunctional orders: Russia's rubbish protests and Putin's limited access order', *Post-Soviet Affairs*, 37(5): 470–88.

Fondahl, G., V. Filippova, A. Savvinova, A. Ivanova, F. Stammler and G. Hoogensen Gjørv (2019), 'Niches of agency: Managing state-region relations through law in Russia', *Space and Polity*, 23(1): 49–66.

Forrat, N. (2018), 'Shock-resistant authoritarianism: Schoolteachers and infrastructural state capacity in Putin's Russia', *Comparative Politics*, 50(3): 417–49.

Foucault, M. and J. Miskowiec (1986), 'Of other spaces', *Diacritics*, 16(1): 22–7.

Friedman, G. (2014), 'Workers without employers: Shadow corporations and the rise of the gig economy', *Review of Keynesian Economics*, 2(2): 171–88.

Fröhlich, C. and K. Jacobsson (2019), 'Performing resistance: Liminality, infrapolitics, and spatial contestation in contemporary Russia', *Antipode*, 51: 1146–65.

Frye, T. (2017), *Property Rights and Property Wrongs: How Power, Institutions, and Norms Shape Economic Conflict in Russia*, Cambridge: Cambridge University Press.

Fuller, S. (2014), 'Conatus', in M. Grenfell (ed.), *Pierre Bourdieu: Key Concepts*, 181–90, Abingdon and New York: Routledge.

Fürst, J. (2021), *Flowers through Concrete: Explorations in Soviet Hippieland*, Oxford: Oxford University Press.

Gabowitsch, M. (2017), *Protest in Putin's Russia*, Cambridge and Malden: Polity.

Gabowitsch, M. (2018), 'Are copycats subversive? Strategy-31, the Russian runs, the immortal regiment, and the transformative potential of non-hierarchical movements', *Problems of Post-communism*, 65(5): 297–314.

Gago, V. (2017), *Neoliberalism from Below: Popular Pragmatics and Baroque Economies*, Durham, NC: Duke University Press.

Gagyi, A. (2015), 'Social movement studies for East Central Europe? The challenge of a time-space bias on postwar western societies', *Intersections. East European Journal of Society and Politics*, 1(3): 16–36.

Gagyi, A. (2017), 'What it takes to compare non-core movements: A world-systems perspective. Two cases from contemporary East Central European movements', *Interface: A Journal for and about Social Movements*, 9(2): 61–82.

Gal, S. (1995), 'Review essay: Language and the "arts of resistance"', *Cultural Anthropology*, 10(3): 407–24.

Garner, I. (2023), *Z Generation: Into the Heart of Russia's Fascist Youth*, La Vergne: Hurst Publishers.

Garo, I. (2008), 'Molecular Revolutions: The Paradox of Politics in the Work of Gilles Deleuze', in I. Buchanan and N. Thoburn (eds), *Deleuze and Politics*, 54–73, Edinburgh: Edinburgh University Press.

Gaufman, E. (2023) *Everyday Foreign Policy: Performing and Consuming the Russian Nation after Crimea*, Manchester: Manchester University Press.

Gel'man, V. (2004), 'The unrule of law in the Making: The politics of informal institution building in Russia', *Europe-Asia Studies*, 56(7): 1021–40.

Gel'man, V. (2016), 'The vicious circle of post-Soviet neopatrimonialism in Russia', *Post-Soviet Affairs*, 32(5): 455–73.

Gel'man, V. (2018), 'Politics versus policy: Technocratic traps of Russia's policy reforms', *Russian Politics*, 3(2): 282–304.

Gilbert, A. (2019), 'Beyond nostalgia: Other historical emotions', *History and Anthropology*, 30(3): 293–312.

Gilliam, C. (2017), *Immanence and Micropolitics: Sartre, Merleau-Ponty, Foucault and Deleuze*, Edinburgh: Edinburgh University Press.

Gimpelson, V., R. Kapelyushnikov and A. Lukyanova (2010), 'Employment protection legislation in Russia: Regional enforcement and labor market outcomes', *Comparative Economic Studies*, 52: 611–36.

Gledhill, J. (2000), *Power and Its Disguises. Anthropological Perspectives on Politics*, London: Pluto Press.

Golubev, A. (2020), *The Things of Life: Materiality in Late Soviet Russia*, Ithaca: Cornell University Press.

Golubev, A. and O. Smolyak (2013), 'Making selves through making things: Soviet do-it-yourself culture and practices of late Soviet subjectivation', *Cahiers Du Monde Russe*, 54: 517–41.

Goode, J., D. Stroup and E. Gaufman (2022), 'Everyday nationalism in unsettled times: In search of normality during pandemic', *Nationalities Papers*, 50(1): 61–85.

Goode, P. (2018), 'Everyday Patriotism and Ethnicity in Today's Russia', in P. Kolstø and H. Blakkisrud (eds), *Russia before and after Crimea: Nationalism and Identity, 2010-2017*, 258–81, Edinburgh: Edinburgh University Press.

Gorbach, D. (2020), 'Changing patronage and informality configurations in Ukraine: From the shop floor upwards', *Studies of Transition States and Societies*, 12(1): 3–15.

Gorbach, D. (2024), *The (un)making of the Ukrainian Working Class: Everyday Politics and Moral Economy in a Post-Soviet City*, New York and Oxford: Berghahn.

Graeber, D. (2001), *Towards an Anthropological Theory of Value: The False Coin of Our Own Dreams*, New York and Basingstoke: Palgrave.

Greene, S. (2013), 'Beyond Bolotnaia', *Problems of Post-Communism*, 60(2): 40–52.

Greene, S. (2019), '*Homo Post-Sovieticus*: Reconstructing citizenship in Russia', *Social Research*, 86(1): 181–202.

Greenfeld, L. (1990), 'The formation of the Russian national identity: The role of status insecurity and ressentiment', *Comparative Studies in Society and History*, 32(3): 549–91.

Grundvall, S. (2018), 'Inside the Brotherhood: Some Theoretical Aspects of Group Dynamics in Biker Clubs', in T. Kuldova and M. Sánchez-Jankowski (eds), *Outlaw Motorcycle Clubs and Street Gangs*, 205–23, Cham: Palgrave Macmillan.

Günel, G., S. Varma and C. Watanabe (2020), 'A manifesto for patchwork ethnography', *Member Voices, Fieldsights*. Available Online: https://culanth.org/fieldsights/a-manifesto-for-patchwork-ethnography (Accessed 2 May 2024).

Gupta, A. (1995), 'Blurred boundaries: The discourse of corruption, the culture of politics, and the imagined state', *American Ethnologist*, 22(2): 375–402.

Gurkov, I. and S. Zokirzhon (2017), 'Current strategic actions of Russian manufacturing subsidiaries of Western multinational corporations', *Journal of East-West Business*, 23(2): 171–93.

Gurova, O. (2009), 'The life span of things in soviet society', *Russian Social Science Review*, 50(4): 49–60.

Gusterson, H. (1993), 'Exploding anthropology's canon in the world of the bomb: Ethnographic writing on militarism', *Journal of Contemporary Ethnography*, 22(1): 59–79.

Hale, H. (2015), *Patronal Politics: Eurasian Regime Dynamics in Comparative Perspective*, Cambridge: Cambridge University Press.

Hale, H. (2018), 'How Crimea pays: Media, rallying round the flag, and authoritarian support', *Comparative Politics*, 50(3): 369–91.

Halse, J. (2018), 'Ethnographies of the Possible', in W. Gunn, T. Otto and R. Smith (eds), *Design Anthropology: Theory and Practice*, 180–96, London and New York: Bloomsbury.

Harvey, C. (2020), 'Principal–agent dynamics and electoral manipulation: Local risks, patronage and tactical variation in Russian elections, 2003–2012', *Europe-Asia Studies*, 72(5): 837–62.

Harvey, D. (2005), *A Brief History of Neoliberalism*, Oxford and New York: Oxford University Press.

Hawkins, H. and L. Price (2018), 'Towards the Geographies of Making: An Introduction', in L. Price and H. Hawkins (eds), *Geographies of Making, Craft and Creativity*, 1–30, Oxford and New York: Routledge.

Hay, C. (2004), 'The normalizing role of rationalist assumptions in the institutional embedding of neoliberalism', *Economy and Society*, 33(4): 500–27.

Haynes, N. and J. Hickel (2016), 'Introduction: Hierarchy, value, and the value of hierarchy', *Social Analysis*, 60(4): 1–20.

References

Helmke, G. and S. Levitsky (2004), 'Informal institutions and comparative politics: A research agenda', *Perspectives on Politics*, 2(4): 725–40.

Hemment, J. (2009), 'Soviet-style neoliberalism? Nashi, youth voluntarism, and the restructuring of social welfare in Russia', *Problems of Post-Communism*, 56(6): 36–50.

Hendley, K. (2013), 'The puzzling non-consequences of societal distrust of courts: Explaining the use of Russian courts', *Cornell International Law Journal*, 45(3): 517–67.

Hendley, K. (2017), *Everyday Law in Russia*, Ithaca: Cornell University Press.

Henke, C. (2000), 'The mechanics of workplace order: Toward a sociology of repair', *Berkeley Journal of Sociology*, 43: 55–81.

Henry, L. (2006), 'Shaping social activism in post-soviet Russia: Leadership, organizational diversity, and innovation', *Post-Soviet Affairs*, 22(2): 99–124.

Henry, L. (2012), 'Complaint-making as political participation in contemporary Russia', *Communist and Post-Communist Studies*, 45(3–4): 243–54.

Herzfeld, M. (2016), *Cultural Intimacy: Social Poetics and the Real Life of States, Societies, and Institutions*, Abingdon and New York: Routledge.

Hilgers, M. (2012), 'The historicity of the neoliberal state', *Social Anthropology*, 20(1): 80–94.

Hirsch, F. (2000), 'Toward an empire of nations: Border-making and the formation of Soviet national identities', *The Russian Review*, 59(2): 201–26.

Hobson, J. and L. Seabrooke (2009), 'Everyday international political economy', in M. Blyth (ed.), *Routledge Handbook of International Political Economy (IPE): IPE as a Global Conversation*, 300–16, London and New York: Routledge.

Höjdestrand, T. (2009), *Needed by Nobody: Homelessness and Humanness in Post-Socialist Russia*, Ithaca: Cornell University Press.

Holland, E. (2013), *Deleuze and Guatarri's A Thousand Plateaus*, London and New York: Bloomsbury.

Hughes, S. (2016), 'Beyond intentionality: Exploring creativity and resistance within a UK Immigration Removal Centre', *Citizenship Studies*, 20(3–4): 427–43.

Humphrey, C. (1983), *Karl Marx Collective: Economy, Society and Religion in a Siberian Collective Farm*, Cambridge and Paris: Editions de la Maison des Sciences de l'Homme and Cambridge University Press.

Humphrey, C. (2002), *The Unmaking of Soviet Life: Everyday Economies in Russia and Mongolia*, Ithaca: Cornell University Press.

Humphrey, C. (2007), 'Alternative freedoms', *Proceedings of the American Philosophical Society*, 151(1): 1–10.

Ingold, T. (2000), *The Perception of the Environment: Essays on Livelihood, Dwelling and Skill*, London and New York: Routledge.

Irby, M. (forthcoming), 'Next year i'll have a red passport: Citizenship-migrant illegibility in Russia', *PoLAR: Political and Legal Anthropology Review*.

Ishchenko, V. and O. Zhuravlev (2022), 'Imperialist ideology or depoliticization? Why Russian citizens support the invasion of Ukraine', *HAU: Journal of Ethnographic Theory*, 12(3): 668–76.

Ismailbekova, A. (2025), *Mobilisation of Kinship in the Context of Migration*, New York and Oxford: Berghahn.

Jackson, M. (1996), 'Introduction: Phenomenology, Radical Empiricism, and Anthropological Critique', in M. Jackson (ed.), *Things as They Are: New Directions in Phenomenological Anthropology*, 1–50, Bloominghton: Indiana University Press.

Jackson, M. and A. Piette (2015), 'Introduction: Anthropology and the Existential Turn', in M. Jackson and A. Piette (eds), *What Is Existential Anthropology?*, 1–29, New York and Oxford: Berghahn.

Jacobsson, K. (2015), 'Introduction: The Development of Urban Movements in Central and Eastern Europe', in K. Jacobsson (ed.), *Urban Grassroots Movements in Central and Eastern Europe*, 1–32, Farnham and Burlington: Ashgate.

Jasarevic, L. (2015), 'The thing in a jar: Mushrooms and ontological speculations in post-Yugoslavia', *Cultural Anthropology*, 30(1): 36–64.

Jasper, J. (2004), 'A strategic approach to collective action: Looking for agency in social movement choices', *Mobilization*, 9(1): 1–16.

Jasper, J. (2007), 'Cultural Approaches in the Sociology of Social Movements', in B. Klandermans and C. Roggeband (eds), *Handbook of Social Movements across Disciplines*, 59–109, New York: Springer.

Jasper, J. (2018), *The Emotions of Protest*, Chicago: University of Chicago Press.

Jehlička, P. (2021), 'Eastern Europe and the geography of knowledge production: The case of the invisible gardener', *Progress in Human Geography*, 45(5): 1218–36.

Jessop, B. (2007), *State Power: A Strategic-Relational Approach*, Cambridge: Polity.

Jessop, B. (2016), *The State: Past Present Future*, Cambridge: Polity.

Jokūbas, A. (2020), 'Ressentiment as a function of memory: Nietzsche, Deleuze, Jankelevitch', *Problemos*, 98: 71–82.

Jonsson, S. (2013), *Crowds and Democracy: The Idea and Image of the Masses from Revolution to Fascism*, New York: Columbia University Press.

Kalb, D. (2013), 'Financialization and the capitalist moment: Marx versus Weber in the anthropology of global systems', *American Ethnologist*, 40: 258–66.

Kalb, D. and H. Tak (2005), 'Introduction: Critical Junctions – Recapturing Anthropology and History', in D. Kalb and H. Tak (eds), *Critical Junctions: Anthropology and History beyond the Cultural Turn*, 1–28, New York and Oxford: Berghahn.

Kangas, A. and S. Salmenniemi (2016), 'Decolonizing knowledge: Neoliberalism beyond the three worlds', *Distinktion: Journal of Social Theory*, 17(2): 210–27.

Kapferer, B. and C. Taylor (2012), 'Forces in the Production of the State', in A. Hobart and B. Kapferer (eds), *Contesting the State: The Dynamics of Resistance and Control*, 1–20, Canon Pyon: Sean Kingston Publishing.

Katz, C. (1996), 'Towards minor theory', *Environment and Planning D: Society and Space*, 14(4): 487–99.

Katz, C. (2001), 'Vagabond capitalism and the necessity of social reproduction', *Antipode*, 33(4): 709–28.

Kay, R. (2006), *Men in Contemporary Russia: The Fallen Heroes of Post-Soviet Change?*, London and New York: Routledge.

Kazharski, A. (2019), 'Civilizations as ontological security?: Stories of the Russian Trauma', *Problems of Post-Communism*, 67(1): 24–36.

Keat, R. (2008), 'Ethics, Markets and MacIntyre', in K. Knight and P. Blackledge (eds), *Revolutionary Aristotelianism: Ethics, Resistance and Utopia*, 243–57, Stuttgart: Lucius & Lucius.

Kerkvliet, B. (2009), 'Everyday politics in peasant societies (and ours)', *The Journal of Peasant Studies*, 36(1): 227–43.

Kesküla, E. (2014), 'Disembedding the company from Kinship: Unethical families and atomized labor in an Estonian mine', *Laboratorium: Journal of Social Research*, 2: 58–76.

Khmelnitskaya, M. (2017), 'The social budget policy process in Russia at a time of crisis', *Post-Communist Economies*, 29(4): 457–75.

Kleman, K. (2021), *Patriotizm snizu. 'Kak takoe vozmozhno, choby liudi zhili tak bedno v bogatoi strane?'*, Moscow: Novoe Literaturnoe obozrenie.

Knight, K. (2008), *Aristotelian Philosophy: Ethics and Politics from Aristotle to MacIntyre*, Cambridge: Polity Press.

Kolářová, K. (2017), 'The Inarticulate Post-Socialist Crip: On the Cruel Optimism of Neoliberal Transformations in the Czech Republic', in A. Waldschmidt, H. Berressem and M. Ingwersen (eds), *Culture – Theory – Disability: Encounters between Disability Studies and Cultural Studies*, 231–64, Bielefeld: transcript Verlag.

Kolstø, P. (2016), 'Marriage of convenience? Collaboration between nationalists and liberals in the Russian opposition, 2011–12', *Russian Review*, 75(4): 645–63.

Komin, M. (2023), 'Bor'ba za dannye. Chto meshaet sozdat' tsifrovoi reestr voennoobiazannykh' [The struggle for data. What is hindering the creation of a digital register of those liable for military mobilization], *Carnegie politika*, 19 April, Carnegie Endowment for International Peace. Available online: https://carnegieendowment.org/politika/89567 (Accessed 2 May 2024).

Kononenko, V. (2011), 'Introduction', in V. Kononenko and A. Moshes (eds), *Russia as a Network State: What Works in Russia When State Institutions Do Not?*, 1–18, Basingstoke and New York: Palgrave MacMillan.

Kordonsky, S. (2012), 'Norma otkata', *Otechestvennye zapiski*, 2(47): 71–80.

Kordonsky, S. (2016), *Socio-Economic Foundations of the Russian Post-Soviet Regime. The Resource-Based Economy and Estate-Based Social Structure of Contemporary Russia*, Stuttgart: Ibidem-Verlag.

Kourachanis, N. (2020), *Citizenship and Social Policy: From Post-War Development to Permanent Crisis*, Cham: Palgrave MacMillan.

Kozlov, V. (1996), 'Denunciation and its functions in Soviet governance: A study of denunciations and their bureaucratic handling from Soviet police archives, 1944–1953', *The Journal of Modern European History, 1789–1989*, 68(4): 867–98.

Kozlova, N. (2005), *Sovetskie liudi: Stseny iz istorii*, Moscow: Evropa. Seriia 'Imperii'.

Krause, J. (2021), 'The ethics of ethnographic methods in conflict zones', *Journal of Peace Research*, 58(3): 329–41.

Krause, R. and M. Rölli (2008), 'Micropolitical Associations', in I. Buchanan and N. Thoburn (eds), *Deleuze and Politics*, 240–54, Edinburgh: Edinburgh University Press.

Krinsky, J. (2007), 'Constructing workers: Working-class formation under neoliberalism', *Qualitative Sociology*, 30(4): 343–60.

Kruglova, A. (2017), 'Social theory and everyday Marxists: Russian perspectives on epistemology and ethics', *Comparative Studies in Society and History*, 59(4): 759–85.

Kruglova, A. (2019), 'Driving in Terrain: Automobility, modernity, and the politics of statelessness in Russia', *American Ethnologist*, 46(4): 457–69.

Krupets, Y and Y. Epanova (2023), 'Developing craft business in Russia: Capitals and tactics of young cultural entrepreneurs', *Cultural Trends*, 32(1): 20–34.

Kuksa, T. (2020), 'Cherezvychainoe gosudarstvennoe regulirovanie rasprostraneniia Covid-19 v Rossii: Biurokraticheskaia logika priniatiia reshenii i medikalizatsiia posvednevnosti v nachale pandemii' [Emergency state regulation of the spread of Covid-19 in Russia: Bureaucratic logic in decision-making and the medicalization of everyday life at the beginning of the Pandemic], *The Journal of Sociology and Social Anthropology*, 23(4): 183–203.

Kuksa, T. (forthcoming), 'V poiskakh (pravo)sub'ektnosti i ISD v deistvii: paternalistskoe bezmolvie versus neoliberal'naia/dogovornaia agentnost' beremennykh i rozhenits' [In search of (legal) subjectivity and Informed Voluntary Consent in action: paternalistic silence versus neoliberal/contractual agency of pregnant women and women in labour], draft article presented at the Anthropology *kruzhok* hosted by Nikolai Ssorin-Chaikov, 16 June 2024.

Kulmala, M., M. Kainu, J. Nikula and M. Kivinen (2014), 'Paradoxes of agency: Democracy and welfare in Russia', *Demokratizatsiya*, 22(4): 523–52.

Kuzio, T. (2016), 'Nationalism and authoritarianism in Russia: Introduction to the special issue', *Communist and Post-Communist Studies*, 49(1): 1–11.

Kuzmina, Y. (2023), 'The Defenders of Shiyes: Traditionalism as a mobilisation resource in a Russian protest camp', *East European Politics*, 39(2): 260–80.

Lambek, M. (2008), 'Value and virtue', *Anthropological Theory*, 8(2): 133–57.

Lambek, M., ed. (2010), *Ordinary Ethics: Anthropology, Language, and Action*, New York: Fordham University Press.

Lampland, M. (2010), 'False numbers as formalizing practices', *Social Studies of Science*, 40(3): 377–404.

Lankina, T. (2016), 'It's not all negative: Russian media's flexible coverage of protest as a regime survival strategy', *Ponars Policy Memo*. Available online: https://www.ponarseurasia.org/it-s-not-all-negative-russian-media-s-flexible-coverage-of-protest-as-a-regime-survival-strategy/ (Accessed 2 May 2024).

Laruelle, M. (2019), *Russian Nationalism: Imaginaries, Doctrine, and Political Battlefields*, London and New York: Routledge.

Laruelle, M. (2022), 'What is the ideology of a mobilized Russia?', *Ponars*, 4 October. Available online: https://www.ponarseurasia.org/what-is-the-ideology-of-a-mobilized-russia (Accessed 2 May 2024).

Lazarev, E. (2023), *State-building as Lawfare: Custom, Sharia, and State Law in Postwar Chechnya*, Cambridge: Cambridge University Press.

Ledeneva, A. (1998), *Russia's Economy of Favours: Blat, Networking and Informal Exchange*, Cambridge: Cambridge University Press.

Ledeneva, A. (2013a), *Can Russia Modernise? Sistema, Power Networks and Informal Governance*, Cambridge: Cambridge University Press.

Ledeneva, A. (2013b), 'Russia's practical norms and informal Governance: The origins of endemic corruption', *Social Research: An International Quarterly*, 80(4): 1135–62.

Lefebvre, H. (1991 [1974]), *The Production of Space*, trans. D. Nicholson-Smith, Oxford: Blackwell.

Levada, I. (2003), 'Homo Post-Sovieticus', *Russian Social Science Review* 44(1): 32–67.

Levashov, V., N. Velikaia, I. Shushpanova, O. Grebniak and O. Novozhenina (2023), 'Kak zhivesh, Rossiia?' [How are you, Russia?] in *Ekspress-informatsiia 53 etap sotsiologicheskogo monitoringa*, June, Moscow: Russian Academy of Sciences.

Lewis, D. G. (2020), *Russia's New Authoritarianism: Putin and the Politics of Order*, Edinburgh: Edinburgh University Press.

Leykin, I. (2019), 'The History and afterlife of Soviet demography: The Socialist roots of post-Soviet neoliberalism', *Slavic Review*, 78(1): 149–72.

Leykin, I. and M. Rivkin-Fish (2022), 'Politicized demography and biomedical authority in post-Soviet Russia', *Medical Anthropology*, 41(6–7): 702–17.

Limonov, L. and K. Vakhrusheva (2010), 'Zemel'nyi rynok i stroitel'stvo v Sankt-Peterburge: Problemy nepolnoi spetsifikatsii prav i gosudarstvennoi kvazimonopolii na zemliu' [Land market and construction in St. Petersburg: problems of incomplete specification of rights in state quasi-monopoly on land], *Finansy i Biznes*, 3: 128–43.

Linkon, S. (2018), *The Half-Life of Deindustrialization: Working-Class Writing about Economic Restructuring*, Ann Arbor: University of Michigan Press.

References

Lipman, M. (2016), 'How Putin silences dissent: Inside the Kremlin's crackdown', *Foreign Affairs*, 95: 38–46.

Liu, M. (2005), 'Post-Soviet Paternalism and Personhood: Why 'Culture' Matters to Democratization in Central Asia', in Birgit Schlyter (ed.), *Prospects of Democracy in Central Asia*, 225–38, Stockholm and London: Swedish Research Institute in Istanbul & I.B. Tauris.

Mac Carron, P., K. Kaski and R. Dunbar (2016), 'Calling Dunbar's numbers', *Social Networks*, 47: 151–5.

MacIntyre, A. (1981), *After Virtue: A Study in Moral Theory*, Notre Dame: University of Notre Dame Press.

Malinova, O. (2014), 'Obsession with status and *ressentiment*: Historical backgrounds of the Russian discursive identity construction', *Communist and Post-Communist Studies*, 47(3–4): 291–303.

Manuilova, A. (2022), 'Biopolitics of Authoritarianism. The Case of Russia', in M. Piasentier and S. Raimondi (eds), *Debating Biopolitics New Perspectives on the Government of Life*, 151–70, Northampton, MA and Cheltenham: Edward Elgar.

Marneros, C. (2021), 'The an-archic nomos of the nomads: Preliminary thoughts on the relationship between law and anarchy', *Critical Legal Thinking*. Available online: https://criticallegalthinking.com/2021/04/16/the-an-archic-nomos-of-the-nomads-preliminary-thoughts-on-the-relationship-between-law-and-anarchy (Accessed 2 May 2024).

Martin, D. (2021), 'Corporation, education, and knowing your station: Social estates between a closed city and an Oxbridge College', *Laboratorium. Russian Review of Social Research*, 13(1): 104–26.

Massumi, B. (1996), 'Becoming-Deleuzian', *Environment and Planning D: Society and Space*, 14(4): 395–406.

Mattingly, C. (2012), 'Two virtue ethics and the anthropology of morality', *Anthropological Theory*, 12(2): 161–84.

Mattingly, C. (2019), 'Defrosting concepts, destabilizing doxa: Critical phenomenology and the perplexing particular', *Anthropological Theory*, 19(4): 415–39.

Matveev, I. (2019), 'State, capital, and the transformation of the neoliberal policy paradigm in Putin's Russia', *International Review of Modern Sociology*, 45(1): 27–48.

Matza, T. (2010), 'Subjects of freedom: Psychologists, power and politics in postsocialist Russia', PhD diss., Stanford University.

Matza, T. (2012), '"Good individualism"? Psychology, ethics, and neoliberalism in postsocialist Russia', *American Ethnologist*, 39(4): 804–18.

Mau, S. (2023), *Mute Compulsion: A Marxist Theory of the Economic Power of Capital*, New York: Verso.

McAdam, D. (2003), 'Beyond Structural Analysis: Toward a More Dynamic Understanding of Social Movements', in D. McAdam and M. Diani (eds), *Social Movements and Networks: Relational Approaches to Collective Action*, 281–98, Oxford: Oxford University Press.

McAdam, D., S. Tarrow and C. Tilly (2001), *Dynamics of Contention*, Cambridge: Cambridge University Press.

McGlynn, J. (2023), *Memory Makers: The Politics of the Past in Putin's Russia*, London: Bloomsbury.

McKean, B. (2020), *Disorientating Neoliberalism: Global Justice and the Outer Limit of Freedom*, New York: Oxford University Press.

Melucci, A. (1989), *Nomads of the Present: Social Movements and Individual Needs in Contemporary Society*, ed. John Keane and Paul Mier, Philadelphia, PA: Temple University Press.

Melville, A. (2022), 'State Capacity and Russia', in G. Gill (ed.), *Routledge Handbook of Russian Politics and Society*, 193–206, London: Routledge.

Migdal, J. (2004), *State in Society: Studying how States and Societies Transform and Constitute One Another*, Cambridge: Cambridge University Press.

Mitchell, K., S. Marston and C. Katz (2004), 'Life's Work: An Introduction, Review and Critique', in K. Mitchell, S. Marston and C. Katz (eds), *Life's Work: Geographies of Social Reproduction*, 1–26, Malden and Oxford: Blackwell.

Mitchell, T. (1991), 'The limits of the state: Beyond statist approaches and their critics', *The American Political Science Review*, 85(1): 77–96.

MKRU [no author] (2021), 'Rossiiu nazvali stranoi, skryvaiushchei real'noi uroven' smertnosti ot koronavirusa' [Rossia is named as a country hiding the real level of deaths from Coronavirus], *Moskovskii komsomolets*, 4 August. Available online: https://www.mk.ru/social/2021/08/04/rossiyu-nazvali-stranoy-skryvayushhey-realnyy-uroven-smertnosti-ot-koronavirusa.html?utm_source=yxnews&utm_medium=desktop&nw=1628245349000 (Accessed 2 May 2024).

Moliarenko, O. (2013), 'Raspredelennyi obraz zhizni i kontrurbanizatsionnye protsesy kak faktory razvitiia sel'skikh i gorodskikh poselenii' [Distributed lifestyles in contraurbanization processes as factors in the development of rural and urban settlements], *Voprosy gosudarstvennogo i munitsipal'nogo upravleniia*, 1: 48–71.

Moliarenko, O. (2016), 'Tenevaia gosudarstvennoe i munitsipal'noe upravlenie' [Shadow public administration], *Monitoring obshchestvennogo mneniia: Ekonomicheskie i sotsial'nye peremeny*, 3: 120–33.

Moliarenko, O. (2018), 'Ownerless automobile roads in Russia', *Problems of Economic Transition*, 60(1–3): 220–42.

Monticelli, L. (2021), 'On the necessity of prefigurative politics', *Thesis Eleven*, 167(1): 99–118.

Morozov, V. (2015), *Russia's Postcolonial Identity: A Subaltern Empire in a Eurocentric World*, New York: Palgrave Macmillan.

Morris, J. (2011), 'Socially embedded workers at the nexus of diverse work in Russia: An ethnography of blue-collar informalization', *International Journal of Sociology and Social Policy*, 31(11/12): 619–31.

Morris, J. (2012), 'Unruly entrepreneurs: Russian worker responses to insecure formal employment', *Global Labour Journal*, 3(2): 217–36.

Morris, J. (2013), 'Beyond coping? Alternatives to consumption within a social network of Russian Workers', *Ethnography*, 14(1): 85–103.

Morris, J. (2014), 'The warm home of cacti and other Soviet memories: Russian workers reflect on the socialist period', *Central Europe*, 12(1): 16–31.

Morris, J. (2016), *Everyday Post-Socialism: Working-Class Communities in the Russian Margins*, London: Palgrave Macmillan.

Morris, J. (2017), 'Cheesed off, but not because of sanctions. Immiseration, elite disconnect and neoliberal convergence', *Postsocialism.org*. Available online: http://postsocialism.org/2017/11/16/cheesed-off-but-not-because-of-sanctions-immiseration-elite-disconnect-and-neoliberal-convergence (Accessed 2 May 2024).

Morris, J. (2019a), 'People as the new oil?', *Riddle Russia*, 22 February. Available online: https://ridl.io/people-as-the-new-oil/ (Accessed 2 May 2024).

Morris, J. (2019b), 'A tax paying autocracy?', *Riddle Russia*, 8 July. Available online: https://ridl.io/a-tax-paying-autocracy/ (Accessed 2 May 2024).

Morris, J. (2019c), 'The informal economy and Post-Socialism: Imbricated perspectives on labor, the state, and social embeddedness', *Demokratizatsiya: The Journal of Post-Soviet Democratization*, 27(1): 9–30.

Morris, J. (2021a), 'From prefix capitalism to neoliberal economism: Russia as a Laboratory in capitalist realism', *Sotsiologiia vlasti*, 33(1): 193–221.

Morris, J. (2021b), 'Russian vaccine hesitancy and the paradox of state-society relations', *Postsocialism.org*. Available online: https://postsocialism.org/2021/08/27/russian-vaccine-hesitancy-and-the-paradox-of-state-society-relations/ (Accessed 2 May 2024).

Morris, J. (2023a), 'How homophobic propaganda produces vernacular prejudice in authoritarian states', *Sexualities*, online first.

Morris, J. (2023b), 'Coproducing the Car and the Stratified Street: Automobility and Space in Russia', in G. Duijzings and T. Tuvikene (eds), *If Cars Could Walk: Postsocialist Streets in Transformation*, 89–105, Oxford and New York: Berghahn.

Morris, J. (2023c), 'Activists and Experiential Entanglement in Russian Labor Organizing', in J. Morris, A. Semenov and R. Smyth (eds), *Varieties of Russian Activism: State-Society Contestation in Everyday Life*, 143–65, Bloomington: Indiana University Press.

Morris, J. and M. Garibyan (2021), 'Russian cultural conservatism critiqued: Translating the tropes of "Gayropa" and "Juvenile Justice" in everyday life', *Europe-Asia Studies*, 73(8): 1487–507.

Morris, J. and S. Hinz (2017), 'Free automotive unions, industrial work and precariousness in provincial Russia', *Post-Communist Economies*, 29(3): 282–96.

Morris, J. and A. Polese (2016), 'Informal health and education sector payments in Russian and Ukrainian cities: Structuring welfare from below', *European Urban and Regional Studies*, 23(3): 481–96.

Mouffe, C. (1999), 'Deliberative democracy or agonistic pluralism?', *Social Research*, 66(3): 745–58.

Munro, K. (2019), '"Social reproduction theory," social reproduction, and household production', *Science & Society*, 83(4): 451–68.

Nadkarni, M. and O. Shevchenko (2004), 'The politics of nostalgia: A case for comparative analysis of post-socialist practices', *Ab imperio*, 2: 487–519.

Narvselius, E. (2016), 'Tusovka Died– Long Live Tusovka! Post-Soviet Culturally Polyphonic Youth Groupings in L'viv (Ukraine)', in B. Törnquist-Plewa (ed.), *History, Language and Society in the Borderlands of Europe: Ukraine and Belarus in Focus*, 185–214, Malmö: Sekel Bokförlag.

Nielsen, F. (1986/2006), *The Eye of the Whirlwind. Russian Identity and Soviet Nation-Building. Quests for Meaning in a Soviet Metropolis* [Unpublished MS]. Available online: http://www.anthrobase.com/Txt/N/Nielsen_F_S_03.htm#200_Chapter%20Two:%20Life%20on%20the%20Islands (Accessed 2 May 2024).

Nikinova, O. (2010), 'Soviet patriotism in a comparative perspective', *Studies in East European Thought*, 62: 353–76.

North, D. (1990), *Institutions, Institutional Change and Economic Performance*, Cambridge: Cambridge University Press.

Odierna, B. (2024), 'Assembling Bits and Pieces: From Patchwork to Ethnography', in T. Burger, U. Mahar, P. Schild and A-M Walter (eds), *The Multi-Sided Ethnographer: Living the Field beyond Research*, 73–92, Bielefeld: transcript Verlag.

Ong, A. (2006), *Neoliberalism as Exception*, Durham, NC: Duke University Press.

Orlova, G. (2004), 'Apologiia stranoi veshchi: "malen'kie khitrosti" sovetskoi cheloveka' [Apologia for a strange thing; 'Small tricks' of the Soviet person], *Neprikosnovennyi zapas*, 34(2); 84–90.

Orlova, G. and J. Morris (2021), 'Pandemiia i (bez)umnom gorode: tsifrovye protezy i affordansy moskovskoi samoizoliatsii' [Pandemic in the in(sane) city: digital prostheses and affordances of Moscow self-isolation], in E. Lapina-Kratasiuk, O. Zaporozhets and A. Voz'ianov (eds), *Seti goroda. Liudi. Tekhnologiia. Vlasti*, 135–79, Moscow: Novoe literaturnoe obozrenie.

Orlova, G., K. Tanis, M. Balakhonskaya, A. Balyakova, A. Berlov, A. Zaripova and M. Lukin (2022), 'How to turn towards Soviet temporality? Setting the analytical optics', *Basic Research Program Working Papers*, National Research University Higher School of Economics Moscow. Series: Humanities WP BRP 211/HUM/2022.

Orlova, V. (2021), 'Malfunctioning affective infrastructures: How the "broken" road becomes a site of belonging in postindustrial eastern Siberia', *Sibirica*, 20(1): 28–57.

Østbø, J. (2021), 'Hybrid surveillance capitalism: Sber's model for Russia's modernization', *Post-Soviet Affairs*, 37(5): 435–52.

Oushakine, S. (2010a), 'Somatic Nationalism: Theorizing Post-Soviet Ethnicity in Russia', in C. Bradatan and S. Oushakine (eds), *In Marx's Shadow: Knowledge, Power, and Intellectuals in Eastern Europe and Russia*, 155–74, Lanham, MD: Lexington Books.

Oushakine, S. (2010b), *The Patriotism of Despair*, Ithaca: Cornell University Press.

Ovsyannikova, A. (2016), 'Is neoliberalism applicable to Russia? A response to Ilya Matveev', *Open Democracy*, 20 May. Available online: https://www.opendemocracy.net/en/odr/is-neoliberalism-applicable-to-russia-response-to-ilya-matveev/ (Accessed 2 May 2024).

Palomera, J. and T. Vetta (2016), 'Moral economy: Rethinking a radical concept', *Anthropological Theory*, 16(4): 413–32.

Papadopoulos, D. (2018), *Experimental Practice: Technoscience, Alterontologies, and More-than-social Movements*, Durham, NC: Duke University Press.

Parsons, M. (2014), *Dying Unneeded: The Cultural Context of the Russian Mortality Crisis*, Nashville: Vanderbilt University Press.

Pavlovskaya, M. (2018), 'Ontologies of Poverty in Russia and Duplicities of Neoliberalism', in S. Schram and M. Pavlovskaya (eds), *Rethinking Neoliberalism: Resisting the Disciplinary Regime*, 84–103, London and New York: Routledge.

Peck, J. (2004), 'Geography and public policy: Constructions of neoliberalism', *Progress in Human Geography*, 28(3): 392–405.

Pellizzoni, L. (2022), 'A different kind of emancipation? From lifestyle to form-of-life', *European Journal of Social Theory*, 25(1): 155–71.

Pesmen, D. (2000), *Russia and Soul: An Exploration*, Ithaca: Cornell University Press.

Petukhov, V. (2018), 'Dinamika sotsial'nykh nastroenii rossiian i formirovanie zaprosa na peremeny' [The dynamic of social mood of Russians in the formation of demand for change], *Sotsiologicheskie issledovaniia*, 11(415): 40–53.

Petukhov, V. and R. Petukhov (2019), 'Zapros na peremeny: prichiny aktualizatsii, kliuchevye slagaemye i potentsial'nye nositeli' [Demand for change: causes of actualization, key components and potential media], *Polis. Politicheskie issledovaniia*, 5: 119–33.

Piano, E. (2018), 'Outlaw and economics: Biker gangs and club goods', *Rationality and Society*, 30(3): 350–76.

References

Pilkington, H. (2002), 'Farewell to the *tusovka*: Masculinities and Femininities on the Moscow Youth Scene', in H. Pilkington (ed.), *Gender, Generation and Identity in Contemporary Russia*, 243–70, London and New York: Routledge.

de Pina-cabral, J. (2013), 'The two faces of mutuality: Contemporary themes in anthropology', *Anthropological Quarterly*, 86(1): 257–75.

Pina-Cabral, J. (2017), *World: An Anthropological Examination*, Chicago: Malinowski Monographs. Hau Books/University of Chicago Press.

Piskunov, M. and T. Rakov (2020), 'Kommunisticheskii trud? Subbotnik mezhnu pozdnesovestskim ritualom i ekologicheskoi praktikoi' [Communist labour? The subbotnik between late-Soviet ritual and ecological practice], *Vestnik Surgutskogo gosudarstvennogo pedagogicheskogo universiteta*, 6(69): 113–20.

Plueckhahn, R. (2017), 'The power of faulty paperwork', *Inner Asia*, 19(1): 91–109.

Plusnin, J., Y. Zausaeva, N. Zhidkevich and A. Pozanenko (2015), *Wandering Workers. Mores, Behavior, Way of Life, and Political Status of Domestic Russian Labor Migrants*, Stuttgart: ibidem-Verlag.

Pokrovskii, N. and S. Bobylev (2003), *Sovremennyi rossiiskii sever. Ot kletochnoi globalizatsii k ochagovoi sotsial'noi strukture* [Contemporary Russian North. From cellular globalization to the focal social structure], Moscow: GU-VShE.

Pottinger, L. (2017), 'Planting the seeds of a quiet activism', *Area*, 49(2): 215–22.

Prozorov, S. (2013), 'Living ideas and dead bodies: The biopolitics of stalinism', *Alternatives*, 38(3): 208–27.

Raikhel, E. (2016), *Governing Habits: Treating Alcoholism in the Post-Soviet Clinic*, Ithaca, NY: Cornell University Press.

Rancière, J. (2001), 'Ten theses on politics', trans. D. Panagia and R. Bowlby, *Theory & Event*, 5(3).

Rancière, J. (2016), *The Method of Equality: Interviews with Laurent Jeanpierre and Dork Zabunyan*, trans. Julie Rose, Cambridge and Malden: Polity.

Rancière, J. (2017), 'Jacques Rancière: Democracy, equality, emancipation in a changing world', *Babylonia*, Speech of Jacques Rancière at B-FEST (International Antiauthoritarian Festival of Babylonia Journal), 27 May. Available online: https://www.babylonia.gr/2017/06/11/jacques-ranciere-democracy-equality-emancipation-changing-world (Accessed 2 May 2024).

Read, J. (2008), 'The Age of Cynicism: Deleuze and Guattari on the Production of Subjectivity in Capitalism', in I. Buchanan and N. Thoburn (eds), *Deleuze and Politics*, 129–59, Edinburgh: Edinburgh University Press.

Reeves-Evison, T. and M. Rainey (2018), 'Ethico-aesthetic repairs', *Third Text*, 32(1): 1–15.

Reid, S. (2006), 'The Meaning of Home: "The Only Bit of the World You Can Have to Yourself"', in L. Siegelbaum (ed.), *Borders of Socialism: Private Spheres of Soviet Russia*, 145–70, New York: Palgrave Macmillan.

Remington, T. F. (2018), 'Russian economic inequality in comparative perspective', *Comparative Politics*, 50(3): 395–416.

Ries, N. (1997), *Russian Talk: Culture and Conversation During Perestroika*, Ithaca and London: Cornell University Press.

Robbins, J. (2013), 'Beyond the suffering subject: Toward an anthropology of the good', *Journal of the Royal Anthropological Institute*, 19(3): 447–62.

Roberts, C. and T. Sherlock (1999), 'Bringing the Russian State Back In: Explanations of the derailed transition to market democracy', *Comparative Politics*, 31(4): 477–98.

Robertson, G. (2010), *The Politics of Protest in Hybrid Regimes: Managing Dissent in Post-Communist Russia*, New York: Cambridge University Press.

Robinson, A. (2010), 'Why Deleuze (still) matters. States, war-machines and radical transformation', *Ceasefire*. Available online: https://ceasefiremagazine.co.uk/in-theory-deleuze-war-machine/ (Accessed 2 May 2024).

Rogers, D. (2011), 'Community, symbolic order, and the exclusion of the social in Serguei Oushakine's *Patriotism of Despair*', *Ab Imperio*, 1: 247–61.

Rogers, D. (2015), *The Depths of Russia: Oil, Power, and Culture after Socialism*, Ithaca and London: Cornell University Press.

Romanov, P. (2008), 'Quality Evaluation in Social Services: Challenges for New Public Management in Russia', in B. Peters (ed.), *Mixes, Matches, and Mistakes: New Public Management in Russia and the Former Soviet Republics*, 9–51, Budapest: Local Government and Public Service Reform Initiative, Open Society Institute.

Roy, A. (2009), 'Why India cannot plan its cities: Informality, insurgence and the idiom of urbanization', *Planning Theory*, 8(1): 83.

Rupprecht, T. (2020), 'Global varieties of neoliberalism: Ideas on free markets and strong states in late twentieth-century Chile and Russia', *Global Perspectives* 1(1): 1–13.

Rupprecht, T. (2022), 'The Road from Snake Hill: The Genesis of Russian Neoliberalism', in S. Quinn and D. Plehwe (eds), *Market Civilizations: Neoliberals East and South*, 109–38, New York: ZONE BOOKS.

Sakwa, R. (2010), 'The dual state in Russia', *Post-Soviet Affairs*, 26(3): 185–206.

Sakwa, R. (2021), 'Heterarchy: Russian politics between chaos and control', *Post-Soviet Affairs*, 37(3): 222–41.

Sassen, S. (2014), *Expulsions: Brutality and Complexity in the Global Economy*, Cambridge, MA and London: Harvard University Press.

Saunders, R. (2013), 'Pagan places: Towards a religiogeography of neopaganism', *Progress in Human Geography*, 37(6): 786–810.

Sayer, A. (2005), *The Moral Significance of Class*, Cambridge and New York: Cambridge University Press.

Scharff, C. (2016), 'The psychic life of neoliberalism: Mapping the contours of entrepreneurial subjectivity', *Theory, Culture & Society*, 33(6): 107–22.

Schechner, R. (1988), *Performance Theory*, New York: Routledge.

Scheler, M. (2003 [1913]), *Ressentiment*, Milwaukee: Marquette University Press.

Schenk, C. (2021), 'Producing state capacity through corruption: The case of immigration control in Russia', *Post-Soviet Affairs*, 37(4): 303–17.

Schlögel, K. (2023), *The Soviet Century: Archaeology of a Lost World*, trans. R. Livingstone, Princeton and Oxford: University of Princeton Press.

Schwenkel, C. (2015), 'Spectacular infrastructure and its breakdown in socialist Vietnam', *American Ethnologist*, 42(3): 520–34.

Scott, J. (1976), *The Moral Economy of the Peasant: Rebellion and Subsistence in Southeast Asia*, New Haven and London: Yale University Press.

Scott, J. (1990), *Domination and the Arts of Resistance: Hidden Transcripts*, New Haven and London: Yale University Press.

Secor, A. and J. Linz (2017), 'Becoming minor', *Environment and Planning D: Society and Space*, 35(4): 568–73.

Seleev, S. and A. Pavlov (2016), *Garazhniki*, 2(6) Fond podderzhki sotsial'nykh issledovanii 'Khamovniki'. Moscow: Strana Oz.

Semenov, A. (2017), 'Against the stream: Political opposition in Russian regions in the 2012–2016 electoral cycle', *Demokratizatsiya: The Journal of Post-Soviet Democratization*, 25(4): 481–502.

Serebrennikov, D. (forthcoming), 'Tekhnologii i izmenenie povsednevnykh praktik sledovatelei i politseiskikh posle tsifrovizatsii ikh raboty na premere g. Moskvy' ['Shift or flow? Changes in the daily Moscow law enforcers practices after its digitalization'], unpublished MS.

Sharafutdinova, G. (2016), 'Managing National Ressentiment: Morality Politics in Putin's Russia', in A. Makarychev and A. Yatsyk (eds), *Vocabularies of International Relations after the Crisis in Ukraine*, 130–51, London and New York: Routledge.

Sharafutdinova, G. (2019), 'Was there a "simple soviet" person? debating the politics and sociology of "Homo Sovieticus"', *Slavic Review*, 78(1): 173–95.

Sharafutdinova, G. (2020), *The Red Mirror: Putin's Leadership and Russia's Insecure Identity*, New York: Oxford University Press.

Sharafutdinova, G. (2023), *The Afterlife of the 'Soviet Man': Rethinking Homo Sovieticus*, London and New York: Bloomsbury Academic.

Sharma, A. and A. Gupta (2006), 'Introduction: Rethinking Theories of the State in an Age of Globalization', in A. Sharma and A. Gupta (eds), *The Anthropology of the State: A Reader*, 1–42, Malden and Oxford: Blackwell.

Sherlock, T. (2020), 'Russian society and foreign policy: Mass and elite orientations after Crimea', *Problems of Post-Communism*, 67(1): 1–23.

Shevchenko, O. (2009), *Crisis and the Everyday in Postsocialist Moscow*, Bloomington: Indiana University Press.

Shevchenko, O. (2015), 'Resisting Resistance: Everyday Life, Practical Competence, and Neoliberal Rhetoric in Postsocialist Russia', in C. Chatterjee, D. Ransel, M. Cavender and K. Petrone (eds), *Everyday Life in Russia: Past and Present*, 52–71, Bloomington: Indiana University Press.

Shevchuk, A. (2020), 'From factory to platform: Autonomy and control in the digital economy', *Sotsiologiia vlasti*, 32(1): 30–54.

Shields, S. (2019), 'The paradoxes of necessity: Fail forwards neoliberalism, social reproduction, recombinant populism and Poland's 500Plus policy', *Capital & Class*, 43(4): 653–69.

Shirikov, A. (2022), 'Opium for the masses: How propaganda won Russians' trust', *Russia.Post*, 28 October. Available online: https://www.russiapost.info/society/opium (Accessed 2 May 2024).

Shleifer, A. and D. Treisman (2005), 'A normal country: Russia after communism', *Journal of Economic Perspectives*, 19(1): 151–74.

Sigman, C. (2013), 'The "new public management" in Russia. The tribulations of a transposition', *Government and Public Action*, 3(2): 441–60.

Slabinski, D. (2022), 'Mechanisms of movement emergence and sustainability in Russia: A case study of the shiyes protests in Arkhangelsk region, 2018–2020', Unpublished Masters Thesis, University of Oslo. Available online: https://www.duo.uio.no/handle/10852/100328 (Accessed 2 May 2024).

Slobodian, Q. (2018), *Globalists: The End of Empire and the Birth of Neoliberalism*, Cambridge, MA: Harvard University Press.

Smith, A., A. Stenning, A. Rochovská and D. Świątek (2011), *Domesticating Neoliberalism: Spaces of Economic Practice and Social Reproduction in Post-socialist Cities*, Malden and Oxford: Wiley-Blackwell.

Smith, M. B. (2010), *Property of Communists: The Urban Housing Program from Stalin to Khrushchev*, DeKalb: Northern Illinois University Press.

Smyth, R. (2002), 'Building state capacity from the inside out: Parties of power and the success of the president's reform agenda in Russia', *Politics & Society*, 30(4): 555–78.

Smyth, R. (2006), 'Strong partisans, weak parties? assessing the assumptions of cohesiveness within Russian party organisations', *Comparative Politics*, 38(2): 202–28.

Smyth, R. (2021), *Elections, Protest, and Authoritarian Regime Stability: Russia 2008–2020*, Cambridge: Cambridge University Press.

Smyth, R., M. McCann and K. Hitchcock (2023), 'From Neighbors to Activists: Shared Grievances and Collective Solutions', in J. Morris, A. Semenov and R. Smyth (eds), *Varieties of Russian Activism: State-Society Contestation in Everyday Life*, 70–92, Bloomington: Indiana University Press.

Sokolov, B., R. Inglehart, F. Ponarin, I. Vartanova and W Zimmerman (2009), 'Disillusionment and Anti-Americanism in Russia: From Pro-American to Anti-American attitudes, 1993–2009', *International Studies Quarterly*, 62: 534–47.

Sparke, M. (2013), *Introducing Globalization: Ties, Tensions, and Uneven Integration*, Malden and Oxford: Wiley-Blackwell.

Ssorin-Chaikov, N. (2003), *The Social Life of the State in Subarctic Siberia*, Stanford: Stanford University Press.

Stephenson, S. (2015), *Gangs of Russia: From the Streets to the Corridors of Power*, Ithaca, NY: Cornell University Press.

Stewart, S. and J. Dollbaum (2017), 'Civil society development in Russia and Ukraine: Diverging paths', *Communist and Post-Communist Studies*, 50(3): 207–20.

Strathern, M. (1984), 'Subject or Object? Women and the Circulation of Valuables in Highlands New Guinea', in R. Hirschon (ed.), *Women and Property – Women as Property*, 158–75, London: Croom Helm.

Strathern, M. (2018), 'Relations', in F. Stein, S. Lazar, M. Candea, H. Diemberger, J. Robbins, A. Sanchez and R. Stasch (eds), *The Cambridge Encyclopedia of Anthropology*. Available Online: http://doi.org/10.29164/18relations.

Strathern, M. (2020), *Relations: An Anthropological Account*, Durham, NC: Duke University Press.

Sztompka, P. (2004), 'The Trauma of Change: A Case of Post-Communist Society', in J. Alexander, R. Eyerman, B. Giesen, N. Smelser and P. Sztompka (eds), *Cultural Trauma and Collective Identity*, 155–95, Berkeley and London: University of California Press.

Tacchetti, M., N. Toro, D. Papadopoulos and M. de la Bellacasa (2022), 'Crafting ecologies of existence: More than human community making in Colombian textile craftism', *EPE: Nature and Space*, 5(3): 1383–401.

Tarrow, S. (1993), 'Modular collective action and the rise of the social movement: Why the French Revolution was not enough', *Politics and Society*, 21(1): 647–70.

Taylor, B. (2011), *State Building in Putin's Russia: Policing and Coercion After Communism*, New York: Cambridge University Press.

Taylor, S. (2017), 'Psychosocial Research', in B. Gough (ed.), *The Palgrave Handbook of Critical Social Psychology*, 225–42, London: Palgrave Macmillan/Springer Nature.

Tereshina, D. (2019a), 'Managing Firms and Families: Small Businesses in Provincial Russia in Times of Flexible Accumulation', Dissertation Zur Erlangung des Doktorgrades der Philosophie, Halle-Wittenberg: Max Planck Institute for Social Anthropology.

Tereshina, D. (2019b), '"Shiyes is our Stalingrad": Garbage riots and moral outrage in northwest Russia', *Max Planck Institute for Social Anthropology*, 10 December. Available Online: https://www.eth.mpg.de/5353781/blog_2019_12_10_01#:~:text=A%20wave%20of%20public%20rallies,Pomorye%20ne%20pomoika (Accessed 2 May 2024).

Thelen, T. (2011), 'Shortage, fuzzy property and other dead ends in the anthropological analysis of (post)socialism', *Critique of Anthropology*, 31(1): 43–61.

References

Thelen, T. (2018), 'Socialism, Marxist-Leninist-Maoist', in H. Callan (ed.), *The International Encyclopaedia of Anthropology*, London: John Wiley & Sons.

Thelen, T. and E. Alber, eds (2017), *Reconnecting State and Kinship*, Philadelphia: University of Pennsylvania Press.

Thelen, T., L. Vetters and K. von Benda-beckmann, eds (2017), *Statography: Towards a Relational Anthropology of the State*, New York and Oxford: Berghahn.

Thévenot, L. (2020), 'How does politics take closeness into account? returns from Russia', *International Journal of Politics, Culture and Society*, 33: 221–50.

Toal, G. (2017), *Near Abroad: Putin, the West and the Contest over Ukraine and the Caucasus*, New York: Oxford University Press.

Tomášková, E. (2017), 'Influence of hashtag on formation of new phraseological units in political journalism of online media', *Caracteres: estudios culturales y críticos de la esfera digital*, 6(2): 245–58.

Tooze, A. (2018), 'Neoliberarlism's world order', *Dissent Magazine*, summer. Available online: https://www.dissentmagazine.org/article/neoliberalism-world-order-review-quinn-slobodian-globalists (Accessed 2 May 2024).

Topolski, A. (2015), *Arendt, Levinas and a Politics of Relationality*. London: Rowman & Littlefield.

Torsello, D. (2018), 'Corruption', in H. Callan (ed.), *The International Encyclopaedia of Anthropology*, London: John Wiley & Sons.

Trickett, N. (2023), 'Pavlov's stimulus: understanding "military Keynesianism" in Russia', *Riddle Russia*, 15 August. Available online: https://ridl.io/pavlov-s-stimulus-understanding-military-keynesianism-in-russia/ (Accessed 2 May 2024).

Trickett, N. (2025), *Empire of Austerity: Russia and the Breaking of Eurasia*, London: Hurst Publishers.

Tsing, A. (2015), *The Mushroom at the End of the World*, Princeton and Oxford: Princeton University Press.

Tsipursky, G. (2016), *Socialist Fun: Youth, Consumption, and State-Sponsored Popular Culture in the Soviet Union 1945–1970*, Pittsburgh, PA: University of Pittsburgh Press.

Tsygankov, A. (2015), 'Vladimir Putin's last stand: The sources of Russia's Ukraine policy', *Post-Soviet Affairs*, 31(4): 279–303.

Urinboyev, R. (2021), *Migration and Hybrid Political Regimes*, Oakland, CA: University of California Press.

Ushakin, S. (2009), '"Nam etoi bol'iu dyshat?" O travme, pamiati i soobshchestvakh' [Do we have to breathe this pain? On Trauma, memory in communities], in S. Ushakin and E. Trubina (eds), *Travma: Punkty*, 5–47, Moscow: NLO.

Vanke, A. (2024), *The Urban Life of Workers in Post-Soviet Russia: Engaging in Everyday Struggle*, Manchester: Manchester University Press.

Vanke, A. and I. Tartakovskaya (2016), 'Transformatsii maskulinnosti rossisskikh rabochikh v kontekste sotsial'noi mobil'nosti' [The transformation of Russian working class masculinities in the context of social mobility], *Mir Rossii*, 25(4): 136–53.

Virno, P. (2004), *A Grammar of the Multitude: For an Analysis of Contemporary Forms of Life*, trans. I. Bertoletti, J. Cascaito and A. Casson, Los Angeles: Semiotext(e).

Volkov, V. (2002), *Violent Entrepreneurs: The Use of Force in the Making of Russian Capitalism*, Ithaca: Cornell University Press.

Vorbrugg, A. (2019), 'Not about land, not quite a grab: Dispersed dispossession in rural Russia', *Antipode*, 51(3): 1011–31.

Vorbrugg, A. (2022), 'Ethnographies of slow violence: Epistemological alliances in fieldwork and narrating ruins', *Environment and Planning C: Politics and Space*, 40(2): 447–62.

Walker, C. (2015), '"I don't really like tedious, monotonous work": Working-class young women, service sector employment and social mobility in contemporary Russia', *Sociology*, 49(1): 106–22.

Walker, C. (2016), 'In Search of "Stability": Working-class Men, Masculinity and Wellbeing in Contemporary Russia', in A. Cornwall, N. Lindisfarne and F. Corioris (eds), *Dislocating Masculinity (revisited): Comparative Ethnographies*, 51–65, London: Zed Books.

Wedeen, L. (1999), *Ambiguities of Domination: Politics, Rhetoric, and Symbols in Contemporary Syria*, Chicago and London: University of Chicago Press.

Wengle, S. (2012), 'Engineers versus managers: Experts, market-making and state-building in Putin's Russia', *Economy and Society*, 41(3): 435–67.

Wengle, S. and M. Rasell (2008), 'The monetisation of l'goty: Changing patterns of welfare politics and provision in Russia', *Europe-Asia Studies*, 60(5): 739–56.

Wexler, P. (1996), 'The internal critique of social psychology', *Counterpoints: Critical Social Psychology*, 16: 13–23.

White, A. (1990), *De-Stalinization and the House of Culture: Declining State Control over Leisure in the USSR, Poland and Hungary, 1953–1989*, London: Routledge.

White, D. (2018), 'State capacity and regime resilience in Putin's Russia', *International Political Science Review*, 39(1): 130–43.

Wood, E. (1982), 'The politics of theory and the concept of class: E. P. Thompson and his critics', *Studies in Political Economy*, 9(1): 46–75.

Yudin, G. (2020), 'Governing through polls: Politics of representation and presidential support in Putin's Russia', *Javnost – The Public*, 27(1): 2–16.

Yurchak, A. (2003), 'Soviet hegemony of form: Everything was forever, until it was no more', *Comparative Studies in Society and History*, 45(3): 480–510.

Yurchak, A. (2005), *Everything Was Forever, Until It Was No More: The Last Soviet Generation*, Princeton and Oxford: Princeton University Press.

Zakharova, A. (2023), 'Moral cartography: Classifications of villagers in the working life of rural bureaucrats', *Anthropological Forum*, 19(59): 103–29.

Zakharova, A. (2024), 'Speaking simply and remembering people: The affective labor of Rural Bureaucrats', Conference Paper *Vectors*, MSSEES, Moscow 19 April.

Zdravomyslova, E. and V. Voronkov (2002), 'The informal public in Soviet society: Double morality at work', *Social Research*, 69(1): 49–69.

Zhelnina, A. (2023), 'The River of Urban Resistance: Renovation and New Civic Infrastructure in Moscow', in J. Morris, A. Semenov and R. Smyth (eds), *Varieties of Russian Activism: State-Society Contestation in Everyday Life*, 120–42, Bloomington: Indiana University Press.

Zhikharevich, D. and D. Savchenko (2023), '"I don't know, I wasn't there": The possibility of knowing in a depoliticized society', *Russian Analytical Digest*, 302(13): 2–5.

Zubarevich, N. and S. Safronov (2019), 'People and money: Incomes, consumption, and financial behavior of the population of Russian regions in 2000–2017', *Regional Research of Russia*, 9: 359–69.

INDEX

activism 189–208
  communicative 78
  decentralized 190
  ecological 183, 198–201
  graffiti 188, 198, 201, 204–5
  political 19, 23, 77
  pro-war 60, 203–4
adminresurs 130
affect, political 13, 27, 29, 32, 45, 57, 76, 79, 192, 196–7, 206, 208
Agamben, Giorgio 102, 185
Arendt, Hannah 191–2
authoritarian capitalism 14
authoritarian personality 5
authoritarianism
  ordinary 10
  resilience of 131

Baathism 10
bezperspektivnost and *bezyskhodnost* 27–8, 63, 66–7, 79, 95, 101, 209
biopolitics 91–3, 98, 102, 133, 213
blat (favour exchange) 134, 171, 173
Bolotnaia protests in 2011 206
Bourdieu, Pierre 63, 66, 130, 161, 172
Burawoy, Michael 8

cadastral services 74, 122, 127, 135–6, 138, 141, 149–50, 157, 186
capitalist realism 15, 21, 87–9, 94–5, 98, 101–2, 106–7, 212–13
carers (nannies) 14–15
Charlesworth, Simon 66
Cherkaev, Xenia 118, 134, 170–3, 181, 211
China 14, 32, 33, 42, 96, 111, 155, 214
Chukhrov, Keti 21, 46–7, 49, 57, 67, 71, 81–2, 216
Clastres, Pierre 5, 153
Clément, Karine 10, 12, 43, 96, 189, 192, 206, 210
clientelism, political 16, 18

Cohen, Stanley 38
Collier, Stephen 91–2, 118
commonality, *see under obshchnost* concept
communication, qualitative 47, 70, 74–5, 79, 119, 128, 135, 196, 211–2, 216
composites, ethnographic 8
conatus, *see under* striving
connectiveness, *see under obshchnost* concept
corporate social responsibility 109–10
corporatism 90, 110–13, 212
COVID-19 34, 77, 94, 112, 130, 134, 143
craft concept 167–88
Crimean annexation 1–2, 4, 17, 28–9, 35, 201

dealienation, *see under* USSR
defensive consolidation 20, 29–30, 32, 35, 37–8, 41–4, 60, 100, 110, 190, 193–4, 210
Deleuze, Gilles (and Félix Guattari) 63, 129, 207, 214
  on Foucault 68
Deleuzian concepts of
  antiproduction 22, 214
  control society 20, 111–2, 155–6, 164, 213
  deterritorialization 76, 133, 152, 154–60, 162, 164, 203, 205, 215
  lines of flight 4, 15, 19, 102, 154–60, 162, 164, 179, 182, 214, 217
  minoritarian 154–5, 210, 216
  nomadism 19, 155–8, 160–5, 179, 192, 204, 206–7, 214–15
  ressentiment 46
de-regulation, *see also* governance 117, 131, 134, 138
desire, socially-connective 14–15, 46–7, 62, 68, 74, 76, 81, 153, 155, 157, 161, 169, 193, 204, 209–11, 214

240   *Index*

discourses, official
    gender 3–4
    geopolitical 9, 12, 29, 31, 38
    anti-LGBT 3, 34
    anti-Ukraine 31, 37–8, 46
    anti-West 3, 29, 34–5
dispossession 14, 52–3, 66, 71–2, 103, 161, 172, 182
DIY practices 68, 168, 173, 178
domestication, neoliberal 21, 87–8, 102, 108, 111–2
Donbas conflict 2, 15–16, 201
drive, *see under* desire
Dumont, Louis 49
Dunbar, Robin 7–8

emotion, *see under* affect
enthusiasm, war 28
entrepreneurialism 105, 110
    'bare' 88, 102, 105, 110, 113, 154
    'unruly' 98, 100, 108, 110, 154
ethnic solidarity 15
ethnicized labour 64, 90, 105–6
extended networks of practice 68, 170, 177–8

Fassin, Didier 21, 52–3, 56
fatalism, *see under* pofigizm
feeling, *see under* structure of feeling
Fisher, Mark 15, 94
Foucault, Michel 18, 91, 132, 153, 155, 217

Gago, Verónica 63, 67–8
garages 149–52, 158–60
gig economy 94, 104–5
gleaning 22–3, 169–71, 174, 182, 186
governance 119–21, 126–31, 137, 153
    as care relation 18–19, 78, 119, 121, 128, 137, 144–5, 213
    coproduced 119–20, 123, 128, 133–8, 142, 145, 213
    'devolved' 22, 128–9, 135
    municipal 123–4, 150
    'shadow' 141–2, 213–14
governmentality 91, 98, 102, 105, 118, 142, 155
grievance narratives 9, 39, 45–6, 60, 206

habitability 67–8
haunting, socialist 13, 47, 51–2, 59, 73, 77, 162, 211
heating plant 115–16
heterotopia 23, 217
higher education 2–3
hopelessness, *see under bezperspektivnost* and *bezyskhodnost*
House of Culture 169, 171, 177–9, 188
Humphrey, Caroline 14, 71, 76, 83, 90, 151
'hustle' 98, 99, 102, 107

identity, national 28, 30–1, 33, 46
imperial-mindedness 32, 49
incoherence, of state 122–3, 126–7, 132, 138–42, 145, 213–14
individualism, methodological 13, 46–7, 52, 61–2, 88, 173, 211
inequality 33, 39, 42, 46, 51, 56, 87, 102
informal economy 20, 66, 91, 89, 103, 107–8, 131, 149, 159, 162–5
intergenerational communication 32–3, 70–3, 82, 212
interlocutors, key ethnographic
    Alla (IT worker, Moscow) 3
    Denis and Katya (woodworkers) 174–6
    Dima (schoolboy patriot) 2–3
    Felix (biker activist) 190–1, 194–5, 201–4
    Igor (Izluchino man) 88, 96–102
    Julia (Moscow pensioner) 35–6
    Kirill (factory worker) 125–6, 132
    Lena and sisters (crafters) 176–7
    Lyova (plumber in fifties) 1–2, 4, 17, 63
    Natasha (memory activist 55–6)
    Nikita (Kaluga metal turner) 90, 106–10
    Nikolai Viktorovich (heating engineer) 115–18, 140–2
    Olga (citizen journalist) 125, 160
    Polina (anti-war activist) 190, 192, 197–9, 204–6
    Rahimjon (Kyrgyz worker) 90, 103–5
    Sasha (forklift driver) 1–2, 12, 17, 68–9, 169, 171
    Svetlana Grigorievna (cultural worker) 179, 185
    Svetlana Sergeevna (cadastral worker) 74, 136–7

Index

Tamara (Kaluga politician) 21, 60, 62, 70–5, 77–80, 143, 188
Tanya (yard beautifier) 117, 179–81, 185, 210
Valera (mechanic) 158–9
Vanya 21, 59, 62–6, 68–70, 80, 122–3, 134, 138, 186
Viktor (retired engineer) 39–41
intersubjectivity 4, 60–2, 68, 77, 81, 99, 119, 155–6, 177–8, 184–5, 187, 189–90, 192, 196, 211
intimacy, political 10

Jessop, Bob 132

Kaluga city 6, 8, 89, 103, 106–7, 109, 122
Kharkiv 3
kinship, fictive 90, 108–11, 119, 122, 135, 137, 212
Kozlova, Natalya 52, 216
Kropotkin, Peter 184

labour migration, *see under vakhta*
Levada, Yuri 89
'loser' identity 61, 64–7, 93, 101, 187
loyalism, political 4, 32

MacIntyre, Alasdair 171–2
Mariupol 28
Mattingly, Cheryl 74, 192
Matveev, Ilya 91
McAdam, Doug 196, 207
media consumption, *see under* television consumption
memory, *see also* nostalgia 99, 211
metaoccupational community 68–9, 77–8, 100, 162, 173
methodology, *see also* composites
    elliptical ethnographic 9, 189
    ethnographic 6–8, 163
    extended case method 8
    polyphonic 7
    social media 37
    triangulation 5, 109, 200
microproletarianization 111
mobility, population, *see also vakhta* 8
mobility, social 15, 31, 41, 57, 112

mobilization, military 3, 10, 19, 27, 30, 79, 98, 101, 125–6, 157–8, 164, 213
monetization, *see under* welfare state
moral economy 69–70, 106, 144–5, 150, 162, 170
Moscow 2–3, 8, 14, 33–6, 96–8, 101, 103–5, 125, 154, 160
motherland, 'small' 76, 177
Mouffe, Chantelle 5, 161, 214
mutual aid 18, 69–70, 90, 170, 184–7, 191, 203–4

nationalism 29, 31–2, 38, 45, 51
NATO expansion 32, 35
Navalny, Alexei 31, 33, 100, 156, 183, 199, 205–7
neo-colonialism 15–16
neoliberalism, *see also* domestication 87–113, 118, 129, 145, 177
    authoritarian neoliberalism 94, 112
Nietzsche, Friedrich 45–6, 52, 55–6, 153
North, Douglass 16
nostalgia, Soviet 5, 13, 32–3, 35, 42, 45, 49, 67, 74–6, 211–2

obshchnost (commonality) concept 12, 21, 32, 81–3, 167, 182, 209, 211
    frustration of 29–30, 43, 45
orientalism 78, 121, 155
Orlova, Galina 12, 81, 187–7
Oushakine, Serguei 39, 54, 211

paternalism 107–8, 110, 113, 117, 120, 145
    enterprise 90
    state 39, 50
patriotic education 2–4
patriotism
    everyday or vernacular 1, 43, 55, 194–5, 203
    pro-war 194–5
    social media 3, 203–4
    Soviet 53
    state-sponsored 31, 51
patron-client relations 88, 106, 111, 118, 120–1, 127, 130, 141
personhood 62, 82, 90, 144, 205
Peter the Great 4

phenomenological approaches
(anthropology) 8, 47–8, 60, 62, 66,
74, 156, 206, 196–7, 207–8
pofigizm (fatalism) 56, 65, 78, 125, 174
Polanyi, Karl 113
political economy
critical 13–15, 209
of Russia 33–4
political subjectivity 4, 11, 98, 189, 207
politics
accelerationist 182
as craft 192
as demobilization 43, 61
as experiential entanglement 23, 184,
192, 197, 205–8, 216
as micropolitics 17–20, 22, 153, 155,
161, 164, 168–9, 192, 195, 198,
206–8, 214, 216
electoral 130
everyday 193
opportunity structure of 184
pragmatic 192
prefigurative 181–2, 184, 201
quiet 22, 203
vernacular 12
versus 'the political' 5, 56, 155, 161,
164, 189, 203, 214
postsocialism 14, 51, 72–3, 87, 93, 131,
170–1, 173, 210
poverty in Russia 42, 95
practice, extended networks of 68, 170,
178
preferences, political 10
Prigozhin mutiny 210, 213
Procuracy service 2, 120, 138–9, 141, 143
propaganda effects 37
provisioning, social 22, 170, 180, 217
public opinion polling 9–10, 28–9, 39,
42, 51
Putin period in context 33–4, 39, 41–2,
111, 128
Putin, Vladimir 4, 9, 28, 32, 42, 57, 206
ideology of 31, 43
voters for 100

Rancière, Jacques 56, 161–2, 164, 169, 172,
187
notion of political asideness 4, 161–2,
214

religion 4, 179
resentment, geopolitical, *see also*
discourses 5, 9, 12, 21, 32, 34–5, 38,
40, 45–6, 50, 54, 56, 61
ressentiment 21, 45–6, 52, 54–7, 61,
211–2
as social hurt 9, 56, 65, 67, 71–3, 78–9,
81
Rostov-on-Don 3
russification 16, 36

salvage 167, 170, 173, 180–2, 185–6
Sassen, Saskia 14
Sayer, Andrew 172
Schutz, Alfred 61, 208
Scott, James C. 17, 150–3
Sharafutdinova, Gulnaz 28–9, 41, 46,
50–2, 144, 216
Shevchenko, Olga 29, 33, 83, 87, 94, 98,
181, 211
siloviki (security personnel) 64, 139
Sobyanin, Sergey 128, 200
social Darwinism 16, 18, 33, 61, 87, 93,
106, 113
social media use 30, 37, 77, 193, 199–200,
202, 204
social psychology, critique of 50–1, 54,
56, 81
social reproduction theory 15, 88–9, 95,
112–13, 164–5, 181, 209–10
socialism, vernacular, *see also* haunting
78, 119, 134, 168, 170, 194–5, 203,
211–2
Sovietization, *see under* USSR
Special Economic Zones 6, 106–8
Spinoza, Baruch 63, 82, 153
state capacity 18, 22, 119, 128–31, 138,
144, 183, 213
state conceptualization
as kinship 19
incoherence of 18, 22
stick system (*palochaia sistema*) 136–7
Strathern, Marilyn 62, 82, 186–7
striving 63, 65, 67–9, 72, 77–8, 212, 216
structure of feeling 4, 11–13, 38, 43, 50–1,
54, 83, 101–2, 126, 142, 144, 149,
197, 211–2, 216
subbotniki 47, 109, 154, 182
suffering, postsocialist 29, 53, 71–4

Index

television consumption 1, 10, 37, 40, 140
Thelen, Tatjana 22, 121, 131, 135, 144–5, 173, 212
Thompson, E. P. 11, 52, 150, 161, 182
Tilly, Charles 195–6, 205, 207
trauma, social 39, 43, 53–4, 60–1, 65, 67, 89
Tsing, Anna 185–6

Ukraine
    attitudes towards 35–7, 41, 55, 79, 100, 191, 194, 200
    reactions in Russia to 2022 invasion 9, 19, 27–8
unipolarity 32
USSR, *see also* nostalgia
    economism 91, 118
    homemaking 167–8
    multinational discourses of 36–7
    ontology 21, 43, 47–9, 51–2, 62, 68, 81, 90, 128, 137, 142, 144, 162, 170, 186–7, 203, 211–13, 216
    property rights 118, 134, 173
utility services 115, 122–4, 131, 133–43

vakhta (labour migration) 14, 96–7
Vanke, Alexandrina 47, 50, 54, 61, 170, 174, 180, 216
Veterans Association 60, 80, 200
violence, structural 15, 19, 94–5, 100, 178, 210
volunteering for war 40–1, 57

Wagner fighters 19
Weber, Max 113, 121, 128, 135, 144
Wedeen, Lisa 10
welfare state 92–3
Western companies' exit from Russia 3, 106
Williams, Raymond 11, 50, 52, 102, 182, 216
WWII memory politics 9, 55, 200, 202–3

Yamal 88–9, 96, 99
Yurchak, Alexei 48–9, 76, 82, 211

Z-patriotism 9, 40, 55–6, 79, 202–3